Leading a Worthy Life

LEON R. KASS

Leading a Worthy Life

Finding Meaning in Modern Times

ENCOUNTER BOOKS

NEW YORK · LONDON

CONTENTS

Introduction

"MAY YOU LIVE in interesting times!" This ancient Chinese curse appears to have landed on us – we whose lives have spanned the end of the twentieth century and the beginning of the new millennium. In addition to the usual run of crises, foreign and domestic, we face genuinely novel prospects both for good and for ill, the harms often emerging tragically as unavoidable consequences of the benefits. Ours is the age of atomic power but also of nuclear proliferation, of globalized trade but also worldwide terrorism, of instant communication but also fragmented communities, of free association but also marital failure, of limitless mobility but also homogenized destinations, of open borders but also confused identities, of astounding medical advances but also greater worries about health, of longer and more vigorous lives but also protracted and more miserable deaths, of unprecedented freedom and prosperity but also remarkable anxiety about our future, both personal and national. In our age of heightened expectations, many Americans fear that their children's lives will be less free, less prosperous, or less fulfilling than their own, a fear that is shared by the young people themselves. Like their forebears, our youth still harbor desires for a worthy life. They still hope to find meaning in their lives and to live a life that makes sense. But they are increasingly confused about what a worthy life might look like, and about how they might be able to live one.

In less interesting times, a dominant and confident culture was able to provide many young people with authoritative guidance for how to live. Religious traditions and inherited customs and mores pointed the way to a good life. Adults, quite comfortable with their moral authority, were not stingy with their praise and blame, reward and punishment, nor did they neglect the effort to model decent conduct for the young to follow. In the post–World War II years of my boyhood, the prevailing culture took pains to turn children into grown-ups. It offered guidance for finding work and vocation, customs of courtship for finding a suitable spouse, and a plethora of vibrant local institutions and associations – religious, fraternal, social, political, charitable, cultural – for finding meaningful participation in civic and communal life. The institutions of higher learning proudly believed in light and truth, and were pleased to initiate the next generation into the intellectual and artistic treasures of the West. To be sure, those less interesting times also offered fewer opportunities for women and minorities and less room for individual divergence from the norm, and the more imaginative and independent people among us sometimes felt stifled. But there were at least norms to be rebelled against, and most people acquired at least some beginning ideas about what makes a life worth living.

No longer. Young people are now at sea – regarding work, family, and civic identity. Authority is out to lunch. Courtship has disappeared. No one talks about work as vocation. The true, the good, and the beautiful have few defenders. Irony is in the saddle, and the higher cynicism mocks any innocent love of wisdom or love of country. The things we used to take for granted have become, at best, open questions. The persons and institutions to which we once looked for guidance have ceased to offer it successfully. Today, we are supercompetent when it comes to efficiency, utility, speed, convenience, and getting ahead in the world; but we are at a loss concerning what it's all for. This lack of cultural and moral confidence about what makes a life worth living is perhaps the deepest curse of living in our interesting time.

I do not mean to imply that my fellow Americans are living empty or meaningless lives. Far from it. Many people today are fulfilled in their work, their families, their communities, and their religious devotions. But they live their worthy lives in the absence of strong and confident cultural support. Indeed, they do so in the face of relentless attacks – from intellectuals, popular culture, and media celebrities – on their core beliefs, practices, and institutions. We are awash in cynicism about work, love, marriage, government, and seeking the truth – and, truth to tell, not without cause.

Other peoples, in earlier times and places, have also been cursed to live in interesting times. Great nations have experienced crises of confidence, whether from war weariness, declining religious beliefs, or cultural disarray. Consider ancient Athens, for example, a city-state that came to prominence in the Persian Wars, after which it found itself in possession of an empire, more by default than by design. Athens predominated for several decades, only to enter upon interesting times as a consequence of the Peloponnesian War with Sparta and her allies, the plague of Athens, and a decline in manners and morals at home. Cynical public intellectuals and wise guys (my translation of *sophistes*) ran around undermining belief in the gods and in traditional mores, also teaching the young how to make the weaker argument appear the stronger. The conservative elders – their equivalent of our American Legion – looked back nostalgically to the glory days of Marathon, even as demagogues swayed the multitude and as public speech and morals headed for the sewer.

Yet precisely because the old orthodoxies were crumbling, these troubled times in Athens offered great opportunities for renewal and growth, at least for individuals. It was then that Socrates, calling philosophy down to earth from its preoccupation with the heavens, made famous the question "How to live?" He gathered around him the finest youths, who warmed to his insistence that the unexamined life was not worth living. Instead of receiving authoritative answers, his students were encouraged to discover genuine and weighty questions, and to undertake real quests in search of a worthy and flourishing life. Never mind that the city fathers, mistaking Socrates for one of the subversive Sophists, convicted and executed him for impiety and for corrupting the young; his influence lives to the present day as the supreme model of a thoughtful life, thanks to the divine Plato, who commemorated the life of his teacher in his famous dialogues. Though Socrates professed no substantive teaching, he exemplified – and still exemplifies – what it means to live thoughtfully and worthily, fully open to the world, fully present to his friends and his city. His example underscores the opportunity that we still enjoy today, in part because we too live in interesting and open-ended times, to seek and find a worthy life for ourselves. We can begin by rejecting the despair and cynicism that often surround us and cloud our vision.

This book is written in a Socratic spirit. Recognizing both the fatigue of our inherited ways and the opportunities it opens up, I aim to encourage our flagging moral confidence by illuminating key aspects of a worthy life that are still available to us and by defending them against some of their enemies. I hope to be helpful to both secular and religious readers, to people who are looking for meaning on their own and to people who are looking to deepen what they may have been taught or to square it with the spirit of our times.

The book grows out of the two major activities of my professional life, spanning nearly fifty years: examining closely the human meaning of the new biology and its life-altering biotechnologies, and teaching searchingly great books that offer profound but competing accounts of the good life. It also no doubt reflects what I have learned, over a long and blessed life, from lived experience – as a child of unschooled but humanly splendid Jewish immigrants from Eastern Europe, who grew up in an ethnically diverse, lower-middle-class neighborhood on the South Side of Chicago after the Second World War; as a young lover, husband, father, and grandfather, blessed as few have been in his marriage of fifty-four years; as a student of the liberal arts, medicine, and biochemistry, a practitioner of biomedical research at the National Institutes of Health, and (for most of my life) a teacher of the humanities at St. John's College and the University of Chicago; as a member of the National Council on the Humanities and as chairman of the President's Council on Bioethics; as a research scholar at the American Enterprise Institute; and as an engaged citizen of the United States under fourteen of its forty-five presidents. During this time I have witnessed and thought about many large cultural changes in American society, most of them initiated or accelerated by technological innovations introduced or popularized in my lifetime: washing machines and dryers, television, antibiotics, interstate highways and colossal automobilty, commercial aviation, the Pill, the Internet, the Human Genome Project and genetic screening, psychoactive drugs, *in vitro* fertilization, organ transplantation, personal computers, smartphones and instant messaging. More than most of my contemporaries, I have regarded these innovations as mixed blessings, recognizing the ways in which they contribute to bettering human life, but noticing too the challenges they present to our very humanity.

Although I have learned much from experience and from knowledge of times and authors past, I write not with nostalgia for those less interesting days, but rather with both concern and hope for the present and the future: concern lest we diminish our chances for a worthy human life amidst a glut of distracting, addicting, and isolating amusements; hope that we can recover and strengthen our appreciation of the permanent possibilities for a rich and meaningful life. I believe that such a life is, in fact, more accessible to many more people than ever before, thanks to freedom, prosperity, and life-easing technologies, even if the fundamental features and deeper significance of such a life are harder to recognize and sustain in the confusions of our times. My main purpose in writing this book is to shine fresh light on several fundamental and irreplaceable aspects of the good life, as well as on the specific threats they face today and tomorrow: love, family, and friendship; human achievement, human excellence, and human dignity; learning and teaching in search of understanding and wisdom; and fulfilling the enduring human aspirations for the true, the good, and the beautiful, for the righteous and the holy, and for freedom, equality, and self-government. I seek to provide an articulate defense of what many Americans tacitly believe or seek in their heart of hearts but have forgotten how to articulate or defend. And I wish to suggest how these aspects of a worthy life, once recognized and defended, can still be pursued under present circumstances, as goals toward which we may continue to steer our voyages over turbulent waters, in newfangled and ever-changing conveyances.

* * *

The chapters in this book were originally separate essays, written for different occasions over a period of twenty years. They have all been revised and updated, and organized into a coherent structure, informed by the purposes just reviewed. The first chapter, "Finding Meaning in Modern Times: An Overview," introduces the theme of the book and presents a synoptic view of four domains in which people can and do find meaning in their lives: in fulfilling work, in love and family, in love of country and public service, and in seeking the truth about ourselves and the world. Activities in these domains (especially the second and the fourth) are explored in greater detail in the subsequent chapters.

The first section, "Love, Family, and Friendship," deals with the domain of deep interpersonal intimacy and familial flourishing, the aspect of a worthy life that is in principle most accessible to, and most sought by, the largest number of people. In my experience, most young people – despite the cheap cynicism they hear about the dim prospects for enjoying happy and enduring marriage – still harbor a desire to find a soulmate with whom they might make a life. They want to be taken seriously; they want to love and be loved. Although chastened by the sad experience of their parents' generation, and therefore fearful of failure, they would gladly, if they could, pledge "In sickness and in health, until death do us part" to a worthy partner.

There are many obstacles in the way of their meeting the right – or a right enough – one, but perhaps none greater than the lack of cultural forms and social encouragement on a path that points to marriage. This deficit is the point of departure for the chapters in this section. Chapter Two, "The End of Courtship," identifies and discusses the numerous impediments in modern American life to the nearly extinct practice of "courting" – finding and winning a life partner – and seeks to explain why so many young people are "loveless in Seattle." It shows why those now defunct forms were well adapted to getting people to the altar, where lives could be joined under a promise of fidelity, loyalty, and enduring care; and it suggests which aspects of those old forms of courting might find practical modern substitutes, even if courtship itself is not revivable as a widespread cultural practice.

The next chapter, "The Higher Sex Education" (adapted from an essay written with my late wife, Amy), offers a correction to the way our culture now educates young people about our sexuality. For the true goal of sex education is not the prevention of pregnancy and (other) unwanted sexually transmitted consequences – the useful but limited purpose of today's *low* sex education – but rather the elevation and education of the heart, achieved by refining its sensibilities, enlarging its imaginings, ennobling its erotic desires, educating its judgments of prospective beloveds. This chapter illustrates by example how such edifying education is still available to present-day would-be lovers, through the wise use and thoughtful exploration of literature that we have inherited from less interesting times.

Chapter Four, "Virtually Intimate," looks at the strengths and weaknesses of Internet matchmaking services. For many people today, these are the best available means of meeting a worthy life partner, and they have already been used successfully to introduce millions of people to their missing other halves. But because Internet matchmaking is a dis-embodied technological remedy for the isolating deformations of our social lives – deformations resulting in large part from prior technological innovations – it carries dangers of its own, potentially adding a new set of impediments to genuine and full intimacy, whether between lovers or friends.

Looking past courtship to marriage and parenthood, Chapter Five, "What's Your Name?" (also taken from an essay written with Amy), raises questions about the culturally controversial "marital name" and about the significance of names that parents give their children. Naming is not only an act of identification by which we become known in the world; it also expresses our hopes and wishes both for ourselves as marital partners and parents, and for the children we name. Against the stream, I (we) argue for the once universal practice of having a common marital name, symbolic of a shared new life, to be shared also with all future children of the union. I also explain why it makes more sense for the bride to accept the offer of the groom's surname than for him to adopt hers, or for both of them to invent some altogether new surname unconnected with a familial past.

The second section of the book moves from private and intimate domains to the more public realm of action, with special attention to human excellence and human dignity, long considered central aspects of a worthy life. According to ancient moral philosophers such as Plato and Aristotle, an especially worthy life was most of all a life of virtuous activity, in fulfillment of our given nature. Cultivation and education provided the *means* to a worthy life; the complete or perfected human being constituted the *end*. Young people were encouraged to keep their eyes on the heights of human possibility and the peaks of human flourishing, as objects of aspiration and emulation.

Modern moral philosophers, in contrast, were less interested in shining examples of human excellence than in the basic *conditions* of a worthy life, especially health and prosperity. Struck by the stinginess of nature and the limitations of our *given* nature, they were more concerned to lift the base of the human condition than to reach the summit of human possibility. They looked to a new quantitative science, pregnant with powerful technological possibilities, to alleviate human misery – to achieve, in Francis Bacon's words, "the relief of man's estate." But they also envisioned ways to overcome *all* human limitations (including our mortality) and to improve upon our given human nature. Their bold dream of mastering human nature has come of age in our time, as novel biotechnologies – based on amazing progress in molecular genetics, developmental biology, neuroscience, and aging research – hold out the promise not only of cures for deadly diseases but also of major enhancements of body and mind, issuing in superior performance, better children, ageless bodies, and happy souls.

Many people will of course want to avail themselves of these enhancing techniques, which offer easier and more effective ways to improve upon their natural gifts and their chances for worldly success. But a little reflection will show that these are, to say the least, mixed blessings. The technologies that promise all sorts of enhancement of our nature may, paradoxically, diminish the chances for genuine human achievement, human virtue, and human dignity.

The first chapter in this section, "Ageless Bodies, Happy Souls," provides an overview of the subject of biotechnical enhancement, with special attention to the dignity of human agency and the difference between technologically attained partial goals and full human flourishing. It argues that the pursuit of an ageless body and longer life will turn out to be a distraction from the possibility of living *well*. And it suggests that the technologically assisted pursuit of an untroubled and self-satisfied soul will turn out to be deadly to all worthy desires.

Chapter Seven explores two accounts of human dignity, often at odds with each other in public discussion. One of these emphasizes the basic dignity of human *being* (called by some the sanctity or inviolability of human life); the other focuses on the full dignity of being *human* (of living humanly and excellently). This chapter seeks to discover the basis for each sort of dignity, and it shows why both need our vigorous defense in this biotechnological age. Finally, it argues that the two dignities are mutually implicated and interdependent, both of them reflections of our unique, "in-between" nature as the one *godlike* animal.

A test case for thinking about human dignity in action is presented in the next chapter, "For the Love of the Game" (written with Eric Cohen). Taking off from the steroid scandal in baseball, this chapter uses the domain of athletics to consider the public pursuit and display of excellence, with and without enhancing technique. It provides a strong defense of the beauty and grace of athletic performance, pursued and appreciated for their own sake, against the deforming single-minded pursuit of victory or statistical records by any means necessary. It articulates the deep humanity of athletic activity (and, by extension, of all embodied human action), and discusses the aesthetics of sport and the character of worthy fandom, concluding with some suggestions about transcendent possibilities in sport (and in many other human activities).

The ninth chapter examines life not at its zenith but at its nadir, with death on the doorstep, as it eventually comes for us all. "A Dignified Death and Its Enemies" argues against giving dehumanization a final victory by embracing a technological fix for our finitude, in the practices of assisted suicide or euthanasia. This chapter aims to show why we esteem the virtues of courage and equanimity in the face of death. It also defends the venerable and intrinsic virtues of the medical profession, which, if it stays true to its calling, will never abandon either its patients or the goodness of their lives. And it argues that a true physician adhering to his ethical calling, especially in difficult straits, can vindicate and preserve the dignity of agent and patient alike, thereby serving as a model of worthy and meaningful work.

Chapter Ten, "A More Perfect Human," deepens our reservations about enhancement biotechnologies and about the technical solutions of assisted suicide and euthanasia, by looking at an earlier national effort to use science and medicine to achieve the perfect human being and to eliminate deficiency, deformity, and disability. Written as a commentary on "Deadly Medicine: Creating the Master Race," the remarkable and disturbing exhibit about German science and medicine between the two world wars, produced by the United States Holocaust Memorial Museum, the chapter shows the devastating consequences of pursuing so-called human perfection by technological means and of trying to "fix" the human condition by science alone. It examines the dangerous *practices* of negative and positive eugenics, a topic creeping back into American conversation as we enter the age of genetic engineering, and it exposes the dangerous *thinking* of "soulless scientism," which looks to health as our salvation and medicine as the messiah.

The third section of the book, "In Search of Wisdom," moves from the domain of action to the realm of thought, where many people still seek and find meaning in the life of wonder, inquiry, learning, and reflection. Here, too, we twenty-first-century Americans face serious challenges and obstacles. In higher education, learning for its own sake is culturally disparaged, partly because the costs of getting an education compel students to focus on practical studies aimed at making a living after college rather than on liberal learning aimed at living well. Computer science, economics, and business majors – yes; classics, literature, and philosophy majors – no. In addition, political correctness and academic trendiness among the faculty, especially in the humanities and social sciences, discourage those who would seek truth and wisdom, and generally result in what Allan Bloom called the closing of the American mind. In place of the love of learning, we get pseudosophisticated cynicism about the search for truth. In place of skeptical science, we get dogmatic scientism. In place of a desire to know, we adopt the knowing pose that snickers at such innocence.

Yet the desire for understanding is hard to eradicate, and many a young person is still interested in the big questions. At most colleges and universities there are still pockets of liberal learning, and great (or good enough) teachers who care about students and nurture their interest in living meaningful lives. It takes only one or two really good teachers to open a mind and turn around a soul. And for students of whatever age, it takes only an openness to learning and a desire not to be self-deceived to make for ourselves a life of thoughtfulness, and to become people who will not sleepwalk through life but will delight in learning whatever we can about the world's limitless mysteries, beauties, and truths.

The first chapter in this section, "The Aims of Liberal Education," is addressed especially to entering college students. It considers several competing goals of a college education, and rejects them in favor of a wisdom-seeking – a *philo-sophical* and liberating – habit of thoughtfulness, through which we seek deeply to understand ourselves in relation to the world around us. Making use of a distinction between two different types of thinking – asking questions (the way of Socrates) and solving problems (the way of modern science) – this chapter argues for the life-giving benefits of questing for what is true and good, of having and honing a mind that is open and hungry, yet also modest and self-critical.

Chapter Twelve, "Looking for an Honest Man," offers as an example my own wisdom-seeking journey, from medicine and biochemical research to philosophy, literature, and Bible study, all in the service of understanding the meaning of our common humanity and of learning how to live a worthy life. Although autobiographical in character, the chapter is meant to convey what *anyone* can learn from a serious engagement with big questions and great authors. It points the way to a revival of humanistic learning, in which the books that we have inherited are treated neither as authoritative guides nor as relics of a no longer relevant age, but as *friends* who will walk with us through life, challenging our assumptions, elevating our sensibilities, and giving us new questions and insights into the things that matter, now and always.

Going beyond philosophy and literature, Chapter Thirteen considers the two great intellectual and cultural edifices that compete for our adherence and that seem to offer the most comprehensive truths: science and religion. The age-old tension between these two complementary but adversarial domains – often mistakenly called the domains of reason and of faith – has for centuries been an animating force of Western civilization. But recent partisan attempts to reduce the tension by eliminating the other side now threaten to mislead us about both. By a careful critique of "scientism" – a quasi-religious faith that natural science can answer all questions about the world and our place within it – I try to rescue the biblical teachings from the belief that science has rendered them unbelievable. Instead, I argue for the compatibility of the Bible, properly read as an account of *what things mean* and of how to live, with science, properly seen as an immensely powerful but ultimately more modest and partial effort to understand (only) *how things work*.

The final section of the book, "The Aspirations of Humankind: Athens, Jerusalem, Gettysburg," comprises three essays, each one focused on a famous text that I love and have often taught, each text associated with a famous city, each city associated with a different strand of Western civilization and culture, each strand displaying and advancing one or another of the great aspirations of humankind.

First, Athens, the leading city of ancient Greece. According to Pericles, her leading statesman, Athens was the school of Hellas, later to become also a major source of Western civilization. Western civilization would hardly be what it is were it not for the Athenians, who at the battles of Salamis and Marathon repulsed the huge Persian invasion, thus saving the ground for Greece's golden age – for democratic self-rule, individual freedom, and the enduring works of Aeschylus, Sophocles, Euripides, and Aristophanes; Herodotus and Thucydides; Phidias and Polycleitus; Plato, Xenophon, and Aristotle. It is from the Greeks that the West inherited the ideas and ideals of human virtue or excellence (*aretê*), as well as a devotion to the beautiful (*to kalon*), both in nature and in art. And it is from the Greeks that the West inherited also the liberal arts of arithmetic and geometry, music and astronomy, grammar, rhetoric, and logic, as well as the passion for truth and the love of wisdom known as *philosophia*. These humanistic teachings – especially about virtue and wisdom, and their relation to human flourishing – received their supreme expression in Aristotle's *Nicomachean Ethics*, the subject of Chapter Fourteen.

Next, Jerusalem, the holy city of ancient Israel – of God's originally chosen people, the People of the Book, who under the leadership of Moses entered into a covenant with the Lord at Sinai in which they bound themselves to pursue righteousness and holiness under His commandments. Jerusalem, final home also of Jesus of Nazareth, the story of whose life and teachings, crucifixion and resurrection became the basis of a new and hugely successful universal religion that spread biblical teachings to all regions of the globe. It is from Jerusalem (that is, Judaism and Christianity) that the West inherited the ideas and ideals of man (and woman) made in the image of God, of loving your neighbor as yourself, and of loving the one God with all your heart and all your soul and all your might. It is from Jerusalem that the West inherited also a devotion to justice and mercy and a belief in the dignity of all human beings – the brotherhood of man under the fatherhood of God. The biblical teachings – especially about the relations among law, justice, and holiness, and between man and God, as presented in the Ten Commandments – are the subject of Chapter Fifteen.

And finally, Gettysburg. To the old trope of "Athens and Jerusalem," long regarded as twin sources of the West, I add – in all seriousness – the site of a justly famous cemetery and an even more justly famous speech. The name of Gettysburg stands for the unique contribution to Western civilization made by the idea and practice of the United States of America. If Greece gave the West virtue, beauty, and philosophy, and if biblical religion gave the West reverence, righteousness, and love of neighbor, America gave the West – and the world – its first enduring political embodiment of the ideas and ideals of freedom and equality and the practice of constitutional self-government in the service of those ideals. Gettysburg is, perhaps, an odd choice to stand as the representative of the United States. Philadelphia, site of the signing of the Declaration of Independence and home of the Constitutional Convention, has an older and more fundamental claim. And Washington, D.C., as the nation's capital, would be a more obvious choice. But it was at Gettysburg that our greatest and wisest president gave the canonical speech that remains to this day the most powerful and most beautiful statement of the American creed and purpose. The concluding chapter offers a close analysis of the Gettysburg Address and reflections on Abraham Lincoln's "refounding" of the American nation.

* * *

Even this cursory summary of what lies in store should alert the reader to the fact that I offer no single account of what makes for a worthy life. The various chapters and sources I rely on point in different, often competing directions. Which is it: private intimacy, public action, or the search for wisdom? Which is the better life: questioning or reverence, giving the law to yourself or living under command, seeking truth or serving others? Whose call should we answer: Athens, Jerusalem, or Gettysburg? As we have many talents and diverging circumstances, the path to a worthy life taken by one of us will rarely match the path taken by another. But in one respect, the goal is, at least formally, the same for all: to have earned in word and deed our place at the banquet of human life to which we have been so graciously (and undeservedly) invited.

I have no idea whether I will someday have to answer for my life before the bar of judgment. I have never lived my life either in hope of heaven or fear of hell. But I have long liked the idea of having to give an account of my life when my time is up, not so much in terms of specific good deeds and bad, virtues and vices, kindnesses and sins, as to explain what I have done with the unmerited gift of a place on our planet, and, to boot, with all the advantages of living in America in the twentieth and twenty-first centuries. Yes, our circumstances have changed greatly. Our streets are no longer paved with cobblestones, and we do not travel by horse and buggy. We no longer write letters or go on dates, and we spend much of our lives in mediated existence before a mesmerizing screen, or two or three. Our culture no longer offers us authoritative guidance on how to live. But we still have our race's age-old longings for love and friendship, meaningful work, understanding and wisdom, a place in our community, an opportunity to serve, and a relationship to something higher or beyond. Let us not sell them short.

CHAPTER ONE

Finding Meaning in Modern Times

An Overview

In 1992, IN HIS Francis Boyer Lecture entitled "The Cultural Revolution and the Capitalist Future," Irving Kristol explored the growing gap between our thriving capitalist economy and our unraveling bourgeois culture. Regarding the economy, he showed how capitalism had produced a widely shared prosperity that put paid to arguments in favor of the socialist alternative. Regarding the culture, he showed how succeeding waves of elitist opposition to our inherited moral, aesthetic, and spiritual norms and sensibilities had issued in a nihilistic anticulture, hostile not only to religion, family, patriotism, and traditional morality, but even to the promise of Enlightenment reason itself.

Concluding with a look to the future, Kristol foresaw both good news and bad. In the short run, he was confident that the nihilism preached by our elites would not prevail politically, because our sensible, bourgeois, property-owning democracy breeds its own antibodies that "immunize it, in large degree, against the lunacies of its intellectuals and artists." For the long run, he was much less sanguine:

> But a society needs more than sensible men and women if it is to prosper: It needs the energies of the creative imagination as expressed in religion and the arts. It is crucial to the lives of all of our citizens, as it is to all human beings at all times, that they

encounter a world that possesses a transcendent meaning, a world in which the human experience makes sense. Nothing is more dehumanizing, more certain to generate a crisis, than to experience one's life as a meaningless event in a meaningless world.

Bourgeois society ... has produced through the market economy a world prosperous beyond all previous imaginings – even socialist imaginings.... [But] this world, with every passing decade, has become ever more spiritually impoverished. That war on poverty is the great unfinished task before us.

Irving Kristol was second to none in his appreciation of America's political genius and commercial spirit. He esteemed the blessings of freedom and prosperity, and he extolled the bourgeois virtues that make them possible. But he also knew that freedom and prosperity are not ends in themselves and do not alone guarantee a life with purpose, a life with meaning, a life of genuine human flourishing. And he was concerned that the very successes of the American enterprise might tragically lead us to neglect higher human goods.

This essay begins where Kristol left off. Twenty-five years on, how fares the struggle against our spiritual impoverishment? Are we Americans, despite our continuing freedom and prosperity, really losing the quest for a meaningful life?

It would be easy to argue that life in America is spiritually more impoverished than ever. As evidence, one might cite the rising respectability of public atheism and the falling off of religious observance; the eclipse of the ideal of work as vocation; the emptiness and coarseness of the popular culture; the weakening of marriage and family ties; the failure of higher education to nurture the hungry souls of our young, and the huge increase in clinical depression among college students; the decline of patriotism and national attachment; and new expressions of doubt about America's future, fueled by a strident cynicism on the left and a growing despair on the right.

But this picture is at best incomplete. As Charles Murray points out in *Coming Apart: The State of White America, 1960–2010*, marriage, industriousness, law-abidingness, and religiosity are alive and well among the cultural elite, even as they are in decline among the lower classes. Nationwide, many of our social indicators show a partial repair of earlier unravelings. Community service is on the rise, as is private philanthropy. There is once again a proper respect for the armed forces. And despite their superficial cynicism, America's young people – not only among the privileged – continue to harbor deep desires for a life that will prove meaningful, a life of love and work, service to God and country, and pursuit of truth or goodness or beauty.

All in all, there is reason to believe that our deeds and practices – if not also our spiritual prospects – are better than the dispiriting speeches and theories that garner the most notoriety. But this hardly means that the campaign against spiritual poverty has been won. What most decent Americans still practice or know in their bones, they do and know despite the strenuous and unceasing efforts of intellectuals and the popular culture to persuade them otherwise – efforts whose doleful consequences are all around us. But to wage a truly winning war on spiritual impoverishment, we need much more. We need a newly inspirited cultural elite, one that, as Murray puts it, confidently preaches what it practices. And we need institutions that will once again educate our elite in the sources, the ideas, and the beliefs that guide us as a people. But first, and most, we need a full-throated intellectual defense and celebration of what most Americans still tacitly know and live by. And this requires an account of *why* and *how* our most worthy practices answer to our deepest human aspirations and longings. In what follows, I offer the outlines of such a defense and such an account.

Before proceeding further, a brief stipulation. For most people in the West over the last two millennia, finding transcendent meaning in life has been centrally linked to biblical religion. For committed Christians and Jews, it is God's will and plan that make order out of chaos, not only in nature, through the Creation, but also in human life, through His moral and spiritual instruction. In Western Europe, much of the growing spiritual malaise and loss of cultural confidence can be attributed to the so-called "death of God," the loss of belief in a superintending deity. But in the United States, the announcement of God's death is premature, to say the least. Although more Americans than ever are religiously unaffiliated, 92 percent say that they believe in God, and 81 percent say that religion is very (55 percent) or fairly (26 percent) important in their lives – this despite tremendous intellectual energy and a slew of best-selling books devoted to undermining this blessed condition.

For present purposes, however, I propose to leave organized religion to one side. Each faith has its proper exponents and defenders, and generic arguments from the outside will not satisfy the doubting Thomases regarding the truth of God's existence or the goodness of His teachings. Let us look instead at the secular realms of human life where many Americans still find deep meaning and in which they live as if life still makes sense. I have in mind four such realms: work; love and family; community and country; and the pursuit of truth. Most of the life-affirming activities in these realms are accessible to most Americans, and all have this in common: we practice and pursue them not as diversions or escapes from reality, but because they answer truly to our deepest aspirations: to live a life that makes sense, a life that is worthy of the unmerited gift of our own existence.

Meaningful Work: Exercising Our Human Powers

Nearly all Americans must work to live. But there is also virtue in this necessity. Above and beyond the benefits of remuneration, there is *dignity* in earning a livelihood, in providing not only for oneself but also and especially for one's family. Among the rising generations, gainful employment is an early sign of maturity and the first step toward self-reliance. Holding down a job requires not only know-how and competence, but also the virtues of diligence, dependability, and the exercise of personal responsibility. Unemployment, even if compensated, is demoralizing, degrading, and dehumanizing to any self-respecting adult who wants to work.

Yet even the moral praise of industriousness and self-reliance comes up short if we are looking at work as a possible source of transcendent meaning. For this we need an account of work as intrinsically satisfying, quite apart from the income it produces or the virtues it engenders. We need to consider work, as Dorothy Sayers put it, "not, primarily, a thing one does to live, but the thing one lives to do." Work enables us to utilize and to most fully express our God-given talents, gaining meaning for our lives from fulfilling our nature, from seeing our work well done, and from delighting in the gifts our work provides to a world that needs and appreciates them.

True enough, work to many people is irksome, a mere "job," worth only the wages it earns or the consumption and leisure it makes possible.

(The word "job," you might like to know, originally meant a mere "piece or gob of work," defined in Samuel Johnson's dictionary as "a low mean lucrative busy affair; petty, piddling work.") True, too, not everyone can find work to which he or she is well suited, never mind called. Still, these empirical difficulties do not affect the main point: real work can – and for many people still does – all by itself provide a life that makes sense, a life of intrinsic meaning and purpose, a life that lifts the worker to the fullness of his or her being, and beyond. Most readers of this book are probably blessed with work of that sort. And all of us have encountered the joy of work among artists and artisans, teachers and nurses, firemen and police, soldiers and social workers, businessmen and clergy, and myriad other occupations, from the lofty to the low. Finding meaning in work generally depends less on the external task than on the attitude and manner in which the work is done. Witness the differing answers of three laborers who were asked to describe the work they were jointly doing: "I'm making a living," said the first. "I'm dragging heavy stones," said the second. Said the third, "I'm building a cathedral." Only for the last laborer did the work possess its full human meaning. Only for him was his work a spiritual as well as a bodily exercise.

That work should be central to life's fulfillment is a very old idea, and it persists because it is rooted in human nature. Aristotle argued that human flourishing is a life of virtuous or excellent *activity*, where "activity" translates a word of Aristotle's own coinage, built from a root meaning "work": *energeia*, literally, "being-at-work." For the fullness of who we *are* is manifested only when we are *active*, when we are "*at work.*" To be truly human is to be humanly-at-work, exercising our humanity to the full. And doing so excellently is the heart of flourishing and fulfillment. The pleasure and subjective satisfaction that we feel as a result is merely secondary and derivative; the essence of our happiness lies in the activity itself, in our being-at-work.

Love and Family: Transcending Our Mortality

We human beings are at work not only when we are occupationally working. We are also deeply at work in the activities of love and friendship, and especially when we are actively engaged in family life, the domain of private life in which most Americans find the greatest meaning – and the second area where we need a revitalization of our thinking. Despite high-profile public controversies about the scope and meaning of marriage, millions of Americans still devote themselves, privately and quietly, to providing decent lives and future opportunities for their children. More to the point, many of us regard our families as the heart of what makes life worthwhile. We do so, in many cases, with greater difficulty and less cultural support than did our grandparents. And many of us openly worry that the American future may not be as bright for our children and grandchildren as its present and past have been for us. Yet this very concern bespeaks the importance of our children's well-being for our own fulfillment.

Why is this so? People offering secular arguments for marriage and family often cite empirical evidence to show that married people are healthier, wealthier, and happier than unmarried people, and that children fare better by every measure when they are reared in a single home by both their parents. These utilitarian arguments are true, but they lack a deeper anthropological account of *why* love, marriage, and family continue to be central to human flourishing.

Such an account begins with human erotic desire. It is erotic desire that powerfully leads the soul away from its purely selfish preoccupations with comfort, safety, and gain. For many a callow youth, falling in love is the first soul-opening event. And while *eros* can be notoriously fickle in its choice of objects, when disciplined – especially by the vows and practice of a solid marriage – it can provide for a private life whose satisfactions are among the most enduring blessings life has to offer. Living life under a promise, husband and wife enjoy the practice of mutually giving and receiving love, one to the other. Through devotion and care, informed by the pledge and practice of fidelity, everyday life takes on the character of a sacrament. To be sure, the busy-ness, cares, and burdens of daily domestic life – not to speak of unforeseen economic and medical woes or difficulties with the in-laws – often obscure its deeper meaning, the profundity of the prosaic. But looking back on life's journey, a well-married couple knows that even – or especially – in facing the most difficult challenges, oar to oar, they have enjoyed fulfillments not available to the unmarried.

But *eros* seeks more than loving companionship and the comforts of home, bulwarks against the loneliness of a solitary existence. *Eros* is at bottom also a longing for immortality in the face of finitude, and it seeks to give birth. Human love is not merely possessive and self-serving, a lack seeking to be filled; it is also generous and generative, a fullness seeking to give birth. Indeed, it is the common project of procreation that holds together what sexual difference sometimes threatens to drive apart. Flesh of their flesh, a child is the parents' own commingled being externalized, and their unification is even more powerfully enhanced by the shared work of rearing. Providing an opening to the future beyond the grave, carrying not only our seed but also our names, our ways, and our hopes that they will surpass us in goodness and happiness, children are a testament to the opportunity for transcendence. A hope-filled repayment forward of the debt we owe backward for our own life and rearing, our children represent also our share in the perpetual renewal of human possibility. In this way, sexual *eros*, which first drew our love upward and outside of ourselves, finally provides for the partial overcoming of the limitation of perishable embodiment altogether.

It is for this deeper reason that marriage, procreation, and especially childrearing are at the heart of a serious and flourishing human life, if not for everyone at least for the great majority. Most of us know from our own experience that life becomes truly serious when we become responsible for the lives of others for whose being in the world we have said "We do." It is fatherhood and motherhood that teach most of us what it took to bring us into our own adulthood, engaged in practices that are most fully rewarded when we live to see our children caring for children of their own. And it is the desire to give not only life but *a good way of life* to our children that opens us toward a serious concern for the true, the good, and even the holy. Parental love of children leads once wayward sheep back into the fold of church and synagogue. In the best case, it can even be the beginning of the sanctification of life – even in modern times.

It is true that many people are denied these blessings, while others practice childless marriage without regret. It is also true that legal definitions of marriage and social designations of "family" are undergoing major transformations. But these facts do not alter the truth of what I have suggested: that we *can* enunciate a deep understanding of love, marriage, and family – on universal anthropological rather than strictly religious grounds – that would both describe and explain the familial ideals to which many Americans aspire and that would make clear just *why* those practices embody a transcendent meaning and purpose for our lives. We all must acknowledge that there will be no going back to more traditional views and practices concerning sex and marriage. But it is still possible for us to articulate – and to celebrate – an account of human love and its generative fruit that can be affirmed under present and future family forms. At the center of such an account will be the insight that children are a gift of love, not a product of our will, and that we are most fulfilled in their rearing when we raise them to serve not *our* present ambitions but *their* future good, and, indeed, the goodness of life itself.

Love of Country: Fulfilling Public Service

Third, the objects of human loves and longings are not restricted to the private sphere of love and its progeny. Cooler than *eros* yet not for that reason less potent are the several forms of human *philia: philopatria* or patriotism, the love of country; philanthropy, the love of fellow human beings; and philosophy, the love of wisdom. Activities animated by these loves and longings still give meaning to the lives of many Americans, even if once again the prevailing common opinions do not do them justice. Patriotism is a good case in point.

Patriotism in the United States, like America itself, is exceptional – and not so easily cultivated. Ours is not an ethnic motherland or fatherland, rooted in soil with bonds of blood. We belong rather to a republic founded on ideas, but ideas that celebrate the individual rather than the collective, private rights rather than public glory. We are a nation of immigrants – today, a truly cosmopolitan nation – and anyone willing to swear allegiance to the United States can become an American, a transformation impossible for someone hoping, by change of residence, to become French or Chinese. But our liberal way of life also makes it possible for people to live among us, even as citizens enjoying our rights, without becoming patriots – that is, without being people who love and serve our country, and who are willing to defend her when necessary with their life, fortune, and sacred honor. Yet remarkably, and especially in critical times – from the American Revolution to our ongoing struggles against Islamist terror and brutality – Americans have risen to the occasion, putting the republic and its ideals before self, serving her nobly and well.

Approximately four million men and women served in the active-duty military in the first ten years after 9/11, and thousands more have joined their ranks every month since. (More than twice as many served during the Vietnam War, and more than four times as many served in World War II.) Less dramatic but much more ubiquitous are the longstanding and still-vibrant American traditions of public and community service, practiced in local governments and through a plethora of voluntary religious, philanthropic, and civic associations. For many an American, the life of service to the nation still makes sense and gives meaning to our lives.

But our thinking about patriotism – as with work and family life – has fallen behind our practice. Compared with the cultural attitudes surrounding World War II, and especially since the 1960s, patriotism has come under suspicion, most regrettably among those who teach the young. Our national heroes are debunked, our national achievements belittled, our every sin magnified. Today, American patriotism faces more explicit challenges, both universalist and parochial. On the one hand, liberal intellectuals decry national distinctions, deny the need for patriotic sacrifice, and urge us to join the party of humanity and to see ourselves as "citizens of the world." On the other hand, many people – including some of the same intellectuals – encourage divisive identity politics at home, accentuating ethnic and racial differences, eschewing assimilation and the melting pot, and celebrating only *hyphenated*-American identities – a matter of deep disappointment to those of us who once fought for civil rights and integration. Finally, in opposition to these tendencies, we are witnessing an upsurge of crude nationalism, an "America First" blood-and-soil nativism, with more than a touch of xenophobia and race-hatred of the sort we fought World War II to destroy. Given these universalist, tribalist, and nativist challenges, there is all the more reason to articulate a sensible patriotism, coupled with efforts to translate it into meaningful civic participation and service – and not primarily during national elections.

It is relatively easy to show that the universalist dream is contrary to possibility, and that the idea of "citizen of the world" is largely empty preening. Honest-to-goodness citizenship exists only for members of a specific polity, and for the foreseeable future the world will remain divided into disparate political communities, each with its own legal system and way of life. What is more necessary is to show why national identity and attachment are not only inevitable but also *desirable*, for individuals as well as for the American nation. Here, the plain truth of the matter is that real life, even for those critics of America who preach liberal universalism, cannot do without the nurturing benefits of strong particularistic attachment. For the vast majority of human beings, life as actually lived is lived parochially and locally, embedded in a web of human relations, institutions, culture, and mores that define us and – whether we know it or not – give shape, character, and meaning to our lives. One's feeling for global humanity, however sincere, is based on an abstraction, hard to translate into the concrete and meaningful concern that leads neighbor to care and work actively for neighbor, Chicagoan for Chicagoan, Texan for Texan, American for American. Civic self-government – the pride of political achievement – is possible only in the communities in which we actually live, and there can be no robust civic life without patriotic attachment. I am not talking about the psychic boost we give ourselves by yelling "USA, USA" at the Olympics. I am talking, rather, about the genuine elevation of our lives made possible by belonging freely, feelingly, and actively to something larger and more worthy than our individual selves.

Other nations, of course, can and do lay claim to similar ties and loyalties. But for us Americans, there are special reasons for patriotic attachment, for we are a parochial nation with a universal calling and a most remarkable history in answering it. The principles of human equality, inalienable rights, and government by consent, newly enunciated in the Declaration of Independence, were given operative life in the polity established by the Constitution, under which the United States became and remains a shining example of stable self-government and a beacon of hope for oppressed peoples all over the world. We are the privileged heirs of a way of life that has offered the blessings of freedom and dignity to millions of people of all races, ethnicities, and religions, and that extols the possibility of individual achievement as far as individual talent and effort can take it. We are also a self-critical nation, whose history is replete with efforts to bring our practices more fully in line with our ideals. And our national history boasts hundreds of thousands of heroic men and women who gave their lives that the nation might live and flourish. To belong to such a nation is not only a special blessing but a special calling: to preserve freedom, dignity, and self-government at home and to encourage their spread abroad. As Abraham Lincoln put it, in a call to perpetuate our political institutions: "This task of gratitude to our fathers, justice to ourselves, duty to posterity, and love for our species in general, all imperatively require us faithfully to perform."

It should now also be clear why American patriotism and national service can and do provide a life of transcendent meaning. We love our country not only because it is ours, but also because it is good – not perfect, but very good. We love her all the more when we undertake to serve and preserve her, for then she becomes also the embodiment of our efforts and our very being, as we extend our being-at-work onto a larger and more enduring canvas, and our own vitality is lifted to a higher plane. Service to our country, rightly understood, is not a form of self-sacrifice in the name of freedom, but a freely chosen form of self-fulfillment. For this reason, those who spend their lives in America's cause are never victims or martyrs. They are heroes, and we honor them rightly when we gratefully esteem the blessings they have safeguarded and when we emulate their example. The Army motto has it right: Patriotic service, in peace as well as war, enables each of us to "Be all that you can be."

Seeking Truth: Minding Self and World

Being all that we can be includes a concern with truth. A full life encompasses the life of the mind, exercised not only in solving practical problems but also in an active quest for understanding, desired for its own sake. Across the nation, esteemed institutions of higher learning, charged with seeking knowledge and educating the young, operate under mottos such as "Veritas" or "The Truth Shall Make You Free." Thus it is beyond sad that for several decades these would-be homes of truth seeking have been betraying their own mission.

The natural scientists, who show us how things work, for the most part still adhere to a disinterested pursuit of knowledge. But many humanists and social scientists, who should be showing us what things mean, have largely abandoned the standard of truth. In place of an appropriate truth-loving skepticism, which insists on seeing evidence and assessing arguments before accepting an opinion as true, they peddle the mind-deadening and self-indulgent poison that truth, like beauty, lies only in the eye of the beholder, with each person freely "constructing" reality according to his own tastes. Thus they turn what should be shared inquiry in search of understanding into mere fighting in pursuit of victory. Their trendy and shallow scholarship is bad enough, but they deserve the hemlock for corrupting the hearts and minds of the young. The best of our youth, who still come to college hungering for guidance in how to live, and who would be greatly helped by an introduction to the best of what has been thought and said, are promptly urged to give up such naive views and "childish dreams." They are encouraged instead to busy themselves with a careerist curriculum, and all too commonly a subversive one that, in the name of a vulgar relativism disguised as sophistication, teaches them to mock their own decent beliefs about God, vocation, love and family, morality, patriotism, even about the very existence of truth and goodness – all this for their parents' $50,000-plus a year.

And yet, we should not despair. The desire to know and the passion for truth are hard to eradicate, and there must come a reckoning for those who seek to crush these aspirations. As was said long ago, all human beings by nature desire understanding; witness the delight that all healthy children take in hearing stories, seeing new sights, and learning the names and ways of things. Most of us, no matter how sophisticated, do not really want to be self-deceived about matters of human importance, and especially about what it means to live well. We want to see clearly; we want to appreciate the complexities and wonders and mysteries of the world and our place within it; we want to be taken seriously and to learn to live a life that makes sense. Wonder of wonders, our desire for such knowledge is matched by the (at least partial) knowability of the world, and, with effort, genuine learning is possible. Despite the lazy lure of relativism, we really do know in our bones that some opinions are truer, some books better, some lives and nations more admirable than others. And anyone who has even once tasted the exhilaration of discovery is a witness to the existence of truth and the value of seeking it.

Fortunately, we do have some educational institutions – first among them, St. John's College – fully devoted to seeking truth and wisdom. And if we know how to look, we can find truth seekers and pockets of liberal learning even in the most decadent of institutions. Outside of the universities, other institutions still uphold the banner of truth and goodness, as did Irving Kristol's journal, *The Public Interest*, and as does its replacement, *National Affairs*. At the American Enterprise Institute, my own current home, the president, Arthur Brooks, declared in his inspiring annual address to the staff that truth is more important than victory at AEI – though victory is also sweet.

But it is mainly evidence gained from forty years of teaching undergraduates and watching their delight in learning that sustains my belief that our intellectual and spiritual prospects are much better than we might think from listening to the nihilistic preaching of the professoriate. Despite extensive cultural rot and a shortage of edifying encouragement, American society still tosses up superb young people who want more from life, and from their teachers, than they are now getting. They understand, albeit dimly, that the open-minded yet passionate search for understanding is itself an integral part of a flourishing human life. If we treat them as better than they think they are, if we legitimize their spiritual hunger and feed it properly, they will more often than not rise to the occasion and vindicate our best hopes for them. Is it not only a matter of time before some radical young Turks rebel against their professorial elders, rejecting the sawdust and cheap tinsel of nihilism and showing again how honest concern with truth and goodness and beauty really does answer to the deepest longings of the soul? Will we not live to see the great day when serious students, with their parents' blessings, decide to Occupy the Campus and demand real value for their time and money? We can only hope and pray so.

Our Theotropic Nature and the Virtue of Hope

Two concluding remarks, the first about religion. The discerning reader will have noticed that even in traveling only on secular terrain I have not exactly left religion behind. While deliberately avoiding any specific doctrine, I have presented a picture of our humanity that emphasizes the aspirations and longings of the human soul, aspirations that are distinctively ours because we alone among the creatures stand in the world as beings in quest of a calling. Unless and until our aspirations are crushed by the cynicism of bad teachers or by devastating defeats, we live looking for an upward path – toward worthy work, love, service, and understanding. Whether we know it or not, we are, as Irving Kristol so aptly put it describing himself, theotropic – oriented toward the divine – because we sense in ourselves and in our fellow human beings a divinelike possibility and a penchant for the good.

And that thought leads to perhaps the most important – and often misunderstood – subject of hope, the one indispensable virtue. Hope is different from optimism, a belief that this is the best of all possible worlds and that everything will turn out well in the end. Hope is also more than a feeling; it is an attitude or disposition, an orientation, a way of being and holding oneself in the world. As a disposition, hope is deeper even than the sum total of our particular hopes for this or that future outcome. For even when – or perhaps especially when – specific future hopes are disappointed, the posture of hope – a strange fusion of trust, belief, and upward orientation of the will – still enables us to live and act trusting that the world is still and always the sort of place that can answer to the highest and deepest human aspirations.

In this most fundamental sense, hope is *not* a hope for *change*, but an affirmation of *permanence*, of the permanent possibility of a meaningful life in a hospitable world. Hope in this sense is not only a Judeo-Christian virtue. It is not only the most essential – and abundant – American virtue. It is the condition of the possibility of all human endeavor and all human fulfillment.

Yes, there is still much spiritual poverty in America. But we go forward with confidence that our spiritual hungers can yet be nurtured in this almost promised land, provided that we have the courage to insist that the well-being of the spirit is central to our notion of national success and personal flourishing. *This* war on poverty – on our *spiritual* poverty – will not add a cent to the national debt. It can enrich our lives beyond measure.

I · Love, Family, and Friendship

Some Reflections on Modern Culture

CHAPTER TWO

The End of Courtship

IN THE ONGOING WARS over the state of American culture, few battle-
grounds have seen more action than that of "family values" – sex, marriage, and childrearing. Passions run high about sexual harassment, con-
dom distribution in schools, pornography, abortion, gay marriage, and
other efforts to alter the definition of "a family." Many people are dis-
tressed over the record-high rates of divorce, illegitimacy, teenage pregnancy, marital infidelity, and premarital promiscuity. On some issues,
there is even an emerging consensus that something is terribly wrong:
Though they may differ on what is to be done, people on both the left and
the right have come to regard the breakup of marriage as a leading cause of
the neglect, indeed, the psychic and moral maiming of America's children.

But while various people are talking about tracking down "deadbeat
dads" or reestablishing orphanages or doing something to slow the rate
of divorce – all remedies for marital failure – very little attention is being
paid to what makes for marital success. Still less are we attending to the
ways and mores of entering into marriage, that is, to wooing or courtship.

There is, of course, good reason for this neglect. The very terms –
"wooing," "courting," "suitors" – are archaic; and if the words barely exist
anymore, it is because the phenomena have all but disappeared. Today
there are no socially prescribed forms of conduct that help guide young
men and women in the direction of matrimony. This is true not just for
the lower classes. Even – indeed, especially – the elite, who in previous
generations would have defined the conventions in these matters, lack a
cultural script whose denouement is marriage. There are still exceptions

to be found, say, in closed religious communities or among new immigrants from parts of the world that still practice arranged marriage. But for most of America's middle- and upper-class youth – the privileged and college-educated – there are no known social paths, explicit or even tacit, directed toward marriage. People still get married, though later, more hesitantly, and, by and large, less successfully. People still get married in churches and synagogues, though often with ceremonies of their own creation. For the great majority, though, the way to the altar is uncharted: It's every couple on its own, without a compass, often without a goal. Those who reach the altar seem to have stumbled upon it by accident.

Then and Now

Things were not always like this; in fact, one suspects things were *never* like this, not here, not anywhere. In this respect as in so many others, we live in utterly novel and unprecedented times. Until what seems like only yesterday, young people were groomed for marriage, and the paths leading to it were culturally set out, at least roughly. Our grandfathers, in polite society, came a-calling and a-wooing at the homes of our grandmothers, under conditions set by the woman, operating from strength on her own turf. A generation later, courting couples began to go out on "dates," in public and increasingly on the man's terms, given that he had the income to pay for dinner and dancing. To be sure, some people "played the field," and dating on college campuses in the prewar years became a matter more of proving popularity than of proving suitability for marriage. But "going steady" was a regular feature of high-school and college life, especially after the war, when the age of marriage dropped considerably, and high-school or college sweethearts often married right after graduation, or even before. Finding a mate, no less than getting an education that would enable him to support her, was at least an unstated goal of many a male undergraduate; many a young woman, so the joke had it, went to college mainly for her MRS. degree, a charge whose truth was proof against libel for legions of college coeds well into the 1960s.[1]

In other respects as well, the young remained culturally attached to the claims of "real life." Though times were good, fresh memory kept alive the poverty of the Great Depression and the deaths and dislocations of the war; necessity and the urgencies of life were not out of sight, even for fortunate youth. Opportunity was knocking, the world and adulthood were beckoning, and most of us stepped forward into married life, readily, eagerly, and, truth to tell, without much pondering. We were simply doing – some sooner, some later – what our parents had done, indeed, what all our forebears had done.

Not so today. Now the vast majority go to college, but very few – women or men – go with the hope, or even the wish, of finding a marriage partner. Many do not expect to find there even a path to a career; they often require several years of postgraduate "time off" to figure out what they are going to do with themselves. Sexually active – indeed, hyperactive – they flop about from one relationship to another. To the bewildered eye of this admittedly much-too-old but still-romantic observer, they manage to appear all at once casual and carefree and grim and humorless about getting along with the opposite sex. The young men, nervous predators, act as if any woman were equally good; they are given not to falling in love with one, but to scoring in bed with many. And in this sporting attitude they are now matched by some female trophy hunters.

But most young women strike me as sad, lonely, and confused. Hoping for something more, they are not enjoying their hard-won sexual liberation as much as liberation theory says they should.* Forget about wooing; today's collegians do not even make dates or other forward-looking commitments to see one another. In this, as in so many other ways, they reveal their blindness to the passing of time and its meaning. Those very few who couple off seriously and get married upon graduation, as their parents did, are looked upon as freaks.

After college, the scene is even more remarkable and bizarre: singles bars, personal "partner wanted" ads (almost never mentioning marriage as a goal), men practicing serial monogamy (or what someone has aptly renamed "rotating polygamy"), women chronically disappointed in the failure of men to "commit." For the first time in human history, mature women by the tens of thousands live the entire decade of their twenties –

---

* Readers removed from the college scene should revisit Allan Bloom's profound analysis of relationships in *The Closing of the American Mind* (New York: Simon & Schuster, 1987). Bloom was concerned with the effect of the new arrangements on the possibility for liberal education, not for marriage, my current concern.

their most fertile years – neither in the homes of their fathers nor in the homes of their husbands, unprotected, lonely, and out of sync with their inborn nature. Some women positively welcome this state of affairs, but most do not; resenting the personal price they pay for their worldly independence, they nevertheless try to put a good face on things and take refuge in work or feminist ideology. As age thirty comes and goes, they begin to allow themselves to hear their biological clock ticking, and, if husbands continue to be lacking, single motherhood by the hand of science is now an option. Meanwhile, the bachelor herd continue their youthful prowl, with real life in suspended animation, living out what Kay Hymowitz, a contributing editor of *City Journal*, has called a "postmodern postadolescence."

Those women and men who get lucky enter into what the personal ads call LTRs – long-term relationships – sometimes cohabiting, sometimes not, usually to discover how short an LTR can be. When, after a series of such affairs, marriage happens to them, they enter upon it guardedly and suspiciously, with prenuptial agreements, no common surname, and separate bank accounts.

Courtship, anyone? Don't be ridiculous.

Recent Obstacles to Courtship

Anyone who seriously contemplates the present scene is – or should be – filled with profound sadness, all the more so if he or she knows the profound satisfactions of a successful marriage. Our hearts go out not only to the children of failed marriages or of nonmarriage – to those betrayed by their parents' divorce and to those deliberately brought into the world as bastards – but also to the lonely, disappointed, cynical, misguided, or despondent people who are missing out on one of life's greatest adventures, which brings with it many of life's deepest experiences, insights, and joys. We watch our sons and daughters, our friends' children, and our students bumble along from one unsatisfactory relationship to the next, wishing we could help. Few things lead us to curse "*o tempore, o mores*" more than recognizing our impotence to do anything either about our own young people's dilemmas or about these melancholy times.

Some conservatives frankly wish to turn back the clock, thinking that a remoralization of society in matters erotic is a real possibility. I, on the other hand, am largely pessimistic, much of the time despairing of any improvement. Inherited cultural forms can be undermined by public policy and social decision, but once fractured, they are hard to repair by rational and self-conscious design. Besides, the causes of the present state of affairs are multiple, powerful, and, I fear, largely irreversible. Anyone who thinks courtship can make a comeback must at least try to understand what he is up against.

Some of the obstacles in the way of getting married are of very recent origin; indeed, they have occurred during the adult lifetime of those of us over fifty. Perhaps for this reason they may seem to some people to be reversible, a spasm connected with the "'abnormal" 1960s. But when these obstacles are rightly understood, one can see that they spring from the very heart of liberal democratic society and modernity.

Here is a partial list of the recent changes in our society and culture that hamper courtship and marriage: the sexual revolution, made possible especially by effective female contraception; the ideology of feminism and the changing educational and occupational status of women; the destigmatization of bastardy, divorce, infidelity, and abortion; the general erosion of shame and awe regarding sexual matters, exemplified most vividly in the ubiquitous and voyeuristic presentation of sexual activity in movies and on television; widespread morally neutral sex education in schools; the explosive increase in the numbers of young people whose parents have been divorced (and in those born out of wedlock who have never known their father); great increases in geographic mobility, with a resulting loosening of ties to place and extended family of origin; and, harder to describe precisely, a popular culture that celebrates youth and independence not as a transient stage en route to adulthood but as "the time of our lives," imitable at all ages, and an ethos that lacks transcendent aspirations and asks of us no devotion to family, God, or country, encouraging us simply to soak up the pleasures of the present.

The change most immediately devastating to wooing is probably the sexual revolution. For why would a man court a woman for marriage when she may be sexually enjoyed without it? Contrary to what the youth of the Sixties believed, they were not the first to feel the power of sexual desire. Many – perhaps most – men in earlier times avidly sought sexual pleasure prior to and outside of marriage. But they usually distinguished, as did the culture generally, between women one fooled around with and women one married, between a woman of easy virtue and a woman of virtue simply. Only respectable women were respected; one no more wanted a loose woman for one's partner than for one's mother.

The supreme virtue of the virtuous woman was modesty, a form of sexual self-control, manifested not only in chastity but in decorous dress and manner, speech and deed, and in reticence in the display of her well-banked affections. A virtue, as it were, made for courtship, it served simultaneously (for a man) as a source of attraction and a spur to manly ardor, and (for a woman) as a guard against a woman's own desires and as a defense against unworthy suitors. A fine woman understood that giving her body (in earlier times, even her kiss) meant giving her heart, which was too precious to be bestowed on anyone who would not prove himself worthy, at the very least by pledging himself in marriage to be her defender and lover forever.

Once female modesty became a first casualty of the sexual revolution, even women eager for marriage lost their greatest power to hold and to discipline their prospective mates. For it is a woman's refusal of sexual importunings, coupled with hints or promises of later gratification, that is generally a necessary condition of transforming a man's lust into love. Women also lost the capacity to discover their own genuine longings and best interests. For only by holding herself in reserve does a woman gain the distance and self-command needed to discern what and whom she truly wants and to insist that the ardent suitor measure up. While there has always been sex without love, easy and early sexual satisfaction makes love and real intimacy *less* likely, for both men and women. Everyone's prospects for marriage were – are – sacrificed on the altar of pleasure now.

Sexual Technology and Technique

The sexual revolution that liberated (especially) female sexual desire from the confines of marriage, and even from love and intimacy, would almost certainly not have occurred had there not been available cheap and effective female birth control – the Pill – which for the first time severed female sexual activity from its generative consequences. Thanks to technology, a woman could declare herself free from the teleological meaning of her sexuality – as free as a man (mistakenly) appears to be from his. Her menstrual cycle, since puberty a regular reminder of her natural maternal destiny, is now anovulatory and directed instead by her will and her medications, serving goals only of pleasure and convenience, enjoyable without apparent risk to personal health and safety. Woman on the Pill is thus not only freed from the practical risk of pregnancy; she has, wittingly or not, begun to redefine the meaning of her own womanliness. Her sexuality unlinked to procreation, she no longer needs to be concerned about the character of her partner and whether he is suitable to be the father and co-rearer of her yet-to-be-born children. Female sexuality becomes, like male, unlinked to the future. The new woman's anthem: Girls just want to have fun. Ironically, but absolutely predictably, the chemicals devised to assist in family planning keep many a potential family from forming, at least with a proper matrimonial beginning.

Sex education in our elementary and secondary schools is an independent yet related obstacle to courtship and marriage. Taking for granted, and thereby ratifying, precocious sexual activity among teenagers and even preteens, most programs of sex education in public schools have a twofold aim: the prevention of teenage pregnancy and the prevention of venereal disease, especially AIDS. While some programs also encourage abstinence or noncoital sex, most are concerned with teaching techniques for "safe sex," thus treating offspring and disease as equally avoidable side effects of sexuality, whose true purpose is only individual pleasure. (This I myself did not learn until our younger daughter so enlightened me, after she learned it from her seventh-grade biology teacher.) The entire approach of sex education is technocratic and, at best, morally neutral; in many cases, it explicitly opposes traditional morals while moralistically insisting on the equal acceptability of any and all forms of sexual expression, provided only that they are not coerced. No effort is made to teach the importance of marriage as the true home for sexual intimacy.

But perhaps still worse than such amorality – and amorality on this subject is itself morally culpable – is the failure of sex education to attempt to inform and elevate the erotic imagination of the young. On the contrary, the very attention to physiology and technique is deadly to the imagination. True sex education is an education of the heart; it concerns itself with beautiful and worthy beloveds, with elevating transports of the soul. The energy of sexual desire, if properly sublimated, is transformable into genuine and lofty longings – not only for love and romance but for all the other higher human yearnings. The sonnets and plays of Shakespeare, the poetry of Keats and Shelley, and the novels of Jane Austen can incline a heart to woo, and even show one whom and how. What kind of wooers can one hope to cultivate from reading sex manuals – or from watching the unsublimated and unsublime sexual athleticism of the popular culture?

Decent sex education at home is also compromised, given that most parents of today's adolescents were themselves happy sexual revolutionaries. Dad may now be terribly concerned that his daughter not become promiscuous in high school or college, but he probably remains glad for the sexual favors bestowed on him by numerous coeds when he was on campus. If he speaks at all, he will likely settle for admonitions to play it safe and lessons about condoms and the Pill. And mom, a feminist and career woman, is concerned only that her daughter have sex on her own terms, not her boyfriend's. If chastity begins at home, it has lost its teachers and exemplars.

Crippled by Divorce

The ubiquitous experience of divorce is also deadly for courtship and marriage. Some people try to argue, wishfully against the empirical evidence, that children of divorce will marry better than their parents because they know how important it is to choose well. But the deck is stacked against them. Many of them are frightened of marriage, in whose likely permanence they simply do not believe, and they are often maimed for love and intimacy. They have had no successful models to imitate; worse, their capacity for trust and love has been severely crippled by the betrayal of the primal trust all children naturally repose in their parents, to provide that durable, reliable, and absolutely trustworthy haven of permanent and unconditional love in an otherwise often unloving and undependable world.

Countless students at the University of Chicago have told my wife and me that the divorce of their parents has been the most devastating and life-shaping event of their lives.* They are conscious of the fact that they enter into relationships guardedly and tentatively; for good reason, they believe that they must always be looking out for number one. Accordingly, they feel little sense of devotion to another, and with their own needs unmet they are not generally eager to have children. They are not good bets for promise keeping, and they haven't enough margin for generous service. Many of the fatherless men are themselves unmanned for fatherhood, except in the purely biological sense. Even where they dream of meeting a true love, these children of divorce have a hard time finding, winning, and committing themselves to the right one.

It is surely the fear of making a mistake in marriage, and the desire to avoid a later divorce, that leads some people to undertake cohabitation, sometimes understood by the couple to be a "trial marriage" – although they are often, one or both of them, self-deceived (or other-deceiving). It is far easier, so the argument goes, to get to know one another by cohabiting than by the artificial systems of courting or dating of yesteryear. But such arrangements, even when they eventuate in matrimony, are, precisely because they are a trial, not a trial of *marriage*. Marriage is not something one tries on for size, and then decides whether to keep; it is rather something one decides with a promise, and then bends every effort to keep.

Lacking the formalized and public ritual, and especially the vows or promises of permanence (or "commitment") that subtly but surely shape all aspects of genuine marital life, cohabitation is an arrangement of convenience, with each partner taken on approval and returnable at will. Many are just playing house – sex and meals shared with the rent. When long-cohabiting couples do later marry, whether to legitimate their prospective offspring, satisfy parental wishes, or just because "it now seems right," postmarital life is generally regarded and experienced as a continuation of the same, not as a true change of estate. The formal rite of passage that is the wedding ceremony is, however welcome and joyous, also something of a mockery: Everyone, not only the youngest child present, wonders, if only in embarrassed silence, "Why is this night different from all other nights?"

---

* In years past, students identified with Hamlet because of his desire to make a difference in the world. Today, they identify with him because of his "broken home" – the death of his father and the too-hasty remarriage of his mother. Thus, to them it is no wonder that he, like them, has trouble in his "relationships."

Given that they have more or less drifted into marriage, it should come as no great surprise that couples who have lived together before marriage have a higher rate of divorce than those who have not. Too much familiarity? Disenchantment? Or is it rather the lack of wooing – that is, that marriage was not seen from the start as the sought-for relationship, as the goal that beckoned and guided the process of getting-to-know-you?

Feminism against Marriage

That the cause of courtship has been severely damaged by feminist ideology and attitudes goes almost without saying. Even leaving aside the radical attacks on traditional sex roles, on the worth of motherhood or the vanishing art of homemaking, and sometimes even on the whole male race, the reconception of all relations between the sexes as relations based on power is deadly for love. Anyone who has ever loved or been loved knows the difference between love and the will to power, no matter what the cynics say. But the cynical new theories, and the resulting push toward androgyny, surely inhibit the growth of love.

On the one side, there is a rise in female assertiveness and efforts at empowerment, with a consequent need to deny all womanly dependence and the kind of vulnerability that calls for the protection of strong and loving men, protection such men were once – and would still be – willing to provide. On the other side, we see the enfeeblement of men, who, contrary to the dominant ideology, are not likely to become better lovers, husbands, or fathers if they too become feminists or fellow travelers. On the contrary, many men now cynically exploit women's demands for equal power by letting them look after themselves – pay their own way, hold their own doors, fight their own battles, travel after dark by themselves. These ever-so-sensitive males will defend not a woman's honor but her right to learn the manly art of self-defense. In the present climate, those increasingly rare men who are still inclined to be gentlemen must dissemble their generosity as submissiveness.*

---

* Truth to tell, the reigning ideology often rules only people's tongues, not their hearts. Many a young woman secretly hopes to meet and catch a gentleman, though the forms that might help her do so are either politically incorrect or simply unknown

Even apart from the love-poisoning doctrines of radical feminism, the otherwise welcome changes in women's education and employment have also been problematic for courtship. True, better-educated women (in addition to having more interesting lives and work themselves) can find more interesting husbands and can be more engaging partners for better-educated men; and the possibility of a genuine friendship between husband and wife – one that could survive the end of the childrearing years – is, at least in principle, much more likely now that women have equal access to higher education. But everything depends on the spirit and the purpose of such education, and whether it makes and keeps a high place for private life.

Most young people in our better colleges today do not esteem the choice for marriage as equal to the choice for career, not for themselves, not for anyone. Students reading *The Tempest*, for example, are almost universally appalled that Miranda would fall in love at first sight with Ferdinand, thus sealing her fate and precluding "making something of herself" – say, by going to graduate school. Even her prospects as future queen of Naples lack all appeal, presumably because they depend on her husband and on marriage. At least officially, no young woman will admit to dreaming of meeting her prince; better a position, a salary, and a room of her own.

The problem is not woman's desire for meaningful work. It is rather the ordering of one's loves. Many women have managed to combine work and family; the difficulty is not work but careers, or, more precisely, careerism. Now an equal-opportunity affliction, careerism is surely no friend to love or marriage – neither for women nor for men; and the careerist character of higher education is greater than ever. Women are under special pressures to prove they can be as dedicated to their work as men. In the workplace likewise they must do man's work like a man, and for a man's pay and perquisites. Consequently, they are compelled to regard private life, and especially marriage, homemaking, and family, as

---

to her. In my wife's course on Henry James's *The Bostonians*, the class's most strident feminist, who had all term denounced patriarchy and male hegemonism, honestly confessed in the last class that she wished she could meet a Basil Ransom who would carry her off. But the way to her heart is blocked by her prickly opinions and by the dominant ethos.

lesser goods, to be pursued only by those lesser women who can aspire no higher than "baking cookies."

Besides, many women in such circumstances have nothing left to give, "no time to get involved." And marriage, should it come for careerist women, is often compromised from the start, what with the difficulty of finding two worthy jobs in the same city, or commuter marriage, or the need to negotiate or get hired help for every domestic and familial task. Besides these greater conflicts of time and energy, the economic independence of women, however welcome on other grounds, is itself not an asset for marital stability, as both the woman and the man can more readily contemplate leaving the marriage. Indeed, a woman's earning power can become her own worst enemy when the children are born. Many professional women who would like to stay home with their new babies nonetheless work full-time. Tragically, some cling to their economic independence because they worry that their husbands will leave them for another woman before the children are grown. What are these women looking for in prospective husbands? Do their own career preoccupations obscure their own prospective maternal wishes and needs? Indeed, what understanding of marriage informed their decision to marry in the first place?

Not Ready for Adulthood

There is a more subtle, but most profound, impediment to wooing and marriage: deep uncertainty about what marriage is and means, and what purpose it serves. In previous generations, people chose to marry, but they were not compelled also to choose what marriage meant. Is it a sacrament, a covenant, or a contract based on calculation of mutual advantage? Is it properly founded on *eros*, friendship, or economic and social advantage? Is marriage a vehicle for personal fulfillment and private happiness, a vocation of mutual service, or a task to love the one whom it has been given me to love? Are marital vows still to be regarded as binding promises that both partners are duty-bound to keep, or rather as quaint expressions of current hopes and predictions that can easily be nullified should they be mistaken? Having in so many cases already given their bodies to one another – not to speak of the previous others – how do young people today understand the link between marriage and conjugal fidelity? And what, finally, of that first purpose of marriage, procreation, for whose sake societies everywhere have instituted and safeguarded this institution? For, truth to tell, were it not for the important obligations to care for and rear the next generation, no society would much care about who couples with whom, or with how many, or for how long.

This brings me to what is probably the deepest and most intractable obstacle to courtship and marriage: a set of cultural attitudes and sensibilities that obscure and even deny the fundamental difference between youth and adulthood. Marriage, especially when seen as the institution designed to provide for the next generation, is most definitely the business of adults, by which I mean people who are serious about life, people who aspire to go outward and forward to embrace and assume responsibility for the future. To be sure, most college graduates do go out, find jobs, and become self-supporting (though, astonishingly, a great many return to live at home). But though out of the nest, they don't have a course to fly. They do not experience their lives as a trajectory, with an inner meaning partly given by the life cycle itself. They do not see the carefreeness and independence of youth as a stage on the way to maturity, where they take responsibility for the world and especially, as parents, for the new lives that will replace them. The necessities of aging and mortality are out of sight; few feel the call to serve a higher goal or a transcendent purpose.

The view of life as play has often characterized the young, but today, remarkably, it is not regarded as something to be outgrown as soon as possible. For their narcissistic absorption in themselves and in immediate pleasures and present experiences, the young are not condemned but are even envied by many of their elders. Parents and children wear the same cool clothes, speak the same lingo, listen to the same music. Youth, not adulthood, is the cultural ideal, at least as celebrated in the popular culture. Yes, everyone feels himself or herself to be always growing, as a result of this failed relationship or that change of job. But very few aspire to be fully grown-up, and the culture does not demand it, not least because many prominent grown-ups would gladly change places with today's twenty-somethings. Why should a young man be eager to take his father's place if he sees his father running away from it with all deliberate speed? How many so-called grown-ups today agree with C. S. Lewis: "I envy youth its stomach, not its heart"?

Deeper Cultural Causes

So this is our situation. But just because it is novel and of recent origin does not mean that it is reversible or even that it was avoidable. Indeed, virtually all of the social changes we have so recently experienced are the bittersweet fruits of the success of our modern, democratic, liberal, enlightened society – celebrating equality, freedom, and universal secularized education, and featuring prosperity, mobility, and astonishing progress in science and technology. Even brief reflection shows how the dominant features of the American way of life are finally inhospitable to the stability of marriage and family life, and to the mores that lead people self-consciously to marry.

Tocqueville already observed the unsettling implications of American individualism, each person seeking only in himself for the reasons of things. The celebration of equality gradually undermines the authority of religion, tradition, and custom, and, within families, of husbands over wives and fathers over sons. A nation dedicated to safeguarding individual rights to liberty and the privately defined pursuit of happiness is, willy-nilly, preparing the way for the "liberation" of women, and in the absence of powerful nonliberal cultural forces such as traditional biblical religion that defend sex-linked social roles, the most likely outcome is androgyny in education and employment. Further, our liberal approach to important moral issues in terms of the rights of individuals – for example, contraception as part of a right to privacy, or abortion as belonging to a woman's right over her own body, or procreation as governed by a right to reproduce – flies in the face of the necessarily social character of sexuality and marriage. The courtship and marriage of people who see themselves as self-sufficient rights-bearing individuals will be decisively different from the courtship and marriage of people who understand themselves as unavoidably incomplete and dependent children of the Lord who have been enjoined to be fruitful and multiply.

While poverty is not generally good for courtship and marriage, neither is luxury. The lifestyles of the rich and famous have long been rich also in philandering, divorce, and the neglect of children. Necessity becomes hidden from view by the possibilities for self-indulgence; the need for service and self-sacrifice, so necessary for marriage understood as procreative, is rarely learned in the lap of plenty. Thanks to unprecedented prosperity, huge numbers of American youth have grown up in the lap of luxury, and it shows. It's an old story: Parents who slave to give their children everything they themselves were denied rarely produce people who will be similarly disposed toward their own children. Spoiled children make bad spouses and worse parents; when they eventually look for a mate, they frequently look for someone who will continue to cater to their needs and whims. For most people, the mother of virtue and maturity is necessity, not luxury.

The progress of science and technology, especially since World War II, has played a major role in creating an enfeebling culture of luxury. But scientific advances have more directly helped to undermine the customs of courtship. Technological advances in food production and distribution and a plethora of appliances – refrigerators, vacuum cleaners, washing machines, dryers, etc. – largely eliminate the burdens of housekeeping; not surprisingly, however, homemaking itself disappears with the burdens, for the unburdened housewife now finds outside fish to fry. More significantly, medical advances have virtually eliminated infant mortality and deadly childhood diseases, contributing indirectly to a reduction in family size. The combination of longer life expectancy and effective contraception means that, for the first time in human history, the childbearing and childrearing years occupy only a small fraction (one-fifth to one-fourth) of a woman's life; it is therefore less reasonable that she be solely prepared for, and satisfied by, the vocation of motherhood. Lastly, medical advances quite independent of contraception have prepared the drive toward sexual liberation: the triumph of the sexual is a predictable outcome of the successful pursuit, through medicine, of the young and enduringly healthy human body.

In fact, in his *New Atlantis*, Francis Bacon foresaw that the most likely social outcome of medical success would be a greatly intensified eroticism and promiscuous sexuality, in which healthy and perfected bodies seek enjoyment here and now without regard to the need for marriage, procreation, and childrearing. To counter these dangers, Bacon has his proposed utopian society establish the most elaborate rituals to govern marriage, and give its highest honor – after those conferred on the men of science – to the man who has sired over thirty living descendants (within marital boundaries). Without such countervailing customs, the successful pursuit of longer life and better health would lead to a culture of protracted youthfulness, hedonism, and sexual license, as Bacon clearly understood – and as we have seen in recent decades.

Technology aside, even the ideas of modern science have hurt the traditional understanding of sex. The rejection of a teleological view of nature has damaged most of all the teleological view of our sexuality. Sure, children come from the sex act, but the sex act no longer naturally derives its meaning or purpose from this procreative possibility. After all, a man spends perhaps all of thirty seconds of his sexual life procreating; sex is thus about something else. The separation of sex from procreation achieved in this half century by contraception was worked out intellectually much earlier; and the implications for marriage were drawn in theory well before they were realized in practice. Immanuel Kant, modernity's most demanding and most austere moralist, nonetheless gave marriage a heady push down the slippery slope: Seeing that some marriages were childless, and seeing that sex had no necessary link to procreation, Kant redefined marriage as "a lifelong contract for the mutual exercise of the genitalia." If this be marriage, any reason for its permanence, exclusivity, and fidelity vanishes.

With science, the leading wing of modern rationalism, has come the progressive demystification of the world. Falling in love, should it still occur, is for the modern temper to be explained not by demonic possession (Eros) born of the soul-smiting sight of the beautiful (Aphrodite), but by a rise in the concentration of some still-to-be-identified polypeptide hormone in the hypothalamus. The power of religious sensibilities and understandings fades too. Even if it is true that the great majority of Americans still profess a belief in God, He is for few of us a God before whom one trembles in fear of judgment. With adultery almost as American as apple pie, few people appreciate the *awe-ful* shame of *The Scarlet Letter*. The taboos against the sexual abominations of Leviticus – incest, homosexuality, and bestiality – are going the way of all flesh, the second with religious blessings, no less. Ancient religious teachings on marriage have lost their authority even for people who regard themselves as serious Jews or Christians: Who really believes that husbands should govern their wives as Christ governs the church, or that a husband should love his wife as Christ loved the church and should give himself up to death for her (Ephesians 5:24–25)?

The Natural Obstacle

Not all the obstacles to courtship and marriage are cultural. At bottom, there is also the deeply ingrained, natural waywardness and unruliness of the human male. Sociobiologists were not the first to discover that males have a penchant for promiscuity and polygyny; this was well known to biblical religion. Men are also naturally more restless and ambitious than women; lacking woman's powerful and immediate link to life's generative answer to mortality, men flee from the fear of death into heroic deeds, great quests, or sheer distraction. One can make a good case that biblical religion is, not least, an attempt to domesticate male sexuality and male erotic longings, and to put them in the service of transmitting a righteous and holy way of life through countless generations.

For as long as American society kept strong its uneasy union between modern liberal political principles and Judeo-Christian moral and social beliefs, marriage and the family could be sustained and could even prosper. But the gender-neutral individualism of our political teaching has, it seems, at last won the day, and the result has been *male* "liberation" – from domestication, from civility, from responsible self-command. Contemporary liberals and conservatives alike are trying to figure out how to get men to "commit" to marriage, or to keep their marital vows, or to stay home with the children, but their own androgynous view of humankind prevents them from seeing how hard it has always been to make a monogamous husband and devoted father out of the human male.

Ogden Nash had it right: "Hogamus higamus, men are polygamous; higamus hogamus, women monogamous." To make naturally polygamous men accept the conventional institution of monogamous marriage – rightly deemed necessary for the proper care and rearing of the next generation – has been the work of centuries of Western civilization, with social sanctions, backed by religious teachings and authority, as major instruments of the transformation, and with female modesty as the crucial civilizing device. As these mores and sanctions disappear, courtship gives way to seduction and possession, and men become again the sexually, familially, and civically irresponsible creatures they are naturally always in danger of being. At the top of the social ladder, executives walk out on their families and take up with trophy wives. At the bottom, low-status males, utterly uncivilized by marriage, return to the fighting gangs, taking young women as prizes for their prowess. Rebar-barization is just around the corner. Courtship, anyone?

Why It Matters

Given the enormous new social impediments to courtship and marriage, and given also that they are firmly and deeply rooted in the cultural soil of modernity, not to say human nature itself, one might simply decide to declare the cause lost. Indeed, many people would be only too glad to do so. For they condemn the old ways as repressive, inegalitarian, sexist, patriarchal, boring, artificial, and unnecessary. Some urge us to go with the flow, while others hopefully believe that new modes and orders will emerge, well suited to our new conditions of liberation and equality: just as new cultural meanings are today being "constructed" for sexuality and gender, so too new cultural definitions can be invented for "marriage," "paternity and maternity," and "family." Nothing truly important will be lost – so the argument goes.

New arrangements can perhaps be fashioned. As Raskolnikov put it (and he should know), "Man gets used to everything, the beast!" But it is simply wrong to say that nothing important will be lost; indeed, many things of great importance have already been lost, and, as I have indicated, at tremendous cost in personal happiness, child welfare, and civic peace. This should come as no surprise. For the new arrangements that constitute the cultural void created by the demise of courtship and dating rest on serious and destructive errors regarding the human condition: errors about the meaning of human sexuality, errors about the nature of marriage, errors about what constitutes a fully human life.

Sexual desire, in human beings as in animals, points to an end that is partly hidden from, and ultimately at odds with, the self-serving individual: Sexuality as such means perishability and serves replacement. The salmon swimming upstream to spawn and die tell the universal story: Sex is bound up with death, to which it holds a partial answer in procreation. This truth the salmon and the other animals practice blindly; only the human being can understand what it means. As we learn powerfully from the story of the Garden of Eden, our humanization is coincident with sexual self-consciousness, with the recognition of our sexual nakedness and all that it implies: shame at our needy incompleteness, unruly self-division, and finitude; awe before the eternal; hope in the self-transcending possibilities of children and a relationship to the divine.[2] For a human being to treat sex as a desire like hunger – not to mention as sport – is to live a deception.

How shallow an understanding of sexuality is embodied in our current clamoring for "safe sex." Sex is by its nature unsafe. All interpersonal relations are necessarily risky and serious ones especially so. To give oneself to another, body and soul, is hardly playing it safe. Sexuality is at its core profoundly "unsafe," and it is only thanks to contraception that we are encouraged to forget its inherent "dangers." These go beyond the hazards of venereal disease, a reminder and a symbol of the high stakes involved, and beyond the risks of pregnancy and the pains and dangers of childbirth. To repeat, sexuality itself means mortality – equally for both man and woman. Whether we know it or not, when we are sexually active we are voting with our genitalia for our own demise. "Safe sex" is the self-delusion of shallow souls.*

It is for this reason that procreation remains at the core of a proper understanding of marriage. Mutual pleasure and mutual service between husband and wife are, of course, part of the story. So too are mutual admiration and esteem, especially where the partners are deserving. A friendship of shared pursuits and pastimes enhances any marriage, all the more so when the joint activities exercise deeper human capacities. But it is precisely the common project of procreation that holds together what sexual differentiation sometimes threatens to drive apart. Through children, a good common to husband and wife, male and female achieve some genuine unification (beyond the mere sexual "union" that fails to do so): The two become one through sharing generous (not needy) love for this third being as good. Flesh of their flesh, the child is the parents' own commingled being externalized, and given a separate and persisting existence; unification is enhanced also by their commingled work of rear-

---

* This is not to say that the sole meaning of sexuality is procreative; understood as lovemaking, sexual union is also a means of expressing mutual love and the desire for a union of souls. Making love need lose none of its tenderness after the childbearing years are past. Yet the procreative possibility embedded in *eros* cannot be expunged without distorting its meaning.

ing. Providing an opening to the future beyond the grave, carrying not only our seed but also our names, our ways, and our hopes that they will surpass us in goodness and happiness, children are a testament to the possibility of transcendence. Gender duality and sexual desire, which first draws our love upward and outside of ourselves, finally provide for the partial overcoming of the confinement and limitation of perishable embodiment altogether. It is as the supreme institution devoted to this renewal of human possibility that marriage finds its deepest meaning and highest function.

There is no substitute for the contribution that the shared work of raising children makes to the singular friendship and love of husband and wife. Precisely because of its central procreative mission, and, even more, because children are yours for a lifetime, this is a friendship that cannot be had with any other person. Uniquely, it is a friendship that does not fly from, but rather embraces wholeheartedly, the finitude of its members, affirming without resentment the truth of our human condition. Not by mistake did God create a woman – rather than a dialectic partner – to cure Adam's aloneness; not by accident does the same biblical Hebrew verb mean both to know sexually and to know the truth – including the generative truth about the meaning of being man and woman.* For most people, therefore, marriage and procreation are at the heart of a serious and flourishing human life.

The earlier forms of courtship, leading men and women to the altar, rested on an understanding of the deeper truths about human sexuality, marriage, and the higher possibilities for human life. Courtship provided rituals for growing up, for making clear the meaning of one's own human sexual nature, and for entering into the ceremonial and customary world of service and sanctification. Courtship disciplined sexual desire and romantic attraction, provided opportunities for mutual learning about

---

* I recognize that there are happily monogamous marriages that remain childless, some by choice, others by bad luck, and that some people will feel the pull of and yield to a higher calling, be it art, philosophy, or the celibate priesthood, seeking or serving some other transcendent voice. But the former often feel cheated by their childlessness, frequently going to extraordinary lengths to conceive or adopt a child. A childless and grandchild-less old age is a sadness and a deprivation, even where it is a price willingly paid by couples who deliberately do not procreate. And for those who elect not to marry, they at least face the meaning of the choice forgone. They do not reject,

one another's character, fostered salutary illusions that inspired admiration and devotion, and, by locating wooer and wooed in their familial settings, taught the intergenerational meaning of erotic activity. It pointed the way to the answers to life's biggest questions: Where are you going? Who is going with you? How – in what manner – are you both going to go?

The practices of today's men and women do not accomplish these purposes, and they and their marriages, when they get around to them, are weaker as a result. There may be no going back to the earlier forms of courtship, but no one should be rejoicing over this fact. Anyone serious about "designing" new cultural forms to replace those that are now defunct must bear the burden of finding some alternative means of serving all these necessary goals.

Is a Revolution Needed?

Is the situation hopeless? One might see a bit of encouraging news in the great popularity – not just among those over fifty – of the recent Jane Austen movies, *Sense and Sensibility*, *Persuasion*, and *Emma*, and (on public television) the splendid BBC version of *Pride and Prejudice*. This is only a small ray of hope, but I believe that the renewed interest in Jane Austen reflects a dissatisfaction with the unromantic and amarital present, and a wish on the part of many twenty- and thirty-somethings to find their own equivalent of Elizabeth Bennet or Mr. Darcy (even without his Pemberly). The return of successful professional matchmaking services – I do not mean the innumerable "self-matching" services that fill pages of "personal" ads in our newspapers and magazines – is a fur-

---

but rather affirm, the trajectory of a human life, whose boundaries are given by necessity, and our animal nature, whose higher yearnings and aspirations are made possible in large part because we recognize our neediness and insufficiency. But until very recently the aging self-proclaimed bachelor was the butt of many jokes, mildly censured for his self-indulgent and carefree, not to say profligate, ways, and for his unwillingness to repay the gift of life and nurture by giving life and nurturing in return. No matter how successful he was in business or profession, he could not avoid some taint of immaturity.

ther bit of good news.* So too is the revival of explicit courtship practices among certain religious groups; young men are told by young women that they need their parents' permission to come courting, and marriage alone is clearly the name of the game. And – if I may grasp at straws – one can even take a small bit of comfort from those who steadfastly refuse to marry, insofar as they do so because they recognize that marriage is too serious, too demanding, too audacious an adventure for their immature, irresponsible, and cowardly selves.

Frail reeds, indeed – probably not enough to save even a couple of courting water bugs. Real reform in the direction of sanity would require a restoration of cultural gravity about sex, marriage, and the life cycle. The restigmatization of illegitimacy and promiscuity would help. A reversal of recent antinatalist prejudices, implicit in the practice of abortion, and a correction of current antigenerative sex education would also help, as would the revalorization of marriage as both a personal and a cultural ideal. Parents of pubescent children could contribute to a truly humanizing sex education by elevating their erotic imagination, through exposure to an older and more edifying literature. Parents of college-bound young people, especially those with strong religious and family values, could direct their children to religiously affiliated colleges that attract like-minded people.

Even in deracinated and cosmopolitan universities like my own, faculty could legitimize the importance of courtship and marriage by offering courses on the subject, aimed at making the students more thoughtful about their own life-shaping choices. Even better, they could teach without ideological or methodological preoccupations the world's great literature, elevating the longings and refining the sensibilities of their students and furnishing their souls with numerous examples of lives seriously led and loves faithfully followed. (The next chapter offers an illustration of using a great text in this way.) Religious institutions could provide earlier and better instruction for adolescents on the meaning of sex and marriage, as well as suitable opportunities for coreligionists to mix and, God willing, match. Without congregational or communal sup-

---

* The burgeoning use of Internet dating and matchmaking services deserves a separate treatment of its own, which I offer in Chapter Four.

port, individual parents will generally be helpless before the onslaught of the popular culture.

Under present democratic conditions, with families not what they used to be, anything that contributes to promoting a lasting friendship between husband and wife should be cultivated. A budding couple today needs even better skills at reading character, and greater opportunities for showing it, than was necessary in a world that had lots of family members looking on. Paradoxically, encouragement of earlier marriage, and earlier childbearing, might in many cases be helpful – the young couple growing up together, as it were, before either partner could become jaded or distrustful from too much premarital experience, not only of "relationships" but of life. Postcollegiate career training for married women could be postponed until after the early motherhood years – perhaps even supported publicly by something like a GI Bill of Rights for mothers who had stayed home until their children reached school age.

But it would appear to require a revolution to restore the conditions most necessary for successful courtship: a desire in America's youth for mature adulthood (which means for marriage and parenthood), an appreciation of the unique character of the marital bond, understood as linked to generation, and a restoration of sexual self-restraint generally and of female modesty in particular.

Frankly, I do not see how this last, most crucial prerequisite can be recovered, nor do I see how one can do sensibly without it. As Tocqueville rightly noted, it is women who are the teachers of mores; it is largely through the purity of her morals, self-regulated, that woman wields her influence, both before and after marriage. Men, as Rousseau put it, will always do what is pleasing to women, but only if women suitably control and channel their own considerable sexual power. Is there perhaps some nascent young feminist out there who would like to make her name great and who will seize the golden opportunity for advancing the truest interest of women (and men and children) by raising (again) the radical banner, "Not until you marry me"? And, while I'm dreaming, why not also, "Not without my parents' blessings"?

CHAPTER THREE

The Higher Sex Education

Help from an Old Story*

ANYONE INTERESTED in improving relations between men and women today and tomorrow must proceed by taking a page from yesterday, for today's tale regarding manhood and womanhood is, alas, too brief and hardly edifying. Our sexual harassment police do emphatically prescribe how *not* to behave toward the opposite sex, as they multiply taboos on speech and gesture. But outside of certain strongly religious communities, we have no clearly defined *positive* mores and manners that teach men how to be men in relation to women, and women how to be women in relation to men – or, for that matter, how to be gentlemen and ladies. What instruction there is for relations between the sexes is largely gender-neutral: respect the other person's freedom; avoid sexist speech and unwanted advances; be sincere, sensitive, and caring. The common designations for pairings-off are neutered and unerotic: people have a relationship, not a romance, with a partner or a significant other, not a lover or a beloved. Never mind "hooking up," which looks upon casual sex as the joining of cattle cars. In our increasingly androgynous age, our sexual speech and mores are designed to fit all couples, homo- and heterosexual, and all manners of intimacy, serious or frivolous.

Though maleness and femaleness are natural facts, manhood and

---

* This chapter is largely based on an essay written with my wife of blessed memory, Amy A. Kass.

womanhood are, in fashionable opinion, culturally constructed norms, at least to some degree. It is no accident that the meaning of being a man or being a woman has been radically transformed in a society that celebrates freedom and equality, encourages individualism and autonomy, rejects tradition, practices contraception and abortion, sees marriage as a lifestyle, provides the same education and promotes the same careers for men and women, homogenizes fathers and mothers in the neutered work of "parenting," denies vulnerability and dependence, keeps mortality out of sight, and raises its children without any sense of duty or obligation to future generations. As I argued in the last chapter, the roots of these cultural ideas and practices lie deeper than the sexual revolution, feminism, and the Sixties, and it is naive to think that we can easily reverse their influence with some newly designed mores and manners, like the return of ballroom dancing or single-sex dormitories or romantic ballads, welcome though these changes might be. Truth to tell, most of us would not want to roll back the clock even if we could, and we certainly don't want to abandon modern liberal democratic society, equal opportunities for women, or the easier ways of life made possible by the scientific-technological project. This means that even conservatives are looking for reform on the cheap, a revival of good sense and decency in relations between the sexes without sacrificing any of the privileges and luxuries of modern life. We strongly suspect this is impossible.

But even if no one can prescribe a good remedy, we are no longer in denial about whether the patient is sick. In the last few decades we have witnessed the rise of discontent, mainly among women, with the present arrangements between the sexes. Many women, and some men, are revolted by the hookup culture and are looking for alternatives: they want real intimacy, they want enduring relationships, they want marriage. Best-selling advice books for durable relationships, books on modesty, campus projects like "Take Back the Date" and the "Love and Fidelity Network," and the rising popularity of marriage-oriented Internet matching services (examined in the next chapter) are important signs that many people – again, especially women – are eager for lasting relationships with the opposite sex based on romance and mutual respect, fidelity and friendship. Whether they know it or not, what they want is a revival of some form of courtship, with established modes of speech and deed whose goal is marriage.

Anyone interested in developing new mores and manners pointing toward marriage needs to understand what these mores once were, and, even more, what they were trying to achieve. In addition, young people need to acquire the sensibilities, tastes, and skills in reading character that can help them find and judge prospective mates – something they once gained from the study of fine literature and which they can never hope to learn from watching *Seinfeld* or *Sex and the City* or *Two and a Half Men*. To explore the now lost practices of courtship and to encourage the relevant sensibilities, in 1996 we offered a (by invitation only) seminar on the subject at the University of Chicago. We were moved to do so after two decades of observing, with growing sadness, the frustrations and disappointments of our students and former students as they passed through the decade of their twenties (and for some, far into their thirties) failing to find the life partner they longed for or the private happiness that is based on lasting intimacy. The success of our seminar, in which we read and discussed selections mostly from old books, inspired us to prepare an anthology of readings on courting and marrying, designed to help people of marriageable age become more thoughtful about what they are and should be doing. *Wing to Wing, Oar to Oar: Readings on Courting and Marrying*, published in 2000, became the basis for a publicly offered undergraduate course we taught at Chicago in the spring of that year. We were hoping to revive a higher kind of sex education, an education of heart and mind for lasting marital happiness.

We knew that we faced a formidable challenge – a couple of aging dinosaurs discussing sex, love, courting and marrying with a bunch of hairy mammals young enough to have been our grandchildren. And after hearing their opinions in the first class, I was convinced that the enterprise was pure folly. Male student: "The idea of being married to the same woman for twenty-five years is preposterous." (We had then been married almost thirty-nine years.) Female student: "We know that we are not supposed to get married until we are at least twenty-eight, so all of our current relationships with men are *supposed to be* impermanent." Female student: "Casual sex with men is a great improvement, because, by getting the sex thing out of the way, it is now possible to be *friends* with men as it never was before." After that class, I felt like tossing in the towel and never going back.

But my wife, cooler and wiser, knew not to despair. "Not to worry.

They are just blowing smoke. We'll do what we always do: put good readings in front of them and discuss them as if they really mattered. You'll see. They are better than they know." And so for the next ten weeks we read and talked about, for example, the Garden of Eden story, the coupling of Ares and Aphrodite, Aristophanes' speech from Plato's *Symposium*, C. S. Lewis on *Eros*, and the courtships of Darcy and Elizabeth (*Pride and Prejudice*), Emile and Sophie (Rousseau's *Emile*), and Orlando and Rosalind (*As You Like It*).

Surprisingly, perhaps the most helpful reading turned out to be Erasmus's "Courtship: A Colloquy" (written in 1523), a compressed dramatic enactment in which Erasmus depicts not so much what was happening in his day as what he thought *should* happen.[3] It provides a useful mirror in which we can see the deficiencies of our present situation and, at the same time, look for basic principles of courtship that might still be necessary and desirable today. By reviewing and commenting here on major portions of the colloquy, we seek to show by example how pondering old texts can contribute to the search for positive manners and mores, especially in an age where none are available.

On first or even second reading, "Courtship: A Colloquy" will no doubt strike most modern readers as quaint or irrelevant, at best. We hope to demonstrate why it can and should be taken seriously, not because it offers a pattern readily importable to modern times – it doesn't – but because it addresses, whether we recognize them or not, what are still the most important issues: (1) How to transform brutish sexual appetite into human loving? (2) How to make a manly man interested in marriage and (when they arrive) attached to his children? (3) How to help a woman negotiate between her erotic desires and her concern for progeny? (4) How to enable men to find and win, how to enable women to select and hold the right one for lasting marriage? (5) How to locate the relations of men and women in the larger contexts of human life – familial, political, religious? More up-to-date mores and manners that do not come to terms with these issues will not get the job done. The colloquy should command our attention also because it illustrates what may be the central truth about sexual manners and mores: it is women who control and teach mores.

* * *

Pamphilus and Maria meet in the evening in the vicinity of Maria's family home, probably neither by prior arrangement nor entirely by chance. Pamphilus (whose name means "all-loving" or "loving all") appears at first to be a foolish, moonstruck lover, quite beside himself in love. Although it later will emerge that he is willing to marry, Pamphilus is eager to win Maria (named after the Virgin) here and now, and he presses his suit – in speech and manner – after the conventions of love poetry. Maria, by contrast, appears from the start to be utterly sensible and self-possessed; witty, sharp, and charming, she almost immediately assumes control. She will direct the conversation from the conventions of love poetry to the conventions of marriage. The beginning establishes both the tone and the starting points of the courtship. (Readers are encouraged to read the dialogue aloud, and dramatically.)

PAMPHILUS: Hello – you cruel, hardhearted, unrelenting creature!

MARIA: Hello yourself, Pamphilus, as often and as much as you like, and by whatever name you please. But sometimes I think you've forgotten my name. It's Maria.

PAMPHILUS: Quite appropriate for you to be named after Mars.

MARIA: Why so? What have I to do with Mars?

PAMPHILUS: You slay men for sport, as the god does. Except that you're more pitiless than Mars: you kill even a lover.

MARIA: Mind what you're saying. Where's this heap of men I've slain? Where's the blood of the slaughtered?

PAMPHILUS: You've only to look at me to see one lifeless corpse.

MARIA: What do I hear? You speak and walk about when you're dead? I hope I never meet more fearsome ghosts!

PAMPHILUS: You're joking, but all the same you're the death of poor me, and you kill more cruelly than if you pierced with a spear. Now, alas, I'm just skin and bones from long torture.

MARIA: Well, well! Tell me, how many pregnant women have miscarried at the sight of you?

PAMPHILUS: But my pallor shows I've less blood than any ghost.

MARIA: Yet this pallor is streaked with lavender. You're as pale as a ripening cherry or a purple grape.

PAMPHILUS: Shame on you for making fun of a miserable wretch!

MARIA: But if you don't believe me, bring a mirror.

PAMPHILUS: I want no other mirror, nor do I think any could be brighter, than the one in which I'm looking at myself now.

MARIA: What mirror are you talking about?

PAMPHILUS: Your eyes.

Pamphilus opens by greeting Maria not by name but as "you cruel, hardhearted, unrelenting creature": he finds her cruel because she is hard-hearted, and hard-hearted because she is unrelenting. From the man's point of view, the woman's crime in love is her steadfast refusal to yield sexually to a wooer's importunings. Indeed, after Maria greets him by name and playfully reminds him of her own, Pamphilus sees in her name not mainly the Virgin but rather the pagan deity Mars: Maria appears to him not merely unrelenting but positively warlike, martially aggressive in defense of her virginity.

Maria's lighthearted defense and skillful repartee soon make Pamphilus blush ("You're as pale as a ripening cherry") and then be embarrassed by this involuntary self-revelation ("*Shame* on *you* for making fun of a miserable wretch!"); blushing and embarrassment are good signs, indicating that a man seeks not only a woman's acquiescence but also her esteem and approval. Yet even in this respect Pamphilus remains self-absorbed. In looking at Maria's eyes, he literally and figuratively sees only himself. Trafficking in his own wretched, lovelorn state, he seems as much in love with love as he does with Maria.

Despite her steady resistance, Maria is obviously attracted to Pamphilus – just listen to the way she eggs him on – but, serious in her playfulness, she never forgets who she is or what she wants, not only here and now but especially hereafter. Exploiting his ardor and her self-restraint, she employs her considerable wit to bring Pamphilus round to seeing things from her point of view.

MARIA: ... But how do you prove you're lifeless? Do ghosts eat?

PAMPHILUS: Yes, but they eat insipid stuff, as I do.

MARIA: What do they eat, then?

PAMPHILUS: Mallows, leeks, and lupines.

MARIA: But you don't abstain from capons and partridges.

PAMPHILUS: True, but they taste no better to my palate than if I were eating mallows, or beets without pepper, wine, and vinegar.

MARIA: Poor you! Yet all the time you're putting on weight. And do dead men talk, too?

PAMPHILUS: Like me, in a very thin, squeaky voice.

MARIA: When I heard you wrangling with your rival not long ago, though, your voice wasn't so thin and squeaky. But I ask you, do ghosts even walk? Wear clothes? Sleep?

PAMPHILUS: They even sleep together – though after their own fashion.

MARIA: Well! Witty fellow, aren't you?

PAMPHILUS: But what will you say if I demonstrate with Achillean proofs that I'm dead and you're a murderer?

MARIA: Perish the thought, Pamphilus! But proceed to your argument.

PAMPHILUS: In the first place, you'll grant, I suppose, that death is nothing but the removal of soul from body?

MARIA: Granted....

PAMPHILUS: Then you won't deny that whoever robs another of his soul is a murderer?

MARIA: I allow it.

PAMPHILUS: You'll concede also what's affirmed by the most respected authors and endorsed by the assent of so many ages: that man's soul is not where it animates but where it loves.

MARIA: Explain this more simply. I don't follow your meaning well enough....

PAMPHILUS: Men seized by a divine inspiration neither hear nor see nor smell nor feel, even if you kill them.

MARIA: Yes, I've heard that.

PAMPHILUS: What do you suppose is the reason?

MARIA: You tell me, professor.

PAMPHILUS: Obviously because their spirit is in heaven, where it possesses what it ardently loves, and is absent from the body.

MARIA: What of it?

PAMPHILUS: What of it, you unfeeling girl? It follows both that I'm dead and that you're the murderer.

MARIA: Where's your soul, then?

PAMPHILUS: Where it loves.

MARIA: But who robbed you of your soul? – Why do you sigh? Speak freely; I won't hold it against you.

PAMPHILUS: Cruelest of girls, whom nevertheless I can't hate even if I'm dead!

MARIA: Naturally. But why don't you in turn deprive her of *her* soul – tit for tat, as they say?

PAMPHILUS: I'd like nothing better if the exchange could be such that her spirit migrated to my breast, as my spirit has gone over completely to her body.

MARIA: But may I, in turn, play the sophist with you?

PAMPHILUS: The sophistress.

MARIA: It isn't possible for the same body to be living and lifeless, is it?

PAMPHILUS: No, not at the same time.

MARIA: When the soul's gone, then the body's dead?

PAMPHILUS: Yes.

MARIA: It doesn't animate except when it's present?

PAMPHILUS: Exactly.

MARIA: Then how does it happen that although the soul's there where it loves, it nevertheless animates the body left behind? If it animates that body even when it loves elsewhere, how can the animated body be called lifeless?

PAMPHILUS: You dispute cunningly enough, but you won't catch me with such snares. The soul that somehow or other governs the body of a lover is incorrectly called soul, since actually it consists of certain slight remnants of soul – just as the scent of roses remains in your hand even if the rose is taken away....

MARIA: Now don't begrudge an answer to this, too: do you love willingly or unwillingly?

PAMPHILUS: Willingly.

MARIA: Then since one is free not to love, whoever loves seems to be a self-murderer. To blame the girl is unjust.

PAMPHILUS: Yet the girl doesn't kill by being loved but by failing to return the love. Whoever can save someone and refrains from doing so is guilty of murder.

MARIA: Suppose a young man loves what is forbidden, for example another man's wife or a Vestal Virgin? She won't return his love in order to save the lover, will she?

PAMPHILUS: But *this* young man loves what it's lawful and right, and reasonable and honorable, to love....

First, Maria attempts to turn Pamphilus's attention away from his poetic flights of fancy by encouraging him to take stock of his concrete, living self. To his insistence that his soul has fled his body and migrated to hers, she repeatedly calls attention to his own evident and lively embodiment and animation. To his claim that she is responsible for his suffering, she makes him confess that he loves willingly, reminding him of his free agency. ("Then since one is free not to love, whoever loves seems to be a self-murderer.") When he then protests that the girl kills not "by being loved but by failing to return the love," she cunningly asks: "Suppose a young man loves what is forbidden, for example, another man's wife or a Vestal Virgin? *She* won't return his love in order to save the lover, will she?" Pamphilus is compelled, for the first time, to acknowledge that love must bow before what is licit and honorable: "But *this* young man," he barks, "loves what it's lawful and right, and reasonable and honorable, to love."

But he quickly backtracks: "and yet he [that is, Pamphilus the licit lover] *is* slain." When (in passages not quoted here) he next adds to the crime of murder (that is, of not returning his love) the charge of poisoning or sorcery (that is, displaying her charms), Maria denies all responsibility, cleverly pointing out that the witchcraft must be in the eye of the beholder, since only he is smitten by her look. Summoning all his manly wit and ardor, Pamphilus proceeds to bring Maria before the high court of Venus. Borrowing from the tragedians of old, he wants her to recognize the monstrous erotic woes that might befall someone who rejects the love of a worthy suitor, such as himself. Warning her that Eros might punish her by fixing her own passionate attachment on a hideously ugly, bankrupt, and beastly man, and insisting that he as a lover should be rewarded for loving, he concludes with a dire warning and a plea: "Don't provoke Nemesis; return your lover's love." We have reached a major turning point in the courtship.

PAMPHILUS: Then don't provoke Nemesis: return your lover's love.

MARIA: If that's enough, I do return it.

PAMPHILUS: But I'd want this love to be lasting and to be mine alone. I'm courting a wife, not a mistress.

MARIA: I know that, but I must deliberate a long time over what can't be revoked once it's begun.

PAMPHILUS: I've thought it over a very long time.

MARIA: See that love, who's not the best adviser, doesn't trick you. For they say he's blind.

PAMPHILUS: But one who proceeds with caution is keen-sighted. You don't appear to me as you do because I love you; I love you because I've observed what you're like.

MARIA: But you may not know me well enough. If you'd wear the shoe, you'd feel then where it pinched.

PAMPHILUS: I'll have to take the chance; though I infer from many signs that the match will succeed.

MARIA: You're a soothsayer too?

PAMPHILUS: I am.

MARIA: Then by what auguries do you infer this? Has the night owl flown?

PAMPHILUS: That flies for fools.

MARIA: Has a pair of doves flown from the right?

PAMPHILUS: Nothing of the sort. But the integrity of your parents has been known to me for years now. In the first place, good birth is far from a bad sign. Nor am I unaware of the wholesome instruction and godly examples by which you've been reared; and good education is better than good birth. That's another sign. In addition, between my family – not an altogether contemptible one, I believe – and yours there has long been intimate friendship. In fact, you and I have known each other to our fingertips, as they say, since childhood, and our temperaments are pretty much the same. We're nearly equal in age; our parents, in wealth, reputation, and rank. Finally – and this is the special mark of friendship, since excellence by itself is no guarantee of compatibility – your tastes seem to fit my temperament not at all badly. How mine agree with yours, I don't know.

Obviously, darling, these omens assure me that we shall have a blessed, lasting, happy marriage, provided you don't intend to sing a song of woe for our prospects.

MARIA: What song do you want?

PAMPHILUS: I'll play "I am yours"; you chime in with "I am yours."

MARIA: A short song, all right, but it has a long finale.*

PAMPHILUS: What matter how long, if only it be joyful?

Maria, who has all the while been waiting for just the right opening, sees it and moves in. When challenged to "return your lover's love," she responds coolly and almost offhandedly, "If that's enough, I do return it." Nothing more rankles a man bent on a genuine victory than too easy or casual a concession, and so it is with Pamphilus. "But I'd want this love to be lasting and to be mine alone," he insists, and adds, in a first-time confession, "I'm courting a wife, not a mistress." "I know that," Maria replies, again offhandedly, pretending that she had assumed all along that marriage was uppermost in his mind. Maria has gotten his speech to move from the realm of love to the domain of marriage, seen as the home of enduring and exclusive attachment ("love ... lasting and ... mine alone"). She next turns Pamphilus into matrimony's leading defender. By obliging *him* to make the case for marriage, through addressing her feigned reservations and genuine concerns, she deftly compels him to show whether and why he is a suitable husband.

She begins by insisting on the need for careful deliberation if one is interested in lasting marriage: "But I must deliberate a long time over what can't be revoked once it's begun." Pamphilus, taking the bait, confidently steps forward to show his apparent superiority in thoughtfulness: "*I've* thought it over a very long time." In response, Maria sets the hook: "See that love, who's not the best adviser, doesn't trick you." In other words, prove it.

In a lovely ironic twist, Pamphilus, in order to satisfy his own desire for victory, must now explain to Maria why she ought willingly, indeed,

---

* In canon law, the exchange of a three-word pledge, "I am yours," was regarded as binding and accepted as a valid marriage, whether spoken publicly or privately.

ardently, to accept him as a husband. In doing so, he not only explains that his love of Maria is based on esteem and regard – "You don't appear to me as you do because I love you; I love you because I've observed what you're like" – but, more importantly, he defends, over and against Maria's objections, the very things that Maria has all along deemed lawful and right, reasonable and honorable: exclusive love, marital permanence, children and family ties. Pamphilus is made to enumerate the signs that promise marital success: her good birth and good education, the friendship of their respective families, their own lifelong and intimate acquaintance, similar temperaments, equal age, and, especially, the likelihood of friendship based on compatible tastes. In suggesting that these attributes promise marital success, Pamphilus is – even today – hardly mistaken.

Maria, still suspecting that he is moved mainly by her looks, forces him to face the threats that disease and old age pose to her beauty – and that time itself poses to all love of the visibly beautiful:

MARIA: Maybe I'll seem different to you when illness or old age has changed this beauty.

PAMPHILUS: Neither will I always be as handsome as I am now, my dear. But I don't consider only this dwelling place, which is blooming and charming in every respect. I love the guest more.

MARIA: What guest?

PAMPHILUS: Your mind, whose beauty will forever increase with age.

MARIA: Truly you're more than a Lynceus if you see through so much make-up!

PAMPHILUS: I see your thought through mine. Besides, we'll renew our youth repeatedly in our children.

Pamphilus makes a double response to her concern about fading beauty: more than its "dwelling place," he says first, he loves her mind, "whose beauty will forever increase with age"; and he adds, second, "[b]esides, we'll renew our youth repeatedly in our children." In this crucial second remark, Pamphilus, speaking no longer of "I" but of "we," tacitly concedes their mortality and confesses a desire for children, indeed, for "*our* children."

But though these remarks are music to her ears, Maria does not let on that she is pleased; on the contrary, she makes explicit, for the first time, the ever-latent theme of her threatened virginity. Modern readers, tempted here to tune out or roll their eyes, might instead try to discover what the fuss over virginity was once all about.

MARIA: But meantime my virginity will be gone.

PAMPHILUS: True, but see here: if you had a fine orchard, would you want it never to bear anything but blossoms, or would you prefer, after the blossoms have fallen, to see the trees heavy with ripe fruit?

MARIA: How artfully he argues!

PAMPHILUS: Answer this at least: which is the prettier sight, a vine rotting on the ground or encircling some post or elm tree and weighing it down with purple grapes?

MARIA: You answer *me* in turn: which is the more pleasing sight, a rose gleaming white on its bush or plucked and gradually withering?

PAMPHILUS: In my opinion the rose that withers in a man's hand, delighting his eyes and nostrils the while, is luckier than one that grows old on a bush. For that one too would wither sooner or later. In the same way, wine is better if drunk before it sours. But a girl's flower doesn't fade the instant she marries. On the contrary, I see many girls who before marriage were pale, run-down, and as good as gone. The sexual side of marriage brightened them so much that they began to bloom at last.

MARIA: Yet virginity wins universal approval and applause.

PAMPHILUS: A maiden is something charming, but what's more naturally unnatural than an old maid? Unless your mother had been deflowered, we wouldn't have this blossom here. But if, as I hope, our marriage will not be barren, we'll pay for one virgin with many.

MARIA: But they say chastity is a thing most pleasing to God.

PAMPHILUS: And therefore I want to marry a chaste girl, to live chastely with her. It will be more a marriage of minds than of bodies. We'll reproduce for the state; we'll reproduce for Christ. By how little will this marriage fall short of virginity! And perhaps some day we'll live as Joseph and Mary did. But meantime we'll learn virginity; for one does not reach the summit all at once.

MARIA: What's this I hear? Virginity to be violated in order to be learned?

PAMPHILUS: Why not? As by gradually drinking less and less wine we learn temperance. Which seems more temperate to you, the person who, sitting down in the midst of dainties, abstains from them or the one secluded from those things that invite intemperance?

MARIA: I think the man whom abundance cannot corrupt is more steadfastly temperate.

PAMPHILUS: Which more truly deserves praise for chastity, the man who castrates himself or the one who, while sexually unimpaired, nevertheless abstains from sexual love?

MARIA: My vote would go to the latter. The first I'd regard as mad.

PAMPHILUS: But don't those who renounce marriage by a strict vow castrate themselves, in a sense?

MARIA: Apparently.

PAMPHILUS: Now to abstain from sexual intercourse isn't a virtue.

MARIA: Isn't it?

PAMPHILUS: Look at it this way. If it were a virtue per se not to have intercourse, intercourse would be a vice. Now it happens that it *is* a vice *not* to have intercourse, a virtue to have it.

MARIA: When does this "happen"?

PAMPHILUS: Whenever the husband seeks his due from his wife, especially if he seeks her embrace from a desire for children.

MARIA: What if from lust? Isn't it right for him to be denied?

PAMPHILUS: It's right to reprove him, or rather to ask him politely to refrain. It's not right to refuse him flatly – though in this respect I hear few husbands complain of their wives.

Maria here strategically exploits the major weapon in her arsenal, her chastity. By linking the loss of her virginity not to the satisfaction of erotic desire but to procreation, she compels Pamphilus to become simultaneously a respectful defender of her chastity and a proponent of the proper reason for its sacrifice. He is made to argue for the superiority not of *eros* selfishly regarded but of its procreative fruit. Once he does so, Maria herself aggressively turns the tables and makes him speak to the matter of *eros* in the face of lost maidenhood: "*You* answer *me* in turn: which is the more pleasing sight, a rose gleaming white on its bush or plucked and gradually withering?" Translation: Will you still love me once I have yielded, once I am an aging mother, no longer a virginal maiden?

Maria's remark makes clear that chastity has been her prime concern not because she lacks sexual desire; on the contrary, the tenacity of her argument betrays the ardor beneath her outward coolness. Neither does she esteem her virginity because "it wins universal approval and applause," nor because "it is a thing most pleasing to God"; these opinions she puts into the mouths of others ("*they* say …"), and she readily accedes to Pamphilus's rejoinders to both these points, even accepting his implicit argument about the goodness of sexual pleasure. Rather, as one can fully see only at the end, her virginity is in the service of satisfying her own erotic longings, but only with someone who is worthy of being their object and, looking ahead to marriage, of satisfying them long-term.

As the colloquy moves to a close, Maria forces Pamphilus to address certain genuine and enduring worries about married life: loss of liberty, economic hardships, the cares of childrearing, the risks of losing a child or of raising bad children. In all his answers, which we will not rehearse here, Pamphilus speaks the speech of strong, confident, and responsible manhood, willing and able to undertake all the risks of family life in the service of virtue and holiness. He concludes:

PAMPHILUS: We'll try, therefore, to be good ourselves. Next, we'll see that our children are imbued from birth with sacred teachings and beliefs. What the jar is filled with when new matters most. In addition, we'll see that at home we provide an example of life for them to imitate.

MARIA: What you describe is difficult.

PAMPHILUS: No wonder, because it's lovely. (And you're difficult too, for the same reason!) But we'll labor so much the harder to this end.

MARIA: You'll have tractable material to work with. See that you form and fashion me.

Maria, in so many words, appears to have accepted his suit. But she keeps her composure. Pamphilus begs for her pledge; she refers him instead to seek the consent of their parents.

PAMPHILUS: But meanwhile say just three words.*

MARIA: Nothing easier, but once words have flown out they don't fly back. I'll give better advice for us both: confer with your parents and mine, to get the consent of both sides.

PAMPHILUS: You bid me woo, but in three words you can make success certain.

MARIA: I don't know whether I could. I'm not a free agent. In former times marriages were arranged only by the authority of elders. But however that may be, I think our marriage will have more chance of success if it's arranged by our parents' authority. And it's your job to woo; that isn't appropriate to our sex. We girls like to be swept off our feet, even if sometimes we're deeply in love.

PAMPHILUS: I won't be backward in wooing. Only don't let your decision alone defeat me.

MARIA: It won't. Cheer up, Pamphilus dear!

---

* "I am yours," again, constituting a binding vow of marriage.

PAMPHILUS: You're more strait-laced toward me in this business than I should like.

MARIA: But first ponder your own private decision. Judge by your reason, not your feeling. What emotions decide is temporary; rational choices generally please forever.

PAMPHILUS: Indeed you philosophize very well, so I'm resolved to take your advice.

Even though he has spoken well to her in private, Pamphilus must back up his promising speech with courageous deed. He must acknowledge the claims of parents and tradition and demonstrate before sober judges that he is serious about marriage and its public status. He must swallow his pride, going as a petitioner to her parents, while displaying by this very act his manly ability to protect and provide for their daughter. Understandably, he seeks encouragement for his task. She urges him (and no doubt also herself) to be rational.

Pamphilus presses Maria for a goodnight kiss as a token. Maria repairs again to the subject of chastity:

MARIA: Farewell, Pamphilus darling.

PAMPHILUS: That's up to you.

MARIA: I bid you good night. Why do you sigh?

PAMPHILUS: "Good night," you say? If only you'd grant what you bid!

MARIA: Don't be in too great a hurry. You're counting chickens before they're hatched.

PAMPHILUS: Shan't I have anything from you to take with me?

MARIA: This scent ball, to gladden your heart.

PAMPHILUS: Add a kiss at least.

MARIA: I want to deliver to you a virginity whole and unimpaired.

PAMPHILUS: Does a kiss rob you of your virginity?

MARIA: Then do you want me to bestow my kisses on others too?

PAMPHILUS: Of course not. I want your kisses kept for me.

MARIA: I'll keep them for you. Though there's another reason why I wouldn't dare give away kisses just now.

PAMPHILUS: What's that?

MARIA: You say your soul has passed almost entirely into my body and that there's only the slightest particle left in yours. Consequently, I'm afraid this particle in you would skip over to me in a kiss and you'd then become quite lifeless. So shake hands, a symbol of our mutual love; and farewell. Persevere in your efforts. Meanwhile I'll pray Christ to bless and prosper us both in what we do.

This final exchange reveals Maria's understanding of her own womanhood: "I want to deliver *to you* a virginity *whole* and *unimpaired*." She deliberately holds back, it seems, precisely because she knows what she most desires and what it really means to give herself to her beloved, body and soul. For her, virginity is not an empty heroic or Mars-like pose; neither is it an image of divine purity. It is important because it both represents and makes possible the serious, wholehearted, exclusive, unconditional, unsullied, lifelong attachment she most desires; we may even say, because it enables her to achieve her highest aspiration.

And what of Pamphilus's request for a kiss and Maria's refusal? Here, for sure, a modern reader, even one who has played along up until this point, will leave the train – or so we thought. In an effort to forestall any such knee-jerk rejection, we asked the class, quite simply, "What is a kiss?" To our astonishment and delight, the first four answers were as follows: "A kiss is the most erotic thing imaginable." "A kiss is a sharing of the breath, which is the spirit." "A kiss is a promise." "A kiss is a small consummation." From there it was easy for them to see why they might hesitate to treat one's kisses cheaply – though whether they would themselves bestow their kisses differently we are unable to say.*

---

* Of the twenty-seven students in the class, two married each other, a third (along with his wife) credits the class for enabling him to propose marriage, and a fourth, the woman who extolled the virtues of casual sex with men, is now happily married,

The colloquy ends with Maria encouraging Pamphilus to persevere while she herself will seek divine blessing for their endeavors.

* * *

Let us quickly recapitulate ten important elements of the courtship exchange: (1) He must demonstrate concern for her esteem; he must make himself humanly admirable, not merely handsomely attractive. (2) He must woo concretely, "embodiedly," and personally; love cannot remain a lofty, spiritual quest, indifferent to ordinary life. (3) He must see that he woos freely, not from passionate desire alone but also by deliberate choice, thus displaying in advance the free will by which he will later voluntarily bind himself in marriage. (4) He acknowledges the rule of what is lawful and right, reasonable and honorable. (5) He expresses the wish for exclusiveness, permanence, fidelity – for marriage, not an affair. (6) Both he and (especially) she need to be deliberate: to evaluate character, to look for what could support and enhance their desire for lasting union. (7) Both he and she must be mindful of the transience of bodily beauty. (8) Both, but especially he, need to show concern for children and evince devotion to their well-being. (9) Both need to be aware of the costs and risks of married life – in terms of decreased liberty, diminished wealth, and the pains of loss, grief, and disappointment – and show themselves ready to bear them. (10) Finally, he must stand up before, and stand up to, the older generation, seeking parental consent, establishing links to the larger familial world and to the past, acknowledging that marriage is not just a private matter between the lovers. The manners and mores of courtship teach the lovers that *eros*, for all his glory, is not the highest authority.

Stepping back from the colloquy, let us review courtship, looking for general themes and possible generalizations. Unlike earlier mores that regulated relations between the sexes by paternal authority, religious edict, and arranged marriage, courtship took erotic love of man for woman as its starting point, but sought to discipline it and direct it toward monogamous marriage. Erasmus's colloquy was one of the earliest efforts

---

a mother of several children, and herself a teacher of great texts. About the rest, we have no information.

to establish such marital mores based on love, opposing not only arranged marriage but also the two nonmarital ideals, the romantic ideal of love poetry and the celibate ideal of the church. Part of the discipline of erotic love comes from explicit and self-conscious confrontation with certain deep truths that, as we have seen, are embedded in the mores of courtship, truths regarding the promises and perils of sexual desire and erotic love, regarding human neediness and human freedom, regarding finitude and the longing for eternity, regarding marriage as a vehicle to life's higher possibilities. Courtship enables both man and woman to make clear the meaning of their own sexual nature, while elevating that nature by clothing it in sanctifying ceremony and ritual.

By holding back the satisfaction of sexual desire, courtship uses the energy of romantic attraction to foster salutary illusions that encourage admiration and devotion; functioning as ideals, they in turn inspire conduct worthy of admiration and devotion. At the same time, courtship provides opportunities for learning about one another's character, manners, and tastes. It enables man and woman to discover whether they can be friends, not merely lovers, and whether they have enough in common and enough mutual regard to sustain a union even when the erotic ardor of youth subsides. By locating wooer and wooed in their familial settings, courtship teaches the couple the intergenerational meaning of erotic activity and prepares their parents to accept their own new station, no longer in the vanguard of life. The process of courting provides the opportunity to enact the kind of attentiveness, dependability, care, exclusiveness, and fidelity that the couple will subsequently promise each other when they finally wed. For all these reasons, one does not exaggerate much in saying that going through the forms of courtship provides early practice in being married – a very different kind of practice, for a very different view of marriage, than the practice now thought to be provided by premarital cohabitation. Therefore, when they work well, the mores of courtship provide ample opportunity to discover how good a match and a marriage this is likely to be. In addition, as the natural elements of love between man and woman become a path to marriage, these elements are shaped by courtship into marriage's more-than-natural foundation. Courtship, a wisely instituted practice, is meant to substitute for any lack of personal wisdom.

But this summary ignores the important sexual asymmetry of courtship, well represented in this colloquy. The roles are sexually distinct: the man woos, the woman is wooed, and each quite self-consciously takes up the appropriate part. Initiative apparently belongs to the man, and, at least superficially, he takes the more active role. Pamphilus is in love, not just in lust, and while this makes him vulnerable to poetical exaggeration and prone to fantastical excess, his love indicates his capacity to look beyond himself, to be moved by more than selfish calculation, to risk ridicule, rejection, and failure. A lover – unlike a significant other – is fit for the adventure of marriage; he is not a fellow who plays it safe. In contrast to the calculating contractual partner, having given himself to the tempests of *eros*, he is much more likely to be able to promise "in sickness and in health," "for better and for worse." In the lover, sexual desire is sublimated and attached to an idealized beloved; *eros* is focused upon a particular woman, whom the lover wants to possess and enjoy exclusively. Because she resists, his *eros* is enhanced by being linked to his pride. He desires a victory gained through her *willing* submission, granted only when he has won her esteem. As Allan Bloom remarks (in commenting on Rousseau's treatment of the same subject in *Emile*):

> Even the most independent-minded erotic man becomes dependent on the judgment of a woman, and a serious woman, one who is looking not only for an attractive man but for one who will love her and protect her, may be the best possible judge of a man's virtues and thus be regarded even by the most serious man as the supreme tribunal of his worth.[4]

The correlative of manly ardor is womanly modesty, her reticence, her sexual self-restraint. This is the sine qua non of courtship and, we submit, the key to sound manners and mores concerning manhood and womanhood. It is this that makes manly wooing necessary; that makes woman appear more desirable and worth winning; that spurs a man's ardor and inspires his winning speech and conduct. It is feminine modesty that turns men into lovers, not mere sex partners, and that gives the physically weaker sex the more commanding power of judgment and selection. To the extent that she can keep him somewhat unsure of her return of his affection, and hence more eager for it, she helps form on his side the exclusive attachment that she seeks and that is implied in her modestly "saving herself for marriage." No man would truly give his heart permanently to a woman of easy virtue or to one whose submissiveness he can take for granted.

Modesty not only spurs a man to love; equally important, it defends a woman against the hazards of her own considerable erotic desires. She has more at stake in sex than does the man. Even in our age of female contraception and easy abortion, pregnancy remains a concern mainly for women – arguably more so than ever, albeit for different reasons than before: the law now lodges responsibility and choice regarding pregnancy and childbirth entirely with her, and in consequence, men are no longer under social pressure to marry a woman should she become pregnant with or give birth to his child. But female chastity in the past – contrary to popular prejudice – was not mainly contraceptive in intent, rooted only in fear of unwanted pregnancy. Rather, it was intended to serve the woman's *positive procreative* interest in the well-being of her prospective children by securing for them in advance a devoted and dependable father to protect and provide for them. The "reproductive strategy" (to use the term of sociobiologists) is to attach the man exclusively and permanently to the woman through erotic love and to make him thereby also love and care for her – their – children. Women who think of themselves as potential wives and mothers, *and who act accordingly*, are much more likely to get men to think and act as prospective husbands and fathers. Sexual self-restraint enables a woman to find, hold, and win a man who is not only attractive but who is serious about life, serious enough to bind himself freely to the risk-filled adventure of marriage – and, implicitly, fatherhood – as the price for satisfying his erotic desires for her. In addition, her chastity before marriage gives the man confidence that she too is serious about sexual loyalty and fidelity, and, therefore, that the children she will bear for him to rear will be only his own.

But sexual modesty and chastity awaiting marriage are not just strategically sound and psychologically important. They are also an emblem of the unique friendship that is the union of husband and wife, in which the giving of the heart is enacted in the giving of the body, and in which the procreative fruit of their one-flesh bodily union celebrates their loving embrace not only of one another but also of their mortal condition and their capacity self-consciously to transcend it.

Courtship is centrally a matter for the courting couple, for the young man and his maid. But as Erasmus's "Colloquy on Courtship" makes clear, it takes place in cultural and social settings that – when they are sound – give it shape, support its goals, and even provide larger horizons for the fulfillment of the couple's erotic longings. Larger family ties provide enriching links with ancestors and social networks of belonging. The married pair defines itself as a node joining separate lineages and as a link between generations. The establishment of a home for the rearing of decent children also gives man and woman a growing stake in matters political and a deeper interest in and greater openness to matters religious. Others speak of a need to impose top-down religiously based duties on man and woman to make the marriage work. We would rather point out the bottom-up ways in which marriage and especially parenthood may lead people toward the divine. The miraculous gift of new life, the astonishing power of parental love for children, the humility one painfully learns in trying to rear them, and (especially) the desire to give them not only life but also a good way of life open husband and wife to our most serious concern for the true, the good, and the holy.

Two final comments. We are aware that many readers will find this talk about courtship and female chastity quaint at best. People will insist, perhaps rightly, that most women will never wish to return to the mores of an age that knew not female contraception, late marriage, and careers for women. Our critics would like to believe that female chastity, or at least marked sexual self-restraint, is not necessary for sensible manners and mores regarding sex, marriage, and family. We suggest that the burden of proof lies with them to show how the important functions that courtship and modesty once performed can be accomplished in their absence: not only "getting him to commit," but finding out whether you really want him to; learning whether the fellow who is hanging around is someone to make a life with, someone to rear children with, someone who will fly wing to wing on sunny days and also row faithfully oar to oar in rough waters.

Classical courtship was, in fact, a manifestation of the true power of women as women, residing in their modesty. Men were the visible actors, but the serious woman was in command. This implies that the possibility of restoring sensible sexual mores, pointing toward marriage, lies mainly with women – to be sure, only if enough women reassert the powerful virtue of self-restraint. Their willingness to exercise their power of reform depends, of course, on whether they think that a fulfilling marriage and motherhood are of primary importance in their life. Everything depends on whether modern young women will see things this way.

CHAPTER FOUR

Virtually Intimate

Is the Internet Good for Love and Friendship?

They met online, where he called himself "Prince of Joy," and she called herself "Sweetie." Their real names were Sana and Adnan. Each thought they had found a soul-mate with whom to spend the rest of their lives. They poured their hearts out to each other over their marital troubles. Sana, 27, said, "I was suddenly in love. It was amazing, we seemed to be stuck in the same kind of miserable marriages." Finally, they decided to meet in person, and they discovered that they were married to each other. When it dawned on her what had happened, she said: "I felt so betrayed." Adnan, 32, said, "I still find it hard to believe that Sweetie, who wrote such wonderful things, is the same woman who has not said a nice word to me for years."

It would be nice to report that there was a happy ending, in which Adnan and Sana discovered Sweetie and Prince of Joy in each other. But alas, Adnan sued Sana for divorce on the ground that she was unfaithful to him in pursuing a relationship with his online persona.[5]   *– Metro News*

* * *

Facts are better than dreams.   *– Winston Churchill*

MY SUBJECT IS intimacy, virtual and real. My question is this: "Is the Internet good for love and friendship?" Lovers, we know, are face to face. Friends are side by side. What kinds of "being together" are we fashioning in cyberspace and on our screens?

The subject is daunting. In assessing it, we must contend with the enormous complexity of intimacy itself and also with the surrounding circumstances of modern life, which have already created numerous obstacles to love or friendship of the sort we used to know and many of us still seek. We must contend also with the widely different ways in which people employ the Internet in search of "relationships." Some use it only as a dating or matchmaking service, for purposes ranging from one-night stands to lasting marriage, while others get in touch with long-lost friends or lovers, to reconnect with times gone by or to rekindle old flames. Some engage in pornography and cybersex, while still others embark on true affairs of the heart in what amounts to an ethereal replacement for the epistolary romances of earlier times. Some Internet Lotharios are serious online predators, dissembling their identities and purposes, while others are openly indulging their wildest fantasies, simply to enjoy as an avatar the adventures or pleasures they do not or cannot know in real life. The possibilities are limitless, the rules nonexistent, and anyone can play.[6]

To make matters simpler and more manageable for myself, I will concentrate my attention on the more serious and sincere uses of the Internet: people looking for a genuine soulmate with whom to make a life, people seeking genuine and lasting friendship, and people desiring to find love, however we define it, marital or not. Leaving aside the notorious dangers – more prevalent online than off – of insincerity, deliberate deception, and sexual predation, as well as the sordid and revolting practices of pornography and cybersex, I want to assess what the Internet can do in the best cases, for the honest and decent seekers. To be sure, this narrowing of attention ignores the degree to which the more reprehensible uses of the Internet affect the general culture, in turn altering the sensibilities and expectations of all who come browsing for intimacy. As in the popular culture more generally, sewage produced by some will befoul the water drunk by all. But, as the enthusiasts of Internet relationships point out, what you look for and tolerate online is entirely up to you, and there is room for greater individual control and interactivity – but also, let's be honest, for greater self-enslavement through screen addiction – with the Net than with many other aspects of mass culture.

In considering what the Internet means for love and friendship, I do not contend that its features and effects are utterly novel. On the con-

trary, the Internet is continuous with the long list of previous innovations that have given us increasingly remote and mediated
communication – from the letter, through the telegraph, telephone, and
television, to the text-messaging and photo-sending cell phone and
Skype. But innovations differing only in degree may still make an enormous difference, sometimes yielding, eventually, a difference in kind.
And besides, our failure to recognize the deformations in human intimacy caused by previous innovations should not be used as a reason to
welcome the new deformations we might now be embracing.

To consider the meaning of the Internet for love and friendship, one
must think first about the latter. If one does not know love or friendship,
one will be unable to say whether and how going online helps or hinders.
It will be said, not wrongly, that the meanings of love and friendship are,
in part, culturally determined, and as culture changes, so do they. Yet I
insist that such changes do not touch the *heart* of the phenomena. We
still read with understanding and admiration about the friendship of
David and Jonathan, or Jacob's love for Rachel, or the courtship of
Orlando and Rosalind, or the marriage of Kitty and Levin, or Pierre and
Natasha.[7] My students (over forty years of teaching) and I find much of
Aristotle's analysis of friendship in the *Nicomachean Ethics* to be relevant
to our own experience. And regarding the enduring and essential core of
eros and *philia* (and the other two loves), C. S. Lewis's splendid little book
The Four Loves offers accounts that seem to me profoundly true.

Still, for present purposes, I will observe only that relationships of
love and relationships of friendship, however defined and notwithstanding the important differences between them, are both associations or
conditions of *mutual intimacy*. To be intimate – from the Latin *intimus*,
"inmost" – is to be very close, familiar, and attached, person to person, by
bonds of warm affection and deep communion. Erotic relations generally
involve also sexual intimacy, the giving and receiving of bodies, lover and
beloved each to each and from the other. My question now becomes: How
to think about and assess the new forms of *intimacy*, erotic or not, that
exist on, or are assisted by, the Internet (including, of course, email), intimacies that dwell wholly or partly, or that were merely begun, in cyberspace? What does intimacy mean and become for the *virtually intimate*?

In one sense of "virtually" – meaning "in effect," "practically," "to all
intents"; from the Latin *virtus*, "strength or power" – the virtually intimate

are *effectively* intimate, in the same ways that human beings have always been. In this view, Internet friends and lovers are *as good as* intimate, whether formally so recognized or not. Many practitioners report enjoying the same pleasures and feeling the same emotions – often with even greater intensity – for their online partners as they do for their "offline" ones. (Note how our lingo now treats "*on*-line" as the default human condition, and "*off*-line" – that is, real life – as privative.) On the other hand, we still distinguish "the virtual" from "the real" or "the actual," and regard the former *as a simulacrum*, perhaps with *some* of the same attributes, but very much *not* the real thing. This view would not deny that "virtual intimacy" is something "real" and really "something"; it only casts doubt on whether it is really *intimacy – real love* or *real friendship*. Not to beg the question, we should be open to the possibility that virtual intimacy, although different in kind, could be every bit as good, and good for us, as the real intimacy it simulates.

Not surprisingly, this latter view has many champions: lovers of technique and lovers of novelty always find reasons to exalt whatever is latest, quickest, and most convenient. But these theoretic defenses, which I will shortly consider, pale in comparison to those who are voting with their feet – rather, with their fingers – for intimacies online, and not just for pathetic reasons and sordid pleasures. Clearly, even discounting the contributions of fad and fashion, some widespread human needs, desires, and cravings are leading people to the Net. We must begin therefore by recognizing them and by giving the Internet its due.

Why the Internet? Benefits for the Lonely and Lovelorn

People are lonely. People looking for romance and love cannot easily meet suitable or desirable partners and mates. The alternatives of bars, singles clubs, and wild parties are, for the more high-minded, simply unappealing. Most workplaces are inhospitable to meeting someone special. People who do not regularly attend church or synagogue often lack other forms of association with like-minded people. Many people, especially women, are repulsed by or fed up with the hookup scene; they want to get to know someone better before taking off their clothes. Others are in unsatisfactory relationships, either cohabiting without the desired promise of commitment or in unfulfilled or failing marriages, and are looking for something better. Getting to know people takes time, which is in short supply, and people lack the patience required to start from scratch with a parade of strangers, knowing from past experience that they almost never measure up to hopes and expectations. Even the patient ones finally give up: they encounter no parade of strangers and their patience has not brought one forward. For all these people and for all these reasons, the Internet is a welcome ally, and we should acknowledge its real benefits.

Two in particular deserve emphasis. First, paradoxically, are the benefits of physical distance. In a sex-besotted culture, with modesty and restraint in tatters, we should welcome any intervention that might replace them or at least slow things down, placing lust under wraps so that intimacy and love might first emerge. The idea is as old and anthropologically deep as the Garden of Eden story, where the introduction of the fig leaf, mutually sewn by the newly sexually self-conscious pair, humanizes the sexual situation by changing its normal condition from "ready" to "not." With the fig leaf, an obstacle is symbolically presented to immediate gratification of lust. By covering up ugliness and adorning beauty, clothing also allows the imagination to embellish and love to grow in the space provided by the restraint placed upon lust, a restraint opened by shame and ratified by covering it up. When, in the presence of love, clothing is eventually removed, the mutual and willing exposure of sexual nakedness will be understood by each partner as a gift to one's beloved, and it will be received gladly and without contempt.

Kant captured and extended this point, economically and profoundly, in his commentary on the fig leaf:

> In the case of animals, sexual attraction is merely a matter of transient, mostly periodic, impulse. But man soon discovered that for him this attraction can be prolonged and even increased by means of the imagination – a power which carries on its business, to be sure, the more moderately, but at once also the more constantly and uniformly, the more its object is removed from the senses. By means of the imagination, he discovered, the surfeit was avoided which goes with the satisfaction of mere animal desire. The fig leaf ... – rendering an inclination more inward and constant by

removing its object from the senses – already reflects consciousness of a certain degree of mastery of reason over impulse. *Refusal*
was the feat which brought about the passage from merely sensual
to spiritual attractions, from mere animal desire gradually to love,
and along with this from the feeling of the merely agreeable to a
taste for beauty, at first only for beauty in man but at length for
beauty in nature as well.[8]

In place of the psychic and emotional distance once provided by modesty or restraint in the presence of sexual attraction, physical distance
bridgeable only by being available online to speech provides a way to
remain, at least for a while, unavailable offline to touch. This at-least
symbolic barrier to precipitous and sticky entanglements provides
opportunity to get to know someone's soul, without the distractions of
fetching bodily beauty or the arousals of "chemistry." That the slow, safe,
disembodied nearness of cyberspace can play such a role was well illustrated in the cheerful movie *You've Got Mail*, an Internet update on the
epistolary romance in Ernst Lubitsch's classic movie *The Shop around the
Corner*. Unlike the older movie, restraint not being what it used to be, the
characters played by Tom Hanks and Meg Ryan are each cohabiting, but
unhappily, with someone else. In real life there is keen enmity between
the two, yet their spontaneous, patient, warm, anonymous yet heart-to-
heart disclosures as virtual friend to virtual friend enable each to gain
sympathy and admiration for the other; and their gradually maturing
intimacy, fueled by a generous imagination, makes love possible when
they finally learn each other's real identity.*

I do not want to exaggerate the kinship between the fig leaf (or true

---

* It is fruitful to consider some differences between the older epistolary romance and
its electronic replacement. Although both might be mediated affairs of the heart (and
mind), the former is very much still the work of an embodied being: letters are written,
signed, sealed, and delivered by hand. When they are opened and read, I hold the very
pages she touched, handled, and wrote exclusively for me – not quite holding hands,
but a promise of same. How much less concrete to me is the author of my electronic
mail, which shows no personalized or physical marks that distinguish it (or her) from
other email sent (by some other sender) to protest a rent increase, buy a dress on eBay,
or solicit support for a political candidate. Where is her hand, and where mine, in all
this clicking and scrolling?

modesty) and the Internet. The former is an activity of deliberate withdrawal and reticence, undertaken with intuitive wisdom divining higher
possibilities. Using the Internet is, in a sense, the opposite – an advance
into disclosure, albeit from safe and uncommitted distance. But both
cases permit *imagining* someone admirable to love and be loved by; both
cases make it possible for psychic and emotional distance eventually to
be overcome by emerging trust and nascent love. (On this matter of distance, more later.)

The second genuine benefit, not to be dismissed, is the possibility of
successful matchmaking. Long ago, and even now in certain more traditional cultures, the matchmaker was an indispensable member of the
community. To be sure, marriage was differently regarded, connections
to family and larger community were crucial measures of suitability, and
love, if anyone fell into it, came later. The marriage broker, usually older
and wiser, worked not by science but by intuition and prudence, and in
the best case was a good judge of compatibility. Looking beyond superficial triggers of erotic attraction, she had an eye for those qualities of character, class, religious attachment, and economic prospects that are more
germane to the durability of any match than long blond hair, sculpted
abs, or "chemistry." Nowadays, expectations regarding marriage have
changed and, except in very closed and settled communities, no one has
the necessary firsthand knowledge to match prospects well. But given
the high divorce rates, arranged marriages today could hardly have lower
batting averages than the ones the young people are contracting all by
themselves. Moreover, compatibility still ranks higher than sex appeal as
a bellwether for marital success. Thus, it makes sense to proceed on the
assumption that it is better to fall in love with someone who has first
been screened and selected as a likely match, than to try to discover,
under the glow of passion, whether you are well matched with someone
you believe you have fallen in love with – especially under the present
circumstances in which there are no boundaries or courtship rituals to
discipline *eros.*

In the 1980s and 1990s, people began matchmaking for themselves,
as it were, in the personal columns of newspapers, giving self-descriptions that were generally less individuating than the ads for used cars.
Efficiency was improved with the advent of online dating services, where
photographs can easily be added and where speed and interactivity make

the self-selling process seemingly more efficient – though, no doubt, more open to false advertising and predation. A big step up, in my opinion, are the more professionalized and more marriage-oriented matchmaking services, of which eHarmony is one of the most popular and apparently most successful.

Psychologists for eHarmony construct a personal profile on the basis of an extensive, wide-ranging questionnaire in which the client describes himself or herself – personal characteristics, emotional temperament, social style, cognitive modes, relational skills, values, beliefs, interests – and describes also the attributes and qualities deemed important in a potential partner. A computer algorithm matches profiles around a series of measures "scientifically" shown to correlate with happiness in marriage, and then the computer gives you the names of persons, in your chosen range of geographic proximity, with whom you are likely to be highly compatible. It is all handled very discreetly, with respect for privacy, and guidance is also available for how to proceed, slowly, in making the early email contacts. On average (I learned from speaking with an eHarmony scientist), a client will receive two or three such matches at a time, up to twenty or thirty per week. The service functions solely as a winnowing screen, to locate people worth your meeting; it finds prospects you could never reach; it saves time and decreases the likelihood of failure. It assumes, not foolishly, that it is just as easy to fall in love with someone compatible as with someone not: first eHarmony, then chemistry – a revisionist sequence, to be sure, but one more nearly approaching "rational love," one that promises duration and stability if not equal fireworks. Once you get the names, the rest is up to you. Should love or friendship develop, it is likely that the partners will soon more or less forget that the Internet played any significant initiating role.

We old-timers may shrug our shoulders, repelled by the cold-bloodedness of it all, the very antithesis of love's ability to liberate us from calculating self-interest and self-preoccupation: "And Jacob served seven years for Rachel; and they were in his eyes like but a few days, *because of his love for her.*" It seems dehumanizing (1) to be reducing yourself to 29 scientifically tested, match-relevant "dimensions," (2) to be advertising yourself on the Worldwide Web as marriageable material, your two-dimensional digitized self objectified and displayed in the ether 24/7, working for you even while you sleep, and (3) to be working overtime imagining, grading,

and handling your received stable-full of prospects, trying to figure out –
in Christine Rosen's deft metaphor – which ones to test-drive. But once
we concede the facts about our current cultural scene, we must also
acknowledge the genuine benefits that such a service provides to the
lovelorn and looking. As of 2013, more than thirty-three million people
had used eHarmony's services since they were first offered in 2000.
According to a survey conducted by Harris Interactive and published in
the *Proceedings of the National Academy of Sciences*, almost 4 percent of all
new marriages in the United States between 2005 and 2012 were eHarmony couples.[9] Should these marriages prove durable and satisfying,
this could be culturally transforming – not least by providing stable
homes and good examples for their children.

We should also reckon as a benefit, in the realm of friendship, the
Internet's service to all of us rootless cosmopolites who are disconnected
from our own past or who are looking for others of like mind or with
common interests to share. In my own case, a boyhood friend, not seen in
over fifty years, found me on the Internet shortly before he died, and he
apologized in the ether for nearly putting out my eye on his homerun
swing's follow-through at a friend's eleventh birthday party, a blow that
left his silent mark on the face in my mirror ever since. A second boyhood
friend emerged out of the ether, also after fifty years, leading to an annual
sharing of a meal and a White Sox game with a couple of other guys from
the old neighborhood. My best friend from grammar school, whom I had
many times tried to find online, located me on the Web after fifty-five
years, which resulted in a shared meal and wonderful reminiscences with
our wives and his married children. Each holiday season brings many
welcome e-greetings and photographs from old friends and acquaintances far away, as well as news of births and deaths, illnesses and recov-
eries, successes and disappointments.

And yet, acknowledging all this, one cannot avoid the sense that these
benefits of the Internet are beneficial largely, if not solely, because of the
artificial, dispersed, thin and tattered social world that is modern American life, perhaps especially among the prosperous and mobile. Being
Net-connected is a remedy for the distorted and intimacy-shrunken –
even if successful and thrilling – lives that many of us connected people
lead. Paraphrasing Madison, the Internet offers a rootless remedy for
diseases incident to rootless times. But the remedies are not a cure.

Indeed, in several respects they embody and may even exacerbate the underlying disorders.

Actual Harms of Virtual Benefits

Several features of Internet-mediated love and friendship that are highly praised by its partisans may in fact be intrinsically corrupting – not because they embody ill will or stupidity or vice, but because they are formally and materially at odds with the deep structure and deep meaning of love and friendship at their best. I emphasize "at their best," even though the best is rare and not to be counted on, because it is the cultural ideal that informs people's actual aspirations and hopes. If people come to think that friendship is being "liked" on someone's Facebook page or exchanging emails once a year at Christmastime, or if people think that it is normal to enjoy "romance" as avatars or in disembodied words and emoticons sent through the ether, it will affect what everyone understands and how almost everyone proceeds, especially the pubescent young who rarely know possibilities other than the ones ruling the scene when they are hormonally thrust upon the stage.

Please understand: I am not suffering from nostalgia or the foolish belief that we can turn back the clock. But I do insist that a proper understanding of the moral hazards of virtual intimacy could help some individuals to resist them, some groups to create more humanizing forms to facilitate the growth of true intimacy, and everyone to understand yet one more price we are paying for progress. Even in the worst-case scenario, should the *Titanic* go down, it will be good for us to have a song proclaiming, "It was sad."

Here, then, are six of the *alleged* advantages of Internet intimacy claimed by its champions.

1. *The conquest of space and place.* The diminished importance, not to say irrelevance, of physical distance or presence, replaced by beam-me-up onscreen nearness, with you at my place and me at yours, is a great catalyst of emotional closeness. We can be as near as we can possibly be *from the very first moment*, because you and I are "occupying" the same spaceless space of cyberspace. Moreover, possibilities for friendship and love

are globalized, and the whole world can be fished and trolled for intimacy. People can be friends or even lovers without being together, and without even knowing where the other is. Detached attachment, or "detattachment," is a wholly new form of human closeness, especially attractive for risk-free nonmarital or extramarital affairs of the heart.

2. *The conquest of time and unwelcome mediation.* Internet communication is said to be much more immediate, not only because the speed and convenience of exchange quickens the pace of getting to know you, but also because there are no third parties or publics that can interfere in the one-on-one. No one has to contend with the critical eyes of family or friends; no one has to worry about what anyone else sees or hears or says. No strangers intervene to induce corrosive self-consciousness. It is unmediated and unobstructed intimacy, just you and I. In addition, each partner is sole master of the times for responding, and neither partner's daily schedule is exposed to disruption by ringing phones, verbal importunings, or inconvenient synchronous appearances in the flesh.

3. *The advantages of "disembodiment."* With no bodily distractions or exigencies, Internet intimacy can be mind-to-mind, soul-to-soul, and therefore, at least in principle, a more spiritual encounter. Carefully chosen words, the embodiment of pure mind and reason, carry all the weight. To be sure, the cues provided by nonverbal communication are missing, but, as a result, reason and speech can stand forth in all their glory: ideas, thoughts, witticisms, genuine questions, authentic and expansive answers, all composed at leisure, not under the pressure of someone's gaze or desire to interrupt. Each person can have his or her say, at the desired length, without fear of opposition or contradiction and without being distracted by irruptions of the body, yours or mine. Physical investment being little, mental investment can be unadulterated. If only Shakespeare could see how the Internet eliminates all impediments to "the marriage of true minds"!

4. *Directness and sincerity of communication.* For the less (or more) than perfectly rational, the anonymity and safety of the Internet encourage people to be freer in expressing their wishes, their fantasies, their inner hopes and fears. The informality and casualness of all Internet commu-

nication is here extended to obviate the need for politeness or "beating around the bush." Inhibitions fall away more easily, people can be more emotionally transparent with each other, fantasies can be shamelessly shared, explicitness and directness are the norm. There is less noise from outside distractions, less constraint from public norms, more opportunity to say and be who you really are, or who you would like to be, if only the world and your scant self-confidence would allow you.

5. *Control and self-command.* Because all are physically remote, and because one is ever free to respond or not – and to choose how, when, why, and at what length to respond – everyone is more in control of his social relations online than off. There is no sad face, no anxious gestures to constrain you, so you are free to compose your own speech while freely imagining the other's response. When you have something to say, you don't have to be listening or waiting your turn. A few typed words, or many if you prefer, sent whenever you are ready, with a simple click – your offerings are as much under your complete control as are your other online choices and purchases. And getting out is even easier than getting in: all you need do is nothing. Delete the unwanted message or refuse to answer – a clean break. As one cybersex enthusiast puts it: "The cool thing about cybersex is you never have to talk to the other person again if you don't want to. It is a lot harder to do that in real life" – a comment, by the way, that illustrates Dr. Paul McHugh's sage observation that men don't pay prostitutes for sex, they pay them to go away. With online communication, you don't even need to pay. It's low-investment and low-risk, requiring you to surrender little if any of your autonomy.

6. *Greater comfort and safety.* There is less embarrassment for the shy and less pain for the rejected. Anonymity diminishes exposure. Cyberspace cannot transmit venereal disease. To be sure, predators lurk and caution is necessary, especially when it comes time to meet. But while online, you are safe and sound at your computer, hazarding as little as you please, immune to danger and even to the disappointments of offline – that is, real – love.

I want to suggest that all of these alleged advantages are at odds with genuine intimacy. True intimacy requires embodied and exposed human beings, who are grounded and synchronously together in real space and lived time, and who use tacit and tactful rather than explicit and unvarnished modes of communication, including modes of expression that are deeper than speech itself. True intimacies are translucent rather than transparent to one another; self-surrendering rather than controlling; embedded in networks of ties and obligations to families and communities, rather than isolated atoms utterly free to create themselves *ex nihilo*; adventurous rather than playing-it-safe; guided by hope and trust rather than by calculation and information; face to face or side by side, hand in hand or arm in arm, as much as mind to mind; and driven less by the self-centered desire to find what you were missing than by an eagerness to become all you might become by being fully present to, and concerned for, the well-being of the other, who will also be fully present to, and concerned for, you and your well-being.

To defend these intuitions, we need an account of the anthropology of intimacy – an account of the engagement of embodied souls becoming near and dear to one another. I offer here some elements of such an account, relying heavily on a short essay by the late neurologist-psychologist Erwin Straus entitled "Shame as a Historiological Problem."[10]

Toward an Anthropology of Intimacy

I start with a fundamental distinction, learnable from Aristotle. Liking (or the analogous erotic feeling) is an emotion, but friendship and love properly so called are settled dispositions or "holdings" (*hexeis* or *haltungs*, habits) of soul, where not only warm feelings but also good will and mindful concern are directed steadily at the beloved or, to coin a term, the "befriended." Moreover, this settled disposition to love or "to friend" – not in its cyber-meaning – is, though central, merely the *capacity or capability*; the real thing, *loving* or *befriending*, is found fully only in *activity*, in the manifest being-at-work (*energeia*), here and now, of these settled dispositions. Friends who rarely or never see or speak with one another enjoy but a sleeping friendship. Wakeful and energetic friending and loving require active being together, sharing and enjoying one another's company as well as common interests and activities.[11] Effort, attention, and care are of the essence, and good will must become beneficence in times of need and trouble. Sharing thoughts and speech is silver, but deeds of love are golden. This should settle the question of whether the worldwide but millimeter-deep friendships à la Facebook and Friendster deserve the name, and whether the Internet's emotion-generating powers despite physical separation are an asset for true love. While absence makes the heart grow fonder and familiarity often breeds complacency if not contempt, love and friendship thrive in physical closeness, not in separation. We crave that our dear be ever near. We long for and rejoice in the presence – the real and bodily, not merely virtual or verbal, presence – of the other.*

There is, of course, a complication regarding distance in the case of lovers, a complication not present among friends. For potential lovers, as we noted with the fig leaf, sexual attraction is suffused with a concern for approbation and a fear of rejection; each seeks to win not just the body but especially the heart of the other. Each seeks approval, praise, respect, and esteem; correlatively, each seeks to gaze admiringly at the beautiful beloved. A new dialectic is introduced into the dance of sexual desire: approval, admiration, and regard keep lovers at the beholding distance, even as their desire for one another drives them toward fusion at no distance whatever. The special and mirthful intimacy known only to lovers emerges partly out of the delicate need to preserve and negotiate this distance and its closure. The wordless embrace, the deep drink of meeting eyes, and the caressing or playful words of purely private import are among the intimacy-making and intimacy-expressing fruits of this dialectic of the erotic face-to-face – near, nearer, but also not too near.

Notice, please, that the gazing distance requires and permits mutual beholding: by gazing or beholding I mean something other than "looking *at*": it does not objectify the beloved, but is a form of communion. The exchanged look, which today goes by the wretched name "eye contact" – as if eyeballs were billiard balls – is always an invitation to or the

---

* These observations, the reader should note, provide a necessary qualification and correction to my earlier unqualified praise of physical distance as an asset to the development of intimacy in our age of sexual unrestraint, and even to properly knowing the other. Many people who have been acquainted only online are surprised to discover, when they finally meet in the flesh, that "you are not the person I know." They have known only the photographic image and the ethereal words, supplemented by their own imagination.

expression of a mutual meeting of souls. Voyeurs, incapable of giving themselves to love, keep their distance, as do users of pornography. Theirs is a one-way viewing, incommunicado, with the object of their attention treated not as a unique woman to be loved but as a generic woman to possess and to satisfy one's own lusts and fantasies. Says Erwin Straus, "The looking of the voyeur" – and, I add in my own name, the face-browsing of the Internet date seeker – "is as different from the looks exchanged by lovers as medical palpation from a gentle caress of the hand. In viewing, there is a transition from the immediate I-thou encounter, i.e., mutual participation, to a unilateral intention – a transition from the I-thou relationship to the subject-object relationship proper. All looking and being looked at is a lapse from immediate communication."[12]

To be sure, all of us lovers are at risk of lapsing into the psychic mode of the voyeur, seeing the beloved solely from the outside, objectively, as an object to be possessed and enjoyed, not as the living being who graces you with the opportunity to take a lovers' journey into mutual self-revelation and self-discovery. But where love is present, you do not love her for her long dark hair but for herself alone. "There's beggary in the love that can be reckon'd."

The crucial anthropological and psychic fact about intimacy is what Straus called *immediate experience* and the sphere of *immediate becoming*: the important distinction is not between what is public and what is private (in truth, a special case of the public), but between the *public* and *immediate* modes of being.

> We belong to the public in the ways we are described – e.g., by our name, title, position, status, profession, etc.... If we meet a stranger in public, we usually ask two questions: "Who is he?" and "What is he?" The name identifies someone in the social space of the family, of the birthplace, of the chronicles. To the question of the What of his being, we answer by stating his profession, his position, etc. The specification points to something general and repeatable. (*Le roi est mort. Vive le roi.*)* These are general and repeatable functions that the individual assumes in public. The *intimate person* is always initially concealed by his public figure. It

---

* "The king is dead. Long live the king."

is possible to participate in a public figure with a non-committal, one-way kind of general interest; but the intimate person *opens and reveals himself to understanding only in mutual and immediate participation. . . .*

Public being is characterized, as we have seen, by objectification, reflection, generality, repetition; the outcome is non-committal, one-way participation. Immediate being, on the other hand, is not objectified, it is singular, unique becoming and calls for reciprocal sharing.[13]

When we live immediately, we live *on the way*, in process, *in medias res*, unfinished yet seeking, tentatively yet honestly and organically yet responsively disclosing to another – and, a crucial point, *also to ourselves* – not some prefabricated finished "self" but the unfolding mysteries of what we really think and feel, and the translucent truths of who we are aspiring and striving to become – God willing, with your help. As Kurt Riezler remarks, thanks to love, "the relations between human beings can be such that the I and the You build up a We as the whole of an intimate world in which they are obliged to be to themselves what they are to each other and are permitted to be to each other what they are to themselves."[14]

A crucial but silent psychic force, what Erwin Straus calls "protective shame," stands guard over intimacy and the sphere of immediate becoming, keeping out the necessarily objectifying looks both of the outsider and of our own corrosive reflective consciousness.

The secret that shame protects is not, ... as prudery makes the mistake of believing, one that is already in existence and only needs to be hidden from outsiders, for those who are in becoming are also hidden from themselves. Their existence is first made explicit in their shared immediate becoming. Youth keeps its secret still, while age has become knowing. Thus, youth is impelled to youth.[15]

In the Garden of Eden story, the new self-consciousness manifested in the discovery that "their eyes were opened and they saw that they were naked" was a breakdown of protective shame, a new self-reflective doubleness in the soul that shattered the unselfconscious being-together of immediate experience. The act of concealment (the fig leaf) was an effort – an unsuccessful one – to recover the undivided consciousness of living immediately that we human beings so rarely enjoy – save when, thanks to love and friendship, we are able let down our guard, shed our public faces as namable and complete beings, and enter wholeheartedly and unreflectively into life's immediate and present possibilities. But, note well: the dialectic of reticence and exposure that guide the pace and extent of self-disclosure is governed solely by growing trust and intimacy, and it differs greatly from the calculated need- or fear-driven controlled release or withholding of information that governs nonintimate speakers. Indeed – and this is another crucial point overlooked by enthusiasts of virtual intimacy – intimate speech is not a means of exchanging information but rather of disclosing souls, of revealing who we are (also to ourselves) by eliciting the blossoming self-revelation of a friend or beloved.

As already noted, the two modes of being are correlated with two modes of communication: the explicit, clearly articulate, perfectly transparent, no-beating-around-the-bush "speech-about," and the largely tacit, feeling-tinged, translucent and incomplete "speech-to" of mysterious self-disclosure. The desire for clarity and transparency – a form of objectification – is the enemy of intimacy; lovers shun the bright light of the clear and distinct, but relish the concealment of the half-light where their unavoidably incomplete and therefore indistinct thoughts and sentiments can be conveyed, often silently. Those who complain, rightly, that the purely articulate mode of Internet exchange leaves out crucial nonverbal communication do not always appreciate the profundity of what is missing. The so-called nonverbal cues are not just a different way of speaking; they are gifts of spontaneous, unselfconscious, and wholly embodied engagement with the other. An immediate gesture of acceptance and encouragement (or the opposite) is deeper and truer than speech can ever be about the mystery of self and the power of love.

No one knows and shows this truth better than Tolstoy, who fittingly does not argue for it (as I am doing) but enables us to witness and embrace it wholeheartedly. I commend to your attention especially Levin's (successful) proposal to Kitty in *Anna Karenina* and the account of the speech between the married Pierre and Natasha in the First Epilogue to *War and Peace*. (Both are excerpted in Mrs. Kass's and my anthology, *Wing to Wing, Oar to Oar: Readings on Courting and Marrying*.)

Against even this barest sketch of the character of genuine intimacy, we can see how and why the remote, fast and mediated, disembodied, casual and explicit, controlled and safe ways of Internet sociability are all antithetical to what real intimacy requires. Virtual intimacy, and even just the desire for real intimacy that seeks to find its partner online, begins the process voyeuristically, with objectification and detached looking at and looking over. At least at the start, it is driven by purely selfish concerns, a private project looking to fill a void, to satisfy a need, to cure one's own loneliness or unhappiness. It proceeds through acts of will, via controlled decisions of selection, based also on words, words, words – words from and to a prospect chosen, in eHarmony's case, on the basis only of objectified, analytic, and machine-scoreable verbal self-descriptions.

To be sure, the goal in the best case is to replace the objectified view with the immediate one, to replace looking at by being with, to replace self-preoccupation and the activities of selfish finding and getting with other-regard and the activities of generous caring and giving, and to replace the posture of safe control by a surrender to the unsafe but soul-satisfying adventure of sharing a life in process of mutual becoming. But the means, at least at the beginning, are deeply at odds with the end – and it will take greater consciousness of this opposition to overcome the costs of this approach. People who believe that fingers are for clicking are at a disadvantage in learning that they are most beautifully used for caressing a beloved's face or for pointing out a wondrous aspect of the world to a friend jointly seeking the same truth. People whose hands are always on the keyboard may have a harder time converting them to their more human uses of clasping another's, open-handedly offering a gift, or holding them still in prayer. People whose bodies are transcended in the ether are behind the curve in expressing human embodiment, which arms us for embracing, enfolding, and cradling the fruits of one-flesh union, at its best blessed by love. People who meet impersonally (not face to face) and asynchronously (not through the living back-and-forth of unmediated conversation in the same place and time), and through self-advertising and the controlled release of information, will have to shift gears if they are to engage in the mutual, unrehearsed activities of immediate becoming and mutual self-disclosure and spontaneous self-revelation. People who are needily seeking someone to be a match for themselves may have trouble realizing that genuine love generously overflows beyond measure to the beloved, and that a beloved is loved not only or mainly because she fits and matches some specified criteria, like the missing piece of your jigsaw self, but also and especially because she is in herself admirable and lovable.

About few things in matters erotic and friendly is our current cultural scene more confused than about the relation between needy self-serving love and the gracious love of another, not only because narcissism and selfishness have been encouraged by the sexual revolution, or because courtship and other cultural forms that emphasize respect for the other have largely disappeared. We also suffer from a misunderstanding of the relation between acts of love and acts of self-fulfillment. When we lovingly and generously serve the good of another, an at-least-equal benefit redounds to ourselves. The beloved receives our lovingly given benefaction; we receive the joy of being-at-work as a giving lover or friend. Because it is more expressive of the human soul than speech and calculation and choice, loving is its own reward.*

But even this richer account of the relation between self-love and love-of-another neglects – as does the Internet matchmaking business, and indeed much of today's American view of coupling-off – the self-*transcending* and *generative* direction of erotic love: *eros*, however much it promises the lovers self-completion and self-fulfillment – that it will make one out of two, forever – cannot fully or permanently do so: the coupling two cannot really become one flesh or one soul, and, willy-nilly, death will part even the best of pairs. But *eros* itself, rightly understood, has the remedy for these difficulties. For *eros* points ultimately to procreation and the as-yet-unborn children of erotic union, children who, as the genuine one-flesh fruit of their love, will in part redeem the perishable dyad by stepping forward to take their place. Of this, our current Internet dating culture knows nothing and cares less. Roger Scruton puts it well:

> The Internet substitute for intimacy is essentially *non-reproductive.* Unlike erotic love, it is not internally directed to the unborn. It is

---

* For a profound treatment of this point, see Aristotle's discussion of beneficence in the *Nicomachean Ethics*, Book IX, Chapter 7, where he considers why benefactors love their recipients more than recipients love benefactors.

not, so to speak, a summons which calls new life into being, but simply a self-stimulation of existing life…. There is a deeper sterility coming to the surface in the Internet culture: not just the emptiness of human relations, but the severing of those relations from any commitment to the future.[16]

Coda: About Time and the Eternal

Two final comments, the first about the meaning of time and its enemy, speed; the other about eternity. Some people sincerely believe that the Internet is a way of conquering time no less than space. Time, as they say in contracts, is of the essence. But the goal is not to hurry through life, nor, conversely, is it to make time stand still, through technological wizardry. Unlike the time of the physicists, which, being mathematized, is a directionless dimension, the time of our lives is forward, always becoming, never complete; and we live most fully when we immerse ourselves immediately in the invitations of our ever-unfolding present existence. Time is indeed of the essence, but speed is not. Speed kills. Against this all-too-human error, love offers a master speed, speed as from *"spes"* or hope, about which Robert Frost wrote so beautifully on the occasion of his daughter's wedding:

> No speed of wind or water rushing by
> But you have speed far greater. You can climb
> Back up a stream of radiance to the sky,
> And back through history up the stream of time.
> And you were given this swiftness not for haste,
> Nor chiefly that you may go where you will,
> But in the rush of everything to waste,
> That you may have the power of standing still –
> Off any still or moving thing you say.
> Two such as you with such a master speed
> Cannot be parted nor be swept away
> From one another once you are agreed
> That life is only life forevermore
> Together wing to wing and oar to oar.[17]

Frost is not the first to use the language of speed or quickness to show how love may quicken the life of a couple into a vitality that far exceeds what each partner might attain alone. But Frost also plays on the archaic meaning of "speed" as "prosperity or success in an undertaking," as well as on its Latin root, *spes*, meaning "hope," to point to love's capacity to transcend time's "rush of everything to waste," offering rest within motion, permanence within change, the eternal within the perishable. Such possibilities depend on eschewing the freedom to "go where you will" in favor of mutual agreement – a vow that binds and limits freedom – that life now can only mean "life *forevermore together*," whether soaring high or rowing hard against the stream. Does Internet intimacy, and the online culture generally, know or care anything at all about "the power of standing still" or about "forevermore together"?

The final comment gestures toward the theological. In an ancient Hebrew Midrash, a wealthy Roman matron asks Rabbi Jose bar Chalafta how long it took for God to create the world. Informed that it took but six days, she asked him, "What has God been doing since that time?" "The Holy One," answered the Rabbi, "has been sitting in Heaven arranging marriages." "Indeed!" she replied, "I could do as much myself. I have thousands of slaves, and could marry them off in couples in a single hour. It is easy enough." "I hope that you will find it so," said Rabbi Jose. "In Heaven it is thought as difficult as the dividing of the Red Sea." He then took his departure, while she assembled one thousand manservants and as many maidservants, marked them off in pairs, and ordered them all to marry. On the day following this wholesale wedding, the poor victims came to their mistress in a woeful plight. One had a broken leg, another a black eye, a third a swollen nose; all were suffering from some ailment, but with one voice they joined in the cry, "Lady, unmarry us again!" Then the matron sent for Rabbi Jose, admitted that she had underrated the delicacy and difficulty of matchmaking, and wisely resolved to allow Heaven to do its work in its own way.[18]

Given the state of marriages in modern America, one might be forgiven for doubting the matchmaking genius of the Almighty. But the deeper point should not be overlooked. When human beings are open to the world and to the possibility of love, they will know why the Song of Songs exults in this astonishing erotic fact: the wondrous appearance – "leaping upon the mountains, skipping upon the hills" or "coming out of the wilderness" – of the one whom I encounter as my beloved, coming only to me. Miracle of miracles, what, or who, sent her (him) to me?

How likely is it that those who owe their match to an eHarmony algorithm will be moved to such wonder and gratitude? How prepared are they to discover that "Seeing your face is like seeing the face of God"?

CHAPTER FIVE

What's Your Name?*

T HE AUTHORS OF this essay on names have identified themselves. More precisely, they wish to have it understood that they bear the same last name not by coincidence or consanguinity, but because they are married to each other. Some readers may suspect that this biographical fact is responsible for the authors' attitudes toward names and naming. The authors respectfully submit that the reverse is closer to the truth: that their attitudes toward names and naming, and many other things that names imply, are responsible for this paramount biographical fact. At first inchoate, those attitudes have slowly emerged into conscious understanding, and this essay is an attempt to articulate that understanding of what is really in a name.

What's in a Name?

Everybody has a name. Nearly everybody who has a name knows what it is. Our name is as familiar and as close to us as our own skin; indeed, we are more frequently aware of our name than we are of the unique living body that it identifies. We write it, speak it, answer to it – often, immediately, surely, unreflectively. We generally take our name for granted. For this reason, we may not really know our name in a deeper sense – what it means, why we have it, how it should be regarded and used. Because our

---

* This essay was written with my wife of blessed memory, Amy A. Kass.

named identity is so familiar, its mystery may be invisible to us. We name others, and sometimes ourselves, but do we really know what we are doing when we do so?

To name is to identify. But what this means depends on the meaning of names, the meaning of identity, and the relation between the name and the thing named. Most common names, unlike personal names, are merely pointers, holding no deeper meanings for the named. A rose by any other name would surely smell as sweet. The lion were he called a lamb would still be king of beasts. And human beings, whether known as *anthropoi, viri, beney adam,* or *menschen,* remain unalterably rational, animal, and just as mortal. Like the names that Adam gave the animals, these names designate but do not determine the thing. They are conventional handles with which to grasp beings that are already naturally distinct and thus beg only to be recognized with names peculiarly their own. In naming beings distinctively, we do little more than acknowledge the articulated and multiform character of the given world.

Not all acts of naming are so inconsequential. Sometimes they actually shape and form the things they name. Such creative naming is, for example, especially characteristic of the biblical God, Who, in the account of Creation given in the first chapter of Genesis, names five things: light, darkness, the firmament, the dry land, and the gathered waters. As Robert Sacks observes,

> We can best grasp the significance of naming by comparing the things God named with the names God gives them. Light was called day, darkness was called night. The firmament was called heaven, the dry place was called land, the water was called sea. Darkness is not light, water is not dry. What more does a name add? The Hebrew word translated "firmament" which God called heaven comes from the root meaning "to beat." Workmen pound copper until it spreads out into a thin amorphous sheet, then form it and cut it and give it shape. Light and darkness, wet and dry, like the thinly pounded sheet of copper, seem to be an indefinite morass, each having its own quality, but each spreading out beyond the human imagination. But the day ends when night comes and the seas end at the shoreline, and the firmament becomes a whole when it becomes the sky. Without names, there

would still be distinctions. There would be love and there would be hate, but bravery would shade off into foolhardiness, and we would lose the clarity of thought.

God's naming clarifies, delimits, bounds, shapes, and makes intelligible. Like the Creation itself, which proceeds by acts of speech (always acts embodying and producing separations), these acts of naming bring order to chaos, the discrete to the continuous, definition to the indefinite, shapely and recognizable form to the merely qualitative.

Human naming, though perforce an act of speech and hence of reason, is, however, frequently colored by human passions such as fear, pride, hope, and lust. The names that Adam gives the animals may be disinterested, but not so the names he gives to himself and to the woman when she is brought before him: "This now is bone of my bone and flesh of my flesh; and this shall be called woman (*ishah*) because she was taken out of man (*ish*)." Previously called (by God and by the narrator) *adam*, which is not a personal name but a species name (meaning "earthling") for "human being," the man now names himself "male human being," *ish*, in relation to "female human being," *ishah*. It is her (naked) appearance before him ("before him" both literally and lexically in his quoted speech) that makes him feel his maleness; the carnal remark "bone of my bone, flesh of my flesh" strikes us as the verbalization of sexual desire; the man looks upon the woman as if she were his missing half, to which he now feels powerfully drawn in a desire for fusion. At the very least, one must admit that his delight in her leads him to exaggerate the degree to which she is "his own," more same than other, and to see her as an exteriorized portion of himself. This is not the voice of pure reason naming; and the name, born of his desire, has consequences for their relationship.

Later, a different passion will lead the man to rename the woman, this time without reference to himself. Hearing that the woman will bear children, the only good news in God's grim prophecy of the dismal human future (sorrow, sweat, toil, and death), he grasps at this straw of hope, renaming the woman Eve (*Chavah*), because she is the mother of all living (*chai*). From Adam's hopefulness, Eve gets the first genuinely proper name in the Bible.

What meanings are carried in our own proper names, the personal names we bear throughout our lives? Are they arbitrary and conventional handles that serve only to pick us out of a crowd? Or do our names, like those given by God, have power to shape our lives? Which passions do and should govern our acts of naming? When we name, do we express desires for ourselves (*ishah*) or hopes for the future of others (*Chavah*)? Is it a matter of indifference what we are called, what we call ourselves, or what we call others?

As we do not generally name ourselves, we normally do not encounter these questions in our daily lives. True, as Americans, sharing in the English common law of names, we have the right freely to change our names, as often as we please, and not a few young people take advantage of this privilege. But it rarely even occurs to most of us that we could change our names; we accept without question what we have been given, and we unthinkingly regard changing our given name as akin to violating a sacred order. This seemingly "given" order of names is, in fact, the product of conscious human choice, and all the questions about the meaning of naming confront us – whether we realize it or not – when we name our children.

Naming Your Child

The first gift from parents to a child, after the gift of life itself, is a name. The given name is a gift for a lifetime – indeed, for more than a lifetime. When we are gone, our name carved in stone and the memories it evokes will be, for nearly all of us, all that remains. Here is a gift that is not only permanent but possibly life-shaping. Here is a gift that cannot be refused; here is a gift that cannot easily be put aside; here is a gift that must be worn and that straightaway not only marks but constitutes one's identity.

On what basis does one select a gift, especially a gift of such importance? Generally speaking, one gives gifts that one thinks someone will like and appreciate, or one gives gifts that one thinks will be fitting and suitable, or one gives gifts that one thinks will be helpful and good. But in the gift of a name, even more than with other gifts to the newborn (such as clothing or toys), one has no idea which name will prove likable, or suitable, or helpful to the human being who is, at the time of naming, virtually unknown and unknowable, and largely pure potentiality. The awesome mystery of individuated human life announces itself in this nameless and unknowable stranger, who must nonetheless be called by a proper name. Faced with our invincible ignorance, we parents are forced to consult our own thoughts and feelings, though, it is to be hoped, without in the least forgetting the future welfare of our child. Though we necessarily will be moved by what pleases or suits or inspires us, we do well when we remember that it is the child who must live with and live out the identity we thus confer upon him or her.

Some of the considerations that might reasonably enter into choosing a name are obvious. Parents will want a name that is euphonic in conjunction with the family name, or at least will not sound bad. (On this basis we, the authors, rejected our first-choice name for a daughter, Rebekah Kass: too many "ka"s.) Parents will avoid names that could easily become the object of ridicule (and thus we would never have named a son of ours Jack), or that would in other ways be likely to be burdensome to or resented by a typical child. Here parents will no doubt be guided both by their imagination and by their own experience: they will surely remember the miseries inflicted by cruel or insensitive parents on one or another of their childhood acquaintances who had been saddled with a name too unusual, too pretentious, too quaint, too prissy, too foreign, or too stained by a disgraceful namesake. Some parents, to avoid the dangers that befall those who stand out, especially among the conformist young, may well refrain from giving a name that is utterly without precedent – for it may not find in the child that gets it the strength to stand alone and apart. On the other hand, some parents, seeking to avoid the commonplace, may opt for something out of the ordinary, a name with charm or class or appealing novelty, implying thereby the wish to help the child gain distinction. In such matters, different parental choices will no doubt reflect reasonably differing parental attitudes toward the balance between standing out and standing within, between distinction and inclusion, between risk and safety.

Parents who give the matter some thought will try to choose a name that wears well not only during childhood but even more in adulthood, for we bear our names much longer as adults than as children. Some names that are cute on an infant or a child seem ridiculous when attached to a mature or elderly person. Connected with this matter of fitness are considerations of likely nicknames and diminutives, whether given at home or acquired at school or at play. One feels for the little fellow in postwar Shaker Heights whose pretentious, upwardly mobile Jewish parents named him Lancelot, particularly because they could not refrain from calling him by the affectionate (and standard) diminutive form, "Lancelotkele," which resounded through the streets when they called him in from play. (*Latkele*, gentle reader, is Yiddish for a small potato pancake, traditionally eaten at Hanukkah.)

But these considerations are largely negative and serve mainly to prevent mistakes. They do not guide the positive choice. How then do we choose?

Whether we know it or not, the way we approach this serious, indeed awesome, task speaks volumes about our basic attitudes not only toward our children but also toward life. For we can name, just as we can live, in a spirit of self-indulgence and enjoyment, in a spirit of acquisition and appropriation, in a spirit of pride and domination, in a spirit of creativity, in a spirit of gratitude, in a spirit of blessing and dedication. Consider a few of these possibilities.

One could give the child a name that pleases us. How could that be bad? You find your child a delight, so why not celebrate this fact with a name you find delightful? The wanted child is rewarded for being wanted by getting the wanted name, and now proves doubly pleasing to the parents. Granted, no parent who loves a child would choose for it a name he or she does not like. But is this sufficient? And what if the parent has strange tastes? A teacher of our acquaintance once taught twin girls named – we do not jest – Lemonjello and Orangejello, perhaps after the mother's favorite food. The flavors of the parents are visited upon the children. On the principle of pleasing the parental palate, who can criticize? *De gustibus non disputandum.*

One could also give the child a name that pleases us because it pleases others, a name that is fashionable or popular. American fashions in first names change dramatically, especially for little girls. Rarely does one encounter anymore a young woman named Prudence, Constance, Faith, Hope, or Charity – though biblical names have come somewhat back into vogue. No one we knew or had even heard of through our first thirty years was named Tiffany or Chelsea. The fashions change frequently. The top dozen names for the United States from 2000 to 2010 were Emily, Madison, Emma, Olivia, Hannah, Abigail, Isabella, Samantha, Elizabeth, Ashley, Alexis, and Sarah. Long in decline are the popular names from our youth: Mary, Margaret, Helen, Patricia, Deborah, Betty, Susan, Dorothy, Nancy, Carol, Barbara, and Sandra. Since 2010, five new names have crashed the top twelve for the first time: Sophia, Ava, Mia, Chloe, and Charlotte, none of them listed in the top hundred names in the United States for the past century. Over the course of that century, sixty-one different names have appeared in the lists of the top dozen girls' names for a given decade, compared with thirty-nine for boys' names. Only four girls' names have made the top-twelve list in more than two decades: Elizabeth (six times), Emily (four times), Ashley (three times), and Sarah (three times); twenty-four names have appeared only once.

Curiously, the popular boys' names continue to be traditional: The top dozen for the United States from 2000 to 2010 were Jacob, Michael, Joshua, Matthew, Daniel, Christopher, Andrew, Ethan, Joseph, William, Anthony, and David. In eight of the last ten decades, Michael, William, and David have been in the top dozen, as has James, which has returned to the top twelve since 2010. All of these names have been among the top hundred boys' names in the United States for the past century, and all but two of them (Jacob and Ethan) in the top twenty-two.* What this difference in boy-girl naming fashions means, especially in an age that purports at last to take women seriously, we leave for our readers to ponder.

While frivolity, self-indulgence, and love of fashion often inspire naming choices, other parents, more serious, are moved by pride. Indeed, it is natural (but hardly unproblematic) for parents to take pride in the creation of a child, perhaps especially so with the firstborn. Paternal pride in siring a chip off the old block leads many fathers to name their first son after themselves – often saddling Junior with confusion of reference and, more serious, with unreasonable expectations for how he should live his life.

But pride in childbirth is not the prerogative only of fathers. In the first (and therefore, in our view, probably prototypical) human birth presented in Genesis, Eve proudly boasts of her creative power in the birth

---

* Things may be changing for boys' names. Since 2010, five newcomers have crashed the list for the first time: Noah, Mason, Liam, Jayden, and Aiden, none of them listed in the top hundred names in the United States for the past century. (The data from the Social Security Administration can be found here: https://www.ssa.gov/OACT/babynames/decades/index.html.)

of Cain: "And she conceived and bore Cain (*kayin*), saying, 'I have gotten (*kaniti*) a man [equally] with the Lord.'" (Most English translations have Eve say, piously, "with the help of the Lord," but this is an interpolation. The context, in our view, favors this meaning: "God created a man, and now so have I.") And, at first glance, why should she not be proud? She conceived, she carried, she labored, and she delivered; in short, she created a new life out of her own substance, a new life that is her own flesh and blood. Her pride in her creativity and "ownership" of her son is celebrated in the name she gives him: *kayin*, from a root *kanah*, meaning to possess, perhaps also related to a root *koneh*, meaning to shape or make or create.

Cain, the pride of his mother's bearing, bears the name of his mother's pride, and tragically lives out the meaning of the name his mother (unwittingly) gave him. He becomes a proud farmer, the sort of man who lays possessive claim to a portion of the earth, proud of his ability to bring forth fruit from the ground. When his pride is wounded, he kills his brother in anger to reassert his own place as number one. Eve had borne "his brother Abel" almost as an afterthought, with no celebration or boasting, and had given him (also unwittingly) a name meaning "breath that vanishes."

Eve, it seems, learns the folly of her naming ways. Chastened by the death of Abel and bereft by the banishment of Cain, she names her third son in a humbler and more grateful spirit: "And she called his name Seth, 'for God hath appointed [*shath*] me another seed in place of Abel, whom Cain slew.'" With death and the need for replacement now manifest before her, Eve this time enters into the act of naming and parenthood in full awareness of the human condition, in full knowledge that children are not human creations, in full consciousness of what it means to bestow a name. (The word "name" and the phrase "called his name" were not used in the report of the births of Cain and Abel.)

Despite their differences, naming as self-gratification, naming as appropriation, naming as expressing pride, and naming as creativity have this in common: they all take their meaning from and refer back to the activities of the parents. They do not centrally consider the independent being of the child, or the meaning of the child as one who must someday stand forth as the parents' replacement. Such considerations do, at least subconsciously, inform the activity of naming for those parents who seek by means of the name to express, in full seriousness, their best hopes and wishes for the child. These parents will choose a name that imparts personal or human meaning. They may stress continuity of family line by naming a son for the father, a daughter for a grandmother. They may memorialize some worthy friend or ancestor, whose fine qualities they hope to see replicated in the child. They may name after prophets or saints or other historical or literary figures, in the hope of promoting emulation or at least admiration through namesake identification. In these various ways, parents identify their children not with themselves but with what they look up to and respect; they express their fondest hopes, blessing their children, as it were, through names of blessed memory or elevated standing. Beyond this, the best parents will dedicate themselves to making good the promise conveyed in the good name thus bestowed.

The solemnity of such naming, and its meaning as dedication, is most evident when names are given within religious ceremonies. At a baptism, the newborn child is symbolically purified, sanctified, and received by name into the Christian community, obtaining his or her name in an act of christening or baptizing. The child is reborn by being named in the name of the Father, the Son, and the Holy Spirit, an implicit promise by the parents to rear the child in the ways of the Lord. Among its other intentions, baptism denies the parents' natural tendency to think of the child as property or as an object of pride and power. During the ceremony, the parents ritually hand the child over to the minister or to godparents, representatives of the church and community, literally enacting the meaning of naming as dedication. The name given is understood to be eternal, inscribed in the Book of Life.

At a *brith milah*, the Jewish act of ritual circumcision, male children on the eighth day of life enter into the covenant between God and the seed of Abraham, obtaining at this time their given Hebrew name (and here too the boy is handed over to the godfather for the ceremony). Daughters are publicly named in the synagogue soon after birth. Often, the meaning of the name and the reasons for its choice are publicly discussed as the name is given. The prayer for both Jewish sons and daughters that accompanies their naming is for a life that embraces *Torah* (learning and observance), *Chuppah* (marriage and family), and *Maasim Tovim* (good deeds). A name given in such a context is understood, at least implicitly, to be a sanctification and dedication.

It is, of course, not possible to gauge the spirit of the act of naming simply from the name given. The name of a beloved forebear may be perpetuated not because of what made him lovable but, say, because of benefits received by the namer, or as a result of family expectation, or as an expression of mere sentimentality. In a family we know, for example, a man named his son after his deceased father, a man of unrivaled goodness and gentleness, admired and loved by everyone who knew him, without exception or qualification. As it happens, the boy carrying the grandfather's name is the only male child of his generation, so the family name now resides entirely with him. Yet such thoughts are alien to his father, who believes that the past must be happily buried. No attempt has been made to teach the son anything about the grandfather – about his life, his character, his beliefs. Not until the boy was thirteen did he even see a photograph of the man after whom he was named, and then only by accident in another relative's house. The boy's father, a radical, preaches distrust of tradition and authority, and the son has grasped the paternal principle: "the past is dead, follow your likes." Already separating himself from his own past, he sets out to create his own identity, making himself into whatever he wishes. Here we have the name ringing hollow, without a grain of the legacy. The name, like the grandfather, was liked but not revered or even properly appreciated.

When the legacy of a name is truly appreciated and the dream it implies is great, there is a danger that the name will be more a burden than an inspiration to the child. On this ground, a name favored by one of us for a prospective (never born) son, Abraham Lincoln, was vetoed by the more sensible spouse. Parents should be mindful of the gap between hope and fact, between promise and realization: nature may not be cooperative, native gifts may be missing, serious illness or accident may deform and limit. Even in the most propitious circumstances, parental plans and aspirations, however modest, often go unrealized, not least because well-meaning and devoted parents sometimes fail to recognize sufficiently the radical individuality of each child. One names best when one names with modesty and humility, mindful of the child's separate identity and ultimate independence. A name – an identity – given in this spirit is a means of recognizing and celebrating the uniqueness of the life its bearer will live.

Naming a child thus anticipates the central difficulty of childrearing:

how to communicate unconditional love for the child-as-he-now-is, while at the same time doing all in one's power to encourage and help him become better (which is to say, more truly lovable). A name, likable here and now but also bearing hope and promise, fits the good-enough-but-potentially-much-better kind of being that is the human child – indeed, the human being throughout life. Defining the child now but also for later, the given but independent name looks forward to the time when, thanks to good rearing, he will be able to write his own named account in the Book of Life.

The given name, given seriously, provides identity and individuality but within a family and a community; it recognizes continuity with lives of the past but bears hopes and promises for the new life in the future; it embodies general aspiration but recognizes individual distinction; it reflects present affection as well as the desire for future improvement; it acknowledges that one's child is to be one's replacement; it celebrates the joyous wonder of the renewal of human possibility while accepting the awesome responsibility for helping that possibility to be realized; and it pays homage to the mysterious source of human life and human individuality.

In all these ways, the naming of a child is an emblem of the entire parent-child relation, in both its human generality and its radical particularity. Human children are born naked and nameless, like the animals; they become humanized only through rearing, by acts of speech and deed – praise and blame, reward and punishment, custom and habituation, training and education. They become humanized, in the first instance, at the hands of parents, whose duties include teaching them how to call things by their proper name and showing them how to acquire a good name for themselves.

Proper Use of Proper Names

Mention of calling things by their proper name prompts a digression on the proper usage of proper names, itself a central issue of propriety. In fact, it was observations on the prevalent use and misuse of given or first names that long ago aroused our interest in the subject of naming.

As amateur observers of the American social scene, we are struck by how much more of our public social life is nowadays conducted on a first-name basis. The open-faced waiter in the yuppie restaurant begins not with, "Good evening. Are you ready to order?" but with, "Hi, I'm Sherman. I'm your server this evening, and I'd like to tell you about our specials." The gynecologist and all members of his staff (including the barely postadolescent receptionist) call all the patients by first name, even on first encounter. Venerable ladies and gentlemen in homes for the aged are uniformly called Sadie or Annie, Herman or Mike, by people who will never know a tenth of what some of the elderly have forgotten. Small children are not taught to address uncles and aunts as Uncle Leon and Aunt Amy, but plain Leon and Amy. Children of all ages are generally allowed to call all grown-up guests in the home straightaway by their first names. At social mixers, the typical tag has a first name only: "Hello, My Name is Steffie." Total strangers, soliciting for stock brokerages or the local police museum, call during dinner oozing familiarity, asking to speak to Leon or Amy (not knowing that they have thus completely blown their slim chance of success). Students introduce themselves to one another, to their teachers, or to the parents of their friends by first names only. Even some college professors and many members of the clergy prefer to be called by their first names, even when in class or in church or synagogue.

The reasons for this increased familiarity are numerous and sometimes complex, surely varying from case to case. A policy favoring forward but easy amiability, thought useful for putting everyone in a good mood and making them feel at home, is no doubt part of the waiter's conduct; but there is probably also calculation that guests will be more inclined to leave a larger tip for a named "acquaintance" than for an anonymous servant. The gynecologist may believe he is creating a homey atmosphere that will overcome his patient's anxieties and embarrassments; but he is culpably unaware that calling vulnerable strangers by their first names is patronizing, condescending, and unprofessional, that it contributes further to the indignity of being a patient, that most women receiving pelvic examinations will not be made more comfortable by a physician who makes himself improperly familiar, and that the patient's unavoidable exposure is precisely what demands every effort to uphold her dignity. Informality is thought to be a boon to equality and fellow feeling; titles like Uncle and Aunt, or even Mr. or Ms., are distancing and hierarchical.

They get in the way of easy sociability, made possible when everybody, regardless of age or station, is equally just plain Bill.

The change in usage, whatever one thinks of it, is symptomatic of a general breakdown of the boundaries between public and private life, between formal and familiar, between grown-up and childish, between high and low, refined and vulgar, sacred and profane. This leveling of boundaries is itself entirely American, which is to say, it is the result of the relentless march of the democratic spirit, under the twin banners of equality and individualism. But there is something novel and especially revealing – and also especially worrisome – in the self-identification of young students away from home at college.

When we were in college – at the University of Chicago in the 1950s and early 1960s – our teachers called us by our last names, usually prefaced by Mr. or Miss, and we were taught to refer to our peers, even our friends, in the same formal way in class. This civil convention, by the way, applied equally to the faculty: no one was Professor or Doctor, everyone was Mr. or Mrs. or Miss. We did not then fully appreciate the profound good sense of these customs, but we liked them nonetheless. No longer patronized as we had been by our teachers in high school, we were being treated respectfully, like grown-ups – indeed, as nominally the equals of our instructors. This was flattering and encouraging; it induced emulation and a higher level of speech and conduct in the classroom.

But the purpose of this nominal equality was not to flatter the students; it was to mirror and encourage our shared human work. Though we were encouraged to think and speak for ourselves, speech was not personalized and the person of the speaker was not authoritative. What the teacher said or what we ourselves said was given weight not because of the speaker's rank – for we were nominally of the same rank – but only in accordance with its truthfulness or reasonableness. Shared speech and reasoning, and the joint effort to understand, made the classroom a community of fellow learners, not just an aggregate of sometimes overlapping, sometimes clashing personal interests. Objections and criticisms were muted and civil: the casual language of the street, "Leon, you dolt," was replaced by "Mr. Kass, what is your evidence?" Familiarity between teacher and student (or even between student and student) was neither assumed nor promised; like all real friendship, it had to be earned.

Friendships with teachers did occasionally develop, but our eye was not on such personal matters. We were courting the greater self-respect that comes with adult accomplishment. To hear ourselves called after the manner of our parents (and in the case of males, exactly as our fathers were called) dimly reminded us not only who we were and where we came from, but also that we were preparing to take our parents' place.

Now, as teachers at the University of Chicago, we still continue these practices: we are known as Mrs. Kass and Mr. Kass; we call our male students Mr. and our female students Miss, Mrs., or Ms. (as they wish); and we insist that the students in class refer to one another in the same way. Our students do not protest. Nearly all acquire the habit, and some have even told us how much they appreciate the contribution this civility makes to the atmosphere of learning. But we are a vanishing breed.*

In recent years we have also noticed a marked decline in students' use of last names outside of class. If we attend a dinner in the dorms, if unfamiliar students come to office hours, if we overhear them introducing themselves to one another, we hear them give only their first names: "Hello, I'm Susie." To be sure, this is friendliness, this is informality, this is individuality. But in many cases it is also, we believe, a tacit but quite definite denial of their origins, of their roots in families. "Hello, I'm Susie" implicitly means "I am Susie, short for *sui generis*." Changing usages regarding last names reflect changing mores regarding the meaning of last names, which in turn reflect – and may also contribute to – the changing structure of marriage and family life.

The Family Name

Last names or family names are of relatively recent origin in the West. Whereas in China, an emperor in 2852 BC decreed the universal adoption of hereditary family names, this practice became customary in

---

* We were dismayed to learn that the City University of New York has instructed all faculty and staff to desist from referring to any member of the community with the designations of Mr. or Ms., ostensibly to avoid attributing sexual identity to people who might not welcome the attribution. With one blow, the CUNY administrators sought to banish two natural distinctions, recognition of which is fundamental to civilized life everywhere: the difference between males and females, and the difference between children and grown-ups.

England only toward the end of the sixteenth century.* Prior to that time, the given name, usually received at baptism, was the person's full name. To distinguish among persons who shared the same Christian name, surnames would be added over and above the true name (*sur*, from super, "over" or "above"). Surnames had no standard meaning; they could be based on the father's name (John's son or O'Brien), or on one's occupation (Weaver or Hunter), or on place of residence (Bristol, Lyons, At-Water), or they might be an epithet capturing some striking personal trait or achievement (Little, Swift, Arm-Strong).

Only gradually, starting in the early medieval period, were many of these surnames turned into hereditary family names, apparently first in aristocratic families and in large cities. A big impetus toward hereditary family names came with a decree by the Council of Trent (1563) that every Catholic parish keep complete registers of baptisms, including the names of the parents and grandparents along with the name of the child. When Protestant parishes soon followed suit, this practice made the use of family names nearly universal. It was not law but widespread custom that said a woman upon marriage would take the last name of her husband and that their children would then automatically bear the family name.

Despite many variations from country to country – about the order of family and given names, about middle names, about the incorporation of maiden names into a woman's married name, etc. – it is now nearly universally the case that one's personal name includes (at least) one's given or individual name and one's family name. The former, a matter of parental choice, marks one's individuated identity within the larger family and signifies one's path toward a unique life trajectory; the latter, a question of heritable custom, gives one a familial identity in relation to the larger social world and expresses one's connections to a shared ancestral past. Human individuation is contextualized within families – both families of origin and families of perpetuation. Last names are ever-present reminders that we were begotten and that we belong, and, later, that we belong in order to beget.

That a family name is centrally a sign of our connected and dignified

---

* In Norway, hereditary family names began to be commonplace only in the later nineteenth century, and the older custom of patronyms persisted in some rural areas until 1923, when permanent surnames were required by law.

humanity we see when such names are withheld – for example, in the practice of naming slaves in the antebellum South. Slaves were given only first names; if they had to receive a surname to distinguish one from another, it was John's boy, never John's son. The first name individuates, but without a last name it is demeaning, even meaningless. The practice of using only first names, by making one everywhere familiar, renders genuine public life *and* genuine private life impossible. As the slaveholders understood perfectly, it makes the childish station permanent.

Well before there were surnames as family names, the ties of blood and lineage were given expression in the form of patronymics. In their classical or heroic form, the patronym was even more important than the given name, with the son being under lifelong obligation to make himself worthy of his father and thus to earn, as it were, the title to his own name.

Homer, in beginning the *Iliad*, asks the goddess to sing the wrath of Peleus's son Achilles, who is first of interest precisely because he is the son of Peleus, himself the son of Aeacus, himself the son of Zeus. (On his mother's side, Achilles is even closer to the immortals; the goddess Thetis is his mother.) With lesser parents, in Homer's world of heroes, Achilles would have been a nonentity, one from whom nothing much would be expected. But given his pedigree, he is under strenuous obligation to live up to his name, thereby winning great glory also for his father. When Hector, bouncing his infant son Astyanax, wishes for him to become an even greater warrior than his father, this wish must be heard as narcissistic: the son's greatness will pile further glory upon his sire. Homer makes us feel immediately the tragic character of such paternal wishes for one's sons; the reader knows that young Astyanax's future is right here being sacrificed to his father's present thirst for glory, as Hector refuses his wife Andromache's plea, in the name of family, not to return to the fighting. In these heroic cultures, the past throws a long shadow over the present and future, and most men die failing to match the recounted successes of illustrious ancestors. The patronym (or its equivalent family name), and through it the past, continued to exercise hegemony, albeit in somewhat muted form, in European aristocratic societies even into the last century.

We liberal democrats have mercifully escaped from this state of affairs. Our American society and its founding thought begin from the radical equality of each individual, including his inalienable right to practice happiness as he himself defines it. What counts for us is not birth or station, but one's own accomplishments; not who one's parents were, but what one has made (and proposes to make) of oneself. Yet bourgeois democratic family life, with its naming practices, has preserved us, at least until recently, from the rootlessness and isolation to which such individuality might lead. The conventional identity of given name plus inherited family name, in the bourgeois family, represented a sensible mean between the heroic and the anonymous, between the aristocratic tyranny of the past (Peleus's son) and the servile because rootless denial of a dignified adult future (Jim NoName).

Times have changed. Both as a culture and as individuals, we today care even less about where we come from, and also less and less about where we are going, more and more only about the here and now. The ways of the fathers and mothers are not our ways. The ways of our children are unimaginable. Full individualists, and proud of it, we increasingly look solely to ourselves, as Tocqueville remarked over 150 years ago, as the source and reason for things. In the present generation, such individualistic thinking is showing its power against the institution of the family and customs of the family name.

Some time ago, the *New York Times* (January 21, 1993) featured an article by Janice L. Kaplan entitled "Creativity Is Often the Name of This Family Game." In the article, Ms. Kaplan cites numerous examples of novel naming practices to illustrate her thesis that "for more and more of today's parents, choosing a child's last name is a matter of personal decision, a chance to be creative, even an opportunity to make a statement." A few of her examples provide the flavor of them all.

When Elyse Goldstein, a rabbi, married Baruch Browns, a calligrapher and school administrator, they discussed what name they would "pass on" to their offspring. Both "absolutely wanted a family name" but one different from their own respective birth names, "a creative alternative to passing on only the father's surname." The solution: "They took the gold from Goldstein, the brown from Browns, mixed them together and created Sienna, the legal last name of their children." As Mr. Browns explained, "Ocher, or those other muddy yellow colors, didn't seem like nice names."

Dean Skylar and Chris Ledbetter, likewise opposed to "the whole patriarchal tradition," wanted a new name for the child, one that was different from their own names but would "symbolize [their] relationship." Being residents of the state of Florida, which required parents to pass on the father's surname, they faced a court battle to legitimize their choice. Eventually they prevailed, and they combined Ledbetter and Skylar to form Skybetter as the surname of their two children. "All of our names are in the phone book," said Ms. Ledbetter. "That handles most any problem that comes up."

Ms. Van Horn, a commercial photographer and clinical hypnotherapist, and Ms. Hershey, owner of a design and marketing concern, were the first lesbians in Los Angeles County to be granted joint custody of a child. They gave their adopted son both of their last names: hence, Ryan Christopher Hershey-Van Horn. "We're both his parents," Ms. Van Horn explained. "We're both women with careers. And we both have definite identities. It's important that Christopher be real clear about his identity as well."

Whether they made up an entirely new name for their children, or creatively melded their own names, or combined their names with a hyphen, all these parents revealed the same fundamental belief: a child's last name is a matter of free parental choice no less than its first name. Having liberated themselves from the "patriarchal tradition" of women giving up their names – none of the women interviewed by Kaplan took the man's last name – these parents all felt perfectly free to "liberate" their children as well. For what they have creatively managed to "pass on" is a name with no past; and the so-called "family" name is in no case the name of the entire family, but of the children only. The children from birth are already emancipated nominally (in the literal sense of the word) from all links to their parents; they are identified nominally as being unrelated to either parent, let alone to a married couple whose common name would symbolize a union in a new estate and the potential to be a unified family with offspring. These children have essentially been given two first names.

Ms. Kaplan observes that "sometimes, say experts and the children involved, the parents' choices, if not clearly explained, can result in confusion and identity problems." But the worries mentioned are superficial: children who can't fit their names into the boxes on forms; children who can't spell their last names; children at risk of being teased or ridiculed by peers. For the "experts," who want only that the child "develop an appropriate and healthy identity," identity is entirely a subjective matter, but somehow one that yields to "rational understanding." If the origin of the surname is "clearly explained" to the child ("more than once," to be sure), there need be no confusion of identity.

But identity is not just a state of mind. All the explanations in the world cannot alter what the child's name loudly declares: my parents and I belong to different families. Because this is how the child is named and known, his lack of a true family name is now central to his identity, whatever he may feel about it. The parents sometimes justify their practice by pointing out that children of divorced and remarried parents or children of "live-in relationships" also don't share the parental name, but this only proves the point: taking broken or unmarried homes as a suitable norm, and insisting on their own radically individuated identity, they start their children off in life with a broken family identity. It is almost as if they are preparing their children not only for the liberated life they have chosen for themselves, but also for the family fragmentation that now takes its toll of so many of America's children.

These "creative" parents are, we suspect, still a very small minority. Far more common are families in which the children carry the name of the father, even though the mother has kept her maiden name. Here, too, the confusion of identity is obvious: it is not nominally clear who belongs to whom. A friend of ours, a mother of a highly popular first-grader, recently attended her first PTA meeting. Eager to meet the parents of the many frequent visitors to her home, she carefully scanned the nametags of all the people in the room. But on that night the room happened to be full of mothers only, none of whom bore the same last name as her child. Today, it is a wise child who knows his *mother*.

What's wrong with all of this? Leaving aside, for now, the rightness or wrongness of the old so-called patriarchal conventions whereby the wife necessarily takes and the children automatically acquire the husband's name, one can advance powerful arguments why, for reasons of truth and identity, a child's family name should be the same as that of both his parents. The common name identifies the child securely within its nest of origin and rearing, and symbolically points to the ties of parental affection and responsibility that are needed for healthy growth and well-being. Given that the mother-child bond is the most natural foundation of all familial attachments and parental care, it seems especially absurd that mothers should be willing not to have the same last name as their children – unless motherhood is understood as nothing more than a surrogate "social womb," unconnected with nature, and looking after one's children as simply a job or a form of self-fulfillment.

Responsibility for the child, who did not himself ask to be born, is accepted and announced by family naming: the child, individuated from birth (as marked in his given name), also belongs necessarily to his parents, not as a possession to be used but as a precious life to be nurtured. Couples may choose whether to have a child, but they may not morally choose to deny familial responsibility for his care. A shared and transmittable family name, given and accepted rather than invented or chosen, stands perfectly for this shared and transmittable moral reality.

The common name of parent and child stands not only for parental responsibilities, but also for the child's security, filial regard, family loyalty, gratitude, and personal pride. Children are not *sui generis*; we are neither self-made nor self-reared. We begin as dependents, reliant upon the unmerited attention and care lavished on us by our parents. To carry the family name is a constant reminder of what we owe and to whom – and of the fact that what we owe can never be repaid (except, indirectly, by doing the same for our own children). Thus, it represents a special kind of blindness – not to say ingratitude – for our college students to hold themselves familially innominate ("Just Susie") precisely when Mom and Dad are shelling out $50,000 a year to enable them to become educated and independent.

But this backward-looking identification with our family of origin cannot be the whole story. On the contrary, life is forward-going and regenerative; in most cases, we must leave our fathers and mothers and cleave to our spouses, in order to do as our fathers and mothers did before. The given family of origin gives way (not wholly but in very large part) to the chosen family of perpetuation, prepared for and legally sanctioned by the act of marriage. How should this new estate and new identity be reflected in our names? When we marry, what surname or surnames shall we adopt?

Whether we like it or not, choosing surnames at marriage is in today's America almost as much a matter of choice as the giving of first names at childbirth, a reflection (and perhaps also a cause) of novel conceptions of marriage, an institution the meaning of which is itself increasingly regarded as a matter of choice. The traditional bourgeois way of the husband giving and the wife accepting his family name – customary for at least four hundred years in the English-speaking world – is no longer secure as customary. For young American ears, "because that's the way we've always done it" is a losing reason. With the true reasons for the old custom forgotten, its practitioners are impotent to defend it against charges of "patriarchy," "male hegemonism," "sexism," and the like. Thus, with no certain cultural guidance, the present generation (in fact, each couple independently) is being allowed – or should we say compelled? – to think this through for itself.

As a thought experiment, we (the authors) imagined ourselves having to do it over again, but with the benefit of longer views of marriage and of life, and on this condition: to choose not on the basis of what pleases us, but on the basis of what we believe is appropriate to the meaning of marriage and hence, in principle, universalizable.

If marriage is, as we believe, a new estate, one that changes the identities of both partners, there is good reason to have this changed identity reflected in some change of surname, one that reflects and announces this fact. If marriage, though entered into voluntarily, is in its inner meaning more than a contract between interested parties but rather a union made in expectation of permanence and a union open (as no simple contract of individuals can be) to the possibility of procreation, there is good reason to have the commitment to lifelong union reflected and announced in a common name that symbolizes and celebrates its special meaning.

Whether they intend it or not, individuals who individualistically keep their original names when entering a marriage are symbolically holding themselves back from the full meaning of the union. Fearing "loss of identity" in a change of name, they implicitly deny that to live now toward and for one's beloved, as soulmate, is rather to gain a new identity, a new meaning of living a life, one toward which *eros* has pointed us. Often failing to anticipate having their own children, and more generally unable or unwilling to see the institution of marriage as directed toward or even connected with its central generational raison d'être, they create a confused identity for their future children.

The irony is that the clear personal identity to which they selfishly cling (in symbolic denial of their new social identity) is an identity they possess only because their parents were willing and able to create that singular family identity for them. We are, of course, aware that massive numbers of our youth stem from parents who divorce and remarry, and that the insecurity of identity already reflected in their having a different name from a birth parent may lead them to cling tenaciously to their original surname, lest they lose the little identity they have left. Yet if they truly understood their plight, they would be eager to try to prevent such misfortunes from befalling their own children, and would symbolically identify themselves in advance as lifelong parents to their yet-to-be-born children.

It is also ironic that the same young people who live socially on a first-name basis, as though forgetful of where they come from, should at the time of forward-looking marriage turn backward and cling to the name of their family of origin. Faced with the "threat" of "losing themselves" in marriage, they reassert themselves as independent selves by holding on to their original surname as if it were a mark of autonomy and individuality.

The human family, unlike some animal families, is exogamous, not incestuous; it is exogamous not by nature but by the wisest of customs. The near-universal taboo against incest embodies the insight that family means a forward-looking series of generations rather than an inward-turning merging and togetherness. It keeps lineage clear, to distinguish spouses from progeny in the service of tranquil relations, distinct identity, and sound rearing – and above all, to accomplish the family's primary human work of perpetuation and cultural transmission. The legal sanctification and support of marriage, a further expression of the insights embedded in the incest taboo, makes sense only in this view of family. Were sex not generative and families not generational, no one would much care with whom one wished to merge.

In entering a marriage, the partners are bravely stepping forward, unprotected by the family of origin, into the full meaning of human adulthood: they are saying goodbye to father and mother, and cleaving to their spouse. They are tacitly accepting the eventual death of their parents and their own mortality as they embark on the road to the next generation. They express their readiness to discover, by repeating the practice, how their own family identity and nurtured humanity were products of deliberate human choice to affirm and elevate the natural necessity of renewal. A common name deliberately taken at the time of marriage affirms the special union of natural necessity and human choice that the exogamous family itself embodies.

We are well aware that family or social identity is not the whole of our identity, that professional or "career" identity is both psychically and socially important (as are civic and religious identity). The loving and generative aspects of our nature are far from being the whole human story. Yet the familial is foundational, and it cannot without grave danger be subordinated or assimilated to the professional. Our argument for a common social name for the married couple is, however, perfectly compatible with having one partner or the other – or both – keeping a distinct professional name. Some have argued that in today's world of rampant mobility and weakened family ties, and with both husband and wife in the workplace, much is lost and little is gained if professional identity is submerged in a common family name. But precisely to affirm and protect the precious realm of private life from the distorting intrusion of public or purely economic preoccupations, a common social name makes eminent sense – one might say especially under present conditions.

The argument advanced so far does not, of course, yet reach to the customary pattern of the bride taking the groom's name. If anything, it might even call into question the wisdom of allowing either partner to keep the surname of origin. To provide a common last name for themselves, a name that proclaims their social unity and that will immediately confer social identity to their children, the married couple could devise a hyphenated compound that both of them adopt, or they could invent a totally new surname that leaves no trace of either family of origin. But these alternatives are both defective. The first is simply impractical beyond one or at most two generations; the structure of life itself makes impossible the universalizing of the add-and-hyphenate maxim. The second alternative, in our view, too starkly severs the new social ties from the familial past (quite apart from what it means to the public individual identities of each of the partners) and from grandparents still living or remembered. It further accentuates the unraveling of intergenerational connections, symbolizing each little family's atomistic belief in its ability to go it alone. In contrast, a family name that ties the new family of perpetuation to one old family of origin reflects more faithfully the truth about family as a series of generations and the moral and psychological meaning of lineage and attachment.

This leaves only the hard question: shall it be his family name or hers? A little reflection will show why, as a general rule, it should be his.

Although we know from biological science the equal contributions that both parents make to the genetic identity of a child, it is still true to say that the mother is the "more natural" parent, the parent by birth. A woman can give up a child for adoption or, thanks to modern reproductive technologies, can even bear a child not genetically her own. But there is no way to deny out of whose body the new life sprung, whose substance it fed on, who labored to produce it, who wondrously bore it forth. The father's role in all this is minuscule and invisible; in contrast to the mother, there is no naturally manifest way to demonstrate his responsibility.

The father is thus a parent more by choice and agreement than by nature (and not only because he cannot know with absolute certainty that the woman's child is indeed his own). One can thus explain the giving of the paternal surname in the following way: the father symbolically announces "his choice" that the child is his, fully and freely accepting responsibility for its conception and, more importantly, for its protection and support, and answering in advance the vital question: Who's my dad?

The husband who gives his name to his bride in marriage is thus not just keeping his own; he is owning up to what it means to have been given a family and a family name by his own father. He is living out his destiny to be a father by saying yes to it in advance. And the wife does not so much surrender her name as accept the gift of his, given and received as a pledge of (among other things) loyal and responsible fatherhood for her children. A woman who refuses this gift is, whether she knows it or not, refusing the promised devotion or, worse, expressing her suspicions about her groom's trustworthiness as a husband and prospective father.

Patrilineal surnames are, in truth, less a sign of paternal prerogative than of paternal duty and commitment, reinforced psychologically by gratifying the father's vanity in the perpetuation of his name and by offering this nominal incentive to fulfill his obligation to mother and child. This naming custom enables the father to become explicitly the parent-by-choice that he, more than the mother, must necessarily be. Fathers who will not own up to their paternity, who will not "legitimate" their offspring, and who will not name themselves responsible for child-rearing by giving their children their name are not real fathers at all, and their children suffer. The former stigmatization of bastardy was, in truth, meant to protect women and children from such irresponsible behavior by self-indulgent men who would take their sexual pleasures and walk away from the consequences – a behavior probably rooted in natural psychosexual tendencies of the mammalian male, without the discipline imposed by human civilization. The removal of the stigma, prompted by a humane concern not to penalize innocent children by calling them "illegitimate," has predictably contributed mightily to an increase in fatherless children.

The advantage a woman and her children gain from the commitment of the man to take responsibility and to stay the course – the commitment implied in his embracing the woman and her prospective children with his family name – is by itself sufficient reason why it is in a woman's interest as a wife and prospective mother to readily take the bridegroom's name.

But there is a deeper reason why this makes sense. The change of the woman's name, from family of origin to family of perpetuation, is the perfect emblem for the desired exogamy of human sexuality and generation. The woman in marriage not only expresses her humanity in love (as does the man); she also embraces the meaning of marriage by accepting the meaning of her womanly nature as generative. In shedding the name of her family of origin, she tacitly affirms that children of her womb can be legitimated only exogamously. Her children will not bear the same name as her own father – will not "belong to" him. Her new name also allows her father to recognize formally the mature woman she has become. By choosing to accept the gift of her husband's name, by saying yes to customizing her given nature, the woman humanizes the result of her natural prowess and affirms the meaning of her own humanity.

Almost none of what we, the authors, now believe we understand about the meanings and uses of names did we know when, following custom, we first joined our lives together under the bridegroom's family name. We had only partial knowledge, at best, when we deliberately gave our children biblical names. Had we been left to invent our own practices of naming, it is doubtful that we would have gotten it right. In place of our own knowledge, we were guided by the blessed example of the strong, enduring, and admirable marriages and home life of our parents, itself sustained by teachings silently conveyed through custom and ritual. Wisdom in these matters, for individual thinkers, comes slowly if at all. But custom, once wisely established, more than makes up for our deficiencies.

It makes possible the full flourishing of our humanity. William Butler Yeats said it best, in "A Prayer for My Daughter":

> And may her bridegroom bring her to a house
> Where all's accustomed, ceremonious;
> For arrogance and hatred are the wares
> Peddled in the thoroughfares.
> How but in custom and in ceremony
> Are innocence and beauty born?
> Ceremony's a name for the rich horn,
> And custom for the spreading laurel tree.

II · Human Excellence and Human Dignity

Real and Distorted

CHAPTER SIX

Ageless Bodies, Happy Souls

Biotechnology and the Pursuit of Happiness

W E LIVE NEAR the beginning of a golden age of biomedical science and technology. For the most part, we should be mightily glad that we do, as we and our friends and loved ones are many times over the beneficiaries of its cures for diseases, prolongation of life, and amelioration of suffering, psychic and somatic. Since the latter third of the last century, most people in technologically advanced countries have been living healthier and longer lives than even the most fortunate individuals in prior human history. Diphtheria, typhoid, and tuberculosis threaten us no longer. While there is no definitive cure for deadly cancers, half the people who are today treated for those cancers survive more than five years. The average American's life expectancy at birth has increased from forty-seven years in 1900 to seventy-eight in 2000, and millions are now living healthily into their eighties and nineties. Thanks to basic research in neuroscience and new psychotropic drugs, the scourge of major depression and other devastating mental illnesses is finally under effective attack. We have every reason to look forward to new discoveries and new medical blessings. Every one of us should be deeply grateful for the gifts of human ingenuity and for the devoted efforts of scientists, physicians, and entrepreneurs who have used these gifts to make those benefits possible.

Yet, notwithstanding these blessings, present and projected, we have also seen more than enough to make us concerned. For we recognize that the powers made possible by biomedical science can be used for nontherapeutic purposes, serving ends that range from the frivolous and disquieting to the offensive and pernicious. These powers are available as instruments of bioterrorism (for example, genetically engineered drug-resistant bacteria, or drugs that obliterate memory); as agents of social control (for example, drugs to tame rowdies and dissenters, or fertility blockers for welfare recipients); and as means of trying to improve or perfect our bodies and minds and those of our children (for example, genetically engineered supermuscles, or drugs to improve memory). Anticipating possible threats to our security, freedom, and even our very humanity, many people are increasingly worried about where biotechnology may be taking us.

In this chapter I want to discuss only the last and most seductive of these disquieting prospects: the use of biotechnical powers to pursue "perfection," both of body and of mind. I do so partly because it is the most neglected topic in public bioethics, yet it is, I believe, the deepest source of public anxiety, represented in the concern about "man playing God," or about a Brave New World or a "posthuman" future. It raises weighty questions about the ends and goals of the biomedical enterprise, about the nature and meaning of human flourishing, and about the intrinsic threat of dehumanization (or the vaunted promise of superhumanization). It compels attention to what it means to *be* a human being and to be active *as* a human being. And it gets us beyond our narrow preoccupation with the "life issues" of abortion or embryo destruction, important though they are, to deal with what is genuinely novel in the biotechnical revolution, exciting to some but worrisome to many: not the old, crude power to kill the creature made in God's image, but the science-based, sophisticated powers to remake him after our own imaginings.

What exactly are the powers that I am talking about? What sorts of ends are they likely to serve? They are powers that affect the capacities and activities of the human body, powers that affect the capacities and activities of the mind or soul, and powers that affect the shape of the human life cycle, at both ends and in between. We already have powers to prevent fertility and to promote it; to initiate life in the laboratory; to screen human genes, in adults and in embryos, and to select (or reject) nascent life on genetic criteria; to insert new genes into various parts of the adult body, and someday soon also into gametes and embryos; to enhance muscle performance and endurance; to replace body parts with natural or mechanical organs, and perhaps soon, to wire ourselves using computer chips implanted into the body and brain; to alter memory, mood, temperament, appetite, and attention through psychoactive drugs; and to prolong not just the average but also the maximum human life expectancy. The technologies for altering our native capacities are mainly those of genetic screening and genetic engineering; drugs, especially psychoactive ones; and the ability to replace body parts or to insert novel ones. Some of these techniques have been demonstrated only with animals, but others are already being used in humans.

It bears emphasis that these powers, at least for now, are not being developed for the purpose of producing perfect or posthuman beings. They have been produced largely for the purpose of preventing and curing disease, and of reversing disabilities. Even the bizarre prospect of machine-brain interaction and implanted nanotechnological devices starts with therapeutic efforts to enable the blind to see and the deaf to hear. Yet the "dual use" aspect of most of these powers, encouraged by the ineradicable human urge toward "improvement" and the commercial interests that see market opportunities for nontherapeutic uses, means that we must not be lulled to sleep by the fact that the originators of these powers were no friends to Brave New World. Once here, techniques and powers can produce desires where none existed before, and things often go where no one ever intended.

How to organize our reflections? One should resist the temptation to begin with the new techniques or even with the capacities for intervention that they make possible. To do so runs the risk of losing the human import and significance of the undertakings. Better to begin with the human *desires* and *goals* that these powers and techniques are destined to serve: better children, superior performance, ageless bodies, happy souls, a more peaceful and cooperative society, etc.* Here I will leave aside the

---

* These are the organizing principles of *Beyond Therapy: Biotechnology and the Pursuit of Happiness*, A Report by the President's Council on Bioethics (October 2003), with a chapter on each of the first four of these items. Readers who wish to explore these issues in greater depth can find the report in editions with my own introductions published by HarperCollins and The Dana Press, or online at http://bioethics.georgetown. edu/pcbe/reports/beyondtherapy/index.html.

pursuit of optimum children or superior performance (the subject of Chapter Eight) or better citizens, to concentrate on the strictly personal goals of self-improvement, on efforts to preserve and augment the vitality of the body and to enhance the happiness of the soul. These goals are, arguably, the least controversial, the most continuous with the aims of modern medicine and psychiatry (better health, peace of mind), and the most attractive to most potential consumers – indeed, probably to most of us. It is perhaps worth remembering that these were the goals that animated the great founders of modern science, Bacon and Descartes: flawlessly healthy bodies, unconflicted and contented souls, and freedom from the infirmities of age, perhaps indefinitely.

Here are some of the technological innovations that can serve these purposes in varying degrees. With respect to the pursuit of "ageless bodies": We can replace worn-out parts by means of mechanical devices and organ transplantation, or, in the future, through regenerative medicine where decayed tissues are replaced with new ones produced from stem cells. We can improve upon normal and healthy parts, for example via precise genetic modification of muscles, through injections of growth factor genes that keep the transformed muscles whole, vigorous, and free of age-related decline – powers already used to produce "mighty mouse" and "super rat," and soon to be available for treatment of muscular dystrophy and muscle weakness in the elderly but also of interest to football and wrestling coaches and to the hordes of people who spend two hours daily pumping iron and sculpting their bodies. Most radically, we can try to retard or stop the entire process of biological senescence. Recent discoveries in the genetics of aging have shown how the maximum life span of worms and flies can be increased two- or threefold by alterations in a *single* gene, a gene now known to be present also in mammals.

With respect to the pursuit of "happy souls": We can eliminate psychic distress; we can produce states of transient euphoria; and we can engineer more permanent conditions of good cheer, optimism, self-esteem, and contentment. Drugs now available, administered promptly at the time of memory formation, blunt markedly the painful emotional content of the newly formed memories of traumatic events (so-called "memory blunting or erasure," a remedy being sought to prevent post-traumatic stress disorder). Simple euphoriants like Ecstasy, a precursor of Aldous Huxley's "soma," are widely used on college campuses. Powerful antidepressants and mood brighteners like Prozac are wonderful for the treatment of major depression, but also capable in some people of utterly transforming their personalities, changing their outlook on life from that of Eeyore to that of Mary Poppins.

Problems of Description: Therapy or Enhancement?

People who have tried to address our topic have usually approached it through a distinction between "therapy" and "enhancement," the first being the treatment of individuals with known diseases or disabilities, and the second being the directed use of biotechnical power to improve upon the "normal" workings of the human body and psyche. Those who introduced this distinction hoped by this means to distinguish between the acceptable and the dubious or unacceptable uses of biomedical technology: therapy is always ethically fine, while enhancement is, at least prima facie, ethically suspect. Gene therapy for cystic fibrosis or Prozac for psychotic depression is fine; insertion of genes to enhance intelligence or steroids for Olympic athletes is not.

This distinction is useful as a point of departure – restoring to normal does appear to differ from going beyond the normal. But it proves finally inadequate to the moral analysis. Enhancement is, even as a term, highly problematic. Does it mean "more" or "better," and if "better," by what standards? Can improved memory and selective erasure of memory both be enhancements? If "enhancement" is defined in opposition to "therapy," one faces further difficulties with the definitions of "healthy" and "impaired," "normal" and "abnormal" (including "supernormal"), especially in the area of "behavioral" or "psychic" functions and activities. Some psychiatric diagnoses are notoriously vague and their boundaries indistinct: how does "social anxiety disorder" differ from shyness, "hyperactivity disorder" from spiritedness, "oppositional disorder" from the love of independence? Furthermore, in the many human qualities that distribute themselves "normally," such as height or IQ, does the average also function as a norm, or is the norm itself appropriately subject to alteration? Is it therapy to give growth hormone to a genetic dwarf but not to an equally short fellow who is just unhappy to be short? And if the short are brought up to the average, the average, now having become short, will have precedent for a claim to growth hormone injections.

Needless arguments about whether something is or is not an "enhancement" get in the way of the proper question: What are the good and bad uses of biotechnical power? What makes a use "good," or even just "acceptable"? The fact that a drug is being taken solely to satisfy one's desires does not by itself make its use objectionable; consider alcohol consumption as the test case. Conversely, certain interventions to restore natural functioning wholeness – for example, to enable postmenopausal women to bear children or sixty-year-old men to keep playing professional ice hockey – might well be dubious uses of biotechnical power. The moral meaning and assessment of the intervention are unlikely to be settled by the term "enhancement" any more than by the nature of the technique used.

This last observation points to the deepest reason why the distinction between healing and enhancing is insufficient, both in theory and in practice. For the human whole whose healing is sought or accomplished by biomedical therapy is finite and frail, medicine or no medicine. The healthy body declines and its parts wear out. The sound mind slows down and has trouble remembering things. The soul has aspirations beyond what even a healthy body can realize, and it becomes weary from frustration. Even at its fittest, the fatigable and limited human body rarely carries out flawlessly even the ordinary desires of the soul. Moreover, there is wide variation in the natural gifts with which each of us is endowed: some are born with perfect pitch, others are born tone-deaf; some have flypaper memories, others forget immediately what they have just learned. And as with talents, so too with desires and temperaments: some crave immortal fame, others merely comfortable preservation; some are sanguine, others phlegmatic, still others bilious or melancholic. When nature deals her cards, some receive only from the bottom of the deck. But it is often the most gifted and ambitious who most resent their limitations: Achilles was willing to destroy everything around him, so little could he stomach that he was but a heel short of immortality.

Because of these infirmities and shortcomings, human beings have long dreamed of overcoming limitations of body and soul, in particular those imposed by bodily decay, psychic distress, and the frustration of human aspiration. Until now these dreams have been pure fantasies, and those who pursued them came crashing down in disaster.* But the stupendous successes over the past century in all areas of technology, and especially in medicine, have revived the ancient dreams of human perfection. Like Achilles, we beneficiaries of modern medicine regard our remaining limitations with less equanimity, to the point that dreams of getting rid of them can be turned into a moral imperative. Thanks to biomedical technology, people will increasingly be tempted to realize these dreams, at least to some extent: ageless and ever-vigorous bodies, happy (or at least not unhappy) souls, and excellent human achievement (with diminished effort or toil).

Why should anyone be worried about these prospects? What could be wrong with efforts to improve upon human nature, to gain ageless bodies and happy souls with the help of biomedical technology? I begin with some familiar sources of concern.

Common Concerns about Biotechnological "Improvement"

Not surprisingly, the objections usually raised to "beyond therapy" uses of biomedical technologies reflect the dominant values of modern America: health, equality, and liberty.

1. *Health – issues of safety and bodily harm.* In our health-obsessed culture, the first reason given to worry about any new biological intervention is safety. Athletes who take steroids will later suffer premature heart disease. College students who take Ecstasy will damage dopamine receptors in their basal ganglia and suffer early Parkinson's disease. To generalize, no biological agent used for purposes of self-perfection will be entirely safe. This is good conservative medical sense: anything powerful enough to enhance system A is likely to be powerful enough to harm system B. Yet many good things in life are filled with risks, and free people if properly

---

* Dreams of human perfection and the terrible consequences of pursuing it are themes of Greek tragedy and, closer to home, also of "The Birthmark" by Nathaniel Hawthorne, the short story with which the President's Council on Bioethics began its work. http://bioethics.georgetown.edu/pcbe/transcripts/jan02/jan17session2.html.

informed may choose to run those risks if they care enough about what is to be gained thereby. If the interventions are shown to be *highly* dangerous, many people will (later if not sooner) avoid them, and the FDA and/ or tort liability will constrain many a legitimate purveyor.

As an ethical matter, it surely makes sense that one should not risk basic health by pursuing a condition of "better than well."* On the other hand, if the interventions work well and are indeed highly desired, people may freely accept even considerable risk of later bodily harm as a trade-off. But in any case, the big issues have nothing to do with safety; the real questions concern what to think about the perfected powers, assuming that they may be safely used.

2. *Equality – issues of unfairness and distributive justice.* An obvious objection to the use of personal enhancers by participants in competitive activities – such as blood doping or steroids for athletes, or stimulants for students taking the SAT – is that they give those who use them an unfair advantage. But even if everyone had equal access to brain implants or genetic improvement of muscle strength or mind-enhancing drugs, a deeper concern would remain. Were steroid use by athletes to be legalized, most athletes would still be ashamed to be seen injecting themselves before coming up to bat. Besides, not all activities of life are competitive: it would matter to me if she says she loves me only because she is high on "erotogenin," a future brain stimulant that mimics perfectly the feeling of falling in love. It matters to me when I go to a seminar that the people with whom I am conversing are not drugged out of their right minds.

The distributive justice question is less easily set aside than the unfairness question, especially if there are systematic disparities between who will and who will not have access to the powers of biotechnical "improvement." The case against the use of those powers is stronger to the extent that we regard the expenditure of money and energy on such enhancements as a misallocation of limited resources in a world where the basic health needs of millions go unaddressed. It is embarrassing to discover that in 2013, for example, Americans spent two billion dollars

---

* The phrase "better than well" comes from a book by Carl Elliott, M.D., *Better Than Well: When Modern Medicine Meets the American Dream.*

on surgical treatments for baldness, roughly three times the amount spent worldwide for research on malaria.

But once again, inequality of access is not the sole reason for our disquiet over the thing itself, and in discussions of the dehumanizing dangers of, say, eugenic choice, it is paradoxical, to say the least, when people complain that the poor will be denied equal access to the danger: "The food is contaminated, but why are my portions so small?" Huxley's Brave New World runs on an impermeably rigid class system, but would you want to live in that world if offered the chance to enjoy its debased human prospects as an alpha (the privileged caste)? Even an elite can be dehumanized – can dehumanize itself. The central matter is not equality of access, but the goodness or badness of the thing being offered.

3. *Liberty – issues of freedom and coercion, overt and subtle.* This comes closer to the mark, especially with uses of biotechnical power exercised by some people upon other people, whether for social control – say, in the pacification of a classroom of Tom Sawyers – or for their own putative improvement – say, with genetic selection of the sex or sexual orientation of a child-to-be. This problem will of course be worse in tyrannical regimes. But there are always dangers of despotism within families, as parents already work their will on their children with insufficient regard to a child's independence or long-term needs or the "freedom to be a child." To the extent that even partial control over genotype – say, musician parents selecting a child with genes for perfect pitch (to take a relatively innocent example) – adds to existing social instruments of parental control and the risk of despotic rule, this matter will need to be attended to.

There are also more subtle limitations on freedom through peer pressure. What is permitted and widely used may become, for all practical purposes, mandatory. If most children are receiving memory enhancement or stimulant drugs to enable them to "get ahead," failure to provide them for your child might be seen as a form of neglect. If all the defensive linemen are on steroids, you risk mayhem if you go against them chemically pure. And as some critics point out, the enhancement technologies of the future will likely be used in slavish conformity with fashionable, socially defined, and shallow notions of improvement or excellence – as with cosmetic surgery, Botox, and breast implants today.

This problem of conformity – a special kind of restriction on freedom – is in fact quite serious. We are right to worry that the self-selected nontherapeutic uses of the new powers, especially where they become widespread, will move us toward still greater homogenization of human society, perhaps raising the floor but greatly lowering the ceiling of human possibility, and reducing the likelihood of genuine freedom, individuality, and greatness. Indeed, such homogenization may be the most important society-wide concern, if we consider the aggregated effects of the likely individual choices for biotechnical "self-improvement," each of which might be defended, or at least not opposed, on a case-by-case basis. For example, it would be difficult to object to a personal choice for a life-extending technology that would lengthen the user's life by three healthy decades, or a mood brightener that would make the individual more cheerful and untroubled by the world around him. Yet the aggregated social effects of such choices, widely made, could lead to a Tragedy of the Commons, where genuine, sought-for satisfactions for individuals are nullified or worse, owing to the social consequences of granting them to everyone. (I will later argue such a case with respect to the goal of increasing longevity with ageless bodies.) And, as Huxley strongly suggests in *Brave New World*, biotechnical powers used to produce contentment in accordance with democratic tastes threaten the character of human striving and diminish the possibility of human excellence. Perhaps the best thing to be hoped for in that case would be the preservation of pockets of difference – as on the remote islands in *Brave New World* – where the desire for high achievement has not been entirely submerged in the culture of "the last man."

But, once again, important though this surely is as a social and political issue, it does not settle the question regarding individuals. What, then, justifies our disquiet over the individual use of performance-enhancing genetic engineering or mood-brightening drugs for reasons other than medical necessity? Why, if at all, are we bothered by the voluntary *self*-administration of agents that would change our bodies or alter our minds? What is unsettling about our attempts to improve upon human nature, or even our own particular instance of it?

It is difficult to put this disquiet into words. Initial repugnance is hard to translate into sound moral argument. We are probably repelled by the idea of drugs that erase memories or change personalities, or of interventions that enable seventy-year-olds to bear children or play professional sports, or (in some wilder imaginings) of mechanical implants that enable men to nurse infants or computer-body hookups that enable us to download the *Oxford English Dictionary* to our brains. But is there wisdom in this repugnance? Taken one person at a time, with a properly prepared set of conditions and qualifications, it is going to be hard to say what is wrong with any biotechnical intervention that could give us (more) ageless bodies or make it possible for us to have happier souls. If there is a case to be made against these activities on an individual basis, it may have something to do with what is natural, or what is humanly dignified, or with the attitude that is properly respectful of what is naturally and dignifiedly human.

I will come at these essential causes of concern from three directions: (1) the goodness of the ends; (2) the fitness of the means; and (3) the meaning of the overarching attitude of seeking to master, control, and even transform one's own given nature. Three human goods will figure prominently in the discussion: (a) modesty and humility about what we know and can do to ourselves; (b) the meaning of aging and the human life cycle; and (c) the nature of human activity and human flourishing, and the importance of exercising the first and seeking the second through fitting means. I can hope here only to open the questions, starting with the matter of proper attitude.

Hubris or Humility? Respect for "the Given"

A common man-on-the-street reaction to the prospects of biotechnological enhancement is the complaint of "men playing God." An educated fellow who knows Greek tragedy complains rather of hubris. Sometimes the charge means the sheer prideful presumption of trying to alter what God has ordained or nature has produced, or what should, for whatever reason, not be fiddled with. Sometimes the charge means not so much usurping godlike powers, but doing so in the absence of godlike knowledge: the mere *playing* at being God, the hubris of acting with insufficient wisdom.

The case for respecting Mother Nature has been successfully made by environmentalists. They urge upon us a precautionary principle concerning our interventions into all of nature: go slowly, you can ruin everything. The point is certainly well taken. The human body and mind, highly complex and delicately balanced as a result of eons of gradual and exacting evolution, are almost certainly at risk from any ill-considered attempt at "improvement." There is not only the matter of unintended consequences already noted, but also the question about the unqualified goodness of our goals – a matter to which I shall return.

A very interesting version of the hubris objection has been offered by Michael Sandel in a working paper prepared for the President's Council on Bioethics. What is wrong with biotechnological efforts at enhancement and re-creating ourselves is what he calls "hyper-agency, a Promethean aspiration to remake nature, including human nature, to serve our purposes and to satisfy our desires." The root of the difficulty seems to be the failure properly to appreciate and respect the "giftedness" of the world.

> To acknowledge the giftedness of life is to recognize that our talents and powers are not wholly our own doing, or even fully ours, despite the efforts we expend to develop and to exercise them. It is also to recognize that not everything in the world is open to any use we may desire or devise. An appreciation of the giftedness of life constrains the Promethean project and conduces to a certain humility. It is, in part, a religious sensibility. But its resonance reaches beyond religion.[19]

As a critique of the Promethean attitude of the enhancers, Sandel's suggestion is on target. On the side of manipulator, appreciating that the given world – as well as his natural powers to alter it – are not of his own making could induce an attitude of modesty, restraint, humility. But the giftedness of nature also includes smallpox and malaria, cancer and Alzheimer's disease, decline and decay. And, to repeat, nature is not equally generous with her gifts, even to man, the most gifted of her creatures. Modesty born of gratitude for the world's givenness may enable us to recognize that not everything in the world is open to any use we may desire or devise, but it will not by itself teach us *which* things can be fiddled with and which should be left inviolate. The general "giftedness" of things cannot tell us which particular gifts are to be accepted as is, which are to be improved through use or training, which are to be housebroken through self-command or medication, and which opposed like the plague.

The word "given" has two relevant meanings: first, "bestowed as a gift," and second (omitted in Sandel's account), "granted" or definitely fixed and specified, as in mathematical proofs. Most of the bestowals of nature have their given, species-specific *natures*: they are each and all of a given *sort*. Cockroaches and humans are equally bestowed but differently natured. Turning a man into a cockroach would be dehumanizing. Trying to turn a man into something more than a man might be so as well. To avoid this, we need more than generalized appreciation for nature's gifts. We need a particular regard and respect for the special gift that is our own given nature.

In short, only if there is a human givenness that is also *good* and worth respecting – either as we find it or *as it could be perfected without ceasing to be itself* – does the given serve as a positive guide for choosing what to alter and what to leave alone. Only if there is something precious in the given, beyond the mere fact of its giftedness, does what is given serve as a source of restraint against efforts that would degrade it. Coming to human biotechnical engineering, only if there is something inherently good or dignified about natural procreation, human finitude, the human life cycle (with its rhythm of rise and fall), and human erotic longing and striving; only if there is something inherently good or dignified about the ways in which we engage the world as spectators and appreciators, as teachers and learners, leaders and followers, agents and makers, lovers and friends, parents and children, and as seekers of our own special excellence and flourishing in whatever arena we are called to – only then can we begin to see why those aspects of our nature need to be defended. We must move from the hubristic attitude of the powerful designer to look at the proposed improvements as they impinge upon the nature of the one being improved. With the question of human nature and human dignity in mind, we move to questions of means and ends.

"Unnatural" Means and the Dignity of Human Activity

How do, and how should, the excellent ones become excellent? This is a venerable question, made famous by Plato's Meno at the start of the dialogue bearing his name: "Can you tell me, Socrates, whether human excellence is teachable, or if it is not teachable, is it to be acquired by practice or training? Or is it acquired neither by practice nor by learning, but does it originate in human beings by nature or in some other way?" Teaching and learning, practice and training: these are sources in our power. Natural gift or divine dispensation: these are sources not in our power. Until only yesterday, teaching and learning, practice and training exhausted the alternatives for acquiring human excellence, perfecting our natural gift through our own efforts. But perhaps no longer: biotechnology may be able to do nature one better, even to the point of requiring no teaching and little training or practice to permit an improved nature to shine forth. The insertion of the growth factor gene into the muscles of rats and mice bulks them up and keeps them strong and sound without the need for much exertion. Drugs to improve memory, alertness, and amiability could greatly relieve the need for exertion to acquire these powers, leaving time and effort for better things.

What, if anything, is disquieting about such means of gaining improvement? Some people, not thinking very hard, will object to these means because they are artificial, "unnatural." But the manmade origin of the means cannot be the problem. Beginning with the fig leaf and the needle, man has always been the animal that uses art to improve his lot. Ordinary medicine makes extensive use of artificial means, from drugs to surgery to mechanical implants, supplementing the natural remedies of healthy diet, rest, and exercise. If the use of artificial means is absolutely welcome in the activity of healing, it cannot be their unnaturalness alone that upsets us when they are used to make people "better than well."

Yet in those areas of human life where excellence has until now required discipline and effort, the attainment of excellence through biotechnical means looks to many people like cheating. We believe, or believed until only yesterday, that people should work hard for their achievements, and we look down on those who attempt to fly high on the cheap. "Nothing good comes easily." We may prefer the grace of the natural athlete whose performance looks effortless, but we also admire those who struggle to overcome obstacles in order to achieve the same excellence. The merit of disciplined and dedicated striving – a matter of character – may not be the deepest basis of our objection to biotechnological shortcuts, though surely it is pertinent, for character is not only the source of our deeds but also their product. Children whose disruptive behavior is "remedied" by pacifying drugs are not learning self-control; if anything, they are learning to think it unnecessary. People who take pills to block out painful memories will not learn how to deal with suffering and sorrow. A drug to induce fearlessness does not produce courage. An injection to induce aggressiveness does not cultivate the genuine desire to excel.

Yet things are not so simple. There are nontherapeutic interventions that may assist in the pursuit of excellence without cheapening its attainment, and many of life's excellences have nothing to do with competition or adversity. Drugs to decrease drowsiness or increase alertness, sharpen memory or reduce distraction may help people to pursue their natural goals of learning or painting or performing their civic duty. Drugs to steady the hand of a neurosurgeon or to prevent sweaty palms in a concert pianist cannot be regarded as cheating, for they are not the source of the excellent activity or achievement. And for people dealt a meager hand in the dispensing of nature's gifts, it should not be called cheating or cheap if biotechnology could assist them in becoming better equipped, in body or in mind, to meet life's challenges. Even steroids for the proverbial ninety-seven-pound weakling help him get to the point where, through his own effort and training, he can go head to head with those better endowed by nature.

Nevertheless, there is another sense in which the "naturalness of means" does matter: not in that the assisting drugs and devices are artifacts, but in their relation to the nature of truly human activity. Here, in my opinion, is one of the more profound ways in which the use of at least some biotechnological means of seeking perfection – those that work on the brain – come under grave suspicion, as a violation or deformation of the deep structure of natural human activity. In most of our ordinary efforts at self-improvement, by practice or training or study, we sense the relation between our doings and the resulting improvement, between the means used and the end sought. There is an experiential and intelligible connection between means and ends. We can see how confronting fearful things might eventually enable us to cope with our fears. We can see how curbing our appetites produces self-command. The capacity to be improved is improved by using it; the deed to be perfected is perfected by doing it. Human education ordinarily proceeds by speech or symbolic deeds, whose meanings are at least in principle directly accessible to those upon whom they work. Even where the human being is largely passive – say, in receiving praise and blame, or reward and punishment –

both the "teacher" and the "student" can understand how the means used are related to the conduct or activity that they are meant to improve. And all further efforts at self-improvement, spurred by praise and blame, will clearly be the student's own doing.

Biomedical interventions, in contrast, act directly on the human body and mind to bring about their effects in a subject who is entirely passive, indeed, who plays no role at all. At best, he can *feel* their effects, without understanding their meaning in human terms. Whereas a mood brightened in response to the arrival of a loved one or an achievement in one's work is perfectly intelligible in a human sense, a drug that brightened our mood would alter us without our understanding how or why it did so. And this would be true not only about our states of mind. All of our encounters with the world, both natural and interpersonal, would be mediated, filtered, and altered. Human experience under biological intervention becomes increasingly mediated by unintelligible forces and vehicles, separated from the human significance of our activities. The relations between the knowing subject and his activities, and between his activities and their fulfillments and pleasures, are disrupted. The importance of human effort in human achievement is here properly acknowledged: the point is not so much the exertions of good character against hardship, but the manifestation of an alert and self-experiencing agent making his deeds flow intentionally from his willing, knowing, embodied soul.

To be sure, an increasing portion of modern life is mediated life: the way we encounter space and time, the way we "reach out and touch somebody" via the smartphone or Internet. One could make a case that there are changes in our souls and dehumanizing losses that accompany the great triumphs of modern technology. But so long as these technologies do not write themselves directly into our bodies and minds, we are able in principle to see them working on us, and free (again, in principle) to walk away from their use, though sometimes only with great effort. Once they work on us in ways beyond our ken, we are passive subjects, as it were, of what might as well be magic. It makes no difference to the point if we voluntarily choose to subject ourselves to them. The fact that one chooses to drink alcohol or to take a mood-brightening drug does not make one the agent of the change that one thus undergoes (though the law may hold us responsible).

The same point can perhaps be made about enhanced achievements as about altered mental states: to the extent that an achievement is the result of some extraneous intervention, it is detachable from the agent whose achievement it is purported to be. That I can use a calculator to do my arithmetic does not make me a knower of arithmetic. If computer chips in my brain were to download a textbook on physics, would that make me a knower of physics? Admittedly, this is not always an obvious point to make. If I make myself more alert through Ritalin or coffee, or if some other drug compensates for a lack of sleep, I may be able to learn more with my native powers, and in such a way that I can existentially attest that it is *I* who am doing the learning. Still, if human flourishing means not just the accumulation of external achievements and a full curriculum vitae but a lifelong *being-at-work* exercising one's *human* powers *well*, our genuine happiness requires that there be little gap, if any, between the dancer and the dance.

Most of life's activities, to repeat, are noncompetitive. Most of the best of them – loving and working and savoring and learning – are self-fulfilling beyond the need for praise and blame or any other external reward. Indeed, in these activities at their best, there is no goal beyond the activity itself. It is the possibility of unadulterated and for-itself human being-at-work-in-the-world, in an unimpeded and wholehearted way, that we are eager to preserve against dilution and distortion.

In a word: One major trouble with biotechnical (especially mental) "improvers" is that they disrupt the normal character of human being-at-work-in-the-world, what Aristotle called *energeia psyches*, activity of soul, which, when fine and full, constitutes human flourishing (as Chapter Fourteen will discuss more deeply). With biotechnical interventions that skip the realm of intelligible meaning, we cannot really own the transformations or experience them as genuinely *ours*. And we will be at a loss to attest whether the resulting conditions and activities of our bodies and our minds are, in the fullest sense, our own *as human*.

Partial Ends, Full Flourishing

By taking up first the matter of questionable means for pursuing excellence and happiness, we have put the cart before the horse. Here we will consider the more fundamental question of ends, to which the issue of good and bad means must yield. What do we think, in particular, about the goals of ageless bodies and happy souls? Would their attainment improve or perfect our lives as human beings? These are very big questions – too big to be adequately treated here. But the following considerations seem to merit attention.

The case for the goal of ageless bodies seems at first glance to look pretty good. The prevention of decay, decline, and disability, the avoidance of blindness, deafness, and debility, the elimination of feebleness, frailty, and fatigue all seem to be conducive to living fully as a human being at the top of one's powers – of having, as they say, a good quality of life from beginning to end. We have come to expect organ transplantation for our worn-out parts. We will surely welcome stem-cell-based therapies for regenerative medicine, reversing by replacement the damaged tissues of Parkinson's disease, spinal-cord injury, and many other degenerative disorders. It is hard to see any objection to obtaining in our youth a genetic enhancement of all our muscles that would prevent the muscular feebleness of old age and empower us to do any physical task with much greater strength and facility throughout our lives. And, should aging research deliver on its promise of adding not only extra life to years but also extra years to life, who would refuse it? Even if you might consider turning down an ageless body for yourself, would you not want it for your beloved? Why should she not remain to you as she was back when she first stole your heart? Why should her body suffer the ravages of time?

To say no to this offer seems perverse, but I would suggest that it is not. Because this argument is so counterintuitive, we need to begin not with the individual choice for an ageless body, but with what the individual's life might look like in a world where everyone made the same choice. We need to make the choice universal, and see the meaning of that choice in the mirror of its becoming the norm.

What if everybody lived life to the hilt, even as they approached an ever-receding age of death in a body that looked and functioned – let's not be too greedy – like that of a thirty-year-old? Would it be good if each and all of us lived like light bulbs, burning just as brightly from beginning to end, but then popping off without warning at an advanced age but still in our prime, leaving those around us suddenly in the dark? Or is it perhaps better that there be a shape to life, everything in its due season, the shape written, as it were, into the wrinkles of our bodies? What would the relations between the generations be like if there never came a point at which a son surpassed his father in strength and vigor? What incentive would there be for the old to make way for the young if the old slowed down but little and had no reason to think of retiring – if Michael Jordan could play until he was eighty? And might not even a moderate prolongation of life span with vigor lead to a prolongation of functional immaturity in the young – such as arguably has already accompanied the great increase in average life expectancy over the past century? One cannot think of enhancing the vitality of the old without retarding the maturation of the young.

I have tried elsewhere to make a rational case for the blessings of finitude, in "*L'Chaim* and Its Limits: Why Not Immortality?" – the penultimate chapter of my book *Life, Liberty and the Defense of Dignity*. I suggest there that living mindfully with our finitude is the condition for many of the best things in human life: engagement, seriousness, a taste for beauty, the possibility of virtue, the ties born of procreation, the quest for meaning. Though the arguments are made against the case for immortality, they have weight also against more modest prolongations of the maximum life span, in good health, that would permit us to live as if there were always a tomorrow. In what I regard as the most important arguments of that essay, I maintain that the pursuit of perfect bodies and further life extension will deflect us from realizing more fully the aspirations to which our lives naturally point, from living well rather than merely staying alive or living longer. And I argue that a concern with one's own improving agelessness is incompatible with accepting the need for procreation and human renewal: a world of longevity is increasingly a world hostile to children. To covet indefinite prolongation of life for oneself is a narcissistic approach to life, incompatible with devotion to any higher calling or to posterity. And it is arguably a world increasingly dominated by anxiety over health and the fear of death.

What is needed to complete this argument against the pursuit of ageless bodies is an account of the goodness of the natural human life cycle, roughly three multiples of a generation, featuring a time of coming of age, then a time of flourishing, ruling, and replacing of one's self, and finally a time of savoring and understanding, but still sufficiently linked to one's descendants to care about their future and to take a guiding and supporting and sharing role. People who think about life extension think about time only in the way that physicists do, as a continuum in which each portion is identical to every other. But that is not *lived* time, which is choreographed time, shaped time, with a beginning, middle, and end. The big question is whether the shape of our life's time has *human meaning*, and, if so, whether adding many more years to its duration would deform that meaning. It's a long question, and I commend it to your attention.

Finally, what about pharmacologically assisted happy souls? Painful and shameful memories are troubling; guilty consciences disturb sleep; low self-esteem, melancholy, and world-weariness tarnish the waking hours. Why not memory blockers for the first, mood brighteners for the latter, and a good euphoriant (without risk of hangover or cirrhosis) when celebratory occasions fail to be jolly? For let us be clear: if it is imbalances of neurotransmitters – a modern equivalent of the medieval doctrine of the four humors – that are responsible for our state of soul, it would be sheer priggishness to refuse the help of pharmacology for our happiness, when we accept it guiltlessly to correct for a deficit of insulin or thyroid hormone. An answer to this challenge would have three parts, which I can here only sketch out.

First, there is something wrong with the pursuit of utter psychic tranquility, with the attempt to eliminate shame, guilt, and all painful memories. These, it is true, can be crippling in extreme doses. Yet they are also appropriate responses to horror, disgraceful conduct, and sin. The pain of grief is the fitting response to losing a beloved; witnessing a murder *should* be remembered as horrible; doing a beastly deed *ought to* trouble one's soul. Righteous indignation at injustice depends on being able to feel injustice's sting. An untroubled soul in a troubling world is a shrunken human being. More fundamentally, to deprive oneself of one's memory – in its truthfulness of feeling – is to deprive oneself of one's own life and identity.

Second, the positive-feeling states of soul, though perhaps accompaniments of human flourishing, are not its essence. Feelings of pleasure or self-esteem are not the real McCoy when divorced from the human activities that are the essence of flourishing; at best, they are but shadows. Not even the most doctrinaire hedonist wants to have the pleasure that comes from playing baseball without swinging the bat or catching the ball. No music lover would be satisfied with getting from a pill the pleasure of listening to Mozart without ever hearing the music. Most people want to feel good and to feel good about themselves, but only as a result of being good, doing good, and actually experiencing what is fine.

Third, there is a connection between the possibility of feeling deep unhappiness and the prospects for genuine happiness. If one cannot grieve, one has not loved. And to be capable of aspiration, one must know and feel lack. As Wallace Stevens put it, "Not to have is the beginning of desire." There is, in short, a double-barreled error in the pursuit of ageless bodies and factitiously happy souls: human fulfillment depends on our being creatures of need and finitude and hence of longings and attachments.

To sum up: I have tried to make a case for finitude and even the graceful decline of bodily powers. And I have tried to make a case for genuine human happiness, with satisfaction as the bloom that graces unimpeded, soul-exercising activity. The first argument resonates with Homeric and Hebraic intuitions; the second resonates with the Greek philosophers. One would like to think that they might even be connectable, that the idea of genuine human flourishing is rooted in aspirations born of the kinds of deficiencies that come from having limited and imperfect bodies (a suggestion developed further in the next chapter).

Let me suggest, then, that a flourishing human life is not a life lived with an ageless body or an untroubled soul, but rather a life lived in rhythmed time, mindful of time's limits, appreciative of each season and filled first of all with those intimate human relations that are ours only because we are born, age, replace ourselves, decline, and die – and know it. It is a life of aspiration born of the disproportion between the transcendent longings of the soul and the limited capacities of our bodies and minds. It is a life that stretches toward some fulfillment to which our natural human soul has been oriented, and, unless we extirpate the source, will always be oriented. It is a life not of better genes and enhancing chemicals but of love and friendship, song and dance, speech and deed, working and learning, revering and worshipping.

The pursuit of an ageless body is finally a distraction and a deformation. The pursuit of an untroubled and self-satisfied soul is deadly to desire. Finitude, when recognized, spurs aspiration. Fine aspiration acted upon is itself the core of happiness. Not an ageless body, nor a contented soul, nor even a list of external achievements and accomplishments, but rather the engaged and energetic being-at-work of what nature uniquely gave to us is what we need to treasure, and to defend against the devilish promise of technological perfection.

CHAPTER SEVEN

Human Dignity

What It Is and Why It Matters

> It is difficult to define what human dignity is. It is not an organ to be discovered in our body, it is not an empirical notion, but without it we would be unable to answer the simple question: what is wrong with slavery? — *Leszek Kolakowski*

H UMAN DIGNITY has never been a powerful idea in American public discourse, by contrast with continental Europe. We tend instead to favor the language of rights and the pursuit of equality. For the egalitarians among us, the very idea of "dignity" smacks too much of aristocracy, and for secularists and libertarians too much of religion. Moreover, it seems to be too vague and private a matter to serve as the basis for public policy.

Yet we Americans actually care a great deal about human dignity, even if the term does not come easily to our lips. In times past, our successful battles against slavery, sweatshops, and segregation, although fought in the name of civil rights, were at bottom campaigns for treating human beings as they deserve to be treated solely because of their humanity. Likewise, our taboos against incest, bestiality, and cannibalism, as well as our condemnations of prostitution, drug addiction, and self-mutilation – all these, having little to do with defending liberty or equality, seek to uphold human dignity even against voluntary acts of *self*-degradation.

Today, human dignity is of paramount importance in nearly every arena of bioethical concern: in clinical medicine, in research using human subjects, in uses of novel biotechnologies "beyond therapy," particularly for so-called enhancement purposes, and in activities aimed at altering and transcending human nature. Indeed, as we become more and more immersed in a world of biotechnology, we increasingly sense that we neglect human dignity at our peril, not least in light of our gathering powers to alter human bodies and minds in ways that affect our very humanity.

Challenges to Human Dignity: Old and New Concerns

Because ethical concerns differ in the various domains of bioethics, each domain tends to emphasize a particular aspect of human dignity. In clinical medicine, a primary focus is on the need to respect the equal worth of each patient at every stage of life – regardless of race, class, or gender, condition of body and mind, severity of illness, nearness to death, or ability to pay. Every patient deserves equal respect in speech and deed and equal consideration in selecting an appropriate treatment. No life is to be deemed worthier than another, and under no circumstances should we look upon a fellow human being as if he had a "life unworthy of life" and deserved to be made dead. The ground of these opinions, and of the respect for human dignity they betoken, lies not in the patient's autonomy or any other personal qualities but rather in his very being and vitality.

In the domain of research with human subjects, the major ethical issues concern not only safeguarding the subject's life and health but also respecting his humanity, even as this will generally be overlooked in the research protocol. Through the soliciting of their voluntary informed consent, the human subjects are treated also as knowing and willing partners in the research enterprise.

In clinical medicine and research on human subjects, then, appeals to human dignity function explicitly as bulwarks against abuse: patients should not be reduced to "thinghood" or treated as mere bodies; research subjects should not be utilized as mere means or treated only as experimental animals. This "negative" function of the concept of human dignity helps to restrain the strong in their dealings with the weak.*

---

* This "negative" use of the idea of human dignity likely owes its preeminence to the origins of modern biomedical ethics out of the world's horror at the Nazi atrocities, in

But a more robust notion of human dignity is needed when we turn to the moral challenges raised by new biotechnological powers and the novel purposes to which they are being put, and to concerns prompted not by what others may do to us but instead by what we may choose to do to ourselves. After all, the powers of biotechnology to alter body and mind are attractive not only to the sick and suffering but to everyone who desires to look younger, perform better, feel happier, or become more "perfect."

We have already entered the age of biotechnical enhancement: growth hormone to make children taller, preimplantation genetic screening to facilitate eugenic choice, Ritalin to control behavior or boost performance on exams, Prozac and other drugs to brighten mood and alter temperament – not to mention Botox, Viagra, and anabolic steroids. Looking ahead, we can see other invitations already on the horizon: drugs to erase painful or shameful memories or to simulate falling in love. Genes to increase the size and strength of muscles. Nanomechanical implants to enhance sensation or motor skills. Computer-brain interfacing to boost memory and cognition. Techniques to slow biological aging and increase the maximum human life span.

Thanks to these and other innovations, venerable human desires – for better children, superior performance, ageless bodies, and happy souls – may increasingly be satisfied with the aid of biotechnology. A new field of "transhumanist" science is rallying thought and research for the wholesale redesign of human nature, employing genetic and neurological engineering and man-machine hybrids, en route to what has been blithely called a "posthuman" future.

Neither the familiar principles of contemporary bioethics – respect for persons, beneficence, and justice – nor our habitual concerns for safety, efficacy, autonomy, and equal access will enable us to gauge the true promise and peril of the biotechnology revolution. Our hopes for

---

which German scientists and German doctors were deeply implicated. They more than lent a hand with eugenic sterilization, barbaric human experimentation, and mass extermination of the "unfit" – all undertaken, mind you, in order to produce "a more perfect human" (see Chapter Ten below). In post–World War II Europe, the idea of "human dignity," newly expressed in the laws of many nations and especially in the United Nations Declaration of Human Rights, was surely intended to ensure that no human beings should ever again be so abused, degraded, and dehumanized – or, of course, annihilated.

self-improvement and our disquiet about a posthuman future are much more profound. At stake are the kind of human being and the sort of society we will be creating in the coming age.

To be sure, the biotechnological revolution may serve to enhance human dignity, as the optimists believe. It may enable many more human beings – biologically better equipped, aided by performance enhancers, liberated from the constraints of nature and fortune – to live lives of achievement, contentment, and high self-esteem. It might enable more and more people to realize the American Dream. But there are good reasons to wonder whether life will really be better if we turn to biotechnology to fulfill our deepest human desires. We may get more easily what we asked for, only to discover that it was not what we really wanted. Worse, we may get exactly what we asked for and then *fail* to recognize what it costs us in coin of our humanity.

We might get better children, but only by turning procreation into manufacture. We might perform better in the activities of life, but only by becoming mere creatures of our chemists. We might get longer lives, but only at the cost of living carelessly, so obsessed with longevity that we care little about the next generations. We might get to be pharmacologically "happy," but without the real loves, attachments, and achievements that constitute true human flourishing. The supposedly enhanced posthuman future might turn out to be a degenerate hell of cheerful dehumanization.

This is not the place to argue whether we have more to fear than to hope for in biotechnological enhancement and the pursuit of a posthuman future, although I am deeply skeptical. I see no reason to adopt the optimism of the transhumanists, especially because they can offer no standards for judging whether their new "creature" will be better than *Homo sapiens*. But for present purposes, my point is simply this: we cannot evaluate *any* proposed enhancements of our humanity unless we have some idea of what is estimable, worthy, and excellent about being human, unless we have wisdom about human dignity – what it is, and what sustains it, enhances it, and destroys it.

Broadly speaking, and despite the differing emphases among the diverse fields of medical practice, discussions of human dignity in bioethical matters have two main foci: concern for the dignity of life around the edges (the "life and death" issues), and concern for the dignity of life in its fullness and flourishing (the "good life" or the "dehumanization" issues). If one believes that the greatest threat comes in the form of death and destruction – say, in the practices of euthanasia and assisted suicide, embryo research, or denial of treatment to the less than fully fit – then one will be primarily concerned to uphold the equal dignity of every still-living human being, regardless of condition. If, by contrast, one thinks that the greatest danger comes not from killing the creature made in God's image but from self-deifying efforts to redesign him after our own fantasies, or even only from self-abasing practices reflecting shrunken views of human well-being, then one will be primarily concerned to uphold the full dignity of human excellence and rich human flourishing.

These two aspects of human dignity – the basic dignity of human *being*, and the full dignity of being flourishingly *human* – do not always have the same defenders, especially when the two seem to be at odds. Indeed, defenders of one sometimes ignore the claims made in behalf of the other. Thus, certain pro-lifers appear to care little whether babies are cloned or "born" in bottles, so long as no embryo dies in the process; others insist that life must be sustained come what may, even if it means being complicit in prolonging the degradation or misery of loved ones. Conversely, certain advocates of "death with dignity" appear to care little whether the weak and unwanted are deemed unworthy of life and swept off the stage, so long as they get to control how their *own* life ends; and patrons of excellence through biotechnological enhancement often have little patience with the need to care for those whose days of excellence are long gone. Meanwhile, the transhumanist researchers who dream of posthuman supermen care not a fig either for the dignity of human being *or* for the dignity of being human; they esteem not at all the dignity of us ordinary mortals, let alone those of us who are even less than merely ordinary.

Yet there is no reason why friends of human dignity cannot defend at once the dignity of "the low," of human *being*, and the dignity of "the high," of being flourishingly *human*. Properly understood, the two notions are much more intertwined than they are opposed. In order to see why, we need to examine each more closely, beginning with the dignity of human flourishing and living well – of being *human*.

*

Full Human Dignity: The Dignity of Being Human

Among the many moving songs from the American Civil War, one in particular always gives me gooseflesh: the "First Arkansas Marching Song,"
written for and sung (to the tune of "John Brown's Body") by a regiment
made up entirely of ex-slaves fighting on the side of the Union. Here are
the first, third, and last verses of seven:[20]

> Oh we're the bully soldiers of the First of Arkansas,
> We are fighting for the Union, we are fighting for the law;
> We can hit a Rebel further than a white man ever saw,
> As we go marching on.
>
> (*Chorus:* Glory, glory, hallelujah, *etc.*)
>
> We are done with hoeing cotton, we are done with hoeing corn,
> We are colored Yankee soldiers, now, as sure as you are born;
> When the masters hear us yelling, they will think its
>   Gabriel's horn,
> As we go marching on.
>
> Then fall in, colored brethren, you'd better do it soon,
> Can't you hear the drums a-beating the Yankee Doodle tune;
> We are with you now this morning, we'll be far away at noon,
> As we go marching on.

Former slaves, only recently debased and hoeing cotton and corn for
their masters, have transformed themselves into brave soldiers "fighting
for the Union ... fighting for the law." Although formally emancipated by
Lincoln's proclamation months earlier, they have been truly lifted up not
by another's largesse but by their own power and choice. They celebrate
here their new estate, singing out their dignity and beckoning others to
join the cause.

The heart is stirred by this simple display of noble humanity, not least
because it fully refutes the dehumanizing conclusions some may have
drawn from the marchers' prior servitude and submissiveness, namely,
that anyone who accepts a life in slavery must have a slavish soul. I am
particularly moved by their dedication to a cause higher than their own

advantage. And my imagination thrills to the picture of their marching through Southern towns and past slaveholding plantations, summoning their brethren to affirm their own dignity by putting their lives similarly in the service of freedom and union.

Opposite to this example of dignity triumphing over degradation is the self-inflicted dehumanization of Herr Professor Immanuel Rath in the classic German movie *The Blue Angel* (1930). A strict, upright *gymnasium* teacher, Professor Rath goes to the local nightclub to reprimand his wayward students who have been attracted there by the siren singer Lola Lola, and to scold her for corrupting the young. But on entering into her presence, Rath is smitten by Lola's charms, and he returns the next night filled with desires of his own. When he gallantly "defends her honor" against a brutish sea captain seeking sexual favors, Lola, touched by his chivalry, invites him to spend the night.

Exposed in school the next morning by his students, the honorable professor declares his intention to marry Lola Lola, for which decision he is promptly dismissed from his position. Lola, after laughing uproariously at his proposal, unaccountably accepts him; yet at the wedding feast, in front of all the guests, Rath is made to cock-a-doodle-do like a rooster in love. The married professor now joins the traveling show, first as Lola's servant, later as a performing clown.

When the traveling entertainers eventually return to his hometown, Professor Rath is made co-star of the vaudeville show. Lola, with a recently acquired new lover at her side, again forces Rath to play a (now cuckolded) crowing rooster while eggs are cracked upon his skull before a full house of roaring spectators, including his former students and neighbors. It is a scene of human abasement that is unbearable to watch.

What human goods and evils are at issue in these two vignettes? Not liberty or equality or health or safety or justice, but primarily the gain or loss of worthy humanity – in short, the display or the liquidation of human dignity. In the first case, degraded human beings knowingly assert their humanity and their manhood; anyone not humanly stunted will admire and applaud their nobility, courage, and devotion to a righteous purpose higher than themselves. In the second case, an upright and proper man of learning loses his wits and his profession to an infatuation, and finally loses every shred of dignified humanity as he reduces himself to mimicking an inarticulate barnyard animal; anyone not humanly stunted will shudder at his utter degradation, even though he has brought it upon himself.

With these examples before us, let me try to specify what I mean by the dignity of human flourishing – of being actively *human*. Both historically and linguistically, "dignity" has always implied something elevated, something deserving of respect. The central notion etymologically, in English as in the Latin root *dignitas*, is worthiness, elevation, honor, nobility – in brief, excellence or virtue. In all its meanings it has been a term of distinction; dignity is not something to be expected or found in every human being, like a nose or a navel. Even in democratic times, as the soldiers of the First Arkansas Infantry Regiment made clear, "dignity" still conveys the active display of what is humanly best.

Some people maintain that all notions of dignity are but social constructs: mere projections of the prejudices of (aristocratic) societies, and conferred or attributed solely from outside, as are honor and office. Others object that notions of dignity appealing to excellence, being essentially *comparative*, necessarily deny human dignity to many or most people. But if carefully examined, these objections are not justified. Yes, societies accord honor to human excellence; and yes, different societies esteem different virtues differently. But in many (if not most) cases, the virtues esteemed are truly marks of superior and intrinsic humanity: the fireman who rushes into a burning building to save a child or the soldier who falls on a grenade to save his buddies *deserves* and *elicits* our admiration, and he will gain it in many (if not all) societies. Mother Teresa and the Dalai Lama justly earn nearly universal applause; Saddam Hussein and Pol Pot justly earn nearly universal condemnation. The dignity of the First Arkansas Regiment is displayed from within, not conferred from without; the dehumanization of Immanuel Rath is self-evident and intrinsic, not stipulated or attributed.

Moreover, such judgments of excellence and its opposite are only *accidentally* comparative. When we recognize the superior dignity of Mother Teresa we do so not by comparing her against Saddam Hussein or even against moderately virtuous human beings. We judge not that she is better than others (as we do in competitive sports) – though it happens that she is – but rather that she measures up to and even exceeds a high standard of excellent character and dignified conduct. We are not comparing individuals against each other; we are measuring them against a standard of goodness. Courageous or generous deeds would still be courageous or generous – equally dignified and equally honorable – even if everyone practiced them regularly. Thus, the seemingly inegalitarian nature of dignity grounded in excellence of character is not *in its essence* undemocratic, even if ethical virtue is not displayed equally by everyone. Indeed, the fact that most of us esteem and honor conduct better than our own is strong evidence that we do not feel ourselves diminished by it. On the contrary, just as taste honors those who *appreciate* genius almost as much as it honors those who *display* genius, so the appreciation of exemplary human dignity honors also the dignity of those who can recognize and esteem it. Excellence is only accidentally invidious, and the need to make discriminating judgments is no reason to shy away from caring about dignity.

Which intrinsic excellences, then, are at the heart of human dignity and give their bearers special standing? In the view of the ancient Greek poets, the true or full human being is the hero, who draws honor and prizes by displaying his worthiness in noble and glorious deeds. Supreme is the virtue of courage: the willingness to face death in battle, armed only with your own prowess, going forth against an equally worthy opponent – think Achilles against Hector – who, like you, seeks victory not only over his adversary but, as it were, over death itself. Following the Socratic turn in the history of Greek thought, such heroic excellence was supplanted by the virtue of wisdom; the new hero is not the glorious warrior but the man singularly devoted to wisdom, living close to death not on the field of battle but in a single-minded quest for knowledge eternal.

Attractive though these candidates are – we can still read about Achilles and Socrates with admiration – the Greek exemplars are of little practical use in democratic times, especially when it comes to bioethical matters. The dehumanization evident in Aldous Huxley's dystopian *Brave New World* (1932) is not primarily the lack of glorious warriors or outstanding philosophers (or artists or scientists or statesmen). The basic problem is the absence of kinds of human dignity more abundantly found and universally shared.

In Western philosophy, the most high-minded attempt to supply a teaching of universal human dignity belongs to Kant, with his doctrine of respect for *persons*. For Kant, *all* persons or rational beings deserve respect, not because of some realized excellence of achievement but by dint of their participation in morality and their ability to live under the moral law. Through this concept of "personhood," Kant sought to find a place for human freedom and dignity in the face of a Newtonian world-view that reduced even the human being – excepting, for Kant, only the rational will – to a matter of physics. However we may finally judge it, there is something austerely dignified in the Kantian refusal to confuse reason with rationalization, duty with inclination, and the right and the good with happiness (pleasure). Whatever persists of a nonutilitarian ethic in contemporary academic bioethics descends largely from this principled moralistic view.*

But Kant's respect for persons is largely formal, abstracted from how they actually exercise their freedom of will. If universal human dignity is grounded in having a moral life, greater dignity would seem to attach to having a *good* moral life – that is, to choosing well and choosing rightly. Is there not more dignity in the courageous than in the cowardly, in the moderate than in the self-indulgent, in the righteous than in the wicked, in the honest man than in the liar?

And there is a deeper difficulty with the Kantian dignity of "person-hood." It is inadequate not because it is undemocratic or too demanding but because it is, in an important respect, inhuman. In setting up a con-cept of "personhood" in opposition to nature and to the body, it fails to do justice to the concrete reality and particularity of our embodied lives: lives of begetting and belonging no less than of willing and thinking; lives lived always locally, corporeally, and in a unique trajectory from zygote in the womb to body in the coffin. Not all of human dignity con-sists in reason or freedom.

The Kantian dignity of rational choice pays no respect at all to the dignity we have through our natural desires and passions, natural origins and attachments, sentiments and aversions, loves and longings. It pays no respect, in short, to what Tolstoy called "real life," life as ordinarily and concretely lived.

The dignity of being human is perfectly at home in ordinary life, as it is at home in democratic times. Courage, moderation, generosity, righteous-ness, and the other human virtues are not confined to the few. Many of us

---

* The respect for persons so widely celebrated in the canons of ethics governing human experimentation is in fact a descendant of Kant's principle of human auton-omy and the need to protect the weak against the powerful.

strive for them, with partial success, and still more of us do ourselves honor in admiring persons nobler and finer than ourselves. We frequently give even wayward neighbors the benefit of the doubt, and we strongly believe in the possibility of a second chance. No one ever knows for sure when a person hitherto seemingly weak of character will rise to the occasion, actualizing an ever-present potential for worthy conduct. No one knows when, as with the ex-slaves of the First Arkansas, human dignity will summon itself and shine forth brightly. With suitable models, proper rearing, and adequate encouragement – or even just the fitting opportunity – many of us can be and can act in accord with our higher nature.

In truth, if we know how to look, we can find evidence of human dignity all around us, in the valiant efforts that ordinary people make to meet necessity, to combat adversity and disappointment, to provide for their children, to care for their parents, to help their neighbors, to serve their country. Life provides numerous hard occasions that call for endurance and equanimity, generosity and kindness, courage and self-command. Adversity sometimes brings out the best in us, and often shows best what we are made of. Even confronting our own death provides a chance for the exercise of admirable humanity, for the small and the great alike.

Beyond the dignity of virtue and endurance, there is also the simple but deep dignity of human activity – sewing a dress, throwing a pot, building a fire, cooking a meal, dressing a wound, singing a song, or offering a blessing in gratitude. There is the simple but deep dignity of intimate human relations – bathing a child, receiving a guest, embracing a friend, kissing one's bride, consoling the bereaved, dancing a dance, or raising a glass in gladness. And there is the simple but deep dignity of certain ennobling human passions – hope, wonder, trust, love, sympathy, thankfulness, awe, reverence. No account of the dignity of being *human* is worth its salt without them.

Basic Human Dignity: The Dignity of Human Being

The excellence or worthiness that shines forth in human beings is always something that arouses our admiration and respect. Still, there are partisans of human dignity who reject such judgments of excellence or worth, insisting that no one person lives a life more worthy than another's.

Human dignity, they assert, is something every human being – base or noble, wicked or righteous – enjoys equally, simply by virtue of his human *being*.

What is the basis of this claim, and what is its purpose? To begin with, those who advance it seek to prevent the display of contempt, and especially contempt with lethal consequences, toward those who do not "measure up." They wish to ensure a solid level of human worth that no one can deny to any fellow human being; to lean against the widespread tendency to treat the foreigner and the enemy, the misfit and the deviant, or the demented and the disabled as less human or less worthy than oneself – even as unworthy of basic respect and continued existence. And, following the unspeakable horrors perpetrated in the twentieth century, they wish at the very least to provide a moral barrier against the liquidation of human beings often practiced by people acting in the name of their own sense of superior worth.

But even granting the soundness of this purpose (which I embrace wholeheartedly), to assert that we all have "equal dignity" does not, by itself, make it so. Mere assertion will not convince the skeptic or refute the denier of human dignity. We need to establish the *grounds* for thinking that all human beings – whether dignified or not in their conduct – actually have full and equal human dignity, or should be treated as if they did.

The first and perhaps best ground remains practical and political. If you or your government (or my doctor or HMO) wants to claim that, for reasons of race or ethnicity or disability or dementia, I am not your equal in humanity, and, further, if you mean to justify harming or neglecting me on the basis of that claim, the assertion of universal human dignity exists to get in your way. The burden of proof shifts to you, to show why I am not humanly speaking your equal: *you* must prove why you are entitled to put a saddle and bridle on me and ride me like a horse, or to deny me the bread that I have earned with the sweat of my brow, or to dispatch me from this world because I have a "low quality of life."

You will, in fact, face an impossible task: you will be unable to prove that you possess godlike knowledge of the worth of individual souls or that you carry the proper scale of human worth for finding me insufficiently "weighty" to deserve to breathe the air. In this approach, I offer not a metaphysically grounded proof but a rhetorically effective demonstration that I, like you, am a somebody, like you born of woman and destined to die, like you a member of the human species each of whose members knows from the inside the goodness of his own life and liberty.

Mention of life and liberty reminds us that for Americans the doctrine of human equality and equal humanity has its most famous and resounding expression in the Declaration of Independence. Indeed, it is to the principles of the Declaration that some people repair in seeking to ground the dignity of human being, and it makes a certain sense to do so. Americans, in declaring themselves a separate people, began by asserting their belief in the truth that "all men are created equal." However human beings may differ in talent, accomplishment, social station, race, or religion, they are, according to the Declaration, self-evidently equal, at least in this: "That they are endowed by their Creator with certain unalienable rights, that among these are Life, Liberty, and the Pursuit of Happiness."

These passages have always seemed to me self-evidently true, exactly as claimed. But they do not go far enough in providing a ground for the equal *dignity* of human being as such. True, some interpreters suggest that all human beings have dignity because God gave it to them. But the text does not say that the Creator gave all men dignity; it speaks not of equal dignity but of equal rights, and the relation between the two is not as clear as we might wish.

In its eighteenth-century meaning, the natural "right to life" is not a right to be or to stay alive, or even a right not to be killed or harmed. It is, rather, a right to practice active self-preservation, a right to defend, protect, and preserve my life not only against those who threaten it but also in the face of those who would deny the rightfulness of my liberty to do so (for example, by insisting that I must "turn the other cheek"). The right to life is a (negative) right against interference with acts of self-preservation, and it rests not on anything lofty, such as dignity, but on the precariousness of human life and especially on the self-conscious passion that each of us legitimately has for our own continued existence.

It follows that human dignity is not the foundation of these inalienable rights, nor is dignity ours by virtue of the mere fact that we possess them. Instead, the true manifestation of dignity in the American founding appears at the end of the Declaration, where the signers proclaim: "And for the support of this Declaration, with a firm reliance on the protection of Divine Providence, we mutually pledge to each other our lives, our fortunes, and our sacred honor." *Having* equal natural rights is neutral with respect to dignity; *exercising* them in the face of their denial car-ries the dignity of self-assertion; *defending* with one's life and honor the rights of a whole people is high dignity indeed.

Other interpreters of the Declaration, granting that our equal dignity resides not in our rights, locate it in the more fundamental truth that makes those rights necessary: our common mortal fate and our equal capacity to suffer. But there is nothing dignified in vulnerability as such or in the fact of suffering per se. A sufferer merely undergoes, merely receives passively what is inflicted by the active "agent," whether natural, human, or divine. For Christians, Christ on the cross may be regarded as the supreme exemplar of human dignity; but even here it is not suffering as such but suffering understood and accepted as sacrificial and redemp-tive that makes the crucified Jesus, for Christians, the epitome of dignity. If there is dignity to be found in the vicinity of suffering, it consists either in the purpose for which suffering is borne or in the manner in which it is endured. Not everyone has the requisite virtue or strength of soul, and it therefore cannot be the basis of the equal dignity of human *being*.

A deeper ground for our equal human dignity – natural and ontologi-cal, not practical or political – may perhaps be found in our equal mem-bership in the human species. All of us are members of the class *Homo sapiens*, sharing thereby in whatever dignity adheres to the class as a whole, and especially in contrast with the dignity of other animals.

There is surely something to this suggestion. Even when we condemn or show contempt for another person – and even when such condemnation is richly deserved, as, for example, in the case of a Stalin or a Hitler – we cannot help noticing that he is, alas, "one of us." Indeed, the condemnation comes precisely from the great gap between despicable deeds and what we have good reason to expect from another member of our species; we do not find fault with lions and tigers for *their* predatory and lethal conduct.

As it happens, the human "species-form" or gestalt – upright posture, eyes to the horizon, hands fit for grasping, fingers for pointing, arms for embracing or cradling, and mouths for speaking and kissing no less than for eating – functions silently to elicit a primordial recognition from our fellow species members. Such mutual identification is the basis of hospi-tality to strangers, the acts of good Samaritans, or even just a nod of human kinship when we pass one another on the street. This salutary reminder of our common humanity, even in the face of severe deformity or degradation, puts a limit on possible tendencies to banish another person, in thought or in deed, from the realm of human concern and connectedness or even from the world of the living. Preventing many an outrage and many a violation, it also encourages many a sympathetic word and many a charitable deed.

So far, so good. Yet, once again, problems arise if we are compelled to answer just what it is about membership in *Homo sapiens* that justifies allowing our "species pride" to guarantee the inviolability of our life and being. After all, the (higher) animals, too, are not without their special dignity and special standing. Our being alive, and our being members of a closed interbreeding population, are properties that belong also to chimpanzees and cheetahs and kangaroos.

Thus the elevated moral status of the human species must again turn on something else: the special capacities and powers that are ours alone among the creatures. Such distinctively human features include the capacities for thought and image making, freedom and moral choice, a sense of beauty, love and friendship, song and dance, family and civic life, the ethical life, and the impulse to worship.

Yet once we introduce these capacities, we will be hard-pressed not to assess the dignity of particular human beings in terms of the degree to which they actually manifest them. For the universal attribution of dignity to human beings on the basis of specific human attributes pays tribute only to our potentiality, to the possibilities for human excellence. Full dignity will depend on *realizing* these possibilities.

For partisans of the equal dignity of human being, the search for its content has therefore reached a troubling point. The ground of our dignity lies in the humanly specific potentialities of the human species. But this basic dignity is not yet dignity in full, not the realized dignity of fine human activity. What, then, of the dignity of those members of our species who have lost or who have never attained these capacities, as well as those who use them badly or wickedly?

"In-Between": Human Aspiration and Transcendent Possibility

Having now come at human dignity from two directions – first from the dignity of flourishing humanity, beginning at its heroic peak, and then from the dignity of human life at its elemental level of mere existence – we may note a curious coincidence. Once we learn how to find virtue and worthiness in the doings of everyday life, the more "aristocratic" account cannot help being universalized and democratized; and once we are forced to specify what it is about human beings as a class that gives them special dignity, the more "egalitarian" account cannot help introducing standards of particular excellences. This convergence invites the suggestion that the two aspects of dignity may be mutually implicated and interdependent. Let me suggest three ways in which this is so.

First, the (higher) dignity of being human and the (lower) dignity of human being are each dependent on the other, but in different ways. The flourishing of human possibility, in all its admirable forms, depends absolutely on active human vitality, that is, on the mere existence and well-working of the enlivened human body. And just as the higher human powers and activities depend upon the lower for their existence, so the lower depend on the higher for their standing. What I have been calling the basic dignity of human *being* – sometimes expressed as the "sanctity of human life," or the "respect owed to human life" as such – depends on the higher dignity of being *human.*

This mutual dependence can be clearly illuminated if we ask why murder is wrong, and why all civilized people hold innocent life to be inviolable.[21] Particularly helpful here is the biblical story of the Noahide law and covenant in Genesis 9, where, unlike in the more famous enunciation of a similar prohibition in the Ten Commandments ("Thou shalt not murder," Exodus 20), a specific reason is given for why murder is wrong.

Before the Flood, human beings lived without law or civil society. The result appears to be something like what Hobbes called the state of nature, characterized as a condition of the war of each against all. Immediately after the Flood, primordial law and justice are instituted, and a rudimentary civil society is founded. At the forefront of this new order is a newly articulated respect for human life, expressed in the announcement of the punishment for homicide: "Whoever sheddeth man's blood, by man shall his blood be shed; for in the image of God was man made."

In this cardinal law, the threat of capital punishment stands as a deterrent to murder and provides a motive for obedience. But the measure of the punishment is instructive. By equating a life for a life – no *more* than a life for a life, and the life only of the killer and not, for example, also of his wife and children – the threatened punishment implicitly teaches the equal worth of each human life. Such equality can be grounded only in the equal humanity of each human being.

But homicide is to be avoided not only to avoid the punishment. There is a deeper reason why murder is wrong: namely, man's divinelike (image-of-God) status.* Any man's very *being* requires that we respect his life, and human life is to be respected more than animal life because man is more than an animal; man is godlike. Note that the truth of the Bible's assertion here does not rest on biblical authority. Man's more-than-animal status is proved whenever human beings, possessing the godlike powers of reason, freedom, judgment, and moral concern, quit the state of nature and set up life under a law like this one, as only the godlike animal can do. The demand for law-abidingness and for punishing transgression both insists on and demonstrates the superiority of man.

We reach a crucial conclusion: the inviolability of human life rests absolutely on the higher dignity – the godlikeness – of human beings. Yet man is, at most, only god*like*; he is not God or a god. To be an image is also to be different from that of which one is an image. Man is, at most, a mere likeness of God. With us, seemingly godly powers and concerns are conjoined with animality. God's image is tied to blood, which is the life.

This point, too, stands apart from the text that teaches it. Everything high about human life – thinking, judging, loving, willing, acting – depends absolutely on everything low – metabolism, digestion, respiration, circulation, excretion. In the case of human beings, "divinity" needs blood, or "mere" life, to sustain itself. And because of what it holds up, human blood (that is, human life) deserves special respect, beyond what is owed to life as such: the low ceases to be the low. The biblical text elegantly mirrors this truth about its subject, subtly merging both high and low: though the reason given for punishing murder concerns man's godliness, the *injunction*

---

* The second part of verse 9:6 seems to make two points: man is in the image of God (that is, man is godlike), and man was made thus by God. The decisive point is the first. Man's creatureliness cannot be the reason for avoiding bloodshed; the animals too were made by God, yet permission to kill them for food has just been given. The full weight rests on man's *being* "in the image of God," on man's godlikeness.

concerns man's blood. Respect the godlike; do not shed its blood. Respect for anything human requires respecting everything human – respecting human *being* as such.

Second, even as the dignity of being human depends for its very existence on the presence and worth of human vitality, everything humanly high also gets its energizing *impetus* from what is humanly low. Necessity is not only the mother of invention; it is also the mother of excellence, love, and the ties that bind and enrich human life. Like the downward pull of gravity without which the dancer cannot dance, the downward pull of bodily necessity and fate makes possible the dignified journey of a truly human life. Human aspiration depends absolutely on our being creatures of need and finitude, and hence of longings and attachments. Pure reason and pure mind have no aspiration; the rational animal aspires in large part because he is an animal and not an angel or a god.

Once again it is our in-between status – at once godlike and animal – that is the deep truth about our nature, the ground of our special standing, and the wherewithal of our flourishing.

Perhaps the most profound account of human aspiration is contained in Socrates' speech about *eros* in Plato's *Symposium*. *Eros*, according to Socrates' account, is the heart of the human soul, an animating power born of lack but pointed upward. *Eros* emerges as both self-seeking and overflowingly generative – at bottom, the fruit of the peculiar conjunction of, and competition between, two conflicting aspirations joined in a single living body, both tied to our finitude: the impulse to self-preservation and the urge to reproduce. The former is a self-regarding concern for our own personal permanence and satisfaction; the latter is a self-forgetting aspiration for something that transcends our own finite existence, something for the sake of which we spend and even give our lives.

Other animals, of course, live with these twin and opposing drives. But *eros* in the other animals, who are unaware of the tension between the two drives, manifests itself exclusively in the activity of procreation and the care of offspring – an essential aspect of the dignity of all animal life. Socrates speaks of the self-sacrifice often displayed by animals in behalf of their young, and I would add that all animal life, by one path or another, imitates the "noble" model of the salmon, swimming upstream to spawn and die.

But *eros* comes fully into its own as the arrow pointing upward only in the human animal, who is *conscious* of the doubleness in his soul and is driven to devise a life based in part on the tension between the opposing forces. Human *eros*, born of this self-awareness, manifests itself in explicit and conscious longings for something higher, something whole, something eternal – longings that are ours precisely because we are able to elevate the aspiration born of our bodily doubleness and to direct it upward toward the good, the true, and the beautiful. In the human case, the fruits of "erotic giving-birth" are not only human children but also the arts and crafts, song and story, noble deeds and customs, fine character, the search for wisdom, and a reaching for the eternal and divine – all conceived by resourcefulness to overcome our experienced lack and limitation and all guided by a divination of that which would be wholly good and lacking in nothing.

This transcendent possibility is the third aspect of the relationship between what is humanly low and what is humanly high; indeed, it points us to what is both high and highest. And here, too, an ancient story shows us the point.

In the Garden of Eden, the serpent tempts the woman into disobedience by promising that if she and the man eat from the forbidden tree of the knowledge of good and bad, their eyes will be opened and they "will be as gods, knowing good and bad." But, as the text comments with irony, when the human pair disobey, "their eyes were opened and they saw that they were naked." Far from being as gods, they discover their own sexuality, with its shameful implications: their incompleteness, their abject neediness of each other, their subjection to a power within that moves them toward a goal they do not understand, and the ungodly bodily ways in which this power insists on being satisfied – not standing upright contemplating heaven, but lying down embracing necessity.

As in Socrates' account, the discovery of human lowliness is the spur to rise. But here it comes in two stages, one purely human, the other something more. Refusing to accept their shame lying down, the human beings take matters into their own hands: "and they sewed fig leaves and made themselves girdles." In this act of covering their nakedness out of a concern for each other's approbation, human lust is turned into a longing for something more than sexual satisfaction. Shame and love are born twins, delivered with the help of the arts of modesty and beautification.

But there is more. Immediately after covering their nakedness, "they heard the voice of the Lord God walking in the Garden" – the first reported instance of human recognition of and attention to the divine. For it is only in acknowledging our lowliness that we human beings can also discover what is truly high. The turn toward the divine is founded on our discovery of our own lack of divinity, our insufficiency.

It is a delicate moment: having followed their eyes to alluring temptations that promise wisdom, human beings come to see, again through their eyes, their own insufficiency. Still trusting appearances but seeking to beautify them, they set about adorning themselves in order to find favor in the sight of the beloved. Lustful eyes give way to admiring ones, by means of intervening modesty and art. Yet sight and love alone do not fully disclose the truth of our human situation. Human beings must open their ears as well as their eyes; they must hearken to a calling. With eyes opened by shamefaced love, the prototypical human pair are able to hear the transcendent voice.

Awe, too, is thus born twin to shame, and is soon elaborated into a desire to close with and have a relationship with the divine. The dignity of being human, rooted in the dignity of life itself and flourishing in a manner seemingly issuing only in human pride, completes itself and stands tallest when we bow our heads and lift our hearts in recognition of powers greater than our own.

CHAPTER EIGHT

For the Love of the Game

*The Dignity of Sport**

FIRST, THE SUPER BOWL. Next, March Madness. After that, the NBA and Stanley Cup playoffs. Finally, the World Series. Year after year, season by season, sports fans across the country shift their attentions, polish their loyalties, and renew their hopes: maybe this year, just this once, it won't again be "wait till next year."

For many decades, America's most significant athletic contests have been our most popular civic rituals, temporarily removing us from the normal rhythms of everyday life. Medieval Europeans built cathedrals; our ancestors built civic monuments and memorials; we build sports palaces. There we gather to taste vicariously the sweetness of victory, and to celebrate together all that is perennially great in human sport: excellence, grace, and the intense moments that separate triumph from defeat. It is easy to dismiss sport as a triviality, and some highbrows will always do so. Yet these games that youngsters play somehow seem to capture both the lowest and the loftiest possibilities of embodied human life, eliciting in participant spectators and spectating participants the full range of human passions, from rapturous joy to paralyzing despair.

These emotions abound in stadiums and before television screens across America today. But all is not well in the world of sports. One football season began with a superstar banished for killing dogs and ended

---

* This essay was written with my friend and colleague Eric Cohen.

with a United States senator calling for an investigation of spying. Olympians were forced to return their medals. The following baseball season opened under a cloud of steroids and finger-wagging congressional hearings, which put one of the greatest pitchers in the stocks. The world's most beloved cyclist, after years of denial, admitted to blood doping. An all-star footballer was suspended for wife beating. Elite college football and basketball programs have been found guilty of cooking their student-athletes' grades and hiring strippers for their parties.

More generally, many fans today believe that the golden age of sport has long since passed, that modern athletics has become both corrupt and corrupting. Athletes are mercenaries, driven by the love of money – so goes the lament. The pursuit of excellence has been sacrificed to spectacle, shaped more by the demands of television profits than by the dignity of the game. Our heroes are often villains, with no regard for the law of the land or the rules of the game. Sport has morphed into entertainment, and sportsmen into unsportsmanlike trash-talking punks. It was not always thus, the old man sighs, longing for the days of Ruth and Gehrig, Williams and DiMaggio, and the incomparable Jackie Robinson.

Our nostalgia, of course, is something of a distortion, if a noble one. Our ignorance of the sporting past – of the vanity of the original Greek Olympians, the base passions of the ancient Roman fans, the tawdry character of many baseball stars in the early twentieth century, the point shaving and other gambling-related scandals – allows us to forget that much of what we lament about the present is not at all novel. And when it comes to the recent past, the era that today's graying elders remember wistfully from their youth, it is far more pleasant and ennobling to remember the best and forget the worst; and to judge today's athletes against an idealization of those who came before. Tomorrow's elders will no doubt pine for the days of Tim Duncan and Derek Jeter and Peyton Manning.

Yet if nostalgia is a danger, so too is failing to reckon squarely with an adulteration of sports that is unique to our age. For the nature of athletics has indeed changed greatly from the days of the naked runners and wrestlers of ancient Athens and Sparta to the would-be champions of the Rio Olympics of 2016. Even in the modern era we have seen dramatic changes in what it means to be an athlete and to be a spectator.

The first great transformation in the modern era was captured powerfully in the film *Chariots of Fire* (1981), which deals with the Olympics of

1924 and portrays the beginning of a cultural shift from the amateur to the professional athlete. Exercise became training; practice became drills; the pursuit of victory became a science (and a business). The new professionals quickly accomplished feats unheard of in the days of the amateur – with more power, greater speed, and unprecedentedly complex strategies of execution. The original men of the gridiron would find much about modern football unimaginable: the size and skill of the players; the management of the game with satellite photos, helmet headphones, and aging masterminds calling every play from upstairs; the serial loyalties of players who move from one team to the next, abandoning their followers to follow the money.

Combined with the new age of radio and especially big-market television, the professionalization of sport changed the ethic of the players and the outlook of the fans. With team owners raking in billions, players came to expect, and to demand, financial rewards commensurate with their value in the marketplace. They came to see their own achievements, measured quantitatively and enshrined in record books, as assets that may be "monetized" into endorsements. And we, the fans, became ambivalent about the games that we follow with such intensity. We still marvel at the great players, but we question their motives. We hunger for bigger thrills and broken records, but we mourn a lost purity of play that the new professionalism has crowded out. We are devoted unto death to our local teams, but we watch our hometown heroes sign contracts with our archrivals within minutes (or so it seems) of the city's victory parade. We expect to be entertained, but we still want sport to be something more than a circus or a rock concert. We love taking our children to the ballfield, but we fear that today's superstars are bad role models for them.

This ambivalence gave rise to intense and critical – if short-lived – public scrutiny in congressional hearings that resulted in the Mitchell Report, issued in December 2007. The report was a 409-page indictment of the widespread use of performance-enhancing drugs in baseball. Commissioned by Bud Selig, then the commissioner of baseball, and prompted by numerous allegations of illicit drug use by recently active and current players, it was written by former senator George Mitchell after months of thorough investigation, extensive interviews, and private testimony. To no one's surprise, the report declared that we now live in the "steroids era." Although it did little to explain how or why we entered this tawdry era, the report expressed the hope that its findings would help bring it to an end, through stricter oversight, tougher penalties, and better education about the dangerous side effects of performance-enhancing drugs.

Such reforms, however welcome, seem unlikely to halt the glory- or wealth-seeking athlete's turn to biotechnology in the pursuit of superior performance. Indeed, the age of steroids may soon look quaint by comparison with future doping technologies, such as genetic muscle enhancements that could be both impossible to trace and more effective than steroids or growth hormone. If professionalization was the last century's great transformation of sport, biotechnical enhancement looks to be this century's great degradation of sport. And while the Mitchell Report gave voice to a widespread concern about the disturbing effects of performance-enhancing drugs on modern athletics, it also demonstrated our inability (or unwillingness) to confront the deeper sources of the trouble. We seem to know that biotechnological enhancement is a threat to the "integrity of the game," but we cannot really articulate why. The reason is that we have lost an understanding of what makes sports truly admirable and hence worthy of our attention and our allegiance.

Faulty Analysis, Shallow Critique

By devoting nearly all of its 409 pages to documenting who used which drugs and when, the Mitchell Report took for granted that using steroids and other performance-enhancing drugs is a moral and legal offense that should be opposed. It offered a brief list of reasons for the current ban: steroid use unfairly disadvantages honest athletes, undermines the validity of baseball records, harms the human body, sets a bad example for young athletes, and threatens the integrity of the game. These concerns are all genuine, but they were never subjected to rigorous analysis. Only by examining them carefully can we see their inadequacy.

The fact that steroids are illegal is, of course, a good reason not to use them, but not a reason why they should remain illegal, nor does it tell us why they were proscribed in the first place. Declaring that steroids unfairly advantage those who use them, while true, is not a sufficient reason for continuing to prohibit their use. Why not, in the name of fairness, allow those individuals with more limited natural gifts to use steroids and other chemical agents in order to level the playing field, so that victory is not only to the most gifted? Or why not allow all athletes to use performance-enhancing drugs openly and legally, giving everyone free and fair access to whatever enhancements they choose? Indeed, the Mitchell Report itself suggested that one of the solutions to the steroid problem was to promote other kinds of nutritional supplements that would allow players to "achieve the same results." But why are some body-altering supplements to be applauded and others decried?

In its claim that steroid use "victimizes" nonusers by giving them three undesirable choices – lose out to the biologically enhanced, quit the game, or imperil their bodies by becoming users themselves – the Mitchell Report pushed the argument a little deeper. In an age of biotechnical enhancements, many athletes feel that it is impossible to compete on an even playing field without them, and that the choice to forgo performance-enhancing drugs amounts to unilateral disarmament. The pressure to use steroids has certainly become widespread, felt especially by the many marginal players – or by minor leaguers trying to move up – for whom any edge is the difference between staying in the game and losing the big salaries that all major leaguers now earn.

But if the majority of the players, as the report suggests, would truly prefer to stay chemically clean and avoid the need for this unwelcome choice, they could easily and successfully remove such pressures by agreeing collectively to expose the violators, and to shame them – something the Players' Union (which urged players not to cooperate with Senator Mitchell) is light years away from even considering. Moreover, the concern about coercion fails to get to the heart of the matter, since competitive athletes are always forced to measure up to their peers in training and practice or else be left behind.

As for concerns that athletes may subject themselves to health risks from performance-enhancing drugs, many of the sports we find most thrilling – football, hockey, boxing, downhill skiing – require putting one's body in peril. One of the athletic virtues we most admire is "playing hurt," which often means placing excellence in action above bodily well-being. Beginning with Achilles, our most celebrated heroes – in sport as in war – have willingly put their bodies at risk on the field of glory, accepting bodily harm and even a shortened life as a price worth paying for being remembered. If we admire the athlete who risks life and limb in the drive to bring his team to victory, why should we decry the athlete who puts short-term glory above long-term health by using steroids?

Even in sports that entail much less physical risk, like baseball, concerns about adverse health effects hardly seem to capture what really troubles us about steroids. The booing of Barry Bonds and the refusal to elect Mark McGwire to the Hall of Fame had nothing to do with their risking bodily harm. Even if the drugs were legal and safe, one imagines that the record-seeking batter would not like to be seen shooting up before heading to the plate, thus revealing his chemical dependence at the very moment when he is supposed to be demonstrating his personal excellence. He may use such drugs in private, without hesitation or apology, in his quest for fame, fortune, victory, or greatness; but he would be embarrassed to be seen in the act by the very public whose adulation he so craves. Why, exactly, is he ashamed? And would such shame persist for long in a culture that gradually normalized doping because it lacked any better arguments than the risk of bodily harm for maintaining the taboo against it?

The Mitchell Report was surely right to highlight concern about the health effects on youthful athletes who would imitate their steroid-using heroes. The bodies and brains of still-growing young people are especially susceptible to drug-induced harms; a shocking number of teenage and collegiate superstar-wannabes are already placing themselves needlessly at risk, and many more would be endangered should the taboo on these drugs be relaxed. Yet high schools, colleges, and even national Olympic committees, all bent on victory and the money and prestige that it brings, enthusiastically expose young athletes to enormous dangers to life and limb in the service of glory for school and country. Sequestering women's volleyball teams or pubescent gymnasts in drug-free but monomaniacal 24/7/365 training camps for the Olympics arguably deforms young bodies and minds even more than steroid use, cheating, or flouting the law.

In the end, the Mitchell Report left us with a circular argument: we deplore record-breakers like Bonds as cheaters because they broke the rules. It did not articulate the deep ethical and human grounds for preserving the rules that they flouted in their pursuit of athletic glory. In its concern for the "integrity of the game," the report did invite us to think about the meaning of performance-enhancing drugs for the game itself, noting specifically that cheaters win unfairly, baseball records become illegitimate, and drug suppliers can influence the outcome of games by threatening to expose their clients. But these concerns bear only on the *outcome* of the game, not on the authenticity of the game itself.

What is missing is any exploration of why athletic activity and athletic excellence are diminished and dehumanized by the turn to biotechnological enhancements; why the steroid-using athlete cheats not simply his competitor but first and foremost himself and those who cheer for him. The report left unexplored and undescribed what makes doping shameful and degrading, both for the athletes who engage in it and for the culture that fails to oppose it. And it never probed or captured, by image or argument, what makes human sport at its best a realm of excellence and grace, ennobling for participants and spectators alike.

Human Achievement

Like the Mitchell Report, most discussions of biotechnical enhancement are preoccupied with the novel biotechnologies themselves. Commonplace in such discussions are quasi-Talmudic (and inconclusive) arguments about whether and how, for example, steroid use differs from special diets as a means for increasing muscle mass, or how an erythropoietin injection ("blood doping") differs from taking vitamins as a means for increasing the oxygen-carrying capacity of blood. But a deeper analysis of enhancement will begin not from assessments of the technical means but from explorations of the desirable ends. Only if we have a clear idea of the nature and dignity of human activity, in sport and beyond, can we see how that dignity is threatened by the age of biotechnological enhancement. (This was the approach adopted in *Beyond Therapy: Biotechnology and the Pursuit of Happiness*, the 2003 report by the President's Council on Bioethics, which we helped to draft and from which we freely draw in this section of our essay and the next.) We begin by examining athletic activity itself, seeking to illuminate the integrity of the athlete, and then will consider the activity of the spectators, seeking to illuminate the integrity of sport and its value for all of us.

In athletics as in other human activities, excellence has until recently been achievable only by disciplined effort. To many people, victory or excellence attained by means of drugs, genetic engineering, or implanted devices looks like a form of cheating – not only one's opponents but also one's admirers, and the game itself. The reason that cheating should indeed bother us is not simply the principle of fairness, but more fundamentally a respect and admiration for human achievement. We esteem the human doer at his best, especially when he is engaged in activities that invite all to admire the excellence of the few. How did *he* – a human being, just like me – do *that?* If the answer is steroids, then we come to feel as if the body we admire is less like our own, and to believe that the deeds we admire are mere simulations of the human, rather than the human being at his best. The concern about cheating thus points to the deeper concern about the nature and dignity of human activity. What makes human activity truly human, and what makes excellent human activity truly excellent?

Superior performance in sport, as in much else, is generally attained through training and practice. One gets to run faster by running; one builds up endurance by enduring; one increases one's strength by using it on ever-increasing burdens. It is likewise with the complex specific skills of the game – hitting, fielding, and throwing the baseball. The capacity to be improved is improved by using it; the deed to be perfected is perfected by doing it. In many cases, of course, no amount of practice can overcome the limits of one's natural endowments: nature dispenses her unequal gifts with little regard for any abstract principle of "fairness." Yet however mysterious the source and the distribution of natural potential, the individual's cultivation of his natural endowments is intelligible. As agents and as spectators, we can understand the connection between effort and improvement, between activity and experience, between work and result. We appreciate self-achieved excellence because it flows from and manifests the presence of an active, excellence-seeking self.

By contrast, when we use performance-enhancing drugs to alter our native biology – whether to make the best even better or the below average more equal – we make improvements to our performance, paradoxically, less intelligible, in the sense of being less connected to our own self-conscious activity and exertion. The improvements that we might once have made through training alone we now make only with the assistance of stimulants or steroids. Though we might be using rational and scientific means to remedy the mysterious inequality or unchosen limits of our native gifts, we would make the individual's agency less *humanly* or *experientially* intelligible to himself.

The steroid-using athlete certainly gains new physical powers, and the scientist who produced the biological agents of such improvement can certainly understand in scientific terms the genetic workings or physiochemical processes that make it possible. But from the athlete's perspective, he improves as if by magic. True, he must continue to train in order to perform at a higher level even with steroids (or, someday, genetic muscle enhancement). He will still perspire, get tired, and feel his body at work. But the changes in his body, as he can surely attest, are decisively (albeit not solely) owed to the pills he popped or the shots he took, and the relation of those interventions to the changes he undergoes is opaque to his direct human experience. He has the advantages of modern biological science, but he risks a degree of alienation from his own efforts. Precisely because he has chosen to be chemically made into a better athlete, his superior performances are not great athletic *achievements*. Less doer and more done-to, he is dependent on outside agents for "his" performance. His doings become, in a crucial sense, less his own.

Why would an aspiring athlete subject himself to such magical transformations? Why would he adulterate his body and dilute his agency in pursuit of a personal achievement that mocks itself by being less personally his own? The pursuit of an answer will lead us to the heart of athletic activity and why we esteem it. In the process, we shall discover that the use of steroids or other biological enhancers is a symptom of a much deeper adulteration.

In competitive athletics, the goal is victory – the defeat of the opponent, the display of one's own superiority – usually not only in a single contest but over an entire season. Team success is measured by making the playoffs and then winning it all; individual success is measured by batting over .300, driving in more than a hundred runs, or winning more than twenty games in a season. And beyond the contests of this season, the star players also compete against those who excelled in seasons past. Athletes who strive for glory often want to be known as the best ever; and since Mark McGwire or Barry Bonds cannot compete directly against Babe Ruth or Hank Aaron, they do so by compiling higher numbers in the book of records. Over time, athletic excellence becomes defined solely in terms of outcomes: winning rather than losing, breaking previous records, and compiling a stellar *statisticum vitae*. Some old-fashioned connoisseurs may still watch sports for the love of a game well played; but most fans, encouraged by sports media's mania for keeping score, pay and watch largely to learn and celebrate the result.

Once athletic excellence is equated largely with successful outcomes, admired and compensated only for its contributions to the bottom line, it is surely tempting for athletes, by hook or by crook, to seek an extra edge that will increase the chance of victory, boost their individual statistics, and enable them not only to stay in the game but to ascend to the top of the ladder. If their native powers do not suffice, or if they begin to decline, those athletes will be only too happy to seek magical means of getting a better or a different body, in order to attain the longed-for results.

The Full Humanity of Athletic Activity

The dignity and worth of athletic activity are not defined only by winners and losers, faster and slower times, old records and new. It is not simply the measurable, comparative result that makes a performance excellent. It is also the humanity of the human performer. Even when the athlete is competitively engaged, excellent athletic activity seems to have a meaning that is separable from competition: the human body in action, the grace and rhythm of the moving human form, the striving and exertion of the aspiring human athlete. What matters more than the measurable outcome is the lived experience, for doer and spectator alike, of a humanly cultivated gift, excellently at work, striving for superiority and with the outcome in doubt.

Animals also run, often swiftly and gracefully, doer and deed seamlessly united. The average cheetah runs much faster than the fastest human being. But we do not honor the cheetah in the same way we honor the Olympic runner, because the Olympian runs in a human way as a human being. We admire the cheetah's grace and beauty, but we do not esteem its performance. The cheetah cannot help but run fast, and should he catch his quarry he will not have run in vain. The human runner, by contrast, must cultivate his gifts in order to achieve excellence, and although the race is to the swift, his distinctive humanity is on display throughout, win or lose. Racing is itself a human achievement, for each runner alone and for all runners together. For this reason, in assessing athletic performance, we do not separate what is done from how it is done and who is doing it – from the fact that it is being done by a human doer. And we should not separate the score from the purpose of keeping score in the first place: to honor and to promote a given type of human excellence whose meaning is in the doing, not simply in the scored result. Tomorrow's box score is at most a ghostly shadow of today's ballgame. The record book's statistics are anything but vital.

Athletic contests are live human dramas, compressed versions of the overall human drama, in which desire and drive are of the essence. A game comprises more than competing moves calculated for a result or justified solely by it. Consider the best human chess player going up against a chess-playing computer: an outstanding human being facing off against an outstanding human artifact. Are man and machine really "playing chess"? On one level, they are indeed playing the same game, making intelligible moves according to the same rules. Yet the computer "plays" the game rather differently, with no uncertainty, no nervousness, no sweaty palms, no active mind, and, most crucially, with no desires or hopes regarding future success. The computer's way of "playing" is really a kind of simulation – a product of genuine human achievement, to be sure, but not the real thing, playing chess. By building computers that "play" perfect chess, we change the meaning of the activity, reorienting the very character of our aspiration from becoming great chess players to producing the best-executed game of chess.

If chess is no more than the sum of opposing moves that are in principle calculable by a machine, why would human beings wish to play chess at all, especially if the machines can do it better? Why would no one watch a match between two chess-playing computers, or a baseball game that pitted robot pitchers against automatic batting machines? The answer is at once simple and complex: We still play chess because only we can *play chess*, as genuine chess players.

In baseball, similarly, we still run and pitch because running and pitching – while not as fast as roller-skating or using a pitching machine – possess a dignity unique to themselves and to those who engage in these activities. The runner or pitcher on steroids is still, of course, a human being who runs or pitches; but the doer of the deed is, arguably, less obviously himself and less obviously human than his unaltered counterpart. He may be faster, but he may also be on the way to becoming more like an efficient machine or a horse that we breed for the racetrack than a self-willing and self-directing human agent.

To determine what is specific to a human act or performance, and to identify the qualities that make us admire it as a human activity and as the performer's own, a comparison with the doings of other animals again proves helpful. In the activity of other animals, there is necessarily a unity between doer and deed. Acting impulsively and without reflection, an animal – unlike a human being – cannot deliberately feign activity or separate its acts from itself as their immediate source. A cheetah runs, but it does not run a race. Though it senses and pursues its prey, it does not harbor ambitions to surpass previous performances. Though its motion is not externally compelled, it does not run by choice. Though it moves in ordered sequence, it has not planned the course. It owes its beauty and its excellence to nature and instinct alone.

In contrast, the human runner chooses to run a race and sets before himself his goal. He measures the course and prepares himself for it. He surveys his rivals and plots his strategy. He disciplines his body and cultivates his natural gifts to pursue his goal. The end, the means, and the manner are all matters of conscious awareness and deliberate choice. The racer's running is a human act humanly done, because it is done freely and knowingly.

But the humanity of athletic performance resides not only in the chosenness and the intelligibility of the deed. It depends also on the activity of a well-tuned and well-working body. The body in question is a living body, not a mere machine; not just any animal body but a human one; not someone else's body but one's own. Each of us is personally embodied. Each of us lives with, and because of, certain bodily gifts that owe nothing to our rational will. Each of us not only has a body; each of us also is a body.

The truth and the beauty of integrated and embodied human activity are displayed and celebrated in human sport (and also in dance and musical performance). When we see an outstanding athlete in action, we do not see a rational agent riding or whipping a separate animal body, as we do in horse racing. We see instead a body gracefully and harmoniously at work, but at work with discipline and focus, pushing its limits and displaying its powers, all the while obeying the rules and requirements of the game. We know immediately that the human athlete is engaged in deliberate and goal-directed activity, that he is not running in flight moved by fear, or in pursuit moved by hunger. Yet while the human character of his bodily movements is at once obvious, the "mindedness" of the bodily activity is unobtrusive. So attuned is the body to heart and mind that the whole activity of the athlete appears, in the best instance, to flow effortlessly from an undivided being. At such moments the athlete experiences and displays something like the unity of doer and deed one observes in other animals, but with this difference: for humans, such a unity is an achievement. A great sprinter may run like a gazelle and a great boxer may fight like a tiger, but one would never mistake their harmony of body and soul for the brute instinct that spurs an animal toward flight or fight.

In the most complex sports – baseball, football, basketball, hockey, soccer – many of our most sophisticated psychic and physical powers are brought into play, visibly and elegantly united. The athlete goes beyond what is merely animal in man to ascend from acts of the body to acts of mind-body coordination. Man and cheetah both run, but man alone executes a hit-and-run, or dives to catch a sinking liner, or gallops to run down a towering fly ball whose trajectory he has subconsciously calculated correctly after hearing it leave the bat. The expert base stealer knows how to time the pitcher's delivery to gain an undefeatable head start, and the sharp-eyed base runner knows when to extend a double into a triple and how to complete his feat with an artful slide.

Beyond these anatomized acts of mind and body there is the great feat of playing the game itself, from moment to moment and from beginning to end, in light of the larger whole. Players survey the entire scene as they perform in concert with others, attending to where their teammates are heading and how their opponents are defending. They embody the rules, manage the clock, execute their game plans, and make innumerable strategic adjustments when things go badly. At their peak, the great player and the great team reveal the human difference in its glory.

At the root of athletic activity, as of all worthy human activity, is desire or drive or aspiration – every bit as important as talent or training or strategic planning. Our aspiration for excellence, our drive to perform, our desire to do and be something memorable and great, is not finally the product of pure reason or pure will. Neither is it the product merely of our animality. It stems rather from that distinct blending of mind and desire, perhaps peculiar to human beings, that the Greeks called *eros*, which drives us to make of ourselves something less imperfect, something more noble, something beautiful and fine, something that would be fulfilling, as much as is humanly possible. At his heights, the great athlete longs for more than the spirited conquest of his opponents; he longs for "the perfect game" – for perfection itself, the performance that transcends victory alone. And he pursues this aspiration as himself and (at least to begin with) for himself. No admirable human being would seek excellence on the condition that he become someone or something else in order to attain it. No sane person would choose to be the fastest thing on two legs if it required becoming an ostrich. Not the excellence of beast or god, or even the excellence of a magically transformed human being, but the excellence of our own embodied share of mankind's vast potential is the goal we should admire.

In trying to achieve better bodies through biotechnology, we do not honor our given bodies or cultivate our given individual gifts. Instead, whether we realize it or not, we are voting with our syringes to have a different body, with different native capacities and powers. We are giving ourselves new and foreign gifts, not nature's and not our own. Those who retort that nature's original gifts deserve no special claim on our loyalty – why not become someone else, or even something better-than-human? – would diminish the possibility of personal human excellence in the very effort they make to enhance it.

We come here to the great paradox of all human aspiration, which is that it always embraces the given while desiring its perfection. In striving to excel in whatever activity, we must seek to make ourselves better than we now are, but we must also continue to affirm our enduring identity, lest we cease being who and what we are trying to perfect. Every athlete's pursuit of excellence implicitly requires accepting, with grace and gratitude, his own body and its natural endowments, which he cannot escape or change without ceasing to be himself.

The ironies of the biotechnological enhancement of athletic performance should now be painfully clear. By turning to biological agents to transform ourselves in the image that we choose and will, we compromise our choosing and willing identity itself, electing to become less the source or the shaper of our own identity. We take a pill or insert a gene that makes us into something we desire, but only by compromising the self-directed path toward its attainment. By using these agents to transform our bodies for the sake of better bodily performance, we mock the very excellence of our own individual embodiment that superior performance is meant to display. By using these technological means to transcend the limits of our nature, we deform the character of human desire and aspiration, settling for externally gauged achievements that are less and less the fruits of our own individual striving and cultivated finite gifts.

By submitting to the chemists, we become mere placeholders for the tainted records that might one day attach to our name. For what could be more in conflict with athletic excellence, with the body gracefully at work fulfilling its full potential, than the image of the passive patient, chemically dependent on the technological cleverness of others, coveting feats that he can never truly claim as his own and adulation that he does not really deserve? Even should the enhancements of tomorrow prove safe and be kept legal, the shame that now attaches to steroid use would still remain – at least in any honorable society and before any worthy fans.

Fandom, Worthy and Not

Our own worthiness as fans is a largely neglected question, as is the relation of spectator to sport. Athletic activity does not necessarily require spectators. Millions of young and not-so-young people play sports in gyms and on playgrounds, sometimes in organized leagues, often in pickup games, mostly unobserved save by their fellow participants and perhaps a few family members. But spectator sports, both collegiate and professional, are a shared national obsession: they define our perception of sports, and, in turn, they shape the meaning of sport in modern culture. In those realms, the world of the athlete is inseparable from the world of the spectator; the stage on which athletes perform is inseparable from the audience. For the players, the fans provide encouragement, recognition, and the acclaim that confirms their own superiority. For the fans, the players show how the enormously difficult games we try to play can be played by the best, enabling us vicariously to participate in their attainments. As taste is to genius, so appreciative beholding is to superior athletic activity, mirroring and completing it by allowing it to be properly known and properly valued.

Yet there are inherent difficulties in spectator sports, both for the athletes and for the beholders. The fan who comes to see genuine excellence in honorable competition is at the mercy of the integrity – or the lack of integrity – of the athletes and the game. For the athlete who seeks recognition, the honor that he receives is notoriously no better than the judgment and the taste of those who bestow it. The greatest athletes, who know the difference between honor and celebrity, between glory and vainglory, care much more for recognition from a few worthy opponents and connoisseurs than for cheers from an ill-informed mob. Although most professional players take inspiration from the fans as "our extra man," playing to the crowd and satisfying its tastes is at bottom a deformation of athletics, an adulteration imported from the theater. Showing off while playing the part of someone else is the essence of theater; shining forth being oneself at one's best is the heart of sports.

Many of us fans can vividly remember the greatest performances of Roger Clemens on the mound and Marion Jones on the racetrack – the two twenty-strikeout games (against the Seattle Mariners in 1986 and against the Detroit Tigers ten years later), the 100-meter final in Sydney in 2000. We remember Mark McGwire's besting Sammy Sosa in the home-run derby of 1998 to reach a new season record of 70, and we recall seeing it broken only three years later when Barry Bonds hit numbers 71 and 72 in one game, just two days before the end of the season. As spectators, we witnessed human excellence in the flesh – the striving body at work, beautiful to behold, and the spirited competitor at play, dominating opposing batters or rising above his rivals. These performances filled the most devoted fans with euphoric pleasure, and even elicited the admiration of those who cheered for the defeated. Greatness is greatness, even when it is not our own. And some of the spectators whose lives were elevated by these great performances didn't live to see the fall of their heroes. With memories forever sweet, they never saw the curtain lifted to reveal the hidden syringe that gave the steroid-dependent victors their edge.

In a marvelous book entitled *In Praise of Athletic Beauty*, Hans Ulrich Gumbrecht pays moving tribute to the aesthetic excellence of great athletes and describes the deep human satisfactions that great athletic performances give to those who watch them, whether as partisans or as connoisseurs. Is it possible that performance-enhancing drugs might enhance the experience of the spectator – provided that the curtain is never lifted – even as it compromises the integrity of the athlete?

For the beauty-loving fan who watches the game unaware that steroids have been used, the performance of the athlete is no less beautiful or impressive. For the victory-loving fan, the victory is no less sweet. And for the entertainment-loving fan, the pleasure-giving spectacle of sport is not diminished. Yet when we see Marion Jones heading off to prison or Roger Clemens facing his inquisitors in Congress, we as spectators feel wronged. Our heroes turn out to be villains; the retired numbers on the backs of their jerseys get replaced with a scarlet "HGH" on their foreheads. They have soured the pleasure we once took in remembering their feats, and cheated us out of our unadulterated admiration for their excellence.

Right as we are to feel wronged, we spectators may well bear some responsibility for the degradation of our heroes. Right as we are to feel cheated, we ourselves have created a culture that demands new records and greater spectacles and that worships victory at (almost) any cost. To restore the "integrity of the game," we need to recover an understanding of why sport matters to us as a society – why the games men play are a serious business, capable of shaping our character and our souls, for better and for worse.

The adulteration of sport today is owed partly to the fact that spectator sports are, quite literally, a serious business – a multibillion-dollar business – not only for the professional athletes but even more for the agents, the team owners, and the television networks. The tastes of the fans are, to say the least, not entirely of their own making. The huge salaries and bonuses, the marketing of the players and the paraphernalia, the pregame slam-dunk or home-run-hitting contests, the reduction of the game to the highlight reel replayed endlessly on round-the-clock sports channels (the major one, ESPN, originally called the *Entertainment* and Sports Programming Network), the hyping of homer derbies and record chasings, the exploding scoreboards and raucous entertainment between innings or at halftime, the compulsory celebrity appearances before and after the game: all these profit-driven activities help to shape the tastes and judgments of the fans, which in turn reshape the game and the way it is played and appreciated.

Fandom may have become a marketable commodity, but in its essence it remains something noble, and it has deeper roots and significances. Most fans become sports enthusiasts when they are young. And the young are "fan-atics" in the primordial sense: patriots for their team, worshippers of their heroes, amateurs who seek to imitate the pros. The young learn to play the games they watch, and they love to watch the games they play. For many, this loyalty to their team persists for the rest of their lives: as adults they may settle down in New York City, but they remember taking the bus to see Carl Yastrzemski play at Fenway, and they will remain devotees of "Red Sox nation" unto death. Fandom is a kind of patriotism – a devotion to one's own, for better and for worse, combined with a thirst for victory, especially against one's greatest rivals. A few years ago, in a discussion in Washington on "making patriots," Irving Kristol remarked that "if you want to make patriots, make your kids join a sports team."

The fans want to participate in the thrill of victory, even if it means accepting the likelihood of defeat year after year. One of the authors will soon enter his eighth decade of rooting for the White Sox – and against the Yankees – with only one World Series victory to show for it, a victory that he cherishes especially because it proved that not all hope is foolishness. Fans feel part of the game, emotionally and even physically. They jump from their seats, scream at the television, threaten the referees, dance in the streets.

Yet the modern culture of sport complicates the fan's experience of loyalty. Not only do players jump from nation to nation in search of the best salary, so that today's Red Sox god is tomorrow's Yankee devil. Today's hunger for victory easily degenerates into a belief that all is fair in sport and war. Those who feel cheated to learn that Clemens was on steroids may have willfully looked the other way, in the final inning of the final game, so that they could have their victory parade. In sports today, we face the challenge of preserving the virtue of loyalty in a culture of infidelity, and the challenge of moderating the love of victory by the love of honor.

In a culture that rewards or tolerates victory without honor, the fans wrong the players as much as the players wrong the fans. The players do what they must to deliver us the victories that we demand, and we try not to see the infractions and debasements that may have helped to gain those victories – the illegal steroids and corked bats, the practice of "taking out" the quarterback, or pirating your opponent's game plan, or deflating the footballs. When the evidence comes out, we condemn our athletic heroes for taking such measures to gain our admiration, though we may have understood all along that dishonorable means might well be involved. And while we decry their use of performance-enhancing drugs, we are more than a little complicit in their corruption, for we have created a culture that encourages the use of a growing arsenal of bio-magic – cosmetic surgery, Botox, Viagra, and so on – to remake our bodies in the image of our fantasies.

If all we seek from our athletes is entertainment – a good show – we will eventually snicker at the means they use to satisfy us. If what most delights us is seeing the ball fly out into San Francisco Bay or the pitching radar gun recording more than 100 miles per hour, we will be indifferent to how such results are attained. Human sport will become a strange hybrid of dog racing, fantasy wrestling, and the circus freak show, with men and women programmed to perform at the highest levels that science makes possible, and a society of mere spectators who do the wave and roar their approval at feats that defeat the reason anyone plays and honors sports in the first place.

Sport is a species of play, but it is not a frivolous activity. It is true that our games serve no utilitarian purpose; they do not feed the hungry, or cure the sick, or shelter the cold. But sport, like all play, is valuable as an end in itself, not just for the sake of victory or profit or some other result. It belongs to the domain of human activities that are done for their own sake – not the realm of necessity, but that of leisure, of freedom, of cultivation.

Sport is gratuitous, one of the domains (like music and the arts) that set human beings apart from the other animals, as free and perfectible beings who can and do live for more than physical survival and genetic self-perpetuation. Among human societies, those in which play and sport are encouraged have risen above humankind's sober preoccupations with safety, comfort, and gain. Leisure, as Joseph Pieper argued in a beautiful book with that title, is the basis of culture, and the cultivation of our embodied excellences is one of the marks of a cultured society, one whose citizens celebrate being alive and fit, with "mindful" bodies capable of complex and often beautiful movements, improved by the need to test them against worthy rivals.

Play is different from mere amusement or entertainment, other activities that are ends in themselves. A game, though a pastime, does more than pass the time; and though sport entertains us, its meaning is independent of the pleasure we derive from it. A structured activity, governed by rules and filled with risk and uncertainty, sport invites and rewards not only game-specific skills but also indispensable virtues that can be exercised in other realms of life: determination, discipline, courage, endurance, enterprise, perspicacity, and mental toughness. Many a well-coached college athlete in later years praises his coach most for helping him to become a man – responsible, honorable, devoted to making something of himself. Those who watch the game seriously can ratify and admire these virtues more generally.

Sport is not simply artful play; its essence lies somewhere between dance and war. Men meet on a field where only the best men win, and where many of the best are driven primarily by a thirst for victory. The deepest appeal of sport is often the drama of the game – the miracle drive to win as the clock expires, the near-perfect season that ends in tragic defeat, the return of the fallen champion to glory. The fascination of sport lies in the moment of truth, when some rise and some fall, some perform and some choke. Here in microcosm the human drama is on display, with all its pathos and possibility.

For three periods or four quarters or nine innings, away from the cares of our everyday lives, we behold some of life's deepest truths unfolding. Even our best athletes embody both the possibilities *and* the limitations of a finite and vulnerable human body – possibilities they strive to perfect, limitations they struggle to surmount. We watch them accomplish seemingly superhuman things, and our spirits soar with the few who succeed. The kid in us will always love a winner. But as we mature, we come also to respect the many more who strive and fail, as human beings just like us. Even the immortals one day retire, and the best do so with grace, standing aside for the next generation of aspiring heroes.

Because sport is not war, the fight to the finish is marked not by death or surrender, but rather, when played in the right spirit, by gracious celebration and good sportsmanship, displayed by winners and losers alike. This crowning touch of the sporting event is nicely captured in a story Gumbrecht tells about a Japanese baseball superstar named Koji Akiyama, who struck out looking with runners on base at a critical moment of the Japanese championship series. While the fans sighed in disappointment, "Akiyama stayed in the batter's box a second longer than he needed to – and gave a really beautiful smile to the pitcher." Gumbrecht comments:

> Akiyama's smile, I believe, must have come from the feeling that, for a brief moment at least, the opposing pitcher had taken the game of baseball to its highest level, making him, the man at bat who lost the competition, part of this achievement. It was like the smile of the angels that we see sculpted into the stone of medieval cathedrals – art historians believe these smiles signify the angels' happiness at being able to play a role in God's perfect creation.

Sport is a field of grace: the gracious display of beautiful form, the gracious appreciation of worthy opponents, gratitude for native gifts and efforts rewarded. At their best, our greatest athletic events are more than civic rituals; our stadiums become veritable cathedrals and our fandom a kind of worship. Praising athletic beauty is inadequate to the full human and social meaning of sport, which is capable of leading us beyond the aesthetic to the moral and even to the transcendent. The great athlete embodies that perfect unity of gratitude for the given possibilities of his being and pride in the achievements that he alone made possible. If all that matters is athletic beauty, then we should care little about the syringe behind the curtain. But if what matters is the elevation of man through sport, on the field and off, then steroids degrade that which is capable of elevating.

Beyond the Beautiful

With all the problems facing America today, there was perhaps something silly about Congress devoting time to performance-enhancing drugs in sports. The *gotcha* game on Capitol Hill and in the media certainly did little to help us see the deeper issues involved, or to understand what gives athletes and games the integrity that we all presumably seek to defend. But the Mitchell Report and other exposures of drug-enhanced athletes may at least invite us to imagine what kind of society we might become if such biotechnical interventions were to become more powerful and more widespread.

We might come to see Olympic races and dog races, human runners and running horses as little different from one another. Well-bred athletes, increasingly here mostly for our entertainment and amusement, might become little more than expendable props. We might lose sight of the difference between real and false excellence, and eventually no longer care about the distinction. Worst of all, we would be in danger of turning our would-be heroes into slaves – persons who exist only to entertain us and whose freedom to pursue their own human excellence has been shackled by the need to perform for our enjoyment. For a while – perhaps indefinitely – we might relish the superior results that our biotechnical ingenuity makes possible: faster times, better scores, broken records. But we would lose sight of why excellence is worth seeking at all, and would forget how to pursue it as human agents – as proud, aspiring beings.

The danger is greatest for the young fans who grow up in the age of biotechnical enhancement and will want to imitate their steroid-dependent role models, at great harm to themselves. But the deeper danger is that they will come to assume that everything fine is really fake; that human excellence is always compromised; that the greatest performances are always an illusion; that the curtain will inevitably be lifted to reveal the chemist lurking in the shadows. A culture that degrades its heroes, especially the heroes of the young, will destroy the very idea of heroism. A society that gets used to steroids in sport will become even more cynical than it already is. A civilization shaped by the possibilities of biotechnical enhancement will erode the twin possibilities of excellence and gratitude. All that will remain are cartoon heroes and high-tech magic acts, and a life devoted to soul-deforming amusements.

The cure for the adulteration of sports, a cultural disease that is already far along, will require much more than the banishment of steroids and other performance-enhancing drugs. It will require a revival – for contemporary Americans, difficult to achieve – of the athletic ideal as a manifestation of the mysterious powers that make us human. It is useful to recall that the athletic contests of the ancient Greeks, conducted at Olympia, were elements of religious festivals, in which the games were celebrated alongside theatrical productions of great tragedies as well as animal sacrifices to the gods. Apollonian beauty was in the stadium, Dionysian ecstasy was on the stage and in the crowds, and catharsis and edification were all around. Today, without our knowing it, Dionysus still holds court among the fans in our sports palaces (even without the beer and bratwurst), while Apollo still manages to shine between commercial television timeouts and the endless reciting of statistics. The amateur spirit, the love of the game, is not quite dead. Neither is the attitude of gratitude, as many a winning athlete points heavenward after a great play, or gives verbal credit and thanks to God after a thrilling victory, usually to the embarrassment of his television interviewer. In these little gestures – however routine or unthinking they may be – we sports fans are reminded of perhaps the deepest reason why we should honor athletics.

In *Chariots of Fire*, the Scottish runner Eric Liddell, urged by his sister to give up running and return to his work as a Christian missionary in China, explains movingly why he cannot do so: "I believe that God made me for a purpose, but He also made me fast, and when I run I feel His pleasure. . . . To give up running would be to hold Him in contempt." Skeptics may scoff, but the true fans of sports, first listening to Liddell and then watching him perform, nod approvingly, regardless of their theological commitments or even their lack thereof. They know, the believers and the unbelievers, just what he means. And absent such gratitude for our gifts and the correlative desire to cultivate them honorably to the fullest extent possible, the adulteration of sport cannot be overcome, even if the steroid era were to come to an end.

CHAPTER NINE

A Dignified Death and Its Enemies
Why Doctors Must Not Kill

THAT WE DIE is certain. When and how we die is not. Because we want to live and not to die, we resort to medicine to delay the inevitable. Yet in some cases, medicine's success in preserving life has been purchased at a heavy price, paid in the coin of *how* we die: often in conditions of great pain and suffering, irreversible incompetence, and terminal loss of control. In these circumstances, many Americans increasingly seek greater control over the end of life, and some even wish to elect an earlier death in order to avoid the burdens of lingering on. Ironically, they also seek assistance in doing so from the death-defying art of medicine. People no longer talk only of refusing medical treatment, but of physician-assisted suicide and euthanasia. Voters in a few American states have legalized physician-assisted suicide, and legislators in others are actively debating whether to follow suit. A large segment of national public opinion approves the practice of doctor-induced death, and even many physicians appear ready to overturn the centuries-old taboo against medical killing. Euthanasia practiced by physicians seems to be an idea whose time has come.

In my view, it remains a bad idea whose time must not come – not now, not ever. Powerful reasons, both of prudence and of principle, have for centuries supported such a judgment, and, as I will argue, they do so still, despite our changed circumstances – indeed, all the more so because of them. The central argument requires understanding the special moral

202

character of the medical profession and the ethical obligations that it entails – moral character and obligations that rest on deep insights into the human condition and its inherent dignity. Accordingly, I will be considering these interrelated questions: What are the norms that all physicians, *as physicians*, should agree to observe, whatever their personal opinions and private morality? What is the basis of such a medical ethic? What does it say – and what should we think – about doctors intentionally killing? How instead can they truly protect human dignity at the end of life?

Two Ethical Approaches: Autonomy or Compassion

The question about physicians killing appears, at first glance, to be just a special case of this general question: May or ought one kill people who ask to be killed? Among those who answer this general question in the affirmative, two reasons are usually given. First is freedom or autonomy: each person has a right to control his or her body and his or her life, including the end of it. Some go as far as to assert a right to die, a strange claim in a liberal society founded on the need to secure and defend the inalienable right to life. But strange or not, for patients with waning powers too weak to oppose potent life-prolonging technologies wielded by aggressive physicians, the claim based on choice, autonomy, and self-determination is certainly understandable. In this view, physicians (or others) are bound to acquiesce in demands not only for termination of treatment but also for intentional killing through poison, because the right to choose – freedom – must be respected, even more than life itself, and even when the physician would never recommend or concur in the choices made. Physicians, as keepers of the vials of life and death, are morally bound actively to dispatch the embodied person in deference to autonomous personal choice.

The second reason for killing the patient who asks for death has little to do with choice. Instead, death is to be directly and swiftly given because the patient's life is deemed no longer worth living, according to some substantive or "objective" measure. Unusually great pain or a terminal condition or an irreversible coma or advanced senility or extreme degradation is the disqualifying quality of life that pleads – choice or no choice – for merciful termination. Choice may enter indirectly to confirm the judgment: if the patient does not speak up, the doctor (or the relatives or some other proxy) may be asked to affirm that he would not himself choose – or that his patient, were he able to choose, would not choose – to remain alive with one or more of these burdens. It is not his autonomy but rather the miserable and pitiable condition of his body or mind that justifies doing the patient in. Absent such degradations, a request for assisted death would not be honored. Here the body itself offends and must be plucked out – in compassion or mercy, to be sure. Not the autonomous will of the patient, but the doctor's benevolent and compassionate love for suffering humanity justifies the humane act of mercy killing.

These two reasons advanced to justify the killing of patients correspond to the two approaches to medical ethics most prominent in the field today (reflecting the two dominant ethical orientations of the larger American society): the school of autonomy and the school of general benevolence and compassion (or love). Despite their differences, they are united in their opposition to the belief that medicine is intrinsically a moral profession, with its own immanent principles and standards of conduct that set limits on what physicians may properly do. Each school seeks to remedy the ethical defect of a profession seen to be in itself *a*moral – technically competent but morally neutral.

For the ethical school of autonomy, morally neutral technique is morally used only when it is used according to the wishes of the patient as client or consumer. The model of the doctor-patient relationship is one of contract: the physician – a highly competent hired syringe, as it were – sells his services on demand, restrained only by the law. Here's the deal: the patient gets the service he chooses, while the doctor gets money, graced by the pleasure of giving the patient what he wants. If a patient wants to fix her nose or change his gender, determine the sex of unborn children, or take euphoriant drugs just for kicks, the physician can and will go to work – provided that the price is right.*

For the ethical school of compassion, morally neutral technique is

---

* Of course, any physician with personal scruples against one or another of these practices may "write" the relevant exclusions into the service contract he offers his customers.

morally used only when it is used under the guidance of general benevolence or loving charity. Not the will of the patient, but the humane and
compassionate motive of the physician *as human being* makes the actions
ethical. Here, too, there can be strange requests and stranger deeds, but if
they are done from love, nothing can be wrong – provided that the law is
silent. All acts – including killing the patient – done lovingly are licit,
even praiseworthy. Good and humane intentions can sanctify any deed.

In my opinion, both of these approaches misunderstand the moral
foundations of medical practice and therefore provide an inadequate
basis for medical ethics.* For one thing, neither of them can make sense
of some specific duties and restraints long thought absolutely inviolate
under the traditional medical ethic – e.g., the proscription against having
sex with patients. Must we now say that sex with patients is permissible
if the patient wants it and the price is right, or, alternatively, if the doctor
is gentle and loving and has a good bedside manner? Or do we glimpse in
this absolute prohibition a deeper understanding of the medical vocation? Indeed, as I will now try to show, the medical profession has its own
intrinsic ethic, which a physician true to his calling will not violate, either
for love or for money.

An Intrinsically Ethical Profession

Let me propose a different way of thinking about medicine as a profession.
Consider medicine not as a mixed marriage between value-neutral technique and some extrinsic moral principles, but as an inherently ethical
activity in which technique and conduct are both ordered in relation to an
overarching good, the naturally given end of health. This once traditional
view of medicine I have defended at length in *Toward a More Natural Science*.[22] Here I will present the conclusions without the arguments. It will
suffice, for present purposes, if I can render this view plausible.

A profession, as etymology suggests, is an activity or occupation to
which its practitioner publicly professes – that is, confesses – his devotion.

---

* Both are inadequate also for ethics altogether. Human dignity is not reducible to
autonomy and free choice. Neither is unqualified compassion, prompted by human
frailty and weakness, the best or only guide for how to treat our neighbors.

Learning may be required, and prestige may be granted, but it is the profession's intrinsic goal that learning serves and prestige honors. Each of the ways of life to which the various professionals profess their devotion must be a way of life worthy of such devotion – and so they all are. The teacher devotes himself to assisting the learning of the young, looking up to truth and wisdom; the lawyer (or the judge) devotes himself to rectifying injustice for his client (or for the parties before the court), looking up to what is lawful and right; the clergyman devotes himself to tending the souls of his parishioners, looking up to the sacred and the divine; and the physician devotes himself to healing the sick, looking up to health and wholeness.

Being a professional is thus more than being a technician. It is rooted in our moral nature; it is a matter not only of the mind and hand but also of the heart, not only of intellect and skill but also of character. For it is only as a being willing and able to devote himself to others and to serve some high good that a person makes a public profession of his way of life. To profess is an ethical act, and it makes the professional *qua* professional a moral being who prospectively affirms the moral nature of his activity.

Professing oneself a professional is an ethical act for many reasons. It is an articulate public act, a confession before witnesses, not merely a private and silent choice. It is a promise of continuing devotion, not merely an announcement of present preferences. It pledges commitment to a way of life, not just a way to a livelihood; to a life of action, not only of thought. It serves a high good, which calls forth devotion because it is high and good, but which also requires devotion because its service is most demanding and difficult, engaging one's character as well as one's mind and hands.

The good to which the medical profession is chiefly devoted is health, a naturally given although precarious standard or norm, characterized by "wholeness" and "well-working," toward which the living body moves on its own. Even the modern physician, despite his great technological prowess, is finally but an assistant to natural powers of self-healing. As the healing profession, medicine uses artful means to serve the human body's natural efforts to maintain its integrity and its native powers and activities.

But health is difficult to attain and preserve. It can be ours only provisionally and temporarily, for we are finite and frail. Medicine thus finds itself in between: the physician is called to serve the high and universal goal of health, while also ministering to the needs and relieving the sufferings of the frail and particular patient. Moreover, the physician must respond not only to illness but also to its meaning for each individual, who may suffer from self-concern – and often fear or shame – about weakness and vulnerability, neediness and dependence, and the fragility of all that matters to him. Thus the inner meaning of the art of medicine is derived from the pursuit of health and the care for the ill and suffering, guided by an awareness of the delicate, dialectical tension between wholeness and necessary decay.

When the activity of healing the sick is thus understood, we can discern certain virtues requisite for practicing medicine – among them, moderation and self-restraint, gravity, patience, sympathy, discretion, and prudence. We can also discern specific positive duties, addressed mainly to the patient's vulnerability and self-concern – including the demands for truthfulness, instruction, and encouragement. And, arguably, we can infer the importance of certain negative duties, formulable as absolute and unexceptionable rules. Among these, I submit, is this rule: Doctors must not kill. The rest of this chapter attempts to defend this rule and to show its relation to the medical ethic, itself understood as growing out of the inner meaning of the medical vocation.

I confine my discussion solely to the question of direct, intentional killing of patients *by physicians*, in so-called mercy killing. Though I confess myself opposed to such killing even by nonphysicians,[23] I am not arguing here against euthanasia per se. More importantly, I am not arguing against the cessation of medical treatment when such treatment merely prolongs painful or degraded dying; nor do I oppose the use of certain measures to relieve suffering that unavoidably bring an increased risk of death. Doctors may and must allow dying, even if they must not intentionally kill.

Bad Consequences

Although the heart of my argument will turn on my understanding of the special meaning of professing the art of healing, I begin with a more familiar mode of ethical analysis: assessing needs and benefits versus dangers and harms. Still the best discussion of this topic is a now classic essay written by Yale Kamisar in 1958.[24] Kamisar makes vivid the difficulties of ensuring that the choice for death will be freely made and adequately informed, the problems of physician error and abuse, the troubles for human relationships within families and between doctors and patients, the difficulty of preserving the boundary between voluntary and involuntary euthanasia, and the risks to the whole social order from weakening the absolute prohibition against taking innocent life. These considerations alone are, in my view, sufficient to rebut any attempt to weaken the taboo against medical killing; their relative importance for determining public policy far exceeds their relative importance in this essay. But here they serve also to point us to more profound reasons why doctors must not kill.

There is no question that fortune deals many people a very bad hand, not least at the end of life. All of us, I am sure, know or have known individuals whose last weeks, months, or even years were racked with pain and discomfort, degraded by dependency or loss of self-control, or who lived in such reduced humanity that it cast a deep shadow over their entire lives, especially as remembered by the survivors. All who love them would wish to spare them such an end, and there is no doubt that an earlier death could do it. Against such a clear benefit, attested by many a poignant and heartrending true story, it is difficult to argue, especially when the arguments are necessarily general and seemingly abstract. Still, in the aggregate, the adverse consequences of being governed solely by mercy and compassion may far outweigh the aggregate benefits of trying to relieve agonal or terminal distress by direct medical killing.

The first difficulty emerges when we try to gauge the so-called "need" or demand for medically assisted killing. This question is partly empirical, but evidence can be gathered only if the relevant categories of "euthanizable" people are clearly defined. Such definition is notoriously hard to accomplish – and it is not always honestly attempted. On careful inspection, we discover that if the category is precisely defined, the need for mercy killing or assisted suicide seems to be greatly exaggerated, and if the category is loosely defined, the poisoners will be working overtime.

The category always mentioned first to justify mercy killing or assisted suicide is the group of persons suffering from incurable and fatal illnesses, those with intractable pain and little time left to live but still fully aware, who freely request a release from their distress – for example, people rapidly dying from disseminated cancer with bony metastases, unresponsive to chemotherapy. But as experts in pain control tell us, the number of such people with truly untreatable pain is in truth rather low. Adequate analgesia is apparently possible in the vast majority of cases, provided that the physician and patient are willing to use strong enough medicines in adequate doses and with proper timing.*

It will be pointed out that full analgesia induces drowsiness and blunts or distorts awareness. How can that be a desired outcome of treatment? A fair enough question. But then the rationale for requesting death begins to shift from relieving experienced suffering to ending a life no longer valued by its bearer or, let us be frank, by the onlookers. If this becomes a sufficient basis to warrant mercy killing, now the category of euthanizable people cannot be limited to individuals with incurable or fatal and painful illnesses with little time to live. Now persons in all sorts of greatly reduced conditions – from persistent vegetative state to quadriplegia, from severe depression to the condition that now most horrifies, Alzheimer's disease – might have equal claim to have their suffering mercifully halted. The trouble, of course, is that most of these people can no longer request for themselves the dose of poison. Moreover, it will be difficult, if not impossible, to develop the requisite calculus of degradation or to define the threshold necessary for ending life.

In view of the obvious difficulty in describing precisely and "objectively" what categories and degrees of pain, suffering, or bodily or mental impairment could justify mercy killing, advocates repair (at least for the time being) to the principle of volition: the request for assistance in death is to be honored because it is freely made by the one whose life it is, and who, for one reason or another, cannot commit suicide alone. But how free or informed is a choice made under debilitated conditions? Can consent given long in advance – as in so-called living wills – be sufficiently informed about all the particular circumstances that it is meant to cover prospectively? And in any case, are not such choices easily and subtly manipulated, especially in the vulnerable?

---

* The inexplicable failure of many physicians to provide the proper and available relief of pain is surely part of the reason why some people now insist that physicians should (instead) give them death.

Truth to tell, the ideal of rational autonomy, so beloved of bioethicists and legal theorists, rarely obtains in actual medical practice. Illness invariably means dependence, and dependence means relying for advice on physician and family. This is especially true with the seriously or terminally ill, where there is frequently also depression or diminished mental capacity that clouds one's judgment or weakens one's resolve. With patients thus reduced – helpless in action and ambivalent about life – someone who might benefit from their death need not proceed by overt coercion. Rather, requests for assisted suicide can and will be subtly engineered.

To alter and influence choices, physicians and families need not be driven by base motives or even be consciously manipulative. Well-meaning and discreet suggestions, or even unconscious changes in expression, gesture, or tone of voice, can move a dependent and suggestible patient toward a choice for death. Simply by making euthanasia or assisted suicide an option available to gravely ill persons, will we not, as Kamisar wrote long ago,

> sweep up, in the process, some who are not really tired of life, but think others are tired of them; some who do not really want to die, but who feel that they should not live on, because to do so when there looms the legal alternative of euthanasia is to do a selfish or cowardly act?[25]

Anyone who knows anything at all about the real life of the elderly and those who are incurably ill knows that many of them will experience – and be helped to experience – their freedom or right to choose physician-assisted death as an *obligation* or *duty*.

In the great majority of medical situations, the idealistic assumptions of doctor-patient equality and of patient autonomy are false, even when the patient is in relatively good health and where there is an intimate doctor-patient relationship of long standing. But with those who are seriously ill or hospitalized, and, even more, with the vast majority of patients who are treated by physicians who know them little or not at all, many choices for death by the so-called autonomous patient will not be truly free or fully informed. Physicians hold a monopoly on the necessary information: prognosis, alternative treatments, and their costs and burdens. Like many technical experts, they are masters at framing the options to guarantee a particular outcome. This they do already in presenting therapeutic options to the "autonomous patient" for his decision, and there is no reason to think this will change should one of those options become "assistance for death." When the physician presents a depressed or frightened patient with a horrible prognosis and includes among the options the offer of a "gentle, quick release," what will the patient likely choose, especially in the face of a spiraling hospital bill or edgy children? The acceptance of physician-assisted death, ostensibly a measure enhancing the freedom of dying patients, will thus in many cases become a deadly license for physicians to recommend and prescribe death, free from outside scrutiny and immune from possible prosecution.

Contrary to the foolish hopes of advocates for autonomy, the insistence on voluntariness as the justifying principle cannot be sustained. It is naive to think that one can draw and hold a line between, on the one hand, physician-assisted suicide or voluntary euthanasia (practiced by doctors on willing patients) and, on the other hand, *non*voluntary euthanasia (where physicians perform mercy killing without the patient's request). Just think through how the situation would develop in practice. Almost no physician will accede to a request for deadly drugs unless he himself believes there are good reasons to justify the patient's choice for death (too much pain, loss of dignity, lack of self-command, poor quality of life, etc.); otherwise, he will try to persuade the patient to accept some other course of treatment or palliation, including psychotherapy for his suicidal wishes. Thus, in actual practice, physician-assisted suicide and euthanasia will be performed by physicians not out of simple deference to patient choice, but for reasons of mercy: this is a "useless" or "degrading" or "dehumanized" life that pleads for active, merciful termination, and therefore deserves my medical assistance.

But once assisting suicide and euthanasia are deemed acceptable for reasons of "mercy," then delivering those whom illness or dependence have dehumanized will also be acceptable, whether such deliverance is chosen or not. Once legalized, physician-assisted death will not remain confined to those who freely and knowingly elect it – nor do the most energetic backers of "death with dignity" really want it thus restricted. They see the slippery slope and eagerly embrace the principle that will justify the entire downward slide. Why? Because the vast majority of candidates who "merit" an earlier death cannot request it for themselves.

Persons in a so-called persistent vegetative state; those suffering from severe depression, senility, mental illness, or Alzheimer's disease; infants who are deformed; and retarded or dying children – all are incapable of requesting death, but are equally deserving of the new humane "aid in dying."

Lawyers and doctors, subtly encouraged by the cost containers, will soon aim to rectify this inequality regarding the "right to die." Invoking the rhetoric of equal protection, they will ask courts and ethics committees why those who are comatose or demented should be denied a right just because they cannot claim it for themselves. With court-appointed proxy consenters, we will quickly erase the distinction between the right to choose one's own death and the right to request someone else's – as we have already done in termination-of-treatment cases.

Doctors and relatives will not even need to wait for such changes in the law. Who will be around to notice when those who are elderly, poor, crippled, weak, powerless, retarded, depressed, uneducated, demented, or gullible are mercifully released from the lives that their doctors, nurses, and next of kin deem no longer worth living?

Precisely because most of the cases that are candidates for mercy killing are of this sort, the line between voluntary and involuntary euthanasia cannot hold, and it will be effaced by the intermediate case of mentally impaired or comatose persons who are declared no longer willing to live because someone else wills them not to. It is easy to see the train of abuses that are likely to follow the most innocent cases, especially because the innocent cases cannot be precisely and neatly distinguished from the rest.

That the specter of unauthorized euthanasia is not merely scaremongering has been confirmed by reports from the Netherlands, where assisted suicide and voluntary euthanasia practiced by physicians have been encouraged for over thirty years, under guidelines first informally established by the medical profession and later explicitly legalized (in 2002) under the "Termination of Life on Request and Assisted Suicide (Review Procedures) Act." Although the guidelines insist that choosing death must be informed and voluntary, a 1989 survey of 300 physicians disclosed that over 40 percent had already performed *non*voluntary euthanasia and over 10 percent had done so five times or more.[26] Another survey, this one commissioned by the Dutch government, provided even more alarming data: in 1990, besides 2,300 cases of voluntary euthanasia and 400 cases of physician-assisted suicide per year, there were over 1,000 cases of active *non*voluntary euthanasia performed without the patient's knowledge or consent, including roughly 140 cases in which the patients were *mentally totally competent.* (Comparable rates of nonvoluntary euthanasia for the United States would be about 20,000 cases per year.) In addition, there were 8,100 cases of morphine overdose with the intent to terminate life, of which 68 percent (5,508 cases) took place without the patient's knowledge or consent.[27]

Responding to international criticism and concern, the Dutch government commissioned another survey in 1995, which, the researchers claim, showed that the practice of physician-assisted suicide and euthanasia was now well regulated.[28] But Dr. Herbert Hendin and his colleagues, through careful scrutiny of the actual data, found much remaining cause for concern. The incidence of physician-caused death had increased since 1990 (from 3.7 percent to 4.7 percent of all deaths); 59 percent of Dutch physicians, defying the requirement of notification, still were not reporting their death-dealing deeds; more than half felt free to suggest euthanasia to their patients and about 25 percent admitted to ending patients' lives without consent. In 1995, Hendin found, 948 patients were directly put to death without their consent; another 1,896 patients (1.4 percent of all Dutch deaths that year) died as a result of opiates given with the explicit intent to cause death (and in over 80 percent of these cases, no request for death was made by the patient).[29]

And why are Dutch physicians performing nonvoluntary euthanasia? "Low quality of life," "relatives' inability to cope," and "no prospect for improvement" were reasons that physicians gave for killing patients without request; pain or suffering was mentioned by only 30 percent.[30] Is there any reason to believe that Dutch physicians are less committed than their American counterparts to the equal dignity of every life under their care?

Actual abuses aside, the legalized practice of physician-assisted death will almost certainly damage the doctor-patient relationship. True, some may be relieved to know that their old family doctor will now provide suicide assistance when asked. But many – especially those who lack strong social support or a close relationship with a trusted personal doctor – will rightly be suspicious. How can you trust a stranger-doctor to be wholeheartedly devoted to your best interests once he has a license to kill? Imagine the scene: you are old, poor, in failing health, and alone in the world; you are brought to the city hospital after a fall with fractured ribs and pneumonia. The nurse or intern enters late at night with a syringe full of yellow stuff for your intravenous drip. Never mind that, for now, death can be *legally* prescribed only on request. How soundly will you sleep?

Trust will suffer profoundly in subtler ways as well. Should physician-assisted death become a legal and a medical option, it will enter unavoidably – sometimes explicitly, sometimes tacitly – into many a doctor-patient encounter. Though there may be attempts to prevent physicians from introducing the subject, once the choice for active killing exists as a legal right and a medical option, there will be even stronger pressures to make sure that patients know they have it.* Ineluctably, patients will be forced to wonder about their doctor, regardless of how he handles the situation: did he introduce the subject because he secretly or unconsciously wishes to abandon me, or, worse, because he wishes I were dead? Does he avoid the subject for the same reasons, fearing to let me suspect the truth, or is it because he is indifferent to my suffering?

Few will openly express such fears and doubts. Because patients must rely on their doctor, they do not want to risk alienating him by seeming to distrust his motives and goodwill. Anyone who understands even a little of the subtle psychodynamics of the doctor-patient relationship can see immediately the corrosive effects of doubt and suspicion that will be caused by explicit (or avoided) speech about physician-assisted death.

Trust is no mere moral nicety, humanly desirable but medically dispensable. On the contrary, a patient's trust in the physician is a necessary ingredient in the therapeutic relationship and, at least indirectly, in the healing process itself. Mistrust produces stress, anger, and resistance to treatment. In the increasingly impersonal world of modern medicine, patients must simply presume that their caregivers are trustworthy even before they have shown that they deserve to be trusted. Especially under these conditions, the trust given to each physician stems largely from the trustworthiness attached to the profession as a whole. With the taboo

---

* Analogous pressures now operate in the matter of abortion. Even obstetricians opposed to abortion are often compelled to discuss it, if only to avoid later lawsuits should the child be born with abnormalities.

against physician-assisted killing broken, legitimate fears of deadly abuse of the new license will attach even to the most honorable physicians, whose ability to heal and comfort will therefore often be compromised. That your doctor has never yet put anyone to death will not matter; that the profession is legally entitled to do so will make a world of difference.

And it will make a world of psychic difference too for conscientious physicians. How easily will they be able to care wholeheartedly for patients when it is always possible to think of killing them as a "thera-peutic option"? Physicians get tired of treating patients who are hard to cure, who resist their best efforts, who are on their way down – especially when they have had no long-term relationship with them. "Gorks," "gomers," and "vegetables" are only some of the less-than-affectionate names such patients receive from interns and residents. Won't it be tempting to think that death is the best "treatment" for the little old lady "dumped" again on the emergency room by the nearby nursing home? Shall it be penicillin and a respirator one more time, or, perhaps, this time just an overdose of morphine?

Even if the morphine is not given, the thinkability of administering it will greatly alter the physician's attitude toward his patients. Today, hos-pital patients whose charts contain "Do Not Resuscitate" orders are very often treated differently from the rest. This happens not because of offi-cial policy, but despite it. A message is subtly conveyed that such patients are less – or even not at all – worthy of continued life. Should lethal drugs become a medical option, such psychological changes in physicians will be even more difficult to resist. And the consequences will often be deadly.

The taboo against physician-assisted death is crucial not only as a protection against physicians' weaknesses but even more, perhaps, against their arrogance – their willingness to judge, on the basis of *their own private prejudices and attitudes,* whether this or that life is unworthy of continued existence. This most important point is generally over-looked in discussions of assisted suicide because so much attention is focused on the patient's voluntary request for death. But to comply with such a request, the physician must, willy-nilly, play the part of judge, and his judgments will be decidedly nonmedical and nonprofessional, based on his own personal standards. One will choose to assist death over against moderate or impending senility, another against paraplegia, a third against blindness or incurable incontinence or prolonged depression. Only those requests resonating with the physician's own private criteria of "intolerable" or "unworthy" lives will be honored.

True, many people hold opinions and make judgments about which lives are worthier than others and even about which might be unworthy of continued existence. The danger comes when people *act* on these judgments, and especially when they do so under the cloak of professional prestige and compassion. Medical ethics, mindful that medicine wields formidable powers over life and death, has for centuries prevented physicians from acting professionally on the basis of any such personal judgment. Medical students, interns, and residents are taught – and acquire – a profound repugnance to medical killing as a major defense against committing, or even contemplating, the worst action to which their arrogance and/or their weaknesses might lead them.

Even the most humane and conscientious physician psychologically needs protection against himself and his weaknesses and arrogance, if he is to care fully for those who entrust themselves to him. A physician-friend who worked many years in a hospice caring for dying patients explained it to me most convincingly: "Only because I knew that I could not and would not kill my patients was I able to enter most fully and intimately into caring for them as they lay dying." The psychological burden of the license to kill (not to speak of the brutalization of the physician-killers) could very well be an intolerably high price to pay for physician-assisted euthanasia. The point, however, is not merely psychological; it is also moral and essential. My friend's horror at the thought that he might be tempted to kill his patients, were he not enjoined from doing so, embodies a deep understanding of the medical ethic and its intrinsic limits – an understanding of medicine itself.

Medicine's Outer Limits

Every activity can be distinguished from other activities. Sometimes the boundaries are indistinct: it is not always easy, especially today, to distinguish some music from noise or art from smut or some teaching from indoctrination. Medicine and healing are no different: it is sometimes hard to determine the boundaries with regard to both ends and means. Is all cosmetic surgery healing? Are placebos – or food and water – drugs?

There is, of course, a temptation to finesse these questions of definition or to deny the existence of boundaries altogether: medicine *is* whatever doctors *do,* and doctors do whatever doctors can. Technique and
power alone define the art. Since technique and power are ethically neutral, usable for both good and ill, this definition makes clear the need for
limits. Finding or setting limits to the use of powers is especially important when the powers are dangerous: it matters more that we know the
proper limits on the use of medical power – or military power – than the
proper limits on the use of a paintbrush or a violin.

The beginning of ethics regarding the use of power generally lies in
nay-saying. The wise setting of limits on the use of power is based on
discerning the excesses to which the power, unrestrained, is prone.
Applied to the professions, this principle would establish strict outer
boundaries – indeed, inviolable taboos – against those "occupational
hazards" to which each profession is especially prone. Within these outer
limits, no fixed rules of conduct apply; instead, prudence – the wise judgment of the man-on-the-spot – finds and adopts the best course of action
in the light of the circumstances. But the outer limits themselves are
fixed, firm, and nonnegotiable.

What are those limits for medicine? At least three are set forth in the
venerable Hippocratic Oath: no breach of confidentiality; no sexual relations with patients; no dispensing of deadly drugs.[31] These unqualified,
self-imposed restrictions are readily understood in terms of the temptations to which the physician is most susceptible – temptations concerning areas of vulnerability and exposure that the practice of medicine
requires of patients. Patients necessarily divulge and reveal private and
intimate details of their personal lives; patients necessarily expose their
naked bodies to the physician's objectifying gaze and investigating hands;
patients necessarily expose and entrust the care of their very lives to the
physician's skill, technique, judgment, and character. The exposure is, in
all cases, one-sided: the doctor does not reveal his intimacies, display his
nakedness, or offer up his embodied life to the patient. Mindful of the
meaning of such nonmutual exposure and vulnerability, and mindful too
of their own penchant for error and mischief, Hippocratic physicians voluntarily set limits on their own conduct, pledging not to take advantage
of or to violate the patient's intimacies, naked sexuality, or life itself.

The prohibition against killing patients, the first negative promise of

218 LEADING A WORTHY LIFE

self-restraint sworn to in the Hippocratic Oath, stands as medicine's first and most abiding taboo: "I will neither give a deadly drug to anybody if asked for it, nor will I make a suggestion to this effect.... In purity and holiness I will guard my life and my art." In forswearing the giving of poison, the physician recognizes and restrains a godlike power he wields over patients, mindful that his drugs can both cure and kill. But in forswearing the giving of poison *when asked for it*, the Hippocratic physician rejects the view that the patient's choice for death can make killing him – or assisting his suicide – right. For the physician, at least, human life in living bodies commands respect and reverence by its very nature. As its respectability does not depend upon human agreement, revocation of one's consent to live does not deprive one's living being of respectability. The deepest ethical principle restraining the physician's power is not the autonomy or freedom of the patient; neither is it his own compassion or good intention. Rather, it is the dignity and mysterious power of human life itself, and therefore also what the oath calls the purity and holiness of the life and art to which the physician has sworn devotion. A person can choose to be a physician, but he cannot simply choose what physicianship means.*

The Central Core

The central meaning of physicianship derives not from medicine's powers but from its goal, not from its means but from its end: to benefit the sick by the activity of healing. The physician as physician serves only the sick. He does not serve the relatives or the hospital or the national budget, strained by Medicare costs. Thus he will never sacrifice the well-

---

* The ancient Hippocratic physicians' refusal to assist in suicide was not part of an aggressive "vitalist" approach to dying patients or an unwillingness to accept mortality. On the contrary, understanding well the limits of the medical art, they refused to intervene aggressively when the patient was deemed incurable, and they regarded it as inappropriate to prolong the natural process of dying when death was unavoidable. Insisting on the moral importance of distinguishing between letting die (often not only permissible but laudatory) and actively causing death (impermissible), they protected themselves and their patients from their own possible weaknesses and folly, thereby preserving the moral integrity (the "purity and holiness") of their art and profession.

being of the sick to the convenience or feelings or pocketbook of the relatives or society. Moreover, the physician serves the sick not because they have rights or wants or claims, but because they are sick. The healer works with and for those who need to be healed, in order to help make them whole. Despite enormous changes in medical technique and institutional practice, despite enormous changes in nosology and therapeutics, the central purpose of medicine has not changed since the days of Hippocrates. It is just as true today that the ill desire to be whole; that wholeness means a certain well-working of the enlivened body and its unimpaired powers to sense, think, feel, desire, move, and maintain itself; and that the relationship between the healer and the ill is constituted around the desire of both to promote the wholeness of the one who is ailing.

The wholeness and well-working of a human being is, of course, a rather complicated matter, much more so than for our animal friends. Health and fitness seem to mean different things to different people, or even to the same person at different times of life. Yet not everything is relative and contextual. Beneath the variable and cultural lies the constant and organic: the well-regulated, properly balanced, and fully empowered human being. Indeed, only the existence of this natural and universal subject makes possible the study of medicine.

But human wholeness goes beyond the kind of somatic wholeness abstractly and reductively studied by the modern medical sciences. Whether or not doctors are sufficiently prepared by their training to recognize it, those who seek medical help in search of wholeness are not *to themselves* just bodies or organic machines. Each person intuitively knows himself to be a center of thoughts and desires, deeds and speeches, loves and hates, pleasures and pains, but a center whose workings are none other than the workings of his enlivened and mindful body. The patient presents himself to the physician as a psychophysical unity – not just a body, but also not a disembodied person who simply *has* a body. The

---

This view of the matter has been preserved in Western medical ethics to the present day. The proscription of medical killing has been reaffirmed in numerous medical codes and statements of principle. For example, the American Medical Association's current Code of Medical Ethics explicitly rules out physician-assisted suicide on the ground, among others, that it is "fundamentally incompatible with the physician's role as healer."

person and the body are self-identical. True, sickness may be experienced largely as belonging to the body apart from the self, but the healing wanted is the wholeness of one's entire embodied being. Not the wholeness of just soma, not the wholeness of just psyche, but the wholeness of *anthrôpos* as a (puzzling) concretion of soma and psyche is the benefit sought by the sick. This human wholeness is what medicine is finally all about, and what its true practitioners profess themselves duty-bound to protect, promote, and defend.

Can wholeness and healing, thus understood, ever be compatible with intentionally killing the patient? Can one benefit the patient *as a whole* by making him dead? There is, of course, a logical difficulty: how can any good exist for a being that does not? "Better off dead" is logical nonsense – unless, of course, death is not death indeed but instead a gateway to a new and better life beyond. Despite loose talk to the contrary, it is impossible to compare the goodness or badness of one's existence with the goodness or badness of one's nonexistence, because it nonsensically requires treating nonexistence as a condition one is able to experience and enjoy. But the error is more than logical: to intend and to act for someone's good requires his continued existence to receive the benefit.

To be sure, certain attempts to provide benefit may turn out to be lethal. Giving adequate morphine to control pain might induce respiratory depression leading unintentionally to death. But the intent to relieve the pain of the living presupposes that the living will remain alive. This must be the starting point in discussing all medical benefits: no benefit without a beneficiary.

Against this view, someone will surely bring forth the hard cases: patients so ill-served by their bodies that they can no longer bear to live – bodies riddled with cancer and racked with pain, against which their "owners" protest in horror and from which they insist on being released. Cannot the person "in the body" speak up against the rest, and request death for "personal" reasons?

However sympathetically we listen to such requests, we must see them as incoherent. Such person-body dualism cannot be sustained. "Personhood" is manifest on earth only in living bodies; our highest mental functions are sustained by and inseparable from lowly metabolism, respiration, circulation, and excretion. There may be circulating blood without consciousness, but there is never consciousness without blood.

Thus, one who calls for death in the service of personhood is like a tree seeking to cut its roots for the sake of growing its highest fruit. No physician, devoted to the benefit of the sick, can serve the patient *as person* by denying and thwarting his personal *embodiment*. The boundary condition, "No deadly drugs," flows directly from the center, "Make whole."

A number of objections have been raised to counter this defense of the venerable taboo against medical killing. Some critics say that medicine has no central purpose, while others protest that I have defined it too narrowly. For example, Franklin G. Miller and Howard Brody, criticizing an earlier version of this argument, pronounced me guilty of "essentialism," of believing that medicine serves only the goal of healing (despite the fact that I have always held that relief of suffering, along with promoting wholeness, is a necessary part of the medical task).* Instead, they propose that medicine serves a plurality of goals, "which includes healing, promoting health, and helping patients achieve a peaceful death." To achieve this last "important goal for medicine," they argue that in some circumstances "physician-assisted death may become, unfortunately, the best among the limited options."†[32]

Where does this allegedly *medical* goal of "helping patients achieve a peaceful death" come from? Miller and Brody do not say. It surely lacks the support of medical tradition and standard medical ethics. In their discussion, it rather appears out of the blue, simply stipulated and asserted, without an attempt at reasoned justification. Yet even if we place the best construction on their assertion and admit that medicine has something to offer patients regarding the end of life, Miller and

---

* "Essentialism" and "essentialist" often function as terms of abuse in medical ethics and philosophy, not unlike "racist" and "fascist" in political discourse. Even where the terms are given a definite meaning, the name calling often serves in lieu of a refutation. Is it wrong to say that the medical profession is, at its center, the healing profession?

† Miller and Brody are among the few writers who take seriously the need for preserving the intrinsic moral integrity of the medical profession and who share my view that medicine may violate the body only to serve a valid medical goal, not merely to satisfy the patient's requests. We differ in that they regard "achieving a peaceful death" as a legitimate medical goal, and they accept a dualism of person-body that I have criticized. In their view, "respect for the person, who finds his or her continued existence intolerable, takes precedence over the person's embodied life."

Brody are victims of imprecise thought. They have confused helping patients "experience peaceful *dying*" with helping them "*achieve* a peaceful *death*." Medicine surely owes patients assistance in their dying process – to relieve their pain, discomfort, and distress. This is simply part of what it means to seek to relieve suffering, always an essential part of caring *for the living*, even through the process of their dying. But medicine has never, under anyone's interpretation, been charged with *producing or achieving death itself*. Physicians cannot be serving their art or helping their patients – whether regarded as human beings or as persons – by making them disappear.

Despite their errors, Miller and Brody are at least clear that the "achievement of a peaceful death" is a goal *distinct* from healing; they will not try to smuggle euthanasia ("a peaceful death") into medicine under a revisionist idea of healing or relief of suffering. But others are willing to play the sophist. For example, Dr. Else Borst-Eilers, former chair of the Dutch Health Council and former minister of health, welfare and sport, has claimed that "there are situations in which the best way to heal the patient is to help him die peacefully and the doctor who in such a situation grants the patient's request acts as the healer *par excellence*."[33] This kind of euphemistic talk should produce chills in those who remember how a distinguished German jurist, Professor Karl Binding, and a distinguished German psychiatrist, Dr. Alfred Höche, proposed in 1920 the destruction of "life unworthy of life," which they described as "purely a healing treatment" and as a "healing work."[34] (Binding and Höche are discussed further in Chapter Ten below.) Argue if you must that killing those who are infirm and those who are miserable should be acceptable, but for goodness' sake have the decency not to pretend that it is healing.

To say it plainly, to bring nothingness is incompatible with serving wholeness: one cannot heal, or comfort, by making nil. The healer cannot annihilate if he is truly to heal. The physician-euthanizer is a deadly self-contradiction.

When Medicine "Fails"

We must acknowledge a difficulty: the central goal of medicine – health – is, in each case, a perishable good. Inevitably, patients get irreversibly sick, patients degenerate, patients die. Healing the sick is in principle a project that must at some point fail. And here is where all the trouble begins: how does one deal with "medical failure"? What does one seek when restoration of wholeness, or a substantial degree of wholeness, is by and large out of the question?

Contrary to the propaganda of the euthanasia movement, there is much that can be done. Indeed, by recognizing finitude yet knowing that we will not kill, we are empowered to focus on easing and enhancing the lives of those who are dying. First of all, medicine can follow the lead of the hospice movement and – reversing decades of shameful mismanagement – provide truly adequate relief of pain and discomfort, now technically feasible with little blunting of consciousness. Second, physicians (and patients and families) can continue to learn how to withhold or withdraw those technical interventions that are, in truth, merely burdensome or degrading additions to the unhappy end of a life – including, frequently, hospitalization itself. Ceasing treatment and allowing death to occur, when it will, seem to be quite compatible with the respect that life commands for itself. For life can be revered not only in its preservation, but also in the manner in which we allow a given life to reach its terminus. Rightly understood, removing unwanted and burdensome medical interventions serves not a patient's choice for death but rather his choice to continue to live as well as he can, even while he is dying. Doctors may and must allow to die, even if they must not intentionally kill.

Ceasing medical intervention, allowing nature to take its course, differs fundamentally from mercy killing. For one thing, death does not necessarily follow the discontinuance of treatment; Karen Ann Quinlan lived nine more years after the courts allowed the "life-sustaining" respirator to be removed in 1976. Not her physician, but the underlying fatal illness became the true cause of her death.*

What is most important *morally* is that the physician who ceases

---

* The result of the Quinlan case shows that the right to discontinue treatment cannot be part of some larger "right to die" or right "to determine the time and manner of one's own death." Indeed, it is both naive and thoughtless to believe that we can exercise such a "right" short of killing ourselves or arranging to be killed on schedule. The whole notion of the so-called right to die exposes the shallowness of our exaggerated belief in mastery over nature and fortune, a belief that informs our entire technological approach to death.

treatment does not intend the death of the patient. Even if death follows as a result of his action or omission, his intention is to avoid useless and degrading medical additions to the already sad end of a life. By contrast, in assisted suicide and all other forms of direct killing, the physician must necessarily and indubitably intend primarily that the patient be made dead. And he must knowingly and indubitably take on the role of the agent of death. This remains true even if he is merely an assistant in suicide. Morally, a physician who provides the pills or lets the patient plunge the syringe after he leaves the room is no different from one who does the deed himself. "I will neither give a deadly drug to anybody if asked for it, nor will I make a suggestion to this effect."

The same prohibition of killing by physicians continues to operate in other areas of palliative care where some have sought to deny its importance. For example, physicians often and quite properly prescribe high doses of narcotics to patients with widespread cancer in an effort to relieve severe pain, even though such medication carries an increased risk of death. But it is wrong to say that the current use of intravenous morphine in advanced cancer patients already constitutes a practice of medical killing. The physician here intends only the relief of suffering, which, again, presupposes that the patient will continue to live. Death, should it occur, is unintended and regretted.

The well-established rule of medical ethics that governs this practice is known as the principle of double effect, a principle widely misunderstood. It is morally licit to embrace a course of action that intends and serves a worthy goal (like relieving suffering), employing means that may have, as an unintended and undesired consequence, some harm or evil for the patient. Such cases are distinguished from the morally illicit efforts that indirectly "relieve suffering" by deliberately providing a lethal dose of a drug and thus eliminating the sufferer.

True, it may not always be easy to distinguish the two kinds of action from the outside. When death occurs from respiratory depression following administration of morphine, both the outcome and the proximate cause are the same whether the physician intended to kill or only to relieve pain. Physical evidence alone, obtained after the fact, will often not be enough to determine intent. But that is *exactly* why the principle of double effect is so important. Only an ethic opposing the intent to kill, reinforced by the law, keeps the physician from deliberately deadly acts. Such an ethic is necessary to enable physicians to serve and care for our residual wholeness and humanity right to the very end.

Being Humane and Being Human

Once we refuse the technical fix, physicians and the rest of us can also rise to the occasion: we can learn to act humanly in the presence of finitude. What those who are dying need far more than adequate morphine or the removal of burdensome chemotherapy is our presence and our encouragement. Dying people are all too easily reduced ahead of time to "thinghood" by those who cannot bear to deal with the suffering or disability of those they love. Withdrawal of contact, affection, and care is the greatest single cause of the dehumanization of dying. What medicine (and the rest of us) most owes to the dying is not the alleged humaneness of an elixir of death, but the humanness of connected living-while-dying. The treatment of choice is company and care.

The euthanasia movement would have us believe that the physician's refusal to assist in suicide or perform euthanasia constitutes an affront to human dignity. Yet one of their favorite arguments seems to me rather to prove the reverse. Why, it is argued, do we put animals out of their misery but insist on compelling fellow human beings to suffer to the bitter end? If mercy killing is not a contradiction for the veterinarian, why does the medical ethic absolutely rule it out? Is this not simply inhumane?

Perhaps inhumane, but not thereby inhuman. On the contrary, it is precisely because animals are not human that we must treat them (merely) humanely. We put dumb animals to sleep because they do not know that they are dying, because they can make nothing of their misery or mortality, because they cannot live deliberately – that is, humanly – in the face of their own suffering or dying. They cannot live out a fitting end. Compassion for their weakness and dumbness is our only appropriate emotion, and given our responsibility for their care and well-being, we do the only humane thing we can. But when a conscious human being asks us for death, by that very action he displays the presence of something that precludes our regarding him as a dumb animal. Humanity is owed humanity, not humaneness. Humanity is owed the bolstering of the human, even or especially in its dying moments, in resistance to the temptation to ignore its presence in the sight of suffering.

What humanity needs most in the face of evils is courage, the ability to stand against fear and pain and thoughts of nothingness. The deaths we most admire are those of people who, knowing that they are dying, face the fact frontally and act accordingly: they set their affairs in order, they arrange what could be final meetings with their loved ones, and yet, with strength of soul and a small reservoir of hope, they continue to live and work and love as much as they can for as long as they can. Because such conclusions of life require courage, they call for our encouragement – and for the many small acts of speech and deed that shore up the human spirit against despair and defeat.

Many doctors are in fact rather poor at this sort of encouragement. They tend to regard every dying or incurable patient as a failure, as if an earlier diagnosis or a more vigorous intervention might have avoided what is, in truth, an inevitable collapse. The enormous successes of medicine these past fifty years have made both doctors and laymen less prepared than ever to accept the fact of finitude. Physicians today are not likely to be agents of encouragement once their technique begins to fail.

It is, of course, partly for these reasons that doctors will be pressed to kill – and many of them will, alas, be willing. Having adopted a largely technical approach to healing, having medicalized so much of the end of life, doctors are being asked – often with thinly veiled anger – to provide a final technical solution for the evil of human finitude and for their own technical failure: If you cannot cure me, kill me. The last gasp of autonomy or cry for dignity is asserted against a medicalization and institutionalization of the end of life that robs those who are old and those who are incurably ill of most of their autonomy and dignity: intubated and electrified, with bizarre mechanical companions, once proud and independent people find themselves cast in the role of passive, obedient, highly disciplined children. People who care for autonomy and dignity should try to reverse this dehumanization of the last stages of life, instead of giving dehumanization its final triumph by welcoming the desperate goodbye-to-all-that contained in one final plea for poison.

The present crisis that leads to the demand for assisted suicide and active euthanasia is thus an opportunity to learn the limits of the medicalization of life and death, and to recover an appreciation of living with and against mortality. It is an opportunity for physicians to affirm the residual humanity – however precarious – that can be appreciated and cared for even in the face of incurable and terminal illness. Should doctors cave in, and should we allow them to become technical dispensers of death, we would not only be abandoning our loved ones and the duty to care; we would also exacerbate the worst tendencies of modern life, embracing technicism and so-called humaneness where humanity and encouragement are required but sorely lacking. On the other hand, should physicians hold fast, and should we all learn that finitude is no disgrace and that human wholeness can be cared for to the very end, medicine may serve not only the good of its patients but also, by example, the moral health of modern times.

CHAPTER TEN

A More Perfect Human

The Promise and Peril of Modern Science

L ADIES AND GENTLEMEN, please answer truthfully: If you were allowed to choose your own lot in life – or the lot of your children, already born or merely hoped for – which of these binary options would you select: Whole or damaged? Healthy or sickly? Strong or weak? Excellent or mediocre? Smart or stupid? Vigorous or feeble? Perfect or defective? Most of you, I am sure, would unhesitatingly choose the first alternative in each case – not only for yourselves and for your children, but also, since you are philanthropic souls, for the human race as a whole. Let me ask you to reconsider. We all need to be reminded that any actual pursuit of a more perfect human, especially with the help of science, likely comes at a heavy price in coin of our very humanity. We all need to remember how the pursuit of superior human beings can threaten ordinary human decency and humaneness. This lesson was driven home to me by an experience at the United States Holocaust Memorial Museum.

In 2005, while serving as the chairman of the President's Council on Bioethics, I was invited to speak in a lecture series devoted to the museum's important special exhibit, "Deadly Medicine: Creating the Master Race." I found myself intimidated as I had never been before, and even somewhat ashamed to be actually speaking publicly on that subject and in that awe-inspiring place, for opening one's mouth about unspeakable evil risks making it seem banal. And where speech cannot produce intelligibility, sacred memory counsels reverent silence. Yet as the very existence of the Holocaust Memorial Museum implies, some homage to the victims of the Holocaust might yet be rendered if, in remembering their catastrophe, we can also learn something about and for ourselves, gaining both knowledge and resolution to ensure that this will never happen again. In this spirit, I chose to speak little about the abominable uses that the Nazis made of science and medicine. I concentrated instead on the scientific outlook and aspiration that they inherited and exploited, and that dwell robustly among us today.

Science as Salvation: A Cautionary Tale

The "Deadly Medicine" exhibit was structured in a way that invited reflection on how the scientific outlook and aspiration influence us today. The first of its three parts, devoted to eugenic ideas and practices in the Weimar era (1919–1933), was called "Science as Salvation." It was followed by "The Biological State," through which those eugenic ideas were turned into Nazi racial hygiene (1933–1939), and then "The Final Solution," in which Nazi practices of racial hygiene (1939–1945) became mass-murderous. The exhibit thus located the Nazi medical atrocities in the company of an idealistic science that preceded it, and asked us to ponder whether there is any deep connection between them. The true power of the exhibit was the question it implicitly posed about the relation between the last phase and the first: What connection – not only historical but also *logical* – might exist between the Final Solution and the disposition to look to science for salvation? How, if at all, were the optimistic dreams of building a more perfect human through science and medicine related to the actual building of death camps in which real human beings, deemed worthless and worse, were exterminated like so much vermin?

Nothing in the exhibit suggested that the idealistic science of Weimar led necessarily to the Final Solution, though we learned there that the former sowed the seeds that were later used to grow the murderous fruit. And it was surely not the exhibit's intention to suggest even subliminally that noble science must become, however unintentionally, the handmaid of bestiality, or that genetics or medicine or psychiatry should come under suspicion of lending strength to deadly inhumanity. On the other hand, the exhibit – to its great credit – did not allow us lovers of science and progress to rest comfortably in the belief that the Nazis simply corrupted and perverted science, or that *their* science wasn't real science, or that their nefarious purposes were worlds apart from the humanitarian aspirations of modern medicine. The exhibit compelled us to consider whether the Nazi use of medical science might have been less a perversion of science than a logical though monstrously evil conclusion from certain dubious premises and attitudes in the scientific outlook itself, and especially from the prevailing assumptions about the role of science in human affairs. Is there perhaps something wrong – even *deadly* wrong – in seeing science as our salvation? If so, then we might need to be on our guard when this siren song is sung *to us*, as it is today being sung by an ever larger, louder, and more competent chorus.

To reach the ghastly result, the eugenic and perfectionist vision of Weimar had to be politicized by the Nazis, and in a most particular way. The project for the Final Solution depended decisively on the presence of a nearly omnicompetent totalitarian and tyrannical state, enforcing state-sponsored racial and ethnic hatreds, and assaulting the traditional teaching, both biblical and liberal democratic, of the irreducible and equal dignity of every human individual. God willing, we shall not see such a regime again.

Compassionate people like ourselves – enjoying the protections of liberal democratic institutions, a strong cultural prejudice favoring the individual against the collective, and the invaluable Judeo-Christian belief (however much diminished) in the sanctity of human life – may reasonably believe that "it can't happen here," and I agree with this conclusion. But the explicitly Nazi elements of tyranny and race hatred are not absolutely necessary for producing a deadly medicine, even if it never again becomes a "holocaust," and this is the first important point I wish to make. A free people, choosing for ourselves, can and very likely will produce similar deadly fruit from the same dangerous seeds, unless we are ever vigilant against the dangers. This chapter seeks to identify some of the deadly dangers that lurk in the seductive ideas and practices of science as salvation. The essence of the peril lies, ironically, in the zealous pursuit of the more perfect human.

A word of caution against a possible misunderstanding: although I shall be raising questions about the idea and practice of scientism, nothing that I say should be taken as "antiscience" or "antiscientist." The question before us is not the goodness of science and medicine as such, but the goodness of looking to science and medicine as the solution for the human condition, for the relief and salvation of man's estate.

The Holocaust Memorial Museum's exhibit opened with two images that posed the problem and set the stage for all my reflections. The first was the stunning Glass Man, originally displayed at the German Hygiene Museum in Dresden in 1930. The second was photographs of soldiers maimed in World War I.

Many of us are familiar with transparent models of the human body – today widely marketed as science toys for schoolchildren – but it is difficult to exaggerate the excitement that such models generated when they were a novelty. For the first time, the common man could behold a lifelike model of his insides, organ by organ, artery by artery, nerve by nerve, seeing with illuminated brilliance all the parts that made him run. The Glass Man, far from looking ashamed or diminished by this anatomizing invasion of his inner being, stands toweringly over us, fit and proud, with arms uplifted in a gesture of triumph – a model of human perfection, not to say apotheosis. Moreover, this perfect man clearly came not from the hand of God, but from a man even more perfect than himself: the scientific and medical visionary who would someday soon help humankind collectively achieve the healthy perfection here modeled in glass.

Make no mistake, this is serious business. For the Glass Man was the emblem of a new religion: in place of the God who became man, we have here the man become as a god. In place of the suffering Christ, arms stretched in crucifixion, we have the impervious Glass Man, arms elevated in self-exaltation. Behind the scene, in place of a Creator God who it is said sent His son who would, through his own suffering, take away the sins of the world, we have the scientific savior who would take away the sin of suffering altogether. The Glass Man, *in loco crucifixis*, is the perfect icon for salvific science.

The dream of perfect health and fitness is, of course, quite ancient. Indeed, three hundred years earlier, the great founders of modern science, Francis Bacon and René Descartes, summoned humankind to the conquest of nature for the relief of man's estate. Mastery and possession of nature, Descartes announced,

> is desirable not only for the invention of an infinity of artifices which would enable us to enjoy, without any pain, the fruits of the earth and all the commodities to be found there, but also and principally for the conservation of health, which is without doubt the primary good and the foundation of all other goods in this life.

As the sequel makes clear, Descartes had his eye on goals grander than the mere absence of disease or even just ordinary bodily health:

> For even the mind is so dependent on the temperament and on the disposition of the organs of the body, that if it is possible to find some means that generally renders men *more wise* and *more capable than they have been up to now*, I believe that we must seek for it in medicine.... [W]e could be spared an infinity of diseases, of the

body as well as of the mind, and *even also perhaps the enfeeblement of old age*, if we had enough knowledge of their causes and all the remedies which nature has provided us. [Emphasis added.][35]

The ancient dream of perfect health and fitness acquired a new prominence owing to the Great War, which had only recently ended when the Glass Man was created. Images from the aftermath of that war formed the second display of the "Deadly Medicine" exhibit, providing a counterpoint to the Glass Man and an explanation for his great social appeal.

Human deformities, from loss of limbs to loss of mind, came home from the war to Germany (and to all of Europe) by the tens and hundreds of thousands. The maimed and the enfeebled had rarely if ever been seen in such numbers – thanks, please note, to the great technological "advances" in waging war – and the response of the German mind, humiliated in the war, did not take the most compassionate turn. On the contrary, fear and loathing of the deformed and the defective were abundantly expressed, and this hatred of imperfection would fuel the desire to imitate the perfection represented by the Glass Man.

In 1920, right after the war and well before the Nazi period, a distinguished jurist, Karl Binding, and a distinguished physician, Dr. Alfred

Höche, both of them liberals, published a booklet entitled "On Permitting [or Authorizing] the Destruction of Life Unworthy of Life [*Lebensunwerten lebens*]." Beginning modestly with a defense of suicide and assisted suicide as morally acceptable, Binding and Höche move cunningly to a defense of killing those whose miserable condition of body or mind calls for the "healing remedy" of premature death from the hand of medical science. Contemplating the battlefield strewn with thousands of dead youths and comparing this with the mental hospitals dedicated to the long-term care of the demented and the mentally ill, Binding comments:

> One will be deeply shaken by the strident clash between the sacrifice of the finest flower of humanity in its full measure on the one side, and by the meticulous care shown to existences which are not just absolutely worthless but even of negative value, on the other.[36]

And Dr. Höche ends his part of the booklet with a paean to the dawning of a new age:

> There was a time, now considered barbaric, in which eliminating those who were born unfit for life, or who later became so, was taken for granted. Then came the phase, continuing into the present, in which ... preserving every existence, no matter how worthless, stood as the highest moral value. A new age will arrive – operating with a higher morality and with great sacrifice – which will actually give up the requirements of an exaggerated humanism and overvaluation of mere existence.[37]

A vigorous society, comprising only healthy and fit members, is more than justified in doing battle with the evils of deformity and disability by cleansing itself of the disabled and the deformed themselves.

These twin goals – the positive goal of seeking perfection, the negative goal of removing imperfection – are, to repeat, nothing new. They are of ancient pedigree. Indeed, they inspire much of the good that we do in life, and not only in medicine. We pursue virtue or excellence; we stifle vice and improve upon mediocrity. We urge our children to be good and our societies to be better; we try to eliminate the deficiencies and evils to which they are subject. For Christians, the counsel of perfection is even a divine injunction – "Be ye therefore Perfect, even as your Father which is in heaven is Perfect" (Matthew 5:48) – though the perfection Jesus had in mind, I am confident, cannot be pictured in glass.

There is always a danger that we will turn our opposition to deficiency into a rejection of those who bear it – that, for example, the battle against ignorance or impairment will translate into a hatred for the ignorant or the impaired. Indeed, we already call them after their imperfection ("he is a paraplegic," "she is a Down's"), conflating the sin and the sinner. This age-old tendency gallops in an age that not only extols and exhorts to perfection, but also gathers the scientific means to pursue it. The loathing of imperfection fuels the search for perfection, which in turn makes imperfection all the more intolerable. Such is the inner meaning of science seen as salvation, informed by a new idea of human perfection that has, in the end, little patience with human frailty and disability. That attitude is once again gaining strength, and this time it comes with first-rate science and powerful and precise technique. And, in contrast to pre–World War II Germany, it speaks in the seductive voices of freedom, compassion, and self-improvement.

The technologies of interest touch all aspects of human life, from beginning through middle to end. We are only at the dawn of the new age ushered in by deciphering the entire human genome, but already we are widely practicing genetic screening and prenatal and preimplantation genetic diagnosis, capable of identifying and rooting out the genetically unfit before they can be born. Advances in genetics, developmental biology, and neuroscience promise us all sorts of enhancements in human nature that would make us "better than well," both in body and in mind. On the negative side, the prime targets for correction and elimination are mental retardation and mental illness, severe bodily deformity and disability, and, later in life, dementia, debility, and enfeeblement – serious imperfections all. On the positive side, the prime targets for improvement are memory, muscularity, mood, temperament, and intelligence, with the Holy Grail being the conquest of biological senescence and human finitude.

Here I will take a synoptic overview of these promises, with special attention to eugenics. I will briefly review some of the main sources of danger – moral hazards that may be difficult for us to recognize because our practices appear to be governed not by coercive state policy but by free human choice. These moral hazards are of two sorts: dangerous practices and dangerous thoughts. Aiming to present "the big picture," the better to awaken us from our complacency, I will paint with broad strokes. Instead of logical proofs that speak to our analytic reason, I offer showings that appeal to our intuitions.

Dangerous Practices: Negative and Positive Eugenics

In the exciting early days of the genetic revolution, the 1960s and 1970s, both the positive and the negative eugenic goals were enunciated with great gusto. Conferences were held with bold titles like "Genetics and the Future of Man." At one such meeting, the distinguished molecular biologist Robert Sinsheimer enthused that "for the first time in all time a living creature understands its origins and can undertake to design its future.... [W]e can be the agent of transition to a wholly new path of evolution."[38]

About the same time, the Nobel laureate Joshua Lederberg saw in the prospect of human cloning an end to the rule of chance in human reproduction and the opportunity to perpetuate unaltered the genes of genius.[39] Many people looked forward to discovering whether a second Mozart might outdo the first. Also about the same time, the president of the American Association for the Advancement of Science, the gentle geneticist Bentley Glass, enunciated a new right: "the right of every child to be born with a sound physical and mental constitution, based on a sound genotype." Looking ahead to the reproductive and genetic technologies that are today rapidly arriving, Glass proclaimed, "No parents will in that future time have a right to burden society with a malformed or a mentally incompetent child."[*][40]

---

* Notice how Dr. Glass slides shamelessly from a nice-sounding idea ("You have a right to be born fit in body and mind") to a chillier corollary ("We have a right not to be burdened by your presence if you're sickly and stupid"). One suspects that the latter is his real concern, and it was first softened with the disguise of concern for the "right" to be born unflawed. The "right" to be born fit really translates into a duty not to allow "the unfit" to be born. (My thanks to Carol Staswick for this observation.)

Nowadays, we hear almost no such bold eugenics talk from mainstream scientists, though it is bruited about the margins by a small group of bioprophets summoning us to a posthuman future or a remaking of Eden. But eugenic vision and practice are gaining strength behind the fig leaf of "free choice." We are largely unaware that we as a society have already embraced the eugenic principle that "defectives shall not be born," because our practices are decentralized and because they operate not by coercion but by private reproductive choice. Genetic knowledge, we are told, is merely providing information and technique to enable people to make better decisions about their health or reproductive choices.

But our existing practices of genetic screening and prenatal diagnosis – and the newly arriving practices of gene editing to remove unwanted mutations – show that this claim is at best self-deceptive, if not disingenuous. The choice to develop and practice genetic screening and the choices of which genes to target for testing have been made not by the public but by scientists – and not for liberty-enhancing reasons but on eugenic grounds. Many practitioners of prenatal diagnosis refuse to do fetal genetic screening in the absence of a prior commitment from the pregnant woman to abort any afflicted fetus. Many pregnant women who wish *not* to know prenatal facts must withstand strong medical pressures for testing.

Practitioners of prenatal diagnosis, working today with but a fraction of the information now available from the Human Genome Project, already screen for a long list of genetic diseases and abnormalities, from Down syndrome to dwarfism. Possession of any one of these defects, they believe, renders a prospective child unworthy of life. Persons who happen still to be born with these conditions, having somehow escaped the spreading net of detection and eugenic abortion, are increasingly regarded as "mistakes," as inferior human beings who should not exist. Not long ago, at my own university, a physician making rounds with medical students stood over the bed of an intelligent, otherwise normal ten-year-old boy with spina bifida. "Were he to have been conceived today," the physician casually informed his entourage, "he would have been aborted." A woman I know with a child who has Down syndrome is asked by total strangers, "Didn't you have an amnio?" The eugenic mentality is taking root, and we are subtly learning with the help of science to believe that there really are certain lives unworthy of being born.

Not surprisingly, in the face of these practical possibilities, prominent intellectuals are now providing justification for this view of life. The current journals of bioethics, no less, are filled with writings that sweetly sing the song of Binding and Höche, albeit without the menacing German accent. But not all are reticent, either. Here for example are remarks from the writings of Peter Singer, DeCamp Professor of Bioethics in the University Center for Human Values at Princeton, on the question of killing infants with serious yet manageable diseases, such as hemophilia:

> When the death of a disabled infant will lead to the birth of another infant with better prospects for a happy life, the total amount of happiness will be greater if the disabled infant is killed. The loss of a happy life for the first infant is outweighed by the gain of a happier life for the second [even if not yet born]. Therefore, if killing the hemophiliac infant has no adverse effect on others, according to the total view, it would be right to kill him.[41]

In a magazine interview, Singer was asked, "What about parents conceiving and giving birth to a child specifically to kill him, take his organs, and transplant them into their ill older children?" He replied, "It is difficult to warm to parents who can take such a detached view, [but] they're not doing something really wrong in itself." The interviewer then asked, "Is there anything wrong with a society in which children are bred for spare parts on a massive scale?" The Princeton professor of bioethics replied, "No."[42] Do not underestimate what it means for us that such coolly lethal opinions, regarded since 1945 as barbaric, are today again treated with seriousness, and that promoters of such opinions can occupy professorial chairs of ethics at places like Princeton.

Similar ideas and practices are coming into vogue at the other end of life. The practice of physician-assisted suicide and euthanasia has been legal in the Netherlands for several decades and more recently in our own states of Oregon, Washington, Vermont, and California. Other American states are today rethinking their proscriptive laws. In 2015, the Supreme Court of Canada overturned a longstanding legislative ban on physician-assisted suicide, declaring that it violated a basic human right, and gave the legislature one year to come up with a new law governing the practice. For a variety of reasons, an age of legalized euthanasia is likely to be soon upon us. Few are going to speak as openly as Peter Singer about ending worthless lives. But like him, they will promote the deadly practice under the banner of autonomy and choice, graced with slogans of a dignified death – and, of course, utilitarian appeals to cut the costs of care.

To be sure, large familial and social difficulties of a mass geriatric society are already upon us and are destined to become much more severe. Although vast numbers of old people are today healthier and longer-lived than ever before, the price that many of them are paying for the extra decade of vigorous old age between seventy and eighty is often a decade of enfeeblement, debility, and dementia after that. In 2015, over 5.3 million Americans were afflicted with Alzheimer's disease, a number that is predicted to triple before midcentury. Thanks to our ability to treat acute illnesses and crises, roughly 40 percent of us can expect to have about ten frail, enfeebled, and often demented years at the end of our lives, incapable of caring for ourselves in a world of fewer and fewer familial caregivers and, in most cases, without resources to purchase decent home or institutional care. Already we hear the dire statistics about the proportion of health-care costs spent futilely on the last six months of life. Already we hear the call for rationing, for not wasting resources on persons with a "low quality of life" – a gentle Americanism for the German "life unworthy of life."

I do not minimize the ethical anguish that often confronts patients and families when loved ones linger on, their memories gone, their lives little resembling anything like the one they enjoyed. But I still shudder when I hear the call for a technical quick solution to the need for long-term care, for I know what we have to fear when a shallow notion of death with dignity enlists deadly medical force to solve society's demographic and economic problems.

In the Netherlands, as I pointed out in the last chapter, we have seen a foreshadowing of the future. There the "right to die" has flowed down the slippery slope to its most radical meaning and then some: from a right to refuse treatment, to a right to control one's own dying, to a right to be assisted in "becoming dead," to a right to choose euthanasia, to a right to be mercifully dispatched by one's doctor should *he* decide that you are "better off dead." The descent into unauthorized euthanasia is confirmed by official reports from the Netherlands, with roughly a third of Dutch doctors, speaking under immunity, confessing that they have been practicing *non*voluntary euthanasia, without the consent or knowledge of patients, including on a significant number of patients who were mentally totally competent. In 2005, without anyone making a fuss, the Dutch issued a protocol for euthanizing severely ill newborns. If this can happen among the liberal and tolerant Dutch, are we so sure that it cannot happen here?

The battle against imperfection by eliminating the imperfect is only part of our current story. Much more vigorous action is occurring in the scientific and biotechnical quest for human improvement, for doing nature one better and making a more perfect human being. Psychoactive drugs are being developed to increase concentration, to erase troubling memories, or to alter personality. Embryos that are now screened for the presence of disease-causing genetic abnormalities may also soon be screened for the presence of certain desirable genetic traits: greater height, calmer temperament, perfect pitch, and (eventually) also higher IQ. And although precise genetic engineering of designer babies seems to me to be pure science fiction, human cloning (recently achieved for the first time in embryos) does hold out the prospect of perpetuating superior genotypes. Genetic engineering of adults offers the possibility of enhancing muscle bulk and performance. There is active research to increase the maximum life expectancy through hormone treatments or stem-cell-based transplantable tissues, or the ultimate weapon: control of the genes that determine the rate of aging and the age of death. Research is also being done on human-computer interactions, beginning with attempts to enable the deaf to hear and the blind to see, but perhaps leading to computer implants in the brain that would enable us to download entire libraries at the click of a button.

Apart from a few zealots such as the immortalists or the bionics boosters around *Wired* magazine, most people exploring these prospects are not trying to build a superman or a posthuman being. They are, by their own lights, just trying to enhance human performance through biotechnical means, offering a psychophysical route to human improvement that could supplement and extend the improvements we cultivate for ourselves through education or personal training. Yet there is no doubt that such enhancements will be widely desired and used to satisfy age-old dreams of better children, superior performance, ageless bodies, and happy souls – especially with large commercial interests hyping the benefits and creating new demands. Those biotechnical means may even be enlisted to advance certain social goals, such as enabling soldiers and pilots to go long stretches without sleep, or schoolteachers and prison wardens to pacify the unruly.

We have only begun to consider the momentous ethical and social questions in store for us as we head down this road. A report from the President's Council on Bioethics, *Beyond Therapy: Biotechnology and the Pursuit of Happiness* (2003) is an early effort to articulate our unease at these prospects.[43] We are right to be concerned about the meaning of pursuing venerable human goals by "magical" technical means, just as we are right to be concerned about the wisdom of trying to transcend through technology the parameters of our given nature, the delicately balanced product of eons of gradual evolution.

Will human life really be better if we turn to biotechnology to fulfill our deepest human desires? Will those desires be properly satisfied? Will our enhanced activities really be *better*, and better *humanly*? There is an old expression: "To a man armed with a hammer, everything looks like a nail." To a society armed with biotechnology, the activities of human life may come to be seen in purely technical terms, and more amenable to improvement than they really are. Worse, like Midas, we may get more easily what we asked for only to realize it is vastly less than what we really wanted.

We want better children – but not by turning procreation into manufacture or by altering their brains to give them an edge over their peers. We want to perform better in the activities of life – but not by becoming mere creatures of our chemists or by turning ourselves into bionic tools designed to win and achieve in inhuman ways. We want longer lives – but not at the cost of living carelessly or shallowly with diminished aspiration for living well, and not by becoming so obsessed with our own longevity that we care little about the next generations. We want to be happy – but not by means of a drug that gives us happy feelings without the real loves, attachments, and achievements that are essential for true human flourishing.

The pursuit of these perfections, defined scientifically and obtained technologically, not only threatens to make us more intolerant of imperfection, both our own and our neighbor's. It also threatens to sell short the true possibilities of human flourishing, which have always been found in love and friendship, work and play, art and science, service and worship. Our deepest longings are not for artificial contentment and factitious achievements, but for lives that are meaningful, connected, and humanly flourishing. There can be no perfecting of human beings or enhancement of human life without knowing what human flourishing actually is. And no one can presume to judge any change in human nature or human activity to be an improvement – let alone a "perfection" – without knowing what is humanly good.

Dangerous Thinking: Soulless Scientism

The question we must therefore put to the human enhancers and the posthuman futurists is this: What knowledge of the good do you have that entitles you to gamble the human future on your hunches that these proposed alterations will truly make us better or happier? It is a question that science and technology simply cannot answer, and worse, that our bioprophets do not even think to ask. No danger we face in the coming age of biotechnology is greater than the danger of careless and shallow thinking.

If we are to avoid both the deadly and the dehumanizing results from our uses of biotechnology, we will need to be vigilant in our practices and resourceful in our thinking. Everything will depend on whether the technological disposition is allowed to proceed to its self-augmenting limits, or whether it can be restricted and brought under intellectual, spiritual, moral, and political rule. But on this front, I regret to say, the news is not encouraging. For the relevant intellectual, spiritual, and moral resources of our society, the legacy of civilizing traditions painfully acquired and long preserved, are taking a beating – not least because they are being called into question by the findings of modern science itself. The technologies present troublesome ethical dilemmas, but the underlying scientific notions – so we are told – call into question the very foundations of our ethics.

In the nineteenth and the early twentieth century, the challenge came in the form of Darwinism and its seeming opposition to biblical religion, a battle initiated not so much by the scientists as by the beleaguered defenders of orthodoxy. In our own time, the challenge comes from molecular biology, behavioral genetics, neuroscience, and evolutionary psychology, fueled by their practitioners' overconfident belief in the suf-

ficiency of their reductionist explanations of all vital and human phenomena, and in some cases by an explicit intention to overthrow our
venerable moral and religious beliefs.

Such a transformation of moral outlook is welcomed by many of our
leading scientists and intellectuals. In 1997, the luminaries of the International Academy of Humanism – including the biologists Francis Crick,
Richard Dawkins, and E.O.Wilson, and the humanists Isaiah Berlin,
W.V. Quine, and Kurt Vonnegut – issued a statement in defense of cloning research in higher mammals and human beings. Their reasons were
revealing:

> What moral issues would human cloning raise? Some world reli-
> gions teach that human beings are fundamentally different from
> other mammals – that humans have been imbued by a deity with
> immortal souls, giving them a value that cannot be compared to
> that of other living things. Human nature is held to be unique and
> sacred.... As far as the scientific enterprise can determine, ...
> [h]umanity's rich repertoire of thoughts, feelings, aspirations, and
> hopes seems to arise from electrochemical brain processes, not
> from an immaterial soul that operates in ways no instrument can
> discover.... Views of human nature rooted in humanity's tribal
> past ought not to be our primary criterion for making moral deci-
> sions about cloning.... [I]t would be a tragedy if ancient theologi-
> cal scruples should lead to a Luddite rejection of cloning.[44]

In order to justify ongoing research, these intellectuals were willing to
shed not only traditional religious views but *any* view of human distinc-
tiveness and special dignity, their own included. They fail to see that the
scientific view of man they celebrate does more than insult our vanity. It
undermines our self-conception as free, thoughtful, and responsible
beings, worthy of respect because we alone among the animals have
minds and hearts that aim far higher than the mere perpetuation of our
genes. It undermines, as well, the beliefs that sustain our mores, practices, and institutions – including the practice of science itself.

The problem lies less with the scientific findings themselves than
with the shallow philosophy that recognizes no other truths, and with
the arrogant pronouncements of the bioprophets. Here, for example is

the eminent psychologist Stephen Pinker railing against any appeal to the human soul:

> Unfortunately for that theory, brain science has shown that the mind is what the brain does. The supposedly immaterial soul can be bisected with a knife, altered by chemicals, turned on or off by electricity, and extinguished by a sharp blow or a lack of oxygen. Centuries ago it was unwise to ground morality on the dogma that the earth sat at the center of the universe. It is just as unwise today to ground it on dogmas about souls endowed by God.[45]

One hardly knows whether to be more impressed with the height of Pinker's arrogance or with the depth of his shallowness. Pinker is ignorant of the fact that "soul" need not be conceived as a "ghost in the machine" or as a separate "thing" that survives the body, but can be understood (à la Aristotle) to be the integrated powers of the naturally organic body. He has not pondered the relationship between "the brain" and the whole organism, or puzzled over the difference between "the brain" of the *living* and "the brain" of the dead. He seems unaware of the significance of emergent properties, powers, and activities that do not reside in the materials of the organism but emerge only when the materials are formed and organized in a particular way; he does not understand that this empowering organization of materials – the vital form – is not itself material. But Pinker speaks with the authority of science, and few are both able and willing to dispute him on his own ground.[46]

There is, of course, nothing novel about reductionism and materialism of the kind displayed here; these are doctrines with which Socrates contended long ago. What is new is that, as philosophies, they seem (to many people) to be vindicated by scientific advance. Here, in consequence, is perhaps the most pernicious result of our technological progress, more dehumanizing than any actual manipulation or technique, present or future: the erosion, perhaps the final erosion, of the idea of man as noble, dignified, precious, or godlike, and its replacement with a view of man, like nature, as mere raw material for manipulation and homogenization.

Hence, our peculiar moral crisis. We are in turbulent seas without a landmark precisely because we adhere more and more to a view of human life that both gives us enormous power and, *at the same time*, denies every possibility of nonarbitrary standards for guiding its use. Though well equipped, we know not who we are or where we are going. We triumph over nature's unpredictability only to subject ourselves, tragically, to the still greater unpredictability of our capricious will and our fickle opinions. Engineering the engineer as well as the engine, we race our train we know not where. In the absence of any rich view of human flourishing, our pursuit of a more perfect human is at best chimerical. That we do not recognize our predicament is itself a testament to the depth of our infatuation with scientific progress and our naive faith in the sufficiency of our humanitarian impulses.

Let me return to look again at the Glass Man in the light of this discussion. It turns out that the Glass Man is not transparent but opaque. It pretends to show us the innermost man, but in truth it renders his humanity permanently absent. Yes, we see the liver, the kidneys, and the colon, but we learn nothing about the soul. The mysterious character of the human person has not been explained; rather, it has been ignored – nay, banished. The problem is not that anatomizing did not reveal the soul; no one thought it could. It is rather that anatomizing ignores and then denies the soul, denies the wholeness and the inner depth of the human being, even in the very act that seems for the first time to make it visible to him.

In one respect, however, the Glass Man reveals a permanent truth about the human being, ironically driving home a lesson that I do not believe its makers meant to teach. When we look at the head and face, hoping to find evidence of the human soul within, what stares back at us is only the bony skull, universally the mark and symbol of death. Lurking beneath the outer surface of this godlike man is the truth about his vaunted perfection: alas, poor Yorick, death will be his fate, medicine or no medicine. The skull that betokens death for the individual human being betokens also – in a way that the Glass Man's creators surely didn't appreciate – the deadly consequence for a society of pursuing bodily perfection while turning our backs on those who can never reach it.

The idealistic German scientists could not have known that the Glass Man was the harbinger of anything like the Final Solution. But they should have known that the biologizing, soulless account of human life that they were trumpeting is always deadly to humanity, even if not one crematorium is built. A dehumanizing account of human life can all by itself produce a holocaust of the human spirit.

To keep human life human, we need first and foremost a more natural biology and anthropology, a robust account of the nature and meaning of our own humanity that will do justice to life as lived, with its high aspirations, deep longings, and rich possibilities for flourishing. In seeking such an account, we must draw on the wisdom of poets and philosophers and the insights of the great religious traditions. But one thing is clear: our inclination to think only in terms of the American ideals of freedom and equality will not be adequate to the task. In addition, we will need a robust account of *human dignity*, of our special standing, which has been variously captured in terms of the "rational animal," or "made in the image of God," or "higher than the beasts, lower than the angels." Faced with the twin dangers of death and dehumanization, it will be important to advance an account of human dignity that does justice both to (a) the equal dignity we all share by virtue of our common humanity and to (b) the dignity to which we can all aspire by exercising our humanity to the greatest and finest extent possible. Neither the dignity of equal humanity nor the dignity of human excellence is imageable in the Man of Glass.

There is no question that modern science is one of the truly great monuments to the human intellect. Precisely because it is value-neutral and heuristically materialist, it gains the kind of knowledge of how our bodies work that is tremendously helpful in ameliorating disease and relieving suffering. But it cannot even come within hailing distance of human perfection, let alone salvation. In seeking his salvation, if salvation is to be sought, man must continue to look beyond himself, while humbly using his limited powers and still more limited wisdom to try to make our world a little bit better. In the end, the good that we will do with science and medicine can be completed only by avoiding those evils that come from seeing health as salvation, the soul as biochemicals, and medicine as the messiah.

III · In Search of Wisdom

Learning, Teaching, and Truth

CHAPTER ELEVEN

The Aims of Liberal Education

On Seeking Truth

COLLEGIATE LIBERAL EDUCATION in the United States is almost everywhere in retreat, not to say in decline. The reasons are many and the outcome overdetermined. Many people now seeking an education – its so-called "consumers" – regard liberal learning as a luxury at best. With college tuition and postgraduation debt soaring, practical-minded young Americans increasingly concentrate on "more useful" studies in the effort to obtain quickly marketable skills and start building careers. Departments of computer science are booming, while venerable departments of classics are closing down. Larger, more democratized college enrollments have also changed the character of our collegians, with fewer people drawn to education as an end in itself. President Obama seriously proposed that colleges be ranked according to the earning power their bachelor's degree confers upon graduates.

But economic concerns are only part of the story. Liberal education today is languishing largely because of changes in the academy itself over the last half century. Increasingly, science and technology rule the academic roost, partly because of the great success and prestige of research and development, fueled by lavish public and private funding and encouraged from within by the desire to be useful to society. Narrowly educated faculty members, whose rank and reputation rest solely on peer-reviewed publications, stick to their highly specialized lasts. No one will be deflected from his own research by teaching outside of his specialty. No one cares to ask, "What would a liberally educated person need to learn these days?" With some notable exceptions, so-called liberal education at most colleges consists in some minimum distribution requirements across the various fields, allowing students to select among the courses said to satisfy them. Myriad courses exist to advance their careers. We have none to help them think about life's big questions. No one even attempts a rationale for the undergraduate curriculum: who was the last president of a major American university to speak or write thoughtfully about the aims of higher education or the idea of the university?

Academic vision being absent on campus, the void is filled by politics. Across the humanities and social sciences, ideology intrudes itself into the classroom, as teachers seek converts and reward disciples, while intimidating or even silencing those with contrary views. A worrisome illiberality infects many a liberal arts college. Diversity is now the goal of college admissions and faculty hiring, but the most important diversity – the diversity of opinion and belief – is ignored or rejected. Multicultural-ism, once an attempt to broaden the horizons of blinkered American youth, has spawned grievances against the once dominant culture, lead-ing to a rejection of many of the great works that once were the core of a humanistic and liberal education. Never mind requiring people to read these old books: How many English departments even offer a course on Shakespeare or George Eliot or Herman Melville anymore? How many political science departments offer a course on Plato's *Republic* or Locke's *Second Treatise* or the Federalist Papers? Most disheartening is the tri-umph of the postmodern idea that truth is but a social creation, each group entitled to live by its own. With respect to the most important human matters, the university is not a genuine community of fellow truth seekers, sharing common human questions and concerns, but an aggregate of self-promoting identity groups, each bargaining to advance its own sectarian "truths." *Veritas?* Forget about it.

No wonder liberal education is in retreat. Who today can articulate what it is and what it is for?

In its original understanding, liberal education was, first of all, the education befitting a free man, rather than a slave, and by extension the education of a human being free enough from the burdens of meeting necessity to have the leisure to seek self-improvement through learning, and thus to prepare for a life of leadership (largely political, military, or religious) in his community. Liberal education, at first glance, was the education of gentlemen, of a governing elite.

But there was a second and more radical form of liberal education, concerned with liberating people from slavish adherence to their unexamined opinions – the problem made famous by Socrates' image of the cave in Plato's *Republic*. All human beings, wittingly or not, look at the world through opinions inherited from parents and society – ultimately from what we now call "opinion leaders," but once upon a time from poets, statesmen, or prophets. Because it insisted on unearthing and examining these roots of our beliefs and on critical self-examination and reflection, liberal education in this sense was necessarily philosophical. Far from simply endorsing conventional opinion and the status quo, it raised questions about them, fully open to the possibility that the results could be personally upsetting and socially disturbing. A free mind, wanting to avoid self-deception, cares more for truth than for reputation and social approval.

Despite the sad state of liberal education today, and despite the illiberal attempts on many college campuses to silence unorthodox opinions, a concern for truth, I am pleased to say, is hard to eradicate, especially in the young. My forty years of teaching undergraduates and watching their delight in learning sustains my belief that our intellectual and spiritual prospects are much better than we might think from listening to the nihilistic preaching of the professoriate. Despite abundant cultural rot and the lack of edifying encouragement, American society still tosses up superb young people who want more from life, and from their teachers, than they are now getting. Yes, their passions can get the better of them. But high-minded ideas can still appeal to their best aspirations for themselves. If offered opportunities and encouragement for a genuinely liberating education, many of them, in my experience (at St. John's College and at the University of Chicago), will rise to the occasion: they will examine their assumptions, they will search for better understanding, they will try to avoid lying to themselves. They will take to liberal education like a fish to water. What they need most is for their elders – also still fellow seekers, but a little further down the road – to point the way.

In the fall of 1981, at the University of Chicago where I had been a student and was now a young faculty member, I was given such an opportunity. I was asked to deliver the annual "Aims of Education" address to the entering first-year class in the college, assembled in Rockefeller Chapel during orientation week. Here, unmodified, is what I said then, and what I would say again today. Would that other people, at other colleges, were now saying similar things.

The Aims of Liberal Education

This is a rare occasion. Many of you probably will not return again to Rockefeller Chapel, and certainly not together, until you return to graduate. And unless you cut short your summer vacations to attend this annual event, you are unlikely to hear another public lecture on the aims of education. Once classes begin, both students and faculty are usually much too busy getting things done to think much about what they are doing and why, and that is as it must be – though there have been times and may again be times when such collective radical self-scrutiny becomes part of the everyday business of this campus.

Yet though rare, this is nevertheless a typically Chicago occasion. It is the legacy of this university, and especially of this college, to examine fundamental questions, and to do so thoughtfully, reflectively, critically – even self-critically. It is also typical of Chicago that there is no typical Chicago answer to any serious question: two professors, three opinions. We are suspicious of orthodoxy and simple-mindedness. We love diversity, independence, and originality. And having searched our own minds, each of us knows, or thinks he or she knows, what education is all about. Please understand, therefore, that I do not aspire to speak for the university or the college. I merely aspire to speak the truth.

Let me then start closer to the ground with a factual truth. Twenty-seven years ago, early in Orientation Week, I sat in your place here in Rockefeller Chapel, at the close of a tour of the campus, while the secretary of the university's alumni association discoursed on the construction and structure of this august building. I would not have remembered the occasion except that a photograph of the event taken from above later graced the university's alumni magazine, showing our very young and eager faces gazing on high at the tower.

If it were possible to elevate the soul merely by tilting back the head to look aloft on the ceiling, that part of Orientation Week could have been edifying and ennobling. Indeed, though I recall being filled with excitement and some apprehension at starting college, I do not remember that anything elevating was said during Orientation Week, but if it were, I was in all likelihood beneath response. I was too young, too shallow, too ignorant.

If truth be told, I remember altogether little in particular of what my teachers tried to teach me during my four collegiate years. Yet I have known for some time that, in decisive ways, my experience here changed my life. I encountered one skillful teacher who forced me to acknowledge to myself that there were important questions to which the answers I carried around unthinkingly were inadequate. I was introduced to the writings of great thinkers and teachers, nearly all of them dead, from whom in later years I have increasingly drawn sustenance in my pursuit of these questions. I made a few deep and lifelong friendships, friendships based in large measure on sharing in conversation the attempt to understand our experience of the world and of our own humanity. The college's thoroughgoing insistence on self-conscious and philosophical examination of basic assumptions and presuppositions left its mark, and eventually, I am sure, contributed to my exchanging a life of the *practice* of science for one of *thinking* about it and its multiple bearings upon human affairs. Though my liberal education began to grow in earnest only much later, the college planted the seeds. Accordingly, I have it to thank for many of the joys – and the sadnesses – of the life of reflection and self-examination to which it beckoned.

You now know much more than you need to about me. But I know very little about you, taken individually. Yet to speak intelligibly one must know to whom one is speaking. You, of course, know or have been told by others this week how unusual and exceptional you are, individually and collectively. I will begin by assuming that you are common. You are eighteen, plus or minus, and nearly all of you are Americans of the late twentieth century. Because you are young, your experience of the world is limited, largely to home and high school. Almost all of you have watched much television, many of you read the newspapers, some of you have traveled, and a few of you have read good books. You love novelty, care little for the past, and think less about the long-term future. In brief, you are smart, talented, and largely ignorant. Because you are Americans, you are tolerant, easygoing on yourselves and others, usually restless, and by and large concerned with what is useful and practical. Most of all, all of you pride yourselves on your individuality and almost certainly resent my treating you as part of a common group.

Yet there is in fact something uncommon about you, which, alas, you all have in common, and in which I too share. We have all chosen the University of Chicago. For you, it is the first of a series of important choices that will define or delimit your lives – like choices of career, spouse, and place to live – choices that necessarily exclude legions of other possibilities. You have, by choosing a college, closed many a door – to grow up means choosing one way from the myriad ways of life once open to you; but in having chosen Chicago, a road less traveled by, you have passed through a door which, as I hope you will discover, leads to a way of life that will permit you greater understanding of what you are and whither you are tending and will even enable you to appreciate in thought something of the roads you have not taken. The one choice that enriches all other choices is the choice for liberal education, an education open to us all, by the way, because of our *common* humanity. Let us, therefore, say goodbye to you and me, to our individuating differences, and think together about liberal education.

The End of Liberal Education

Let us begin by distinguishing liberal education from other sorts of education. Let us set aside that part of higher education that prepares one for one's future career, whether in the professions of law, medicine, divinity, engineering, or business, or in scholarship or scientific research. In these cases, the mind is specifically prepared in the basic concepts and methods, either of practical arts, say, of legal reasoning or of healing, or of specialized investigation, in each case according to the accepted canons of the profession or discipline. Bodies of accumulated knowledge are transmitted, skills are acquired, and the particular methods of problem solving are learned through practice. Expertise, competence, mastery are the marks of accomplishment. I do not for a moment discount the importance of such achievement and such training, as it is indispensable for our working lives; but it is not liberal education. True, medicine or law or biology or politics *can* be studied, as we shall see, in a liberal way, but when taught professionally or pre-professionally they are not. True, scholarly and scientific research can be an aid to liberal education – and vice versa – but the training or preparation of future scholars and scientists is not what liberal education is about or for. For the aim of liberal education is other than the advancement of the sum of human learning or the discovery of new truths or the growth of knowledge from more to more.

But neither is liberal education just the transmission of accumulated knowledge, the pouring of old learning into new receptacles, or even the initiation of new members into the great tradition, understood as tradition. It is, of course, hard to call someone well educated who is ignorant of the Bible and the writings of Homer and Plato, Shakespeare and Locke, Rousseau and Tolstoy, Newton and Einstein, Darwin and Freud. Indeed, because of their depth, range, and power, these writings are the best materials for the practice of liberal education. But desirable though it is to know one's intellectual forebears, to know them as part of the tradition – or, in the current jargon, as part of the so-called history of ideas – is only to know *about* them and *about* what they thought, not to *think with them*. The history of thought, however valuable, is not itself thinking. And to regard the so-called tradition as authoritative, to accept its authority because of its venerability, is to give over the activity of thinking here and now. The same must also be said for the docile ingestion and unassimilated retention of the fruits of contemporary sciences, whether received authoritatively from written textbooks or even from the mouths of Nobel laureates.

I would also distinguish liberal education from those aspects of education that aspire to or attain a broadening of views, an elevating of sensibilities and tastes, or even the sharpening of intellectual skills. These are, of course, all fine things. It is good to be exposed to and to know about many variations in culture, beliefs, and human activities. Doing so can counteract ethnocentrism and encourage respect for other cultures. But learning is more than exposure, and collecting broad variations does not mean gaining deeper understanding. Liberal education is more than general education, attainable by distribution requirements and a smattering of this and that.

It is also more than aesthetic and cultural enrichment. Our tastes and sensibilities can certainly stand refinement: it should be one of your goals here to learn to recognize and to love the difference between what is noble and beautiful and what is vulgar and ugly. But even the love of Homer and Mozart or the growing taste for the beautiful in nature or in human character is not yet what I mean.

Liberal education also goes beyond acquiring the skills of careful reading, writing, listening, speaking, arguing, calculating, looking, and experimenting. These skills – often called the liberal arts – sharpen the mind and are invaluable *as instruments* for its proper work. But the skills alone are insufficient. When severed from the true work of the free mind, preoccupation with skills can be enslaving, a kind of mental gymnastics which tones one's mental muscles and swells one's vanity, but which in fact is useless and vain. What is the point of knowing "how to think" if one never seriously engages in thinking?

What, then, could be left for the aim of liberal education, if we exclude professional training, research and scholarship, general broadening and culture, the arts of learning, and familiarity with the intellectual tradition? I have already hinted at my answer: Not the adding of new truths to the world, nor the transmission of old truths to the young, but the cultivation in each of us of the disposition actively to seek the truth and to make the truth our own. More simply, liberal education is education in and for thoughtfulness. It awakens, encourages, and renders habitual thoughtful reflection about weighty human concerns, in quest of what is simply true and good. What this means I shall now try to make clear. We need to think about thoughtfulness.

What Is Thoughtfulness?

Thoughtfulness – indeed all thinking, from the most ordinary to the most technical – has its origin in efforts to understand our experience. Its most ordinary beginnings are in wonder or perplexity: we find something in our usually trustworthy experience remarkable, puzzling, or contradictory. Indeed, it is already thought which first recognizes strangeness or contradiction in our perceptions and seeks for clarification. The caterpillar disappears into a cocoon and emerges as a butterfly; the stick dipped into water is straight to the touch but bent to the eye. We are puzzled; we do not understand. Recognition of ignorance is the beginning of thought.

Because much of our experience is filtered through our opinions, thinking also begins with perplexity about opinion. Whether we know it or not, all that we perceive or encounter we interpret – usually unconsciously, that is, without thinking – in the light of our opinions about things, large and small. These opinions usually serve us well. But sometimes we find ourselves in contradiction with ourselves. For example, some of us may believe, as a matter of principle, that one should always be sincere and honest and true to one's beliefs. Some of the same people may also believe that it is wrong – or not nice – knowingly to hurt others. But can one always be both nice and honest? What should you say when your best friend asks what you think of her obnoxious boyfriend? How should you speak if defending your opinions about sex or drugs or the middle class at the family dinner table will only cause pain to your parents? If you take your opinions seriously, you will be troubled by the tension between them. You will be moved to think.

Thinking – all thinking – seeks to liberate us from a slavish adherence to unexamined opinion and an unreasonable trust in our own perceptions and experiences. Make no mistake – thought depends on opinion and experience and does not reject them. Rather, thought seeks to understand what is strange and wonderful and to remove perplexity, doubt, and contradiction.

Yet there are at least two possible responses to the disquieting presence of perplexity and awareness of ignorance. Let me exaggerate and call them the willful and the thoughtful. The willful is *annoyed* with ambiguity, uncertainty, unclarity, and doubt. It seeks clarity and certitude, to make the ambiguity disappear. It wants to be in control of things, not to be puzzled, not to be at a loss. It is painful to be at a loss; it is natural to want to find a way. Willful thinking constructs hypotheses, stipulates definitions and axioms, and tries to deduce from these beginnings an order of relationships in which the various observations or opinions will fit without contradiction. Our modern natural sciences are splendid examples of such hypothetico-deductive thinking. They issue in laws that do indeed permit us to a remarkable degree to give an account of and even to predict and control some natural phenomena.

Yet such willful or constructive thinking differs from thoughtful thinking – though the former is sometimes a necessary preparation for the latter. The thoughtful response to strangeness and perplexity is less interested in dispelling and removing the perplexity than in understanding its true grounds. Less insistent on system or certitude or indubitability, it considers the possibility that ambiguity and mystery are in the nature of things. Though it esteems the exact sciences, it does not forget that their beginnings or first principles were stipulated hypothetically, and that these very hypotheses might themselves contain and conceal objects of the greatest wonder and perplexity, objects especially worthy of thought.

Let me give two examples: physics, our most precise natural science, makes use of concepts of space, time, matter, and motion, and gives them operational definitions, usually thereby foreclosing further thought about what they are. But we may still wonder and ask (and at crucial times, physicists themselves have been compelled to ask), "What *is* time or space or matter or motion?" Or an example from politics: Much modern political discussion begins from the premise that there are certain basic human rights, and it proceeds to think about how they can be secured and made effective. But thought can also ask about what we mean by "a right," about where rights come from, and about what makes rights right. These sorts of questions do not lend themselves to deduction from given and fixed hypotheses. They seek instead the hidden but beckoning unhypothetical ground of these other hypotheses. They seek for what *truly* is and for what *is* truly.

Let me try, in a different way, to say again what I mean by thoughtfulness, this time by identifying thoughtfulness with the activity of questioning, for it is the asking of questions that is the heart of thoughtfulness. Here it will be helpful to distinguish the asking of questions from the setting of problems, two distinct modes of human thinking, which we often confuse. How does a question differ from a problem?*

Etymology provides a clue: "problem" comes from the Greek word *problema,* meaning literally "something thrown out before" us. A problem is any challenging obstacle, from a fence thrown up before an armed camp, to a task set before someone to be done. Problems are publicly articulated tasks that challenge us to solve them, which is to say, to do

---

* This discussion owes much to the educational writings of Eva Brann, St. John's College (Annapolis, Maryland), especially to her lecture "The Student's Problem." See also her *Paradoxes of Education in a Republic* (University of Chicago Press, 1979).

away with them as problems or obstacles. When a problem is solved, it disappears as a problem. Its solution is its dissolution. The solution is usually a construction, put together from elements into which the problem is broken up or, as we say, analyzed. We model the problem into a shape convenient for such analysis and construction; as we say, we *figure it out*. Further, a problem requires a solution *in its own terms;* the solution never carries one beyond the original problem as given.

The model of such problem solving is algebra. The equations containing unknowns are arranged, showing the analyzed elements in their constructed relations. The solutions that identify the unknowns dissolve the problem, and render the equation into an identity or tautology, which invites no further thought.

Consider a sample problem: Our task is to find the length of the side of a square whose area is twice that of the unit square. If we let X equal the length we are seeking, X^2 becomes the measure of the area of the square, which, we are told, is twice the unit. We construct an equation: $X^2 = 2$, and we solve for X. We identify X equal to the positive square root of 2, an irrational number which we cannot write out or speak precisely, but which we represent with the symbol $\sqrt{2}$. Our equation, our construct, now reads $(\sqrt{2})^2 = 2$, or $2 = 2$. It goes no further. It does not invite us to think further, for example, to wonder why or how an irrational number could be the answer to a rational question, or what *number* could *be* if both 2 and $\sqrt{2}$ are equally numbers. Our problem is solved, and our thinking either ceases or goes on to some other problem. In a sense, the goal of all such thinking is to cease to think. It seeks to remove the *need* to think by removing all obstacles to our peace of mind. Its search for clarity and distinctness is, finally, a desire to see through everything, to become clairvoyant, to be untroubled in mind and unfrustrated in action.

Please note: this mode of thought is not confined to algebra or to the doing of homework. It is, in fact, the dominant mode of everyone's thinking. We are always trying to figure something out, to find a way, to calculate the best means to a given end, to solve our problems. How do I get to Rockefeller Chapel? How can I get out of taking a foreign language? What does the teacher want by way of an answer to this essay question? Indeed, so dominant and familiar is this mode of thought that we come to regard it as the only way to think. We treat everything as a problem, from personality problems to the problem of poverty, from the mind-body problem to the problems of life. I leave you to ponder what it would mean to solve the problems of life if living is a problem to be solved.

How does the activity of questioning differ from problem solving or calculating? There are, of course, many kinds of questions. Not every interrogative sentence springs from what I mean by the activity of questioning. We may ask practical questions – Can I borrow the car? Do you have a hammer? – in which our interest is in *action* and in obtaining the means needed to carry it out. We may ask personal or even gossipy questions – How do you like it here? Where are you from? What does she see in him? – in which our true interest, whether real or apparent, whether born of genuine affection, mere politeness, or even envy, vanity, or malice, is in the *person*, which interest we display by means of such questions. We ask rhetorical questions – that is, questions to which we know the answers – whose purpose is only to have others publicly acknowledge the answers.

None of these questions displays what I mean by the activity of questioning; for in none of them is the answer in itself important to the questioner, is the answer itself the true object sought. In contrast, in a genuine question the verbal utterance bespeaks a *desire for an answer*. A true question is a state of mind in which I want to know what I do not know. Please note: a true question presupposes both a recognition of ignorance – somehow an act of intellect – and a desire – somehow an act of emotion or appetite. Indeed, a genuine question shows that the mind is not just an instrument activated by and in the service of the need for survival or the desire for pleasure, power, or recognition. It shows that our intellect also has desires of its own, or better, that *we desire* to know. A genuine question thus gives the lie to that widely believed slander perpetrated on the human soul, which sharply separates reason from emotion or desire, and which sees in the mind only heartless calculation and in the heart only mindless feeling.

Again, etymology is revealing: the English words "question," "query," "inquire" go back to the Latin *quaero*, and via its older form *quaeso* to a Sanskrit root meaning "to hunt out." To question is to quest, to search out and to seek after, to be engaged in passionate pursuit. Like the hunting dogs' search for game – the original meaning of our word quest – questioning is an earnest activity. This insight is preserved in the Latin root: *quaeso* means to seek and search, but also to beg, pray, beseech, entreat. In true questioning, we seek for an answer and by our questions entreat being itself to reveal, to uncover, to make unhidden, the object of our search.

Unlike the solution to a problem, the gaining of an answer to our questions does not dissolve the quest, or at least, does not abolish the desire. Like other forms of genuine love, love does not vanish but even grows when the object is present. As the lover loves to gaze on the beloved, so the questing mind delights in beholding the insights it receives. Further, a true question often leads beyond the terms in which it was first posed. The quest follows the quarry wherever it leads. It refuses to be satisfied with artificial or merely hypothetical constructs, logical or mathematical, or with poetic fictions designed to give it rest. It wants only what is finally true and real. No wonder so much of what educators try to feed us turns unappetizing and stale.

To question has also another meaning, about which a word must be said. To question or to call into question is to raise doubt. It may or may not be part of the other activity of questing. But its main effect is to tear down, to replace belief by confusion or doubt. The first question asked in the Bible is of this sort. The so-called Fall of man begins when the serpent asks the woman: "Yea, has God said, 'You shall not eat of *any* tree of the garden'?" His implication was clear: God *could* be the sort of being whose prohibitions are arbitrary or who even could make commands that would make your life impossible. Depending on what we make of the rest of the story, our susceptibility to the serpent's question led ultimately either to our enlightenment (through eating of the forbidden tree of knowledge of good and evil) or to our permanent separation (through banishment) from the home of true understanding. But, in any event, we all know – and I suspect you will soon know all too well – the doubt-inducing power of a simple question, "How do you know?" or, more simply, just "Why?" Expect such questions and ask them yourselves. But resist the counsel of those – and there are, unfortunately, many such serpents around – who think doubt and skepticism is itself the goal of thought, who reject the existence of knowable truths, and who argue that the discovery that there is always more than one way of looking at things is *the* end of liberal education.

I have already suggested that finding difference of opinion may be the beginning of thoughtfulness, but it cannot be what we seek in our thoughtful and serious activity of questioning. Socrates, an unsurpassed exemplar of questioning himself and others, a man supremely impressed by his own ignorance in almost all matters, insisted that he *knew* that "opinion and knowledge are two different sorts of things." Not the difference of opinion, but the difference between opinion and knowledge makes all the difference for liberal education.

What Is Thoughtfulness Thoughtful About?

Where are we in our search for the aim of liberal education, education in and for thoughtfulness? So far we have tried to say how thoughtfulness is different from other modes of mental activity, especially by pointing to the difference between problem solving or figuring things out and what I have called genuine questioning, or perhaps better, just questing. But I have said almost nothing about the game or quarry, about the *object* of our thoughtful seeking. For what knowledge do we quest? What are we to become thoughtful about? What is the *subject matter* of thoughtfulness?

It should go without saying that there is no single or set curriculum for thoughtfulness. There are and can be no courses called "liberal education," in part because the necessary and proper demands of even the best courses – for example, regular meetings, homework assignments, deadlines, examinations, all given by the instructor – are themselves much closer to the spirit of problem solving than to the spirit of questioning. Moreover, no course can simply teach or impart thoughtfulness; questioning can only begin within the soul of the learner. But, equally important, there is no clearly circumscribed subject for liberal education because it can proceed with any subject, rightly approached.

This answer is both encouraging and discouraging. The good news is that almost anything can become the object of wonder and inquiry. This means that specialization need not be incompatible with thoughtfulness, though many specialists turn out to be thoughtless. Indeed, for some of us, the beginning of thoughtfulness comes only after we have learned a lot about a little and discover that we have not thereby captured its full meaning, often precisely because we have ignored important connections to other matters. In my own case, it was first the prospect of human genetic manipulation that led me to question my onetime conviction that the progress of science and technology would necessarily go hand in hand with an improvement in morals and society, and second, reflection on my activities *as a scientist* that led me to doubt the claims of some of my colleagues that the activities of living organisms, including man, could be fully understood in terms of nonliving matter and the laws of physics and chemistry, or even in terms of behaviorist psychology and neuroscience. But, really, one could start anywhere, and the growth of the various sciences attests to the multiple possible beginnings of human thought, however strongly scientists and scholars now tend to give up thoughtfulness about their own beginnings.

One can ask questions about natural phenomena: What is light and what is seeing, what accounts for the motions of the heavenly bodies or the generation of animals or the origin of species, or, to provide more homely examples, why do dogs wag their tails or human beings blush? Or one can ask about the nature and properties of numbers and geometric figures, ratios and proportions. One can begin with the simple fact that human beings like to tell and hear and make up stories, and even enjoy tragedies and artless tales of plain horror. One can reflect on the common human experience of awe in the presence of overwhelming natural power or architectural grandeur. Or one can think about the power of speech, which enables the intelligibility of thoughts that arise in one mind to fly, as it were, carried on winged words – attached to sounds themselves meaningless – to awaken corresponding intelligibility in another. Why? How? What accounts for these phenomena? What if anything do they mean?

The bad news is, of course, the same as the good news: there is much too much to think about with any care and thoroughness. In our quest to understand, we are usually looking for some larger context in which to locate the disparate phenomena and things whose being and meaning we are pursuing. We intuit that at the end of our quest, beckoning us throughout, is some single and integral intelligible whole into which each of the objects of our inquiry fits. We cross-examine the multiplicity of worldviews, looking for the singleness of the world. Recognizing the vastness of the world and its holdings, the shortness of our life, and especially the weakness of our powers, we are saddened by the thought that perhaps we shall never truly know anything unless, contrary to possibility, we could know everything. Still, once we have tasted the delights of even partial insight, we are encouraged to continue. We want to know just what kind of a world this is and especially what kind of beings we are, and how we do and should relate to that world.

It is this search for *what we are* and *what we can and should become* which, in my view, belongs at the center of our questioning, and therefore at the center of liberal education. True thoughtfulness will include reflection, a looking and thinking back on the thinker and his human situation. The quest for understanding must include the quest for self-understanding. Indeed, the inscription on the ancient temple to Apollo at Delphi, *Know Thyself*, would seem to be a worthy motto of a college devoted to liberal education.

It is no small task to understand (let alone heed) this cryptic and weighty injunction. It would seem to require, at the very least, that we understand not merely our individual peculiarities but also our shared nature as human beings – if, indeed, we have a common human nature; not only who, but *what* are we human beings? That, in turn, would seem to require that we understand not only our human peculiarities – for example, that we are thoughtful animals – but also the nature we share with other living things, not least our embodiment and mortality. On the other side, it would mean asking questions about the relation between our nature and our nurture, that is, about culture – not only in its variety as the plurality of cultures but also in its universality, everywhere shaping human life with rituals and customs governing birth and death, language and song, marriage and education, justice and duty, and beliefs about the divine. It would mean pondering the human propensity to make images and artifacts, tools and stories, statues and temples. It would require looking into the way culture shapes our native passions, our fears, hopes, desires, loves, and hates, and also into why our nature sometimes resists such shaping, leading us often to do that which we would not. And it would involve thinking about thinking. The charge to self-knowledge is admittedly a tall order.

But I believe it is taller still. We need one more addition to our answer to the question "Thoughtfulness about what?" For thoughtfulness about what we *are* includes thoughtfulness about what we can and should become. The quest for self-knowledge, for an answer to the question "What is man?" embraces the further questions: "What is a *good* man?" "What is a *good life* for human beings?" "What is a *good* community and a *good* citizen?" Liberal education must encourage the thoughtful, reflective, self-conscious pursuit of the meaning of what is good.

No doubt this suggestion will cause you difficulty. Most of you are too sophisticated (or is it corrupted?) to believe that there can be truth about good. You know, or think you know, that good is always relative. "Good" is a so-called value: that is, something is deemed good because someone values it; it is not valued because it is good. Just as I like apple pie and you like cherry, what we say is good is a matter of taste, subrational in origin, not amenable to rational inquiry. Some of you know the famous fact-value distinction, and will accord truth – or, as we say, objectivity – only to facts. All of us know that beliefs and tastes are culturally influenced; but some of you are so impressed by the mere fact of cultural differences in beliefs about "good" as to assert that what is deemed "good" is, at best, just a product of culture. Worse, some of you think that beliefs about "good" are a cruel hoax, foisted upon the weak by the strong to enable the strong to exploit and oppress the weak. And many of you have had your fill of those figures of authority whose pronouncements about what's good for you don't square with your own perceptions – though I hasten to add, if the usual experience of mankind is to be trusted, that you will in many cases discover that they were right, and in any case, you will make similar pronouncements to your children.

Nevertheless, I submit, the question about what is good should be open. Despite your professed skepticism, deep down you also know that it *is* open – else in the name of what do you dispute with your parents regarding your own good? You defend and argue about your opinions about justice – about capital punishment, race relations, the status of women, or the war on terror – whereas you would never argue about whether I like apple pie, or even whether I *should* like it. You do not behave as if the differing opinions about the right and the good are just matters of taste, mere preferences. If you really believed that your opinions are good only because they are *your* opinions, you would not argue to defend and justify them with reasons. Does not your willingness to justify your opinions about what is good imply the possibility – and for now I would insist only on its being a possibility – that there *is* an answer, or *better* and *worse* answers, to that all-important question, made famous by Socrates, "How should I live?" If there are possibly better and worse answers, if there are perhaps some objects that would satisfy our longings and would make us truly happy, if there is a way of life that would enable us to say at the end that we had not only lived but lived well, would it not be foolish before you had quested to decide there is no such knowledge to be had by inquiry? Think it over.

A word of caution: this quest for what is good is antithetical to intolerance, self-righteousness, smugness. It requires listening to, respecting, and taking seriously the opinions and ways of others, precisely because almost all opinions seriously held and defended probably embody a certain intimation of what is true, and, at the very least, attest to the human concern with what is true and good, a universal concern more significant than the disparity among the opinions held on these matters. It also means being open to opinions that are unsettling and disquieting, that challenge our complacent and comfortable attachments to our unexamined opinions, especially our opinions about what is right and good.

Yet this open-mindedness and respect for the opinions of others does not imply that all opinions are finally equally worthy or that it does not matter whose opinions or even which books you choose to study. Time is short and our energy is limited. Both are best spent, in my experience, reading slowly and pondering carefully the greatest works of the best writers and thinkers, men and women who have seen more deeply into the permanent human questions or who furnish our imaginations with the richest accounts of human beings struggling to negotiate the promise and the peril of human existence. The great books – philosophical, historical, literary, scientific, theological – are the best companions in pursuit of thoughtfulness, precisely because they are themselves its embodiment. As they demand great effort and as they differ greatly among themselves, their study at once enlivens the mind in its quest for understanding, while encouraging intellectual humility in the face of powerful competing alternatives. Why, for $60,000 a year, seeking an education in thoughtfulness that is to last you a lifetime, should you not spend as much time as you can with the best?

What Good Is Thoughtfulness?

I have now completed, albeit hastily and crudely, an explication of what I mean by *thoughtful reflection about weighty human concerns, in quest of what is simply true and good.* But, on my own principles, our reflection on thoughtfulness and its content must face the question about its worth. What good is thoughtfulness? I offer three suggestions.

First, the habit of thoughtfulness is good, even urgent, for our common life as citizens of the American republic. Our situation early in the twenty-first century finds our effort at self-government, not to say survival, increasingly dominated by technical matters requiring the advice and competence of experts – about, among other things, the economy, defense, energy, health, transportation, communication, and the environment. We steadily are acquiring ever more powerful technologies, including those that increasingly permit deliberate and sophisticated manipulations of the human body and mind. Yet we also recognize, more than we have in some time, and perhaps due to these same dramatic new changes, that the decisions we need to make are never merely technical. They are also always ethical. They all involve judgments of better and worse; they are informed by our opinions, often tacit and unexamined, about what is right and good, for ourselves and for the community. Our technical experts need to be more than technical experts, at the very least in order to know the limits of technical expertise. The technical expert who is liberally educated to the habit of thoughtfulness is less likely to become that most dangerous fellow, a specialist without vision, who knows how to get the rockets up but who cares not where they come down.

These more dramatic social and political problems of our day should serve to remind us that there are always hard choices to be made, that there is no invisible hand that guides destiny in favor of progress or that safeguards liberal democracy. We will live no better than we choose. Our choices are frequently presented as problems to be solved, but some of them are rather questions and difficulties that can only be faced. And even our genuine problems are so thoroughly interconnected that the thoughtless and single-minded pursuit of a solution to one often gives rise to or exacerbates numerous others. If liberal democracy means government by popular choice, if choice involves deliberation about means to ends, if the ends themselves are especially matters for thoughtful reflection, then the habit of thoughtfulness, in its quest for coherence and wholeness and in its willingness and ability to be articulate about matters of better and worse, would seem indispensable if popular government is to be good government.

The usefulness of liberal education for citizens in liberal democracy is, you should note, not confined to national and international affairs. For though few of you will be more than voters – though I hope thoughtful ones – regarding our national government, most if not all of you will be in positions of leadership and responsibility in your local communities, school boards, businesses, or universities. There you will find ample need and opportunity for the exercise of thoughtful citizenship.

Second, thoughtfulness is good not only for our life as citizens. It might also be good for our lives as human beings, in the numerous choices, large and small, that we must make and in our numerous relations with others. I am not sure that you believe me. You certainly believe that professional training or other acquisition of skills will be useful in life, not least because it will enable you to make a living and a good living at that – a fact not to be despised. We can make no such claims for liberal education. Further, on the basis of what you know about formal education from your own experience to date, you probably don't believe that school or book-learning or thinking has much to do with living, as distinguished from making a living. Though your schooling has formed you – and deformed you – in ways you don't even realize, you locate living in the context of family and friends, at home and church, on dance floor and athletic field, and I readily believe that little of what you have studied, in the way you have studied so far, enters into those human relations. Moreover, self-consciousness, in the sense that it is most frequently experienced, is not often welcome, accompanied as it is by feelings of self-doubt, embarrassment, awkwardness, and fear. Indeed, some of our contemporaries like thoughtful self-awareness so little that they deliberately scramble their brains with chemicals in search of some preferable state of mindlessness. Even at Chicago, we sometimes hear, and you probably from time to time will share, a contempt for what is derided as "the so-called life of the mind." Nevertheless, I put it to you that we all in fact believe, deep down, that it is better to know what we are doing than not to know; that ignorance is not bliss, least of all self-ignorance; that thinking through hard choices – no matter how difficult it may be to reach a decision – is sounder and more satisfying than to have these choices made for us or made by us thoughtlessly and blindly.

Moreover, in any serious matter, we would rather have dealings with people who are thoughtful, who are reflective, who have enough detachment from their own inchoate impulses and the immediacy of the moment to respond morally, sensibly, considerately. There would seem to be a connection between thoughtfulness and character. Indeed, as you know, the English language itself makes such a connection: thoughtful means "given to, disposed to, engaged in thinking" or "disposed to consider matters," that is, "prudent, reflective." But thoughtful also means "showing thought or consideration for others; considerate, kindly." Thoughtfulness, in both senses, is the core of the best of friendships.

Now that I have led you to consider favorably the usefulness of thought and reflection for action and your own private lives, I fear I must cause you to reconsider. We all know of circumstances in which too much thinking may lead to indecision or paralysis. Thoughtfulness also requires detachment and may augment it beyond what is reasonable; and there are many occasions in life where detachment seems to be undesirable. Ironically, not even all of the great thinkers have thought that thinking is good for human beings, especially for morals and politics. Says Rousseau, "If nature destined us to be healthy, I almost dare affirm that the state of reflection is a state contrary to nature and that the man who meditates is a depraved animal." He makes a powerful attack on philosophy in the name of decency:

> Reason engenders vanity and reflection fortifies it; reason turns man back upon himself, it separates him from all that bothers and afflicts him. Philosophy isolates him; because of it he says in secret, at the sight of a suffering man: Perish if you will, I am safe. No longer can anything except dangers to the entire society trouble the tranquil sleep of the philosopher and tear him from his bed. His fellow-man can be murdered with impunity right under his window; he has only to put his hands over his ears and argue with himself a bit to prevent nature, which revolts within him, from identifying with the man who is being assassinated. Savage man does not have this admirable talent, and for want of wisdom and reason he is always seen heedlessly yielding to the first sentiment of humanity. In riots or street fights the populace assembles, the prudent man moves away; it is the rabble, the market women, who separate the combatants and prevent honest people from murdering each other.[47]

This challenge cannot be neglected. A college education does not guarantee decency and good character. Perhaps the most profound philosopher of the twentieth century – a man noted in fact for his attempt to restore thoughtfulness – was a member of the German Nazi party and even its articulate defender. Moreover, the dominant source of our Western beliefs about how we should live morally, biblical religion, is rather dubious about the benefits and even about the need for questioning or for autonomous philosophizing, especially about what is good. "The fear of the Lord is the beginning of wisdom," says Psalm 111. And, from Micah: "It has been told thee, O man, what is good, and what the Lord doth require of thee: Only to do justly, and to love mercy, and to walk humbly with thy God." And when Jesus said, "You shall know the truth and the truth shall make you free," I rather doubt that he was thinking of liberal education, or for that matter, of what we mean by free. Is free thought really and always good for morality?

We cannot dissolve this question. Once it is raised, we cannot send it away or solve it by some artful hypothesis and deduction. We really have no choice but to *think* about whether and how thinking is good or bad for character or piety. Those of you attached to one of the religious traditions will no doubt be moved to consider more deeply the traditional teaching about human life and the cosmos in the light of all you learn here. Those of you who are unattached might at least try learning what those religions teach, and to ponder whether so-called unaided human reason is a sufficient guide for human life. We might all consider whether thoughtfulness that does not think on the possibility of the eternal and the divine is thoughtful enough.

Finally, however, the case for the goodness of thoughtfulness cannot rest only on its utility, whether to politics or morals, to public or private life. Thoughtfulness is not only good *for*; it is also simply *good*. It is not only good *for* life; it is also good living. It expresses, in activity, a certain deep longing of the human soul. As Aristotle put it long ago: "All human beings by nature desire understanding." This desire can be thwarted, distorted, and almost crushed – by lack of encouragement or opportunity for its exercise. But anyone who has looked into the eyes of very young children straining to understand, anyone who heard their genuine, spontaneous, and marvelous questions, born of wonder, anyone who has witnessed the delight they manifest when they have understood something, cannot but believe that Aristotle was right. My experience as a teacher assures me that you too are still youthful enough to experience the child's delight in discovery. Happily, the very youthfulness which makes you inexperienced and ignorant also makes you supremely open and eager for learning – much more so, I am afraid, than many of us who will be your teachers, burdened as we are by worldly cares and the care of this university, which makes it possible for you at least freely to learn.

Commit yourselves, therefore, to the careful, disciplined cultivation both of that embryonic desire and of your innate, human powers to understand. Do not be content to be intellectual muscle-men, thinking down all obstacles. Strive not to see *through*, but to see things as they are. Find your questions and follow them. Do not regard college merely as preparation for career or even as preparation for life, if by living you imagine something different from how you can begin to live *here*. Become thoughtful. For the formation of the lifelong habit of thoughtfulness is that preparation for human life which is liveliness itself. Thoughtfulness is the serious – but also playful – business of life. May you make for yourselves a lively time in our college and beyond.

CHAPTER TWELVE

Looking for an Honest Man

The Case for the Humanities

> Life would be no better than candlelight tinsel and daylight rubbish if our spirits were not touched by what has been, to issues of longing and constancy. — *George Eliot*, MIDDLEMARCH

IF ASKED TO IDENTIFY important challenges facing the United States today, few of us would think first – if at all – of the humanities and their condition in contemporary American life. The sorry state of elementary and secondary education would surely make the list, as might the need to improve scientific literacy and technological competence, so that America (we are often told) may remain "competitive" in the globalized economy and high-tech world of tomorrow. Attention might be invited also to political correctness in college classrooms or campus restrictions on free speech. But the larger and more important educational issue of what college students should be learning and why – especially in the humanities – is a subject below the radar for nearly everyone.

It was not always thus. Not quite sixty years ago, when Europeans and Americans still distinguished high culture from popular culture, and when classical learning was still highly esteemed in colleges and universities, C. P. Snow triggered widespread debate over the purposes of higher education. In his famous Rede Lecture at Cambridge University in 1959, "The Two Cultures and the Scientific Revolution," Snow warned of a growing split between the old culture of the humanities and the rising culture of science. He also took Britain's literary aristocracy to task for its dangerous dismissal of scientific and technological progress, which he believed held the solutions to the world's deepest problems. The literary critic F. R. Leavis fired off a vitriolic response, defending the primacy of the humanities for a civilizing education, and insisting that science must not be allowed to operate outside the moral norms that only a first-rate humanistic education could provide. The Snow-Leavis debate traveled to this side of the Atlantic, in serious and searching discussions about the aims of higher education and the importance of the humanities.

Such discussions have, alas, largely disappeared from public discourse and even from the academy. Most professors in nearly all of our leading universities prefer to leave and be left alone, rationalizing their indifference to the goals and requirements of a liberal education by proclaiming for their students the American value of choice, and trumpeting for themselves the maxim of Chairman Mao: "Let a thousand flowers bloom." Few licensed humanists today embrace any view of the humanities that could justify making them the centerpiece of a college curriculum. This abdication is especially regrettable because it comes precisely at a time when – thanks largely to the successes of science and technology – the meaning and future of our humanity cries out for thoughtful attention.

I have devoted most of my career to addressing this challenge. Although formally trained in medicine and biochemistry – fields in which I no longer teach or practice – I have been engaged with liberal education for forty-five years, teaching philosophical and literary texts as an untrained amateur, practicing the humanities without a license. Perhaps precisely because I am an unlicensed humanist, I have pursued the humanities for an old-fashioned purpose in an old-fashioned way: I have sought wisdom about the meaning of our humanity, largely through teaching and studying the great works of wiser and nobler human beings who have bequeathed to us their profound accounts of the human condition.

This chapter traces my adopted career as unlicensed humanist in an effort to suggest, by its form and its substance, what purpose a humanistic education might serve. I offer it not as an *apologia pro vita mea*, but rather in the belief that my own intellectual journey is of more than idiosyncratic interest. Although I generally deplore public trafficking in personal matters, I present a first-person account partly because I believe that true education takes place only in individual souls and in relation to genuine questions and personal concerns, and partly because I hope that an autobiographical thread, manifesting such questions and concerns, will make it easier for readers to join me on a journey to their own discoveries and insights about the indispensability – and limits – of humanistic inquiry today. Although the path I have followed is surely peculiar, the quest for my humanity is a search for what we all have in common. The point is not what *I* have learned, but rather what I have *learned*, and therefore what *anyone* can learn with and through the humanities – and why it matters.

Seeking Human Being

Everyone has heard the story of Diogenes the Cynic, who went around the sunlit streets of Athens, lantern in hand, looking for an honest man. This same Diogenes, when he heard Plato being praised for defining man as "an animal, biped and featherless," threw a plucked chicken into the Academy, saying, "Here is Platonic man!" These tales display Diogenes' cynicism as both ethical and philosophical: He is remembered for mocking the possibility of finding human virtue and for mocking the possibility of knowing human nature. In these respects, the legendary Diogenes would feel right at home today in many an American university, where a professed interest in human nature and human excellence – or, more generally, in truth and goodness – invites reactions ranging from mild ridicule for naiveté to outright denunciation for entertaining such discredited and dangerous notions.

Tracing the stories about Diogenes the Cynic to their source, in *Lives of Eminent Philosophers* by Diogenes Laertius, one discovers that the apocryphal story is somewhat embroidered, if not incorrect. Yes, Diogenes lit a lantern in broad daylight, but he did not say he was looking for an honest man. What he said was, "I am looking for [or seeking] human being," *anthrôpon zêtô* – either *a* human being or *the* human being, either an exemplar of humanity or the idea of humanity, or both. To be sure, purporting to seek the answer by means of candlepower affirms Diogenes' badge as cynic. But the picture also suggests a man who refuses to be taken in by a complacent popular belief that we already know human goodness from our daily experience, or by confident professorial claims that we can capture the mystery of our humanity in definitions. Whether mocking or not, and perhaps speaking better than he knew, Diogenes gave elegantly simple expression to the humanist quest for self-knowledge: I seek the human being – my human being, your human being, our humanity. In fact, the embellished version of his question comes to the same thing: To seek an *honest* man is, at once, to seek a human being worthy of the name, an honest-to-goodness exemplar of the idea of humanity, a truthful and truth-speaking embodiment of the animal having the power of articulate speech.

I confess myself an inheritor of Diogenes' quest, although I have undertaken his search without a grain of cynicism. In place of a lantern, I have lit my journey with the light of books great and good, and, equally important, with the company of teachers and students, friends and loved ones who were on a similar quest.

It began for me with what could be regarded as an answer to Diogenes' question, in the lessons I absorbed in a secular Jewish home of Yiddish-speaking immigrants. My parents of blessed memory – a saintly father and a moralist mother – had come to America via Canada from the Ukraine and from Poland. God having been left behind, along with the czar and the Russian Revolution, "humanity" was the focus of all that my parents tried to teach. The Yiddish translation of *anthrôpos* or "human being" is *mentsch*, a wonderfully capacious notion, at once prosaically descriptive and inspiringly normative. To be *mentschlich* is to be *humane*, behaving decently and considerately toward others; but it is also to be *human*, displaying in one's own character and conduct the species-specific dignity advertised in our uniquely upright posture. *Mentschlichkeit*, "humanity," the disposition and practice of both "humaneness" and "humanness," was thus the quasi-religious teaching of my home. Its content, wholly moral and wholly appealing, went unquestioned: personal integrity and honesty, self-respect and personal responsibility, consideration and respect for every human person (equally a *mentsch*), compassion for the less fortunate, and a concern for fairness, justice, and righteousness. To become and to be a *mentsch*: that was the conscious and articulated goal toward which all of my early rearing was directed.

Two things I did not understand until much later. First, I did not know that the *Yiddishkeit* of my youth – with its universalism and quasi-socialism – represented a deliberate cultural alternative to traditional Judaism, on whose teachings it was parasitic: the Prophets, one might say, without the Law. Second, I did not appreciate that the content of *mentschlichkeit* was in fact a disputable question, and that there were (and are) large differences of opinion, and even irresolvable tensions, regarding its meaning. The latter error was the first to be corrected. Indeed, my foray into the humanities would begin in earnest only when I discovered that the injunction to "be a *mentsch*" required serious reflection, both philosophical and ethical, on the meaning of our humanity.

Science and Its Discontents

The seeds of this reflection were planted at the University of Chicago. There, in the still-living remains of the college created by Robert Hutchins, I first encountered philosophical questions beyond the domain of ethics, as well as some of the competing answers to questions about human nature and human good. I was introduced to the idea of learning as an end in itself, fulfilling our human capacity for understanding. I acquired an educational prejudice in favor of discussing the great questions and reading the great books, though it would take years before I learned why these prejudices were justified. I witnessed up close the dignity of the life of teaching, for we were taught by an exemplary faculty, tenured not for their record of publication but for their devotion to devising and teaching an integrated course of study that could place young ignoramuses on the path of becoming liberally educated men and women. In Socratic spirit, they insisted that we examine *all* our intellectual assumptions and starting points, and they encouraged us to put fundamental philosophical questions even to the natural sciences: What is the relation between matter and form? What makes an organism a unified and living whole? What is the nature of the psyche or soul?

Questions of this sort lay dormant as I entered upon a brief career in medicine, in retrospect another important station on the path to the human. Preclinical studies left me in awe of the marvel that is the human body, and of the stunning events beneath the surface that sustain our existence and enable our remarkable interactions with the world. Clinical experience left me in awe of the privilege – and the peril – of offering a helping hand to fellow human beings in times of crisis. Although I could not then articulate it, I was also mindful of the rare privilege to be admitted to the inner sanctum of the patient's world, to witness human beings – stripped of pretense and sustained only by hope, trust, and the love of kith and kin – attempting to negotiate sicknesses, suffering, and the anxiety of coming face to face with their own mortality. Not for nothing were medieval textbooks of medicine entitled *De Homine*, "On Man," or "On the Human Being." Not for nothing was medicine once an honored branch on the humanistic tree.

Yet precisely around the subject of our humanity I found something missing. The science was indeed powerful, but its self-understanding left much to be desired. It knew the human parts in ever-finer detail, but it concerned itself little with the human whole. Medicine, then and now, has no concept of the human being, of the peculiar and remarkable concretion of psyche and soma that makes us the strangest and most wonderful among the creatures. Psychiatry, then and even more now, is so little chagrined by its failure to say what the psyche or soul is that it denies its existence altogether. The art of healing does not inquire into what health is, or how to get and keep it. The word "health" does not occur in the index of the leading textbooks of medicine. To judge from the way we measure medical progress, largely in terms of mortality statistics and defeats of deadly diseases, one gets the unsettling impression that the tacit goal of medicine is not health but rather bodily immortality, with every death today regarded as a tragedy that future medical research will prevent.

Coming down from theory to practice, I found that I loved my patients and their stories more than I loved solving the puzzle of their maladies. Where my colleagues found disease fascinating, I was fascinated more by the patients – how they lived, how they struggled with their suffering. Above all, I hated the autopsy room, not from fear of death, but because the postmortem exam could never answer *my* question: What happened to my *patient*? The clot in his coronary artery, his ruptured bowel, or whatever diseased body part the pathologist displayed as the explanation of his death was utterly incommensurable with the awesome, massive fact: the *extinction* of this never-to-be-repeated human being, for whom I had cared and for whom his survivors now grieved.

Despite these inchoate reservations, I continued to follow the path of science – indeed, to an even more molecular level. I entered the Ph.D. program in biochemistry at Harvard and was privileged to share in the great excitement of the golden age of molecular biology. Working happily on my own project, I tasted the great pleasures of independent discovery. But my biggest discovery came outside the laboratory.

The Limits of Enlightenment

In summer 1965, interrupting my research, my wife Amy and I went to Mississippi to do civil rights work. We lived with a farmer couple in rural Holmes County, in a house with no telephone, hot water, or indoor toilet. We visited many families in the community, participated in their activities, and helped with voter registration and other efforts to encourage the people to organize themselves in defense of their rights. This deeply moving experience changed my life, but not in any way I would have expected.

On returning to Cambridge, I was nagged by a disparity I could not explain between the uneducated, poor black farmers in Mississippi and many of my privileged, highly educated graduate-student friends at Harvard. A man of the left, I had unthinkingly held the Enlightenment view of the close connection between intellectual and moral virtue: Education and progress in science and technology would overcome superstition, poverty, and misery, allowing human beings to become at last the morally superior creatures that religion and social oppression, in addition to nature's stinginess, had kept them from being. Yet in Mississippi I saw people living honorably and with dignity in perilous and meager circumstances, many of them illiterate, but sustained by religion, extended family, and community attachment, and by the pride of honest farming and homemaking. They even seemed to display more integrity, decency, and strength of character, and less self-absorption, vanity, and self-indulgence, than many of my high-minded Harvard friends who shared my progressive opinions. How could this be?

In summer 1966, my closest friend had me read Rousseau's explosive *Discourse on the Sciences and the Arts*, for which my Mississippi and Harvard experiences had prepared me. Rousseau argues that, *pace* the

Enlightenment, progress in the arts and sciences does *not* lead to greater virtue. On the contrary, it necessarily produces luxury, augments inequality, debases taste, softens character, corrupts morals, and weakens patriotism, leading ultimately not to emancipation but to servitude.

Rousseau complains that writers and "idle men of letters" – the equivalent of our public intellectuals, not to say professors – subvert decent opinion and corrupt the citizens:

> These vain and futile declaimers go everywhere armed with their deadly paradoxes, undermining the foundations of faith and annihilating virtue. They smile disdainfully at the old-fashioned words of fatherland and religion, and devote their talents and philosophy to destroying and debasing all that is sacred among men.

Rousseau also complains that cultivation of the arts and sciences leads to inequality and contempt for the common man:

> One no longer asks if a man is upright, but rather if he is talented; nor of a book if it is useful, but if it is well written. Rewards are showered on the witty, and virtue is left without honors.... We have physicists, geometers, chemists, astronomers, poets, musicians, painters; we no longer have citizens.

And Rousseau complains also that formal education corrupts the young:

> I see everywhere immense institutions where young people are brought up at great expense, learning everything except their duties.... Without knowing how to distinguish error from truth, [your children] will possess the art of making them both unrecognizable to others by specious arguments. But they will not know what the words magnanimity, equity, temperance, humanity, courage are; that sweet name fatherland will never strike their ear; and if they hear of God, it will be less to be awed by him than to be afraid of him.

Nowadays, a resurrected Rousseau might say instead, "If they hear of God, it is less to be awed by him than to mock him."

Could Rousseau be right? Is it really true that the natural home of intellectual progress is not the natural home of moral and civic virtue? Is it really true that as the arts and sciences climb upward, so morals, taste, and citizenship slide downward, and, what's worse, that the rise of the former causes the fall of the latter? If so, all that I had believed about the simple harmony between intellectual and moral progress was called into question. And if the Enlightenment view was not correct, what should I think instead? For the first time in my life, I acquired some real questions, pressing questions, more challenging than those one can answer in the laboratory. A crevice had opened in my understanding of *mentschlichkeit*, between the humane commitments of compassion and equality and the human aspiration to excellence and upright dignity.

This crevice would widen with the two books I read right after Rousseau: Aldous Huxley's *Brave New World* and C. S. Lewis's *Abolition of Man*. The first depicts a future society that has succeeded – through genetic engineering, psychoactive drugs, and applied psychology – in ridding the world of all the evils against which compassionate humanitarianism today does battle. Gone are war, poverty, and disease; anxiety, suffering, and guilt; hatred, envy, and grief; but the world thus "perfected" is peopled by creatures of human shape but stunted humanity. They consume, fornicate, take "soma," enjoy the "feelies" and "centrifugal bumble-puppy," and operate the machinery that makes it all possible. They do not read, write, think, love, or govern themselves. Art and science, virtue and religion, family and friendship are all passé. Precisely because "progress" has eliminated both the need for struggle and the call to greatness and adventure, no one aspires to anything higher than bodily health and immediate gratification. Worst of all, the denizens of the Brave New World are so dehumanized that they have no idea what they are missing.

According to Lewis, the dehumanization threatened by the mastery of nature is caused not so much by the emerging biotechnologies that might directly denature bodies and flatten souls as by the underlying value-neutral, soulless, heartless accounts that science proffers of living nature and of man. By expunging any notion of soul, aspiration, and purpose from its account of life, and by setting itself against the evidence of our lived experience, modern biology ultimately undermines our *self-understanding* as creatures of freedom and dignity, as well as our inherited teachings regarding how to live – teachings linked to philosophical anthropologies that science has now seemingly dethroned.

For me, the search for *anthrôpos* suddenly acquired genuine urgency and poignancy, as these threats to our humanity came not from bigots and tyrants but from the rightly celebrated well-wishers and benefactors of humankind. Could we continue to reap the benefits of our new biology and our emerging biotechnologies without eroding our freedom and dignity? What features of our humanity most needed defending, both in practice and in thought? What solid ideas of human nature and human good could be summoned to the cause?

Pursuit of these questions would require a change of direction and a different approach to human affairs. In 1970, I put away scalpel and microscope to take up directly Diogenes' search for *anthrôpos*, hoping better to understand the honest-to-goodness humanity of the human being by studying not the hidden parts but the manifest activities of the whole, visible in broad daylight, and thereby to help promote his true flourishing. Without realizing it, I became a humanist.

At that time, some scientists and humanists, not a few of them enthusiasts of a "posthuman" future, were addressing the gap between our science and our ethics by proposing a new, "science-based ethic" and calling upon us to "keep up" with the massive changes in human life caused by galloping scientific and technological advance. My intuitions led me in the opposite direction: to try to correct the deficiencies of our scientific understanding of human nature, and to reinforce, where possible, the best of what we have learned about human goodness and human flourishing. In these pursuits, I have sought out the best that has been said and thought by those who have gone before, who might help us discover vital truths that we would otherwise not see. No friend of humanity should trade the accumulated wisdom about human nature and human flourishing for some half-cocked promise to produce a superior human being or human society, never mind a posthuman future, before he has taken the trouble to look deeply into the matter of our humanity – what it is, why it matters, and how we can become all that we are capable of being.

As I look back over the decades since I left the world of science to reflect on its human meaning, three distinct but related pursuits stand out: First, addressing the conceptual danger (stressed by Lewis) of a soulless science of life, I sought a more natural science, one that is truer to life as lived. Second, addressing the practical danger (stressed by Huxley) of dehumanization resulting from the relief of man's estate and the sacrifice of the high to the urgent, I sought a richer picture of human dignity and human flourishing. And third, addressing the social and political dangers (stressed by Rousseau) of cultural decay and enfeeblement, I sought cultural teachings that could keep us strong in heart and soul, no less than in body and bank account. Here are a few high points from these three inquiries.

The Human Animal

Finding a "more natural science" would serve two important goals. First, by doing justice to life as lived, it would correct the slander perpetrated upon all of living nature, and upon human nature in particular, by treating the glorious activities of life as mere epiphenomena of changes in the underlying matter or as mere devices for the replication of DNA. Second, and more positively, by offering a richer account of human nature faithful both to our animality *and* to the human difference, it might provide pointers toward how we might best live and flourish. Toward both goals, a "more natural science" examines directly the primary activities of life as we creatures experience them. It revisits some now neglected notions once thought indispensable for understanding the being and doing of all higher animals: aliveness, neediness, and purposive activity to preserve life and to meet need; openness to and awareness of the world; interest in and action on the world; felt lack of, and appetite for, desirable things from the world; selfhood and inwardness in combination with active communication and relations with other beings, of the same and different species.

Against the materialists who believe that all vital activities can be fully understood by describing the electrochemical changes in the underlying matter, a more natural science would insist on appreciating the activities of life in their own terms, and as known from the inside: what it means to hunger, feel, see, imagine, think, desire, seek, suffer, enjoy. Against those humanists who locate our humanity solely in consciousness or will or reason, having conceded to mechanistic science all truths about our bodies, a more natural science would insist on appreciating the profound meaning of our distinctive embodiment.

From Erwin Straus, a phenomenologist, I learned the humanizing significance of the upright posture: how our standing in the world, gained only through conscious effort against the pull of gravity, prefigures all our artful efforts to overcome nature's indifference to human aspiration; how our supremely mobile arms fit us for the socializing activities of embracing, cradling, pointing, caressing, and holding hands, no less than for the selfish activities of grasping, fighting, and getting food to mouth; how our eyes, no longer looking down a snout to find what is edible, are lifted instead to the horizon, enabling us to take in an entire vista and to conceive an enduring world beyond the here and now; how our refashioned mammalian mouth and respiratory system equip us for the possibility of speech – and kissing; and how our expressive face is fit to meet, greet, and sometimes love the faces that we meet, face to face, side by side, and arm in arm.

From Adolf Portmann, a zoologist, I discovered the deeper meaning of the appearance of animals, whose intricate surface beauty, not fully explained by its contributions to protective coloration or sexual selection, serves also to communicate inward states to fellow creatures and to announce, in the language of visibility, each animal's particular species dignity and its unique individual identity. I even found evidence for natural teleology in, of all places, *The Origin of Species*, where Darwin makes clear that evolution by natural selection requires, and takes as biologically given, the purposive drives of all organisms for self-preservation and for reproduction – drives whose existence is a mystery unexplainable by natural selection.

But the greatest help in pursuit of a more natural science came, most unexpectedly, from studying premodern philosophers of nature, in particular Aristotle. I turned to his *De Anima* ("On Soul") expecting to get help with understanding the difference between a living human being and its corpse, a difference relevant to the difficult task of determining whether some persons on a respirator are alive or dead. I discovered to my amazement that Aristotle has almost no interest in the difference between the living and the dead. He finds that life and soul are best understood not, as we moderns might suspect, from the boundary conditions when an organism comes into being or passes away, but rather when the

organism is at its peak, with its body actively at work in energetic relation to the world – when it is "souling" the world in the activities of sensing, imagining, desiring, moving, and thinking. More surprisingly,
instead of our dualistic ideas of soul as a "ghost in the machine," invoked
by some in order to save the notion of free will, or as a separate immortal
entity that departs the body at the time of death, invoked by others to
address the disturbing fact of apparent personal extinction, Aristotle
offers a holistic idea of soul as the empowered and empowering "*form* of
a naturally organic body," a still-defensible view. "Soul," for Aristotle,
denotes the unified powers of aliveness, awareness, action, and appetite
that living beings all manifest.

This is not mysticism or superstition, but biological fact, although it
goes against current prejudice in that it recognizes the difference between
mere material and its empowering form. Consider, for example, the eye.
Like any organ, it has extension, takes up space, can be touched and
grasped by the hand. But neither the power of the eye – sight – nor sight's
activity – seeing – is extended, touchable, corporeal. The power of sight
"resides in" material and is inseparable from material, but is not itself
material. The eye's light-absorbing chemicals do not *see* the light they
absorb. Sight and seeing are a power and an activity of soul, dependent
on the underlying materials but not reducible to them. Moreover, sight
and seeing are not knowable through our objectified science, but only
through lived experience. A blind neuroscientist could give precise quantitative details about electrical discharges in the eye produced by the
stimulus of light, and a blind craftsman could, with instruction, fashion a
good material model of the eye; but sight and seeing can be known only
by one who sees.

Likewise, the passions of the soul are not reducible to the materials of
the body. It is true that ancient naturalists used to say that anger, for
example, is a heating of the blood around the heart or an increase in the
bilious humor, and today we might describe it as a rising concentration
of certain neurotransmitters in an anger-specific region of the brain. But
these partial accounts, stressing only the material conditions, cannot
reveal the larger truth about anger: Anger, *humanly understood*, is a painful feeling that seeks revenge for a perceived affront. To understand the
human truth about anger and its serious consequences, we must instead
listen to the poets, beginning with Homer's *Iliad*: "Wrath, sing, o goddess,

of Peleus' son Achilles, and the woes thousand-fold it brought upon the Achaians, sending to Hades strong souls of heroes but leaving themselves to be the delicate feastings of dogs and birds." And to understand how we come to know this or any other truth, we can never stop wondering how – marvel of marvels – Homer's winged words carry their intelligible and soul-shaping meanings, hitched to meaningless waves of sound, from the soul of genius to the hearts and minds of endless generations of attentive and sympathetic readers.

The Flourishing Human

My second major pursuit was a richer account of the human good and the good human, one that would reflect a richer anthropology and one that could counter the shrunken views of human happiness and goodness represented by the Brave New World. Not surprisingly, the disagreements of the great authors regarding the human good are even greater than those regarding human nature. Yet once again, ancient philosophers offer soul-expanding teachings, and none more than Aristotle in his *Nicomachean Ethics*, a book that I have taught a dozen times and that transformed how I look at ethics and human flourishing.

Americans usually discuss ethical matters either in utilitarian terms of weighing competing goods or balancing benefits and harms, looking to the greatest good for the greatest number; or in moralist terms of rules, rights, and duties, "thou shalts" and "thou shalt nots." Our public ethical discourse is largely "other-directed" and negative: We focus on condemning misconduct by other people, or on correcting and preventing injustice to other people, rather than on elevating or improving ourselves. How liberating and encouraging it is, then, to encounter an ethics that is focused on the question "How to live?" and that situates what we call the moral life in the larger context of human flourishing. How eye-opening it is to find arguments suggesting that happiness is not a state of passive feeling but a life of fulfilling activity, and especially the unimpeded and excellent activity of our specifically human powers – of doing and making, of thinking and learning, of loving and befriending. How illuminating it is to see the ethical life discussed not in terms of benefits and harms or rules of right and wrong, but in terms of character, and to understand that good character, formed through habituation, is more than holding right opinions or having "good values"; it is a binding up of heart and mind that frees us *from* enslaving passions and frees us *for* fine and beautiful deeds. How encouraging it is to read an account of human life – the only such account in our philosophical tradition – that speaks at length and profoundly about friendship, culminating in the claim that the most fulfilling form of friendship is the sharing of speech and thoughts. And how exhilarating to verify that claim, precisely when Aristotle utters it in the text, because we readers have already experienced the delights of sharing reflectively the illuminating speech and thoughts of the author, offered to us in philosophical friendship.*

But perhaps the most remarkable feature of Aristotle's teaching concerns the *goals* of ethical conduct. Unlike the moralists, Aristotle does not say that morality is a thing of absolute worth or that the virtuous person acts in order to adhere to a moral rule or universalizable maxim. And unlike the utilitarians, he does not say that morality is good because it contributes to civic peace or to private gain and reputation. Instead, Aristotle says over and over again that the ethically excellent human being acts *for the sake of the noble, for the sake of the beautiful.* The human being of fine character seeks to display his own fineness in word and in deed, to show the harmony of his soul in action and the rightness of his choice in the doing of graceful and gracious deeds. The beauty of his action has little to do with the cause that his action will serve or the additional benefits that will accrue to himself or another – though there usually will be such benefits. Rather, it has everything to do with showing forth in action the beautiful soul at work, exactly as a fine dancer dances *for the sake of dancing finely.* As the ballerina both exploits and resists the downward pull of gravity to rise freely and gracefully above it, so the person of ethical virtue exploits and elevates the necessities of our embodied existence to act freely and gracefully above them. Fine conduct is the beautiful and intrinsically fulfilling being-at-work of the harmonious or excellent soul.

---

* Begging the reader's pardon, in the next few paragraphs I quote extensively from an essay I wrote earlier, now presented as Chapter Fourteen. The duplicated material is indispensable for the argument in each essay: here, for the truthful account of my intellectual journey into the humanities; there, for the unfolding account of the teachings of the *Nicomachean Ethics.*

With his attractive picture of human flourishing, Aristotle offers last-ing refuge against the seas of moral relativism. Taking us on a tour of the museum of the virtues – from courage and moderation, through liberality, magnificence, greatness of soul, ambition, and gentleness, to the social virtues of friendliness, truthfulness, and wit – and displaying each of their portraits as a mean between two corresponding vices, Aristotle gives us direct and immediate experience in seeing the humanly beautiful. Any-one who cannot see that courage is more beautiful than cowardice or rash-ness, or that liberality is more beautiful than miserliness or prodigality, suffers (one might say) from the moral equivalent of color-blindness.

But to act nobly, having a noble heart is not enough. It needs help from a sharp mind. Though the beginnings of ethical virtue lie in habitu-ation, starting in our youth, and though the core of moral virtue is the right-shaping of our loves and hates by means of praise and blame, reward and punishment, the perfection of character ultimately requires a certain perfection of the mind. Aristotle's *Ethics* famously teaches the indispensability of prudence or practical wisdom (*phronêsis*) for the supreme sort of ethical virtue. Strictly speaking, one cannot be ethically good unless one is practically wise.

Prudence is, to begin with, the ability to deliberate well about means to ends. But it also involves *intuitive apprehension*, both of the goodness of the ends that one is seeking *and* of the myriad particulars of each human situation, enabling the prudent man to seek and find the best possible action under the circumstances – even if it is a far cry from the best simply. Prudence is more than mere shrewdness. The soul's native power of cleverness can lead to the utmost knavery if not tied down to the noble and just ends that one has been habituated to love. Just as one cannot be ethically excellent without being practically wise, so one can-not be practically wise unless one is ethically excellent.

Today, utilitarians esteem the shrewd and cunning man who knows how to get what he wants, while moralists praise the man of good will, the well-intentioned or good-hearted fellow bent on doing good. These views are both inadequate, as Aristotle shows us. The highest human excellence in the realm of action requires both that one's intentions be good *and* that one's judgment be sound. The prudent man is never a slave to abstract principles or rules of conduct, never a moral preener espousing "ideals" or doctrines; he knows that excellence really consists in finding and enacting the best thing to do *here and now*, always with a view to the good but always as seen in the light of circumstances. He is truly a man for all seasons and for all occasions.

The Wisdom of the Ages

Despite its power and beauty, the picture of human excellence and human flourishing presented in the *Nicomachean Ethics* leaves something to be desired, especially given the needs of modern readers in modern times. What help in thinking about their own possible flourishing, I wonder, are my democratic students really getting from learning to appreciate Aristotle's great-souled man? The virtues of civic life in the polis, beautiful though they still are, seem rather remote from everyday life in urban America, where sympathy, decency, consideration, integrity, and personal responsibility – *mentschlichkeit* – are more relevant and needed than battlefield courage, magnificence, or magnanimity. Yet, sad to report, many of today's students have had little rearing in foundational *mentschlichkeit*, and lifting their gaze to the summits of human greatness sometimes seems chimerical when the ethical ground on which they stand culturally is rather unstable. Moreover, a preoccupation with personal nobility often ignores matters of social justice and the larger public good. Looking only toward the beautiful best also shortchanges the loveliness and especially the obligations of ordinary human lives, lived in families, friendships, neighborhoods, schools, and houses of worship – all of which, as Aristotle himself points out, are surely more efficacious in forming our character than is studying the great philosophers. The best liberal education, though a jewel in the human crown, cannot *by itself* a good human being or a good citizen make.

Accordingly, in my third pursuit, I shifted my anthropological quest from the side of nature to the side of culture, seeking to know the human being not directly, in his nakedness, but indirectly, through an examination of the clothes that fit him best – the clothes of custom and law, song and story, the works of culture and the materials of tradition that bring out the best of which we are capable. The goal was still the same, but my focus turned to the civil and civilizing habits, mores, and opinions that regulate everyday life and that make for human self-command and human flourishing in the domains of work, family, and the multiplicity of human affairs constituting civil society today. One result of this pursuit was a book, *The Hungry Soul: Eating and the Perfecting of Our Nature*, that began with philosophical reflections on human nature and its moral ambiguity, but moved quickly to discussions of the perfecting customs governing human appetite and eating – from the taboo against cannibal-ism and the duties of hospitality, to table manners and the virtue of mod-eration, to festive dining elevated by refinements of taste and wit, to the sanctification of the meal, begun with grace and experienced in gratitude. These explorations were greatly assisted by insights available in the writ-ings of Homer and Herodotus, Plato and Erasmus, Tolstoy and Isak Dinesen, and in the Bible.

In a second project, an interest in the cultural forms that can trans-form mere sexual desire into human *eros* and that can discipline *eros* in the direction of happy marriage resulted in *Wing to Wing, Oar to Oar*, an anthology (produced jointly with my wife) on courting and marrying. Once again, humanistic works and literary examples from across the ages – from Plato's *Symposium* to Erasmus's *On Courtship* and Kierkegaard's reflections on lasting love, from the Bible's Jacob and Rachel to Shake-speare's Rosalind and Orlando, Jane Austen's Elizabeth and Darcy, and Tolstoy's Pierre and Natasha – challenge our unexamined assumptions, sharpen our vision, and educate our desires by illuminating the goals of human longings and the more promising pathways to their fulfillment.

Any humanist seriously interested in the norms and customs govern-ing everyday life cannot help noticing, later if not sooner, the prominent – not to say preeminent – role that our scriptural traditions have played and still play, often invisibly, in the opinions and teachings that guide us, as well as in the humanistic writings of our remote and recent past. And any-one devoted to teaching the *great* books of our tradition would surely want to see for himself just what the Good Book has to say for itself, not relying on hearsay. So it was that my search for the well-clothed human being eventually led me to study – at first, because I had to teach them – the books of the Hebrew Bible. Suspending disbelief, approaching the Bible with open mind and trying to allow the text to teach me how it wishes to be read, I have been astonished to discover an account of human life that can more than hold its own alongside the anthropological and ethical teachings offered by the great poets and philosophers.

I have discovered in the Hebrew Bible teachings of righteousness, humaneness, and human dignity – at the source of my parents' teachings of *mentschlichkeit* – undreamt of in my prior philosophizing. In the idea that human beings are equally godlike, equally created in the image of the divine, I have seen the core principle of a humanistic and democratic politics, respectful of each and every human being, and a necessary correction to the uninstructed human penchant for worshipping brute nature or venerating mighty or clever men. In the Sabbath injunction to desist regularly from work and the flux of getting and spending, I have discovered an invitation to each human being, no matter how lowly, to step outside of time, in *imitatio Dei*, to contemplate the beauty of the world and to feel gratitude for its – and our – existence. In the injunction to honor your father and your mother, I have seen the foundation of a dignified family life, for each of us the nursery of our humanization and the first vehicle of cultural transmission. I have satisfied myself that there is no conflict between the Bible rightly read and modern science, and that the account of Creation in the first chapter of Genesis offers "not words of information but words of appreciation," as Abraham Joshua Heschel put it, "not a description of how the world came into being but a song about the glory of the world's having come into being" – the recognition of which glory, I would add, is ample proof of the text's claim that we human beings stand highest among the creatures.

Thanks to my biblical studies, I have been moved to new attitudes of gratitude, awe, and attention. For just as the world as created was summoned into existence under command, so to be a human being in that world – to be a *mentsch* – is to live in search of our summons. It is to recognize that we are here not by choice or merit, but as an undeserved gift from powers not at our disposal. It is to feel the need to justify that gift, to make something out of our indebtedness for the opportunity of existence. It is to stand in the world not only in awe of its and our existence but under an obligation to answer a call to a worthy life, a life that does honor to the special powers and possibilities – the divinelikeness – with which our otherwise animal existence has been endowed.*

---

* Again begging the reader's pardon, I have stolen the last four sentences, more or less verbatim, from Chapter Thirteen below. Here they are an important marker in my

Much more needs to be said about the relation between the wisdom(s) offered by the Bible – Jewish or Christian – and the wisdom sought by the philosophers or taught by the poets, and about the relation of each to the complexities of modern life. But with our humanity in the balance, it is imperative that we be willing to take help wherever we can find it in our search for self-understanding and guidance. To say the least, no honest quest for the human can afford to turn a blind eye or a deaf ear to the wisdom of the prophets.

The humanities today profit but mainly suffer from having forgotten that they took their origin and point of departure in contradistinction to the "divinities," the inquiry into matters metaphysical and ultimately theological. At first, this separation liberated humanists from dogma and censorship, allowing for several centuries of profound thought and beautiful writing about the human condition and its possible flourishing. But the direction of humanistic learning in my lifetime has culminated in a cynical tendency to disparage the great ideas and to deconstruct the great works inherited from ages past. Can the humanities preserve their true dignity and answer their true calling if they close off or ignore questions of ultimate concern: the character and source of the cosmic whole and the place and work of the human being within it? Can we humanists complete our search for the human being without lifting our gaze, without looking beyond what human beings have wrought, to contemplate the powers that are the condition for the possibility of the world and of our special place within it?

The Case for the Humanities

What can this unlicensed humanist finally say about his search for the human being? As with Diogenes, the quest continues, though the progress achieved makes cynicism even more unjustified. True, the hunt has not captured the quarry, in the sense that I have not found an answer, neatly formulated, sprawling on a pin, that serves as an improved substitute for Plato's "animal, biped and featherless." Instead, I have acquired a

---

intellectual journey; there, they show why the account of Creation in Genesis is not at all embarrassed by the findings of modern natural science.

deeper understanding of the question itself and of the hidden depths of its object. I am much more aware of what a full account of our humanity would entail, including attention to the larger whole – communal, natural, and beyond – in which we human beings are embedded and only in relation to which can we gain any fully flourishing humanity. I can attest to the incomparable value of living with the humanizing gifts of the great books, and the Good Book, open to every one of us regardless of race, class, or gender. In the company of poets and playwrights, philosophers and prophets, novelists and naturalists (deeper human beings all), I have enlarged my vision, furnished my imagination, and deepened my awareness far beyond what I had reason to expect from books.

Grappling with real-life concerns – from cloning to courtship, from living authentically to dying with dignity – has made me a better reader. Reciprocally, reading in a wisdom-seeking spirit has helped me greatly in my worldly grapplings. Not being held to the usual dues expected of a licensed humanist – professing specialized knowledge or publishing learned papers – I have been able to wander freely and most profitably in all the humanistic fields. I have come to believe that looking honestly for the human being, following the path wherever it leads, may itself be an integral part of finding it. A real question, graced by a long life to pursue it among the great books, has been an unadulterated blessing.

But the main key to my flourishing has been the living human company I have enjoyed on my journey. For unlike Diogenes, I have neither needed nor wanted to travel alone. I have been blessed with wonderful teachers and colleagues from whose speech and thoughts I have learned enormous amounts in friendly conversation. I have been supremely blessed in my wife, Amy, co-author and co-teacher – a real humanist, she – from whose literary studies, teaching collaborations, and lifelong conversations my quest has benefited enormously. And I have been blessed in my students, at St. John's College and at the University of Chicago, where serious, thoughtful, smart, eager, engaged, and generous young people have been my most reliable companions in all phases of my journey of inquiry.

It is especially in the relation of one generation to the next that we are best able to understand the true worth of the humanities and the true calling of the humanist. Our students remind us that we too were once at the start of our own journeys, and that we have profited in the search for our humanity from the great cultural inheritance bequeathed to us by countless generations of past seekers, an inheritance opened for us by our own best teachers. Reflection on these unmerited gifts reminds us that we owe a comparable gift to those who will follow us on the path to self-knowledge, in search of wisdom. Too often, those passing for humanists today seek to cut their students off from their inheritance, or they deny its value and significance. But scholars and teachers of the humanities are entrusted above all with sustaining that gift in good order, perhaps adding to it another edifying layer or two, and showing the young why they too should value it and should make use of it in their own searches.

Most young people, in my experience, want to be taken seriously. Despite their facile sophistication and easygoing cynicism – largely a defense against disappointment – most of them are looking for a meaningful life or listening for a summons. Many of them are self-consciously looking for their own humanity and for a personal answer to Diogenes' question. If we treat them uncynically and respectfully, as people interested in the good, the true, and the beautiful, and if we read books with them in search of the good, the true, and the beautiful, they invariably rise to the occasion, vindicating our trust in their potential. And they more than repay our efforts by contributing their own remarkable insights and discoveries to our quest.

The search for our humanity, always necessary yet never more urgent, is best illuminated by the treasured works of the humanities and the "divinities," read in the company of open minds and youthful hearts, together seeking wisdom about how to live a worthy human life. To keep *this* lantern lit, to keep alive *this* quest: Is there a more important task for higher education today? Is there a more important calling for those of us who would practice the humanities, with or without a license?

CHAPTER THIRTEEN

Science, Religion, and the Human Future

NAOMI (age 4): Where did the first person come from?

POLLY (age 7): Well, there are two answers, but what do you think?

NAOMI: I think there was a big tree that broke in half, and, POP, out came a person.

POLLY: Oh, that's interesting. You might be right, but here are the two answers. The Jewish answer is that God created Adam and Eve, and all people came from them. The Public answer is that people came from monkeys.

MOTHER: And where did the monkeys come from?

POLLY: (quick as a wink) From God!

FATHER: But what was before the monkeys?

POLLY: Tehom.

PARENTS: (confused looks on their faces)

POLLY: You know, like the first part of *Bereshith* [Genesis], "*Veha'arets hayeta tohu vavohu vehoshekh 'al-peney tehom.*" ["And the earth was unformed and void, and darkness was on the face of the deep (*tehom*).]

WESTERN CIVILIZATION would not be Western civilization were it not for biblical religion, which reveres and trusts in the one God, Who has made known what He wants of human beings through what is called His revelation, that is, through scripture. Western civilization would not be Western civilization were it not also for science, which extols and trusts in human reason to disclose the workings of nature and to use the knowledge gained to improve human life. These twin sources of Western civilization – religion and science (or, before science, philosophy), divine revelation and human reason – are, to say the least, not easily harmonized. One might even say that Western civilization would not be Western civilization without the continuing dialectical tension between the claims and demands of biblical religion and the cultivation of autonomous human reason.

In the United States today, the age-old tension between science and scriptural religion is intensifying. Recent debates over stem-cell research and the teaching of evolution are but small skirmishes in a larger contest of worldviews, a contest heating up especially because of the triumphant emergence of the new sciences of genetics, neurobiology, and evolutionary psychology. As the findings of these biological sciences are elevated into scientistic challenges to traditional understandings of human nature and man's standing in the universe, religious teachings are increasingly under attack and suspicion. Biblical religion finds itself intellectually on the defensive, in the face of attacks from an aggressive scientific and intellectual elite eager to embarrass it.*

Let us be clear: the stakes in this contest are high. At issue are the moral and spiritual health of our nation, the continued vitality of science, and our own human self-understanding as human beings and as children of the West.

In this chapter, I will examine the challenge of the scientific worldview and consider whether biblical religion can meet that challenge. Before proceeding, however, I need to enter a few preliminary stipulations about the terms "religion" and "science," each of which is complicated and ambiguous.

*

---

* See, for example, recent books by the biologist and bioprophet Richard Dawkins (*The God Delusion*) and the philosophy professor Daniel Dennett (*Breaking the Spell: Religion as a Natural Phenomenon*). Both offer purely naturalistic and evolutionary accounts of the origin of human religions and document what they regard as the evils that belief in God has wrought.

Preliminary Distinctions

What do we mean by referring to "religion"? The world knows innumerable *religions,* and even the so-called great religions of East and West differ profoundly in their conceptions of divinity, nature, man, reason, morals, spirituality, and the purpose of it all. In speaking of religion, we are not talking about a contest between *faith* and *reason,* for religions are about much more than faith, and many of the teachings of biblical religion are neither irrational nor unreasonable. It is true that Christianity emphasizes the supreme importance of belief and the affirmation of doctrine and creed, as compared with matters of practice, ritual, and lawful observance; and Enlightenment rationalists seized upon this emphasis in order to attack religion wholesale as "irrational."

"Science," too, is an ambiguous word, referring in modern usage both to a methodical art for gaining knowledge and to the accumulated knowledge itself. Both these meanings need to be distinguished from a strictly scientific *outlook* on life and the world, which in its full form has been called "scientism," a quasi-religious faith in the sufficiency of modern science to give a complete account of our world, including human life, which itself encompasses man's belief in God. One need not be scientistic to practice science, and most scientists are not. Indeed, many a scientist is also a self-identified member of one or another religious community, though part of what is at issue here is whether any easygoing compatibility of, for example, Darwinism during the week and Judaism or Christianity on the Sabbath is rationally defensible and free of contradiction.

In what follows I will use "religion" to refer to both Judaism and Christianity, overlooking for the most part all of the important differences between them (and within each). By "science" I will mean modern Western science, the globally successful effort – of which mathematical physics is both the jewel and the foundation – to understand how things work, by a method of discovery uniquely invented for this purpose, and ultimately imbued with a philanthropic aspiration to use that knowledge for the relief of man's estate and the betterment of human life.

The relation between religion and science is, of course, neither a scientific nor a religious question. Insofar as it is a genuine question, it is a philosophical one, both subject and object of a quest for wisdom. My philosophical approach carries its own hazards of distortion, since it

risks treating science and (especially) the various religions from the outside, and not in the way they understand themselves. Thoughtful Jews
and Christians and knowledgeable scientists may well not recognize
themselves in my account.* Nevertheless, looking in the mirror that I am
providing should, I hope, stimulate salutary self-reflection.

Although any religion as a human (and more than human) institution
comprises much more than the knowledge or truths it propounds, the primary point of contact and contest between science and religion happens
to be about truth. Hence the central question is this: How do matters
stand between the truths discovered by science and the truths revealed by
biblical religion, between the truths that can send a man to the moon and
the truth spoken in the Torah or the truth that can set you free?

My answer is divided into three parts: first, some remarks about scientific knowledge and truth in general, and its implications for religious
teachings; second, remarks about knowledge of man and his place in the
whole; and third, remarks about knowledge of how human beings ought
to live.

The Limited Knowledge of Modern Science

What kind of knowledge is science, and how is it related to the truths
promulgated by biblical religion? Are these, as Stephen Jay Gould argued,
"non-overlapping magisteria," each having its own canons of evidence
and legitimate claims, yet perfectly compatible domains – despite apparent contradictions between them – neither of which is capable of refuting
or replacing the other? Or should we rather insist that there cannot be
contradictory "truths" about the one world? For either the world is eternal or it came into being; if it came into being, either it was created by
God or it was not; if there is divinity, either there is one God or there are
many gods; either man is the one godlike ("image of God") creature or he

---

* There may also be a deeper problem with allowing the dispute between science
and religion to be adjudicated in the court of philosophy. Both science and
religion, each in its own way, are at odds with the disinterested and unrestrained
pursuit of wisdom: the former arose by rejecting such a pursuit as futile, while the
latter has doubts about the adequacy of unaided human reason.

is not; either his soul is immortal or it is not; either he has free will or he does not; either God has made known to man what He requires of him or He has not. It is, I trust, not just the residual scientist in me that insists there cannot be more than one truth about the one world, even if we human beings can never know it to the bottom.

This premise of a single, universal truth is indeed one of the starting points of modern science, and it is science's reliance on the universal "language" of modern mathematics and on methodical reason to discover such truth that makes possible its transnational and transreligious appeal. If Buddhists or Muslims or Christians want to describe the relation of pressure to volume in a gas at constant temperature or the motion of falling bodies, they will necessarily embrace the equations that are Boyle's law or the law of universal gravitation. Indeed, the quest for *indubitable* knowledge, universally accessible and rationally expressible, was the radical new goal of modern science, rebelling against a two-thousand-year history of intellectual controversy and disagreement on nearly all matters hitherto discussed by scholars. As Descartes put it, "There is nothing imaginable so strange or so little credible that it has not been maintained by one philosopher or other."

By the stringent standard of indubitability, a critique similar to Descartes's could be applied now as well as then to some of the central teachings of the world's great religions. Anyone can doubt or deny the Creation or immortality or the resurrection of the dead without self-contradiction; but no one can deny that the square built on the hypotenuse of a right triangle is equal to the sum of the squares built on the other two sides. In order to gain knowledge as indubitable as mathematics, the founders of modern science had to reconceive nature in objectified (mathematical) terms and to change the questions being asked: no longer the big questions regarding the nature of things, pursued by rare wisdom seekers, but quantifiable problems regarding an objectified nature, soluble by ordinary mathematical problem solvers. If the history of modern science could be viewed not retrospectively from the present, but prospectively from its origins in the early seventeenth century, we would be absolutely astonished at what science has been able to learn about the workings of nature, objectively reconceived.

Nevertheless, despite its universality, its quest for certainty, its reliance on reason purified from all distortions of sensation and prejudice by the use of mathematical method, and the reproducibility of its findings, science does not – and cannot – provide us with absolute knowledge. The reasons are not only methodological but also substantive, and not merely substantive but also intrinsic and permanent.

The substantive limits of science follow from certain fundamental aspects of scientific knowledge and from science's assumptions about what sorts of things are scientifically knowable. They stem from science's own self-proclaimed conceptual limitations – limitations to which neither religious nor philosophical thought is subject. This is not because, science being rational, it is incapable of dealing with the passionate or subrational or spiritual or supernatural aspects of being. It is, on the contrary, because the rationality of science is but a partial and highly specialized rationality, concocted for the purpose of gaining only that kind of knowledge for which it was devised, and applied only to those aspects of the world that can be captured by such rationalized notions. The peculiar reason of science is not the natural reason of everyday life captured in ordinary speech, and it is also not the reason of philosophy or of religious thought, both of which are tied to the world as we experience it, even as they seek to take us beyond it.*

Consider the following features of science and their contrast with the realm of ordinary experience. First, science at its peak seeks laws of nature, ideally expressed mathematically in the form of equations that

---

* It is therefore worth calling into question arguments offered by those who seek to harmonize science and religion by assimilating the rationality of science with the rationality of the biblical God and His creation. They will point out, correctly, that God's creation according to Genesis 1 is based on intelligible principles and proceeds through acts of intelligible speech. Or they will point out that the Christian God is a God of reason, because "In the beginning was the Logos and the Logos was with God." But it bears emphasis that neither the intelligible principles of creation in Genesis 1 (separation, place, motion, and life) nor the Logos spoken of in the Gospel of John is anything like the principles or mathematized *logoi* (ratios) of science. The former are tied to the distinctions of ordinary speech, which names qualitatively different natural kinds; the latter are tied to the concept of quantity, which homogenizes the differences of natural beings (and even the difference between discrete and continuous quantity, between multitudes and magnitudes).

For more on the conceptual peculiarities of modern science, and its radical difference both from ancient science and from ordinary human reasoning about life and the world, see the "Appendix: Observations on Objectivity" at the end of this chapter.

describe precisely the relationships among changing measurable variables; science does not seek to know beings or their natures, but rather the regularities of the changes that they undergo. Second, science – especially in biology – seeks to know how things work and the mechanisms of action in their workings; it does not seek to know what things are, or why. Third, science can give the histories of things but not their directions, aspirations, or purposes; by self-definition, science is nonteleological, oblivious to the natural purposiveness of all living things. Fourth, science is wonderful at quantifying selected *external* relations of one object to another, or an earlier phase to a later one; but it can say nothing at all about *inner* states of being, either of human beings or of any living creature. Fifth, and strangest of all, modern science does not care much about causation; it can often predict what will happen if certain perturbations occur because it knows the regularities of change, but it eschews explanations in terms of causes, especially ultimate causes.

In short, we have a remarkable science of nature that has made enormous progress precisely by its metaphysical neutrality and its indifference to questions of being, cause, purpose, inwardness, hierarchy, and the goodness or badness of things, scientific knowledge included.

Let me illustrate these abstract generalizations with a few concrete examples. In cosmology, we have seen wonderful progress in characterizing the temporal beginnings of the universe as a "big bang" and elaborate calculations to describe what happened next. But from science we get complete silence regarding the status quo ante and the ultimate cause. Unlike a normally curious child, a cosmologist does not ask, "What was *before* the big bang?" or "*Why* is there something rather than nothing?" because the answer must be an exasperated "God only knows!"

In genetics, we have the complete DNA sequence of several organisms, including man, and we are rapidly learning what many of these genes "do." But this analytic approach cannot tell us how the life of a cockroach differs from that of a chimpanzee, or even what accounts for the special unity and active wholeness of cockroaches or chimpanzees, or the purposive effort each living thing makes to preserve its own specific integrity.

In neurophysiology, we know vast amounts about the processing of visual stimuli, their transformation into electrochemical signals, and the pathways and mechanisms for transmitting these signals to the visual cortex of the brain. But the nature of sight itself we do not know scientifically; we know it only from the inside, and only because we are not blind. As Aristotle pointed out long ago (and as I repeated in the last chapter), the eyeball (and, I would add, the brain) has extension, takes up space, can be held in the hand; but neither sight (the capacity) nor seeing (the activity) is extended, and you cannot hold them in your hand or point to them. Although absolutely dependent on material conditions, they are in their essence immaterial: they are capacities and activities of *soul* – hence, not an object of knowledge for an objectified and materialist science.

Implications for Religion

The self-limited character of scientific knowledge is, on the one hand, very good news for Christians and Jews. Eschewing philosophical speculation and metaphysical matters, science leaves those activities and domains free for complementary activities. Human beings will always ask questions of what and why, as well as when and how. Human beings will always ask questions about the first cause and the end of days. Speculative philosophy and religion address these concerns and offer their own answers – albeit on grounds that must, of necessity, be "unscientific." If, for example, Genesis 1 offers a picture of the hierarchy of being, with man perched at its apex, the truth of that claim will not be based on scientific evidence, nor (as I will suggest later) is it likely to be confirmed or denied by scientific findings.

On closer examination, however, Stephen Jay Gould's live-and-let-live suggestion of complementary truths has its own limitations for the seriously religious. This is especially true for those whose reading of scripture is not only literal but literalist: those who think that the truths of scripture belong to the same category of knowledge as that which can be demonstrated or falsified by science or historical research – a misguided hypothesis, in my opinion, but popular nonetheless. So, for example, those who would learn the precise age of the earth from scripture, like Bishop Ussher in the seventeenth century, may be compelled to reconsider the veracity of the Bible, given the abundant evidence for the vast age of the cosmos. The fossil record, despite its lacunae, is an embarrassment to those who believe that the Bible teaches correctly the near-instantaneous appearance of all God's creatures – unless, of course, they retreat to the position (proposed seriously in the nineteenth century) that God seeded the earth's layers with fossils of creatures that never existed, precisely in order to test the faithful.

Then there is that old chestnut of miracles, still a hard one to crack. Few of us in the present age believe in miracles – events that suspend the laws of nature and that we must hold to be "impossible" according to the regularities that science describes for us. In this respect, we are all children of science, at least regarding our contemporary life on earth. So little do we believe in the possibility of miracles that many of us even have trouble imagining any occurrence so unusual or momentous as to shake our faith in the *im*possibility of miracles.

I once discussed this issue with a class of brilliant high-schoolers studying Descartes's *Discourse on Method*. They were dogmatically insisting that their faith in nature's abiding lawfulness could never be shaken, come what may, when I confidently asked: "What if Descartes himself were suddenly to appear in the flesh right before us, not some Madame Tussaud dummy but the real René? Would you change your mind?" To my astonishment, no one was the least bit moved. Instead, invoking the laws of probability and the always non-zero chance of even the rarest of events, the smart scientists in the class averred that the molecules that once accompanied the genius that was Descartes might, on their own, accidentally reunite to give us his reincarnation. I found their faith as touching as it was preposterous.

Yet the irrationality of their zeal does not solve the problem for believing Christians and Jews, to whom big miracles surely matter, and attempts to harmonize science and religion cannot make this issue disappear. Either God gave the Law to the Israelites at Mount Horeb or He didn't; if not, the six hundred thousand witnesses were deluded, and those who accept that His Torah was His gift may need to reconsider. Either the Red Sea parted and the sun stood still or they didn't, in which case God's providence on behalf of His people is less than it is cracked up to be – not an uncommon opinion among some post-Holocaust Jews. And, abundant claims for the harmony of faith and reason notwithstanding, either Jesus rose from the dead or he did not – a miracle from the point of view not only of science but of all reasonable human experience. Yet on the truth of his resurrection rests the deepest ground for the Christian faith in the divinity of Jesus and the promise of man's ultimate salvation in him.

Science not only casts doubt on such astounding "irregularities," it cannot abide them. For science, this is no idle prejudice. If a willful and powerful God were capable of intervening in worldly affairs and suspending the laws of nature, genuine science would be impossible.* Its regularities would be mere probabilities, and its predictions would be entirely contingent on God's being out to lunch.

To my mind, it is a limping rejoinder to this challenge to say that an omnipotent God could still perform miracles and may someday do so again, but that He binds His power by His will for His own good purposes – hence, among other things, making science possible. This is too neat and too ad hoc to be satisfying. And there is, I should add, nothing in scripture to support these apologetic fancies.

On top of this rather old difficulty about miracles in general – a difficulty that Christians and Jews have apparently learned to live with – biblical religious teachings today face newer and more particular difficulties in relation to specific scientific developments, of which the possible tension between evolution and the Bible is only the best-known example. Here I have in mind present and projected discoveries in genetics and neuroscience, and, even more, the *interpretations* of these findings in the theoretical (and often explicitly antireligious) pronouncements of evolutionary psychologists: interpretations and pronouncements that are supported but, in my view, hardly necessitated by those scientific discoveries. Today and tomorrow, major challenges are coming that affect not only specific religious dogmas, unique to each faith, but also the biblical understanding of human nature and human dignity, central ideas in all scriptural religion. This is where the next big battles may be anticipated.

*

---

* Although Descartes gained a great deal of fame for his proofs of the existence of God, the god to whose existence he was devoted is not the God of scripture. Far from being omnipotent, the god of physics is bound by nature's immutable laws and nature's lawful motion. The divine, defined as "eternal changelessness," is indistinguishable from eternal, unchanging nature, acting according to those immutable laws and therefore utterly immune to the sorts of miracles that are indispensable to scriptural teaching.

Science, Human Nature, and Human Dignity

For most of us, most of the time, the limitations of the scientific understanding of the world are not a source of disquiet. Who cares, really, that
according to our physics this most solid table at which I am writing is
largely empty space, or that beautiful colors are conceived of as mathematized waves? Almost no one even notices that science ignores the being of
things, even living things, and approaches them in objectified and mechanistic terms. We start to fret only when the account comes home to
roost, to challenge our self-understanding as free and self-conscious
beings with a rich inner life.

This venerable self-conception, rooted in everyday human experience,
has been reinforced by centuries of philosophical and religious teachings.
Yet the challenge to it has been coming for a long time; indeed, it emerged
with the origins of modern science in the seventeenth century and has
been there for all to see. For centuries, giants of Western philosophy,
including Leibniz, Spinoza, and Kant, labored mightily to find a home
for human freedom and dignity, now that all of nature had to be ceded to
mechanistic physics. Today, those philosophical defenses are no longer
being attempted, whereas the challengers – all adherents of scientism –
have become increasingly bold.

The strongest summonses today come from an increasingly unified
approach to biology and human biology – evolutionist, materialist, deter-
minist, mechanistic, and objectified – combining powerful ideas from
genetics, developmental biology, neuroscience, and evolutionary biology
and psychology. At issue are not only what we think we are, but also our
standing vis-à-vis the rest of living nature. Darwinism in its original version, over 150 years ago, already appeared to challenge our special standing: how could any being descended from subhuman origins, rather than
created directly by the hand of God, claim to be a higher animal, let alone
a godlike one? Indeed, orthodox evolutionary theory even holds that animals should not be called "higher" or "lower," but only more or less complex: since all animals are finally in the same business of individual
survival for the sake of perpetuating their genes, the apparent differences
among them are, at bottom, merely more or less complicated ways of getting the job done.

Materialistic explanations of vital events, even psychic events, leave no room for soul, understood as life's animating principle. Remarkably, our science of life has no interest in the question of what life *is* or what is responsible for it. Likewise, our science of the psyche has no interest in its proper subject: does any psychologist ask, "What is soul, that we are mindful of it?" Deterministic and mechanistic accounts of brain functions seem to do away with the need to speak of human freedom and purposiveness. The fully objectified and exterior account of our behavior – once the province of B. F. Skinner, today the grail sought by neuroscience – diminishes the significance of our felt inwardness. Feeling, passion, awareness, imagination, desire, love, hate, and thought are, scientifically speaking, equally and merely "brain events." Even religious experiences and thoughts about God, according to published reports by "neurotheologians," are rooted in heightened activity of certain well-localized regions of the human brain.

Never mind "created in the image of God": what elevated *humanistic* view of human life or human goodness is defensible against the belief, trumpeted by biology's most public and prophetic voices, that man is just a collection of molecules, an accident on the stage of evolution, a freakish speck of mind in a mindless universe, fundamentally no different from other living or even nonliving things? What chance have our treasured ideas of freedom and dignity against the reductive notion of "the selfish gene" (or, for that matter, "genes for altruism"), the belief that DNA is the essence of life, or the teaching that all human behavior and our rich inner life are rendered intelligible only in terms of neurochemistry and their contributions to species survival and reproductive success?

To repeat, there is nothing novel about reductionism, materialism, or determinism. What is new is that, as philosophies, they seem (to many people) to be vindicated by scientific advance, in an age that respects no authority higher than science. Here, in consequence, would be the most pernicious result of our technological progress: the erosion, perhaps the final erosion, of the idea of man as noble, dignified, precious, or godlike, and its replacement with a view of man, no less than of nature, as mere raw material for manipulation and homogenization (a view illustrated with examples in Chapter Ten).

As a *cultural* matter, the challenge of soulless scientism is surely daunting, even dispiriting. With philosophical anthropology in hibernation, only religious teachings appear to support the intuitions of uninstructed human experience of the human. Our secular elite – in the service of a rational, universal science – is only too happy to charge these teachings with parochialism, dogmatism, and narrow cultural prejudice. The same elite is above all determined to banish all such teachings and (especially) their proponents from public discourse about such "scientific" matters as cloning or euthanasia.

But take heart: as a *philosophical* matter, these challenges should not bother us. Each of them can be met without for a moment calling into question the elegance or accuracy of any genuine scientific findings, and even without turning to religion. An adequate philosophy of nature would know what to say. The subject is long, but the following summary points show once again the limits of any merely scientific approach.[48]

First, regarding our origins: a history of coming-into-being is no substitute for knowing directly the being that has come to be. To know man, we must study him especially as he is (and through what he does), not by how he got to be this way. For understanding either our nature – what we are – or our standing, it matters not whether our origin was from the primordial slime or from the hand of a Creator God: even with monkeys for ancestors, what has emerged is more than monkey business.

Second, regarding our inwardness, freedom, and purposiveness, we must repair to our inside knowledge. Even if scientists were to "prove" to their satisfaction that inwardness, consciousness, and human will or purposive intention are all illusory – at best, epiphenomena of brain events – or that what we call loving and wishing and thinking are merely electrochemical transformations of brain substance, we should proceed to ignore them. For life's self-revelatory testimony with regard to its own vital activity is more immediate, compelling, and trustworthy than are the abstracted explanations that evaporate meaningful lived experience by identifying it with some correlated bodily event. The most unsophisticated child knows red and blue more reliably than a physicist with his spectrometers. And anyone who has ever loved knows that love cannot be reduced to neurotransmitters. Regarding our life – passionate, responsive, appetitive, thoughtful, and active – we have inside knowledge that cannot be denied.

Third, scientists will be unable, on their own ground, to refute our intransigent insistence on our own freedom and psychic awareness. How are they going to explain our resistance to their subversive ideas, save by conceding that we must be hardwired by nature to resist them? If all truth claims of science – and the philosophical convictions that some people derive from them – are merely the verbalized expressions of certain underlying brain states in the scientists who offer these claims, then there can be no way to refute the contrary opinions of those whose nervous systems, differently wired, see things the opposite way. And why, indeed, should anyone choose to accept as true the results of someone else's "electrochemical brain processes" over his own? Truth and error, no less than human freedom and dignity, become empty notions when the soul is reduced to chemicals.

The possibility of science itself depends on the immateriality of thought. It depends on the mind's independence from the bombardment of matter. Otherwise, there is no truth, there is only "it seems to me." Not only the possibility for recognizing truth and error, but also the *reasons* for doing science rest on a picture of human freedom and dignity (of the sort promulgated by biblical religion) that science itself cannot recognize. Wonder, curiosity, a wish not to be self-deceived, and a spirit of philanthropy are the *sine qua non* of the modern scientific enterprise. They are hallmarks of the living human soul, not of the anatomized brain. The very enterprise of science – like all else of value in human life – depends on a view of humanity that science cannot supply and that foolish scientistic prophets deny at their peril, unaware of the embarrassing self-contradiction.

Science and the Moral Life

The deepest limitation of a scientized account of the human condition concerns not so much man as knower but man as an ethical and spiritual being – a being whose existence is defined not only by Kant's first great question, "What can I know?" but by his second and third great questions: "What ought I do?" and "What may I hope?" Man alone among the animals goes in for ethicizing, for concerning himself with how to live, and with better and worse answers to this question. Science, notwithstanding its great gifts to human life in the form of greater comfort and safety, is notoriously unhelpful in satisfying these deeper longings of the human soul.

One should acknowledge straightaway that science is not an immoral or nonmoral activity. On the contrary, although the motivations and characters of individual scientists run the usual human gamut, the enterprise of science taken as a whole is animated by noble purpose: a philanthropic desire to alleviate human misery and to improve human life. In addition, the successful practice of science requires the exercise of many virtues: enterprise (in imagining new possibilities), self-discipline and perseverance (in doggedly pursuing a line of experimentation), courage (in risking failure), measure and judiciousness (in weighing evidence), and intellectual probity and integrity (in reporting data, crediting others, and giving an honest account to one's sources of financial support).

Science is also a social activity: much scientific research involves direct collaboration, and nearly all of it rests on explicit and tacit networks of cooperation; it therefore requires openness, trust, and (within the limits of scientific competition) generous sharing of materials and data. In my own experience, I have found that personal integrity, group morale, and the ease of interpersonal relations in a research laboratory are several cuts above what I have encountered in any other domain of academic life (including philosophy departments and divinity schools).

But these private virtues of scientists, as well as the overall ethical character of the scientific project, are not products of science. Science is notoriously (and deliberately) morally neutral, silent on the distinction between better and worse, right and wrong, the noble and the base. Though it seeks universal knowledge, it has no answer to moral relativism. It can offer no standards to guide the use of the awesome powers it places in human hands. It can do nothing to ensure that the uses made of its findings will be governed in charity, as Francis Bacon prophesied. Science does not know what charity is, what charity requires, or even whether or why it is good. It can neither confirm nor support its own philanthropic assumptions.

Such moral poverty need not be embarrassing, either to science or to religion. After all, science never claimed to speak on moral matters,* and religion remains available to speak where science is silent – to teach us

---

* More than a few of today's scientists, however, are not constrained by such modesty. Taking advantage of their elevated reputation (based on their superior knowledge of how dumb nature works), and falling prey to the tyranny of expertise, they pronounce authoritatively how human beings should act and how they should live – in matters ranging from eating or sex to crime and punishment or war and peace.

our duties, to restrain our vices, to lead us to righteousness and holiness. But the ability of religion to guide us in these ways depends in part on its ability to withstand not the morally neutral discoveries of science but the morally freighted, antireligious campaigns that rely on and make use of a strictly scientific view of human life. And here, the news is hardly good.

No one should underestimate the growing cultural power of scientific materialism and reductionism. As we have seen, the materialism of science, useful as a heuristic hypothesis, is increasingly being peddled as the one true account of human life, on the evidence of the powers obtainable through just such reductive approaches. Many laymen, ignorant of any defensible scientific alternative to materialism, are swallowing and regurgitating the shallow doctrines of "the selfish gene" and "the mind is the brain," because they *seem* to be vindicated by scientific advance. The cultural result is likely to be serious damage to human self-understanding and the subversion of all high-minded views of the good life.

Nowhere will this challenge be more readily felt than in the proposed uses of biotechnical power for purposes beyond the cure of disease and the relief of suffering. Going beyond therapy, we stand on the threshold of major efforts to "perfect" human nature and to "enhance" human life by direct biotechnical alterations of our bodies and minds. As I noted in Chapter Six, we are promised better children, superior performance, ageless bodies, and happy souls – all with the help of the biotechnologies of "enhancement." Bioprophets tell us that we are en route to a new stage of evolution, to the creation of a posthuman society, a society based on science and built by technology, a society in which traditional teachings about human nature will be passé and religious teachings about how to live will be irrelevant.

But what, then, will guide this evolution? How do we know whether any of these so-called enhancements is actually an improvement? Why ought any human being embrace a *post*human future? Scientism has no answers to these critical moral questions. Deaf to nature, to God, and even to moral reason, it can offer no standards for judging scientific progress – or for judging anything else. Instead, it essentially preaches its own version of faith, hope, and charity: faith in the goodness of scientific progress, hope in the prospect of transcending our biological limitations, charity in promising everyone an ultimate victory over the human condition. No religious faith rests on flimsier ground. And yet the project for the mastery of human nature proceeds apace, and most people stand on the sidelines and cheer, thoughtlessly rooting for the abolition of man.

Thus, while there is no philosophical reason to despair, and while a philosophical and religious anthropology could meet the challenge of scientism, there are in fact large cultural reasons to worry. Can our religious traditions rise to the challenge?

The Truth of the Bible

Up to this point, I have largely addressed the relation between religion and science by focusing on the limitations of science. But what about the limits of biblical religion? What new difficulties does it face in the age of science? Can it survive and surmount them?

As an empirical matter, there can be no doubt that the growth of secularism and atheism in the West over the past few centuries, especially in the last fifty prosperous years, is at least in part connected with the success of science and technology – and of modern rationalism more generally – and also with the uses that have been made of science in explicit attempts to embarrass religious beliefs. Just as Lucretius long ago used Epicurus's doctrine of atomistic materialism to combat religious beliefs and to cure men of the fear of the gods, so many modern epicureans enlist the teachings of evolution and neuroscience as battering rams against the teachings of the Bible and the religions built upon it.

Measuring the success of this assault would be a very complicated enterprise, not only sociologically but also philosophically. But it may be helpful, as a test case, to look at what has been a chief target of scientism, the opening chapter of the Bible and its account of Creation. How should the teachings of Genesis 1 be affected by the discoveries of science? Can one still affirm the truths that it purports to teach? Conversely, can the biblical account of Creation – including man's place in it – answer the shortcomings of the scientific account? The answers to these questions depend entirely on what Genesis 1 actually says and what it aims to accomplish in the hearts and minds of its readers.

In writing elsewhere on this subject, I have argued that the teachings of Genesis 1 are indeed untouched by the scientific findings that allegedly make them "plumb unbelievable."[49] Here is a summary of the major points. First, Genesis 1 is not a freestanding historical or scientific account of what happened and how, but rather a (literally) *awe*-inspiring prelude to a lengthy and comprehensive teaching about how we are to live. Second, it is not an account that can be either corroborated or falsified by scientific or historical studies: neither so-called "creation science" nor arguments about "intelligent design," on the one hand, nor evidence regarding the age of the universe or man's evolutionary origins and the workings of his brain, on the other hand, can strengthen or weaken decisively what one is supposed to learn from the Creation story.

This is partly because, third, the Bible addresses its readers not as detached, rational observers moved primarily by curiosity and the desire for mastery over nature, but as existentially engaged human beings who need first and foremost to make sense of their world and their task within it. Genesis speaks immediately and truly to the deepest concerns of human hearts and minds in their normal – and permanent – existential condition. The first human question is not "How did this come into being?" or "How does it work?" The first human question is "What does all this mean?" and (especially) "What am I to do here?"

The specific claims of the biblical account of Creation begin to nourish the human longing for answers to these questions. The world that you, a human being, see around you is orderly and intelligible (albeit against a background of chaos and threat of dissolution); it is an articulated whole comprising distinct kinds. The order of the world is as rational as the speech that you use to describe it, and the speech that summoned it into being right before your (reading) eyes. Most importantly, this noetic (rather than sensual) order of created things intends mainly to demonstrate that the sun, the moon, and the stars, contrary to the belief of uninstructed human experience, are not divine, despite their sempiternal beauty and power and their majestic perfect motion. Nature is neither eternal nor divine;* its beginnings are owed neither to the sexual couplings nor to the warring struggles of gods and goddesses. Moreover, being is *hierarchic*, and man is the highest being in creation,

---

* One cannot exaggerate the importance the Bible attaches to this teaching, for the worship of nature is the "natural way" of human beings in the absence of biblical instruction (see also Deuteronomy 4:15–19). The point has been beautifully made by Harvey Flaumenhaft in "Quest for Order," *Humanities*, January–February 1992.

although not yet perfected or complete. (Unlike all other created things save the heavenly firmament, man is not said by God to be "good.") And man is likewise alone in being *in the image* of God.

What does this mean? And can it be true? In the course of recounting God's creation, Genesis 1 introduces us to His *activities* and *powers*: God speaks, commands, names, blesses, and hallows; God makes, and makes freely; God looks at and beholds the world; God is concerned with the goodness or perfection of things; God addresses solicitously other living creatures and provides for their sustenance. In short, God exercises speech and reason, freedom in doing and making, and the powers of contemplation, judgment, and care.

Doubters may wonder whether this is truly the case about God – after all, it is only on biblical authority that we regard God as possessing these powers and activities. But it is indubitably clear, even to atheists, that we human beings have them, and that they lift us above the plane of a merely animal existence. Human beings, alone among the creatures, speak, plan, create, contemplate, and judge. Human beings, alone among the creatures, can articulate a future goal and use that articulation to guide them in bringing it into being by their own purposive conduct. Human beings, alone among the creatures, can think about the whole, marvel at its many-splendored forms and articulated order, wonder about its beginning, and feel awe in beholding its grandeur and in pondering the mystery of its source.

Note well: these self-evident truths do *not* rest on biblical authority. Rather, the biblical text enables us to confirm them by an act of self-reflection. Our reading of this text, addressable and intelligible only to us human beings, and our responses to it, possible only for us human beings, provide all the proof we need to confirm the text's assertion of our special being. The very act of *reading* Genesis 1 demonstrates the truth of its claims about the superior ontological standing of the human. This is not anthropocentric prejudice, but cosmological truth. And nothing we shall ever learn from science about *how* we came to be this way could ever make it false.*

---

* Modern science should have no real difficulty with this conclusion. The sempiternal heavenly bodies may outlast and outshine us and move in beautiful circular paths; or, if you prefer a modern equivalent, matter-energy may be virtually indestructible. But

In addition to holding up a mirror in which we see reflected our special standing in the world, Genesis 1 teaches truly the bounty of the universe and its hospitality in supporting terrestrial life. Moreover, we have
it on the highest authority that the whole – the being of all that is – is
"very good":

> And God saw every thing that He had made, and, behold, it was
> very good. (Genesis 1:31)

The Bible here teaches a truth that cannot be known by science, even
as it is the basis of the very possibility of science – and of everything else
we esteem. For it truly *is* very good that there is something rather than
nothing. It truly is very good that this something is intelligibly ordered
rather than dark and chaotic. It truly is very good that the whole contains
a being who can not only discern the intelligible order but also recognize
that it is "very good" – who can *appreciate* that there is something rather
than nothing and that he exists with the reflexive capacity to celebrate
these facts with the mysterious source of being itself. As Abraham Joshua
Heschel put it in *Who Is Man?* (1965):

> The biblical words about the genesis of heaven and earth are not
> words of information but words of appreciation. The story of cre-
> ation is not a description of how the world came into being but a
> song about the glory of the world's having come into being. "And
> God saw that it was good." This is the challenge: to reconcile God's
> view with our experience.

There is more. The purpose of the song is not only to celebrate. It is
also to summon us to awe and attention. For just as the world as created
is a world summoned into existence under command, so to be a human
being in that world is to recognize, first of all, that we are here not by
choice or on account of merit, but as an undeserved gift from powers not
at our disposal. It is to feel the need to justify that gift, to make some-

---

only we, not they, can know these facts. Not until there are human beings does the
universe become conscious of itself – a remarkable achievement that should surely
inspire awe and wonder, even in atheists.

thing out of our indebtedness for the opportunity of existence. It is to stand in the world not only in wonder at its existence but under an obligation to answer a call to a worthy life, a life that does honor to the divinelikeness with which our otherwise animal existence has been – no thanks to us – endowed. It is explicitly to feel the need to find a way of life for which we should be pleased to answer at the bar of justice when our course is run, in order to vindicate the blessed opportunity and the moral-spiritual challenge that is the essence of being human.

The first chapter of Genesis – like no work of science, no matter how elegant or profound – invites us to hearken to a transcendent voice. It provides a perfect answer to the human need to know not only how the world works but also what we are to do here. It is the beginning of a Bible-length response to the human longing for meaning and wholehearted existence. The truths it bespeaks – and which are enacted when the text is read respondingly – are more than cognitive. They point away from the truths of belief to the truths of action – of song and praise and ritual, of love and procreation and civic life, of responsible deeds in answering the call to righteousness, holiness, and love of neighbor. Such truths speak more deeply and permanently than any mere doctrine, whether of science or even of faith. As long as we understand our great religions as the embodiments of such truths, the friends of religion will have nothing to fear from science, and the friends of science who are still in touch with their humanity will have nothing to fear from religion. That we should have been given such a life-affirming teaching is, to speak plainly, a miracle.

Appendix: Observations on Objectivity

My discussion of the permanent limitations of science may be helped by some additional philosophical observations, beginning with the radical differences between modern science and ancient science, against which modern science deliberately revolted. The most important differences concern the purpose of science and, therefore, the character of knowledge sought.

Although it is commonplace to distinguish applied from pure science (or technology from science), it is important to grasp the essentially practical, social, and technical character of modern science as such. Ancient science had sought knowledge of *what* things *are,* to be contemplated as an end-in-itself satisfying to the knower. In contrast, modern science seeks knowledge of *how* they *work,* to be used as a means for the relief and comfort of all humanity. Though the benefits were at first slow in coming, this practical intention has been at the heart of all modern science right from the start.

But modern science is practical and artful not only in its end. In contrast with ancient science, its very notions and ways manifest a conception of the interrelation of knowledge and power. Nature herself is conceived energetically and mechanistically, and explanation of change is given in terms of (at most) efficient or moving causes; in modern science, to be responsible means to produce an effect. Knowledge itself is obtained productively: hidden truths are gained by acting on nature, through experiment, twisting its arm to make it cough up its secrets.

The so-called "empirical" science of nature is, as actually experienced, the highly contrived encounter with apparatus, measuring devices, pointer readings, and numbers; nature in its ordinary course and as humanly experienced is virtually never directly encountered. Inquiry is made "methodical," through the imposition of order and schemes of measurement "made" by the intellect. Knowledge, embodied in laws rather than (as in ancient science) theorems, becomes "systematic" under rules of a new mathematics expressly *invented* for this purpose.

This mathematics orders an "unnatural" world that has been intellectually "objectified," re-presented or projected before the knowing subject as pure homogenous extension, ripe for the mind's grasping – just as the world itself will be grasped by the techniques that science will later provide. Even the modern word "concept" means "a grasping-together," implying that the mind itself, in its act of knowing, functions like the intervening hand (in contrast to its ancient counterpart, "idea," meaning "that which can be beheld," implying that the mind functions like the receiving eye). And modern science rejects, as meaningless or useless, questions that cannot be answered by the application of method. Science becomes not the representation and demonstration of truth, but an art: the art of *finding* the truth – or, rather, that portion of truth that lends itself to be artfully found. Finally, the truths that modern science finds –

even about human beings – are value-neutral, in no way restraining technical application, and indeed perfectly adapted for it.

In short, as Hans Jonas put it, modern science contains manipulability at its theoretical core – and this remains true even for those great scientists who are themselves motivated by the desire for truth, and who have no interest in that mastery over nature to which their discoveries nonetheless contribute and for which science is largely esteemed by the rest of us and mightily supported by the modern state.

One special feature of modern biology, itself a cardinal premise of modern science altogether, is both most powerful in yielding new knowledge of biological events and, paradoxically, most untrue to life. This is the principle of objectification. Understanding this fact is the intellectual key to understanding the gulf between scientific knowledge and the world it purports to capture and explain.

The term "objective" has a common colloquial meaning and a precise philosophical meaning, the former descending from the latter but without our knowing the distortions we have swallowed in the process. In common speech, we use "objective" as a synonym for "true" or "real." Not only scientists but any fair-minded person is supposed to "be objective": unprejudiced, disinterested, rational, free from contamination of merely personal – that is, "subjective" – bias or perspective, and able therefore to capture "objective reality." "Objective reality" is the domain especially of the sciences, because the methodical pursuit of reproducible and shareable findings guarantees their objective status.

But this common view is misleading, for "the objective" is not synonymous with "the true" or "the real." Pursuit of the distinction discloses, surprisingly, an unbridgeable gap between science and reality, and, of greatest moment for us, between the science of biology and the living nature it studies. The so-called objective view of nature is not nature's own, but one imposed on nature, imposed by none other than the interested human subject.

Here's how this works. An "object," literally, means that which is "thrown-out-before-and-against" us – thrown by, thrown-before-and-against, and existing for and relative to the human subject who does the throwing. Not the natural world *but the self-thinking human subject* is the source of objectivity. The interested subject's demand for clear and distinct and certain "knowledge" leads him to *re*-present the given world before his mind, in an act of deliberate projection, through concepts (invented for the purpose) that allow him to operate mentally on the world with utmost (usually quantitative) precision. What cannot be grasped through such conceptual re-presentation drops from view. Only those aspects of the world that can be "objectified" (or quantified) become objects for scientific study. The given, visible, and tangible world of our experience is banished into the shadows; the shadowy world of "concepts" gains the limelight and reconfigures everything in sight, giving them an "objectified" character that is at best only partially true to what they *are*.

A concrete example can make more vivid this abstract account of the abstracting character of scientific objectification. The classic instance of objectifying the world concerns the world as visible, and ourselves, by implication, as its experiencing viewers. In a revolution-making passage in the *Rules for the Direction of the Mind*, Descartes sets the program for all of modern science by transforming how we should approach the study of color:

> Thus whatever you suppose color *to be,* you cannot deny that it is *extended* and in consequence possessed of figure. Is there then any *disadvantage,* if, while taking care not to admit any new entity uselessly, or rashly to imagine that it exists ... but merely abstracting from every other feature except that it possesses the nature of figure, *we conceive* the *diversity* existing among white, blue, and red, etc., as being like the difference among the following similar figures?
>
> The same argument applies to *all* cases; for it is certain that the *infinitude of figures* suffices to *express* all the differences in sensible things. [Emphasis added.]

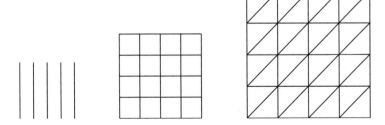

Note the following crucial points:

1. We are told by Descartes to ignore the *being* or *nature* of color, and to concentrate instead only on the "fact" that, because colored *things* are extended (that is, take up space), all *color* has figure or shape. ("Never mind," says Descartes, "what color really *is*. You cannot deny that *it* has figure.")*

2. From "cannot deny" to "forget about everything else": we must *abstract* from every other feature of color except for its having *figure*. Why? For an advantage in knowing, yet a kind of knowing that is indifferent to existence or essence, to what something really *is*. The knowledge gained by objectification is indifferent or neutral to the being or reality of things.

3. Far from representing a reading of nature's own phenomena, objectification is a willful act of mind: Descartes *decides* or *chooses* to conceive color under the concept of figure. We do not, as knowers, try to catch the natural looks of visible things; instead, by decision, *we choose* to *conceive* ("to grasp together") or represent before our grasping minds only *certain* aspects of the world.

4. Which aspects? Not the nature of colors, not the being of colors, but merely the *differences* among them ("the *diversity* existing among white, blue, and red"). We do not seek to know *things* through and through, but only their external – and measurable – *relations*.

5. These natural differences are "translated" – or, rather, *symbolized* – by *mathematical* ones: the differences of color are *re*-presented by differences among similar figures. Why? Because if we con-figure things, we can then "figure them out." We can take their mathematical measure, using the radically new mathematics of quantity (featuring the number line and analytic geometry) that Descartes has invented for this purpose,

---

* Compare the relation of color and shape (*schema*) suggested by Socrates in Plato's *Meno*: "Shape is that which, alone among all things, always accompanies color." Appealing to our primary experience of the visible world, this account integrates shape and color as the two most evident and always related aspects of any visible body, whose shaped surface we come to see only because of color differences between it and its surroundings. To put it crudely, Socrates' philosophizing deepens lived experience; Descartes's turns its back on lived experience.

a mathematics that introduced terms of arithmetic (traditionally the study of *discrete* multitudes) into the study of geometry (the study of *continuous* magnitudes). The analytic geometry of Cartesian space is the perfect vehicle for precise measurement of anything – space, time, mass, density, volume, velocity, energy, temperature, blood pressure, drunkenness, intelligence, or scholastic achievement – that can be treated as a quantity or dimension.

6. Descartes's geometrical figures, standing for the differences among the colors white, blue, and red, may be passé, but the principle he proposes is not: today we still treat color in terms of "wavelengths," purely mathematical representations from which *all the color is sucked out*. This tells the whole story: the objective is purely quantitative. All quality disappears.

7. Objectification can be universalized: *all* the differences (that is, changes or relations) in sensible things (that is, in every being of the natural world) can be expressed mathematically, says Descartes. The world – or more accurately, *changes* in the world – can be represented objectively, as differences among figures (or, eventually, in equations). The multifaceted and profound world of things is replaced by a shadowy network of mathematized relations.

In this classic example, we have the touchstone of all so-called objective knowledge. By design, the objectified world is abstract, purely quantitative, homogeneous, and indifferent to the question of being or existence. Objectified knowledge is ghostly: "things" are "known" only externally and relationally. Moreover, unlike the signifiers of ordinary speech that are its general nouns, the symbolic representations used to handle the objectified world bear absolutely no relation to the things represented: a wavelength or a mathematical equation neither resembles nor points to color.

No one gets very excited about the objectification of color, but we become suspicious when science tries to objectify the *viewing* of color or, worse, the *viewer*. And now we see why. By its very principle, "objective knowledge" will not be – because it *cannot* be – true to lived experience; for lived experience is always qualitative, concrete, heterogeneous, and suffused with the attention, interest, and engaged concern of the living soul. Real sight and seeing can never be captured by wavelengths, absorption spectra of retinal cells, or electrical discharges in the objectified brain. Likewise also the inwardness of life, including awareness, appetite, emotion, and the genuine and interested relations between one living being and others, both friend and foe; or the engaged, forward-pointed, outward-moving tendencies of living beings; or the uniqueness of each individual life as lived in living time, from birth to death; or the concern of each animal (conscious or not) for its own health, wholeness, and well-being – none of these essential aspects of nature alive fall within the cramped and distorting boundaries of nature objectified.

Honesty compels me to add one last and, indeed, astounding part of this tale, one that, I suspect, you already know. Objectification works! For some reason, the many-splendored world of nature allows itself to be grasped by the anemic concepts of objective science. Never mind that it is partial, distorted, and abstract; the quantitative approach has put men on the moon, lights on the ceiling, and pacemakers in our hearts. Somehow, it must be capturing well at least one aspect of being. But this aspect of being is not the whole or the heart of being; not by a long shot.

IV · The Aspirations of Humankind
Athens, Jerusalem, Gettysburg

CHAPTER FOURTEEN

Human Flourishing and Human Excellence

The Truth(s) of Aristotle's Nicomachean Ethics

ARISTOTLE'S *Nicomachean Ethics* is perhaps the most famous and influential book on ethics in the Western philosophic tradition. It is best known for its teachings about human virtue (or excellence), which appears at first glance to be its dominant theme. Of the ten books of the *Ethics*, all but the first and last are about human excellence and its opposites, about virtue and vice. Books II through V are about the virtues or excellences of character, both noble and just – how they are acquired, and what they are. Book VI is about practical wisdom and the other virtues or excellences of intellect. Books VIII and IX are about that quasi-excellence of heart and mind, friendship. And Book VII is largely about that very common falling-short of excellence, incontinence, in which we know the good, but out of moral weakness we fail to pursue it.

But Aristotle's *Ethics* is not about virtue for its own sake. Its overarching concern is human happiness, human flourishing, the explicit subject of Books I and X, the beginning and end of the *Ethics*. The comprehensive question and concern of the *Ethics* is, quite simply, "How to live?" or, better, "How to live well, excellently, flourishingly?" or, yet again, "What is a good, or *the* good, human life, and what is the best?" It is a question that commands the attention of every serious person, and Aristotle's compelling treatment of the subject has for centuries commanded the attention of thoughtful readers, religious and secular, scholars and states-men. Preeminent Christian, Jewish, and Muslim thinkers – Thomas Aquinas, Maimonides, and Averroës and al-Farabi – have embraced much of what Aristotle had to say. Winston Churchill, given the book to read late in his life, declared upon finishing it, "Why, this is what I have always thought." A book having such endorsements, one would think, deserves our attention.

And yet, in my experience, most beginning students do not take well to the *Ethics*. I remember well my own reaction when I read it for the first time as a college sophomore, sixty years ago: I found it abstract, boring, and irrelevant. We did read only part of the book, in a bad translation that made Aristotle seem like a wooden pedant, and the teacher, as I recall, was uninspiring. Nevertheless, I now realize that I was mainly to blame. I was too young, too shallow, not ready. Aristotle himself warns the reader near the beginning of the *Ethics* that his book is not intended for the young and inexperienced, or for those who have been badly brought up. And he tells us at the end that it will be largely useless for those who do not already have a longing for the noble and the good. He knows that he has nothing persuasive to say to those who envy tyrants like Stalin and Saddam Hussein or playboys like Hugh Hefner and Donald Trump.

Nevertheless, when I teach the *Ethics* and invite anyone who is too young, too inexperienced in life, too ruled by his passions, or merely badly brought up, to drop the course and find something more suitable, no one ever leaves. This is not surprising: no young person would admit to being any of these things. Indeed, the book has probably always been read mainly by the young. But to read it well, and with profit, they have had to pretend or imagine that they read with mature minds and with the sensibilities of the well brought up. Today, I suspect, fewer readers are willing and able to engage in such self-flattering discipline, especially to learn from a book by a long-dead Greek white male whose wisdom, if any, is no longer current.

As twenty-first-century Americans, we face special challenges in read-ing the *Ethics*, and we might as well be honest about them. First, living in democratic times, we have trouble forgiving Aristotle for not being a democrat who celebrates equality and for not flattering the reader's com-placent confidence in his own goodness and happiness. Second, living under a liberal – that is, freedom-loving – regime, we bridle at the suggestion that ethics is a branch of politics, meaning that our views of the good life are decisively shaped by the character of the polity and what it looks up to, rather than arising from a strictly private selection of lifestyle made by each of us entirely on our own. Third, thinking we know what a book about ethics should look like, we are perplexed by Aristotle's dialectical manner and his failure to offer foolproof arguments, syllogistic demonstrations, and moral declarations of right and wrong. Finally, and most difficult of all, having embraced the new absolute of moral relativism – "Who's to say what's good and bad?" "All values are subjective, both culturally and personally relative!" – we will resist tooth and nail any suggestion that there really is a better and a worse answer to the question, "How to live, in order to live well?" Let's not beat around the bush: With such cultural prejudices it will be difficult, if not impossible, to learn anything of value from Aristotle.

My short answer to these difficulties: it's your loss. The full answer would be a carefully guided twenty-week reading of the book, trying to make sense of what Aristotle says and means, and considering why it just might be true and important, even for twenty-first-century Americans. For now, I will try instead to persuade you, in two different ways, to suspend your disbelief, and to entertain the possibility that Aristotle's *Ethics* might be offering us the deepest truths about human life and its flourishing. First, drawing on my own long experience of reading and teaching the book, I will discuss some important insights to which it has led me. Second, I will take up one of the most famous chapters in the *Ethics*, and, through some close reading and a concrete example, try to overcome your prejudices against it.

Aristotelian Insights about Human Flourishing and Human Excellence

Some eight years after I had left college, I read the *Ethics* seriously for the first time, in the company of my closest friend, and this reading changed the way I looked at life. Why did I return to the *Ethics*? Because I had acquired some questions about morality: On what does it rest? How can it withstand the challenge of moral relativism? Unlike many young Americans, I never seriously doubted that some things really are better than others, that some actions are just or noble or right, while others are unjust or base or wrong. But could my intuitions be defended, grounded, vindicated? Some experiences had led me to doubt my Enlightenment faith in human perfectibility brought about by reason and science, and Rousseau's *First Discourse* had shocked me by insisting that the cultivation of reason in the form of progress in the arts and sciences necessarily resulted in moral decay. I thus turned to Aristotle hoping to find a demonstrative rational science of ethics, issuing in rules or principles of right conduct, universally valid and rationally defensible, that could be successfully applied in practice.

I instead found something different: a book that is dialectical, not demonstrative; an account not of rules and principles but of lives and characters, better and worse. I found that Aristotle knew all about the challenge of what we call "cultural relativism" but was able to set down some impregnable defenses against it. Indeed, one could say that the entire *Ethics* is an answer to the relativist difficulty, enunciated near the start of Book I: what men call noble and just differs from place to place, so much so that people think nobility and justice exist not by nature but only by arbitrary human agreement. After acknowledging this problem, Aristotle then offers an entirely new way of thinking about ethics, and many important insights for thinking about how to live.* I will mention ten of them as they appear through the book. Though I present them only as distinct truths I have learned from the text, I will try to weave them together to give something of an overview of the whole account.

1. *The three lives.* Everyone agrees, says Aristotle early in Book I, that the ultimate goal we seek in life is happiness (*eudaimonia*), but people disagree about its meaning or content. Discerning their opinions from the way they actually live, Aristotle distinguishes three kinds of human beings whose lives embrace three different understandings of what happiness might be. The many (*hoi polloi*) live as if happiness were having fun and amusing oneself. The refined and ambitious people – especially the political types – live as if happiness were honor or recognition for their personal excellence or achievement. And, third, some rare people

---

* I note again, with apologies, that a few paragraphs of this essay were shamelessly quoted more or less verbatim in Chapter Twelve, to indicate the crucial place of the *Nicomachean Ethics* in my humanistic education.

(not discussed until Book X) live as if happiness consists in learning and seeking wisdom, in philosophizing. Please note: the most revealing distinctions among human beings are not race, class, and gender; neither should we look to wealth or power or culture for explanations of the most basic differences among us. Rather, human beings are fundamentally distinguished by the *ruling passions of their souls*: a passion for fun or pleasure, a passion for honor or recognition, a passion for learning or knowledge or wisdom. Most people are primarily lovers of pleasures; some people are primarily lovers of victory and honor; a few people are lovers of understanding.

In passing, Aristotle notes that there appears to be a fourth kind of life, the life of money-making, embraced by those whose ruling passion is for wealth. But he shows that the life devoted to making money cannot be the humanly flourishing life, inasmuch as money is only an instrumental good – a mere means, useful because it can buy pleasures, or bring honor and power, or be a tool for acting and living well, differently defined. Ever since I learned from Aristotle this distinction of the three (or four) lives, I have found it enormously helpful in examining and understanding the people that I meet.

2. *Happiness is activity.* Happiness, according to Aristotle, is not just contentment; indeed, it is not at all a mere feeling or emotion, but rather an activity. The ordinary Greek word that we translate as happiness, *eudaimonia*, begins to make this clear; it would be better translated as "human flourishing," an enviable way of living-and-being, approaching blessedness. *Eu*, "well," *daimon*, "demon or divinity," *-ia*, "-ness" – *eudaimonia*, "well-demoned-ness" – suggests a condition of high flourishing that, for prephilosophical Greeks, meant that the one who flourishes lives under the tutelage or protection of a benevolent daimon or deity. But unlike those who would therefore equate human flourishing with mere prosperity, Aristotle insists that it is not the possession of some external good like wealth or rank or honor, or of some internal good like beauty or health or even unused virtue, but rather is synonymous with activity – with activity of the *soul*, activity of the human soul *as human*. We human beings flourish when we are *at work*, not when we are asleep, not even when we just wish or plan to be at work. The basketball player as basketball player flourishes only during the game, the

statesman as statesman only when actively engaged in rule, the musician only when making music, the thinker only when thinking. Flourishing *is* activity, and the better we engage in the activity and the more it engages us to the core of our being, the fuller is our flourishing. It is just as the man says: "The human good is a being-at-work* – an activity – of soul in accordance with excellence, and if there is more than one excellence, in accordance with the best and most complete." More succinctly, human flourishing is *souling well*, or *"humaning" excellently*.

3. *The distinction between intellectual and ethical virtue.* If happiness is souling or humaning excellently, what *kind* of excellence is involved? Aristotle is the first to have recorded the difference between the excellences of mind and the excellences of character, that is, between intellectual and ethical (or moral) virtue. Although it turns out that some excellence of mind is necessary for the highest excellence of character (as Aristotle says, one cannot be supremely ethically virtuous if one is not prudent or practically wise), and although some moral virtue is indispensable for improving the intellect (for example, no one strung out on drugs or addicted to booze can learn very much), Aristotle's distinction makes a great deal of sense out of our life and the human world we inhabit.

We all know very intelligent, even learned and brilliant, men and women who are licentious or cowardly or dishonest. And we know very decent and even admirable human beings who are by and large ignorant. In most of our dealings in life, we are far better off in the company of men and women of ethical virtue who know nothing of mathematics or physics or philosophy or theology, than we are in the company of geniuses who have been badly reared. As C. S. Lewis puts it: "I had sooner play cards against a man who was quite skeptical about ethics, but bred to believe that 'a gentleman does not cheat,' than against an irreproachable moral philosopher who had been brought up by sharpers." Of course, excellences of mind and character can be found in the same human being. Perry Mason, that brilliant lawyer of the utmost integrity, was said to be "sharp as a steel trap" (intellectual virtue) and "clean as a hound's tooth"

---

* This cumbersome phrase literally translates *energeia*, a word of Aristotle's own coinage, built on the root *erg*, meaning "work": "in-work-ness" or "being-in-[one's]-work."

(ethical virtue). It is perhaps to increase the chances of such coincidence that Aristotle insists that students of his book should already be well brought up, and that he postpones the discussion of the intellectual virtues until he has spent half the book emphasizing the ethical ones.

4. *Ethical virtue means fine character.* Unlike many modern writers on ethics, Aristotle understands that the moral virtues are states of soul, and not only states of mind. Many people who adhere mentally to the right propositions or maxims turn out not to have them incorporated into the grain of their being. I am not talking just about hypocrites who say one thing but do another. I am talking about the fact that moral excellence is primarily a matter of the *heart* – of the state of our desires, the shape of our wishes, the direction of our intentions. Accordingly, Aristotle's *Ethics* is not an ethics of rules and commandments, of thou shalts and thou shalt nots, of right and wrong, of rights and duties, categorical imperatives, principles, beliefs, opinions, propositions, maxims, faiths, or "values." Rather, it is about that most peculiar grown-togetherness of heart and mind we call someone's character.

Character is not temperament, the natural or physical disposition of the soul. Temperament, literally, "due mixing," is a term from medieval physiology, which taught that the varying mixtures of the four cardinal bodily humors (bile, phlegm, blood, and black bile) determined the basic natural psychic constitution: choleric, phlegmatic, sanguine, melancholic. This humoral theory is in deserved disrepute, but we all know people of such varying natural temperaments, which are often discernable even in infancy.

Neither is character "personality," a term we use to describe the non-intellectual aspects of the people we meet. Personality, from *persona*, "mask," is that mask to the world by which we are identified: we say someone has a nice personality, makes a good impression, is cheerful and easy to get along with, fits in well. But here we are mostly talking about veneered surfaces and mere appearances.

Although character often shines forth in visible deeds, it refers to what is truly at the center, to the shape of the inner soul itself. It is primarily a matter of the orientation and disposition of our power of choosing, a power at once appetitive and mindful.* It is a matter of both our loves and our hates, but also of our discernment, our perspicacity, and our ability to find the way to, and move ourselves toward, what we love as best and right.

When I was younger, I associated mainly with those who shared my so-called "values," my moral and political opinions about the world. Time taught me that many of these fellow travelers were unreliable when the chips were down, and when the virtues of courage or self-restraint or generosity or fairness or self-sacrifice were required. Today, I am always on the lookout for fine character, which never disappoints.

5. *Habituation and habit.* How does fine character develop? How does the choosing power become excellent? The power of choice, Aristotle teaches, is perfected by habituation in choosing well, by repeated actions that accord with what the practically wise would say and do. Many rationalists in ethics, from the Sophists of old to professors of philosophy today, believe that you can make people good by speeches and reasoning. Because they believe that the major obstacle to right conduct is poor thinking and unclarity of mind, they spend all of their attention on analyzing moral argumentation and trying to develop philosophical principles of ethics. Today, ethics is a theoretical subject, whose conclusions one is then supposed to apply to practice. But if the center of the moral life is not reason but character, if the center of character is choice, and if choice hinges not only on thought and opinion but also on the habits of the heart, one discovers that the development of character – and of the most reliable character – comes only through the gradual process of forming one's power to choose into a firm disposition, a formation that results from the repeated practice of choosing well. It may seem circular to say that one comes to be courageous only by acting courageously, but

---

* In giving his deeper account of this power of choosing – in Greek, *proairêsis*, literally, a "taking before" or a "taking ahead of" – Aristotle calls it *orektikos nous* ("appetitive intellect") or *orexis dianoetikê* ("thoughtful appetite"). So grown together are heart and mind in this "faculty" that it is impossible to say whether it is a species of intellection suffused with desire or a species of appetite rendered mindful or thoughtful. Aristotle adds here that such a principle – the source of human action – is the human being (*anthrôpos*): the core of our humanity is none other than this seamless concretion of heart and mind.

that's just the way it is. Thus, it is only as a result of facing the things we fear that we gradually acquire, in the best case, the disposition to fear properly: *as* and *when* and *how much* we ought, and only *what* we ought to fear. Only in this way will we come to act accordingly.

The Greek word for habit or disposition is *hexis*, meaning a having and a holding. A habit is a holding of oneself, a holding fast of oneself, now and in the future. It is an established disposition, a firm bearing or posture toward fear, pleasure, pain, anger, lust, or the love of money and honor. Contrary to our contemporary associations with the word "habit," a *hexis* is not something mechanical or rote, devoid of that spontaneity which alone, allegedly, makes an action humanly praiseworthy. For a virtuous habit is *not* something externally imposed and enslaving, but an *acquired freedom*. It is a self-acquired self-rule, in the absence of which we are slaves to the passions and undisciplined impulses that overtake us.

6. *The noble*. What is the good or use of these excellences of character? We come next to perhaps the most remarkable feature of Aristotle's ethical teaching. Aristotle is neither a moralist (like Kant) nor a utilitarian (like Hobbes or Mill or most Americans) – virtually the only two schools of moral thought we hear about today. Unlike the moralists, Aristotle does not say that morality is a thing of absolute worth, or that the virtuous man does the right thing for its own sake or in order to adhere to a moral rule. Conversely, unlike the utilitarians, he does not say that morality is good because it is useful for civic peace or for private gain or reputation. Although he knows that ethical virtue is useful, he *never* talks about its utility. Most striking in this regard is the discussion of courage, the virtue whose end and justification must have something to do with preserving and defending the city; yet the city is not mentioned in the entire discussion.* Instead, Aristotle says over and over again that the ethically virtuous man acts *for the sake of the noble*.

---

* Part of the reason is this: if benefiting the city were the end, then the goodness of courageous actions would depend on the goodness of the city being served. More important, if virtue is largely defined as what is instrumentally good for the city, what, we must ask, is the city good for? In Aristotle's account, the true goal of the city (politics) is to produce virtuous human beings and citizens. Those virtuous citizens are indeed useful to the city, but the city is itself ultimately useful in producing virtuous human beings.

The noble, *kalon* in Greek, means the beautiful, the fine, the resplendent – not only in body but also and especially in soul. The man of fine character seeks to display his own fineness in word and in deed; he seeks to show the harmony of his soul and the rightness of his choice in the doing of graceful and gracious deeds. The beauty or nobility of his action has little to do with the cause that his action will serve or the benefits that will accrue, to himself or another – though such benefits often obtain. Rather, it has everything to do with showing forth in action the beautiful soul at work, the way a fine dancer dances for the sake of dancing finely. As the ballerina both exploits and resists the downward pull of gravity to rise freely and gracefully above it, so the person of ethical virtue exploits and elevates the necessities of our embodied existence to act freely and gracefully above their downward pull. So, for example, the moderate man satisfies his hunger, born of bodily need, not by stuffing his face, but by mannerly eating, at a well-laid table, sharing food and well-turned conversation with his fellow diners.

There are thus two connected aspects to the noble, one inner, one outer. Inwardly, there is freedom *from* enslavement to the things that weigh us down, like excessive bodily desires for food or sex or the love of money and honor. Outwardly, this inner freedom *from* permits an active freedom *for*, a freedom to act in a seemly and fitting and gracious manner (often also with benefit to others). The outer display manifests the inner state of soul, but goes beyond it by putting it into action. The outer display, the showing forth, is the beautiful being-at-work, the activity, of the harmonious or excellent soul – a high species of human flourishing.

Aristotle, we observe, does not make a sharp boundary between what we would call the moral and the aesthetic. Indeed, as the emphasis on the noble suggests, the ethical turns out to be a species of the aesthetic, as virtuous conduct shines forth in deeds beautiful to behold. In this, I find him right on target. Consider, for example, the problem of the hostess who is entertaining a handicapped guest. Anyone who has thought about it can figure out the maxim: be helpful without causing embarrassment. But it is exceedingly hard to do this well, and very few people can do it perfectly. Yet if we have learned how to look, we also know it when we see it. We know immediately both that it has been well done and that it is beautiful. We admire the freedom, the grace, the tact, the just-rightness, indeed, the beauty of the action of a beautiful soul at work.

A crucial part of Aristotle's answer to the relativist challenge consists in his presentation of what I call the museum of virtues, the virtues of nobility (presented in Books III and IV): courage, moderation, liberality, magnificence, greatness of soul, ambition, gentleness, friendliness, truthfulness, and wit. Aristotle polishes a picture of each of these virtues and places it between two corresponding vices, one of excess, one of deficiency, and in this way – not by argument, but by showing forth – he gives us direct and immediate experience in *seeing* the humanly beautiful. Anyone who cannot see that courage is more beautiful than cowardice and rashness or that liberality is more beautiful than miserliness and prodigality suffers, one might say, from the moral equivalent of color-blindness.

7. *The centrality of prudence.* If one loves and seeks to act nobly, how can one discern exactly what that means in any given circumstance? A beauty-loving heart is not enough. It needs help from a sharp mind. Though the beginnings of ethical virtue lie in habituation, starting in our youth, and though the core of moral virtue is the right-shaping of our loves and hates by means of praise and blame, reward and punishment, the *perfection* of character finally cannot do without a certain perfection of *mind*. Aristotle's *Ethics* is famous for teaching the indispensability of prudence or practical wisdom (*phronêsis*) for the supreme sort of ethical virtue. Strictly speaking, one cannot be ethically good unless one is practically wise.

Prudence is, to begin with, the discursive ability to deliberate well about means to ends. But it also involves direct intellectual apprehension: an intuitive grasp both of the goodness of the ends that one is seeking and of the myriad particulars of each human situation – insights that enable the prudent man to seek and find the best possible action under the circumstances, even if it is a far cry from the best simply. Prudence is not mere calculative shrewdness or cleverness. Just as one cannot be ethically excellent without being practically wise, so one cannot be practically wise unless one is ethically excellent – unless one sees and loves the noble and the just. The soul's native power of cleverness can lead to the utmost knavery if not tied down to the noble and just ends that the virtuous man has been habituated to love. On the other hand, the good intentions of a lover of the noble can lead to equally bad results through well-intentioned foolishness.

Today we are inclined to praise as excellent one or the other of two human types: utilitarians praise the shrewd and cunning man who knows how to get what he wants, while moralists praise the man of good will, the well-intentioned, good-hearted fellow who wants to do good, even if he is a bumbler and frequently gets it wrong. Aristotle shows us that both of these views are mistaken. The highest excellence of a man of action requires both that his intentions be good and that his judgment be sound. Moreover, the man of practical wisdom is not a slave to abstract principles or rules of conduct,* to "ideals" or doctrines. Because of the diverse circumstances and utter particularity of all the choices we make in our lives, the prudent man knows that virtue really consists in finding and enacting the best possible thing to do *here and now*, in the light of the circumstances. He is truly a man for all seasons and for all occasions.

8. *Friendship.* The human being is not just a citizen, and human life comprises more than action in the affairs of the city. There is also private life, in which other aspects of our natural humanity are realized and perfected. Central among these is our capacity for love and friendship.

Aristotle's *Ethics* is the only major work of ethics in the Western world that devotes so much attention (one-fifth of the whole) to the massively important and wonderful human phenomenon of friendship – not erotic or sexual love, but friendship – that lifelong being-together of souls that overcomes, as much as is possible, the isolation and separation of human beings. Two of his insights are worthy of mention for present purposes. First, most of the people we call our friends are merely friends of utility or pleasure, in which the friend is befriended because he is useful or fun to be with, not loved on account of his goodness or for his own sake. But the only true and lasting kind of friendship is of the latter sort, the friendship based on virtue. So it behooves anyone interested in durable friendship to look hard at the people they now think of as their friends, to see what exactly it is that draws them together, and to be on the lookout for good and loveable friends who could be theirs for a lifetime.

What kind of friends are these likely to be? This is shown in the sec-

---

* This is not to say that the prudent man is unprincipled or in doubt about whether murder, adultery, and theft are wrong: Aristotle points out that their very names mean badness. But they are beneath the discussion, for he is discussing human flourishing, not staying out of prison; he is interested not in reforming tyrants but in educating gentlemen for happiness.

ond insight: Considering all the various kinds of activities that friends do together, Aristotle argues his way to the true conclusion that the most durable, most equal, most intimate, and most rewarding kind of friendship is the friendship of sharing speech and thoughts – in other words, the philosophical friendship of mutual learning. To be sure, he also gives proper attention to the friendship of sharing in noble deeds, and notes the importance of friends as mirrors and appreciators of our own virtuous conduct. But he also points out the rivalry inherent in the friendship of those zealous for noble action: only one warrior can be the best of the Achaians, and that aspiration is finally deadly to friendship.* In contrast, speech and thought – both activities of the highest order – are the only truly shareable things in the world, the only things in which my having them doesn't preclude your having them too. Indeed, my having more usually means that you will have more as well.

Here let me point out a most magnificent feature of the structure and rhetoric of the entire book. Aristotle's argument for the superiority of philosophical friendship, made in Book IX, Chapter 9, draws additional evidence for itself from the very act of reading and discussing the book. For Aristotle's *Ethics* is, in my view, an act of Aristotelian friendship for the willing reader. From the very start, Aristotle has been inviting us to examine ourselves, to reflect on our socially cultivated humanity and to ponder the human soul beneath it. Thus, when he describes the delight we have in the activities of sensing and thinking, in self-awareness, in learning about our own aliveness and sharing it with a friend, we can experience exactly what he is describing – for this remark comes on the heels of nine books in which our friend Aristotle has been leading us to this deeper self-knowledge. We are inclined to believe him about the friendship of sharing speech and thoughts precisely because we have been experiencing for ourselves the truth of what he is telling us, and most dramatically at this high point in the text.

---

* In highlighting this rivalry, Aristotle notes that a virtuous man may sometimes nobly stand aside to allow his friend to perform the noble deed, but then adds slyly that he is thus obtaining the greater nobility for himself. The paradigmatic case to which Aristotle no doubt alludes is that of Achilles and Patroclus, in which Achilles, by allowing his friend to go out into battle in his stead (and wearing his armor), is the unwitting cause of his death.

9. *Pleasure.* These remarks about the delights of friendship lead directly to an important conclusion about pleasure, a topic that recurs throughout the *Ethics* and that is the subject of two short thematic treatments, at the end of Book VII and at the beginning of Book X. Here we find that pleasure is not itself bad; on the contrary, it is good. Pleasure is integral to happiness, yet pleasure alone is not happiness. Pleasure bears a deep relationship to activity, on which it is dependent. When we are active, without impediment, when everything goes with the grain and nothing obstructs, when the soul is at work excellently, pleasure comes as a supervening and unbought grace. To use Aristotle's lovely image, it is "like the bloom of youth gracing those who are healthy and in their prime."

Yet although he is finally a spokesman for pleasure, Aristotle is not a hedonist. Indeed, he offers the best refutation of hedonism, of the shallow and always prevalent view that regards pleasure as homogeneous and esteems pleasure as *the* good. He shows us that pleasures differ in kind and in quality because they are derived from and tied to activities. He enables us to see that we do not really want the pleasure without the activity; rather, we want the activity for itself. We do not want the pleasure of playing baseball without playing baseball, the pleasure of listening to music without hearing any music, the pleasure of having learned without knowing anything. Pleasure follows in the wake of the activity and lights it up into consciousness. But without the activity, there can be no happiness. Disconnected pleasure – say, from a bottle or a syringe – is but a fraudulent substitute. Thus Aristotle, and only Aristotle, refutes hedonism without embracing suffering or self-denial.

10. *The life of learning.* Which activity of soul goes to the depth of our being and accordingly offers us the highest pleasure? According to Aristotle, it is the life of learning in pursuit of wisdom. Though very few human beings are capable of living the philosophical life, our friend, the author of the *Nicomachean Ethics*, has led us gradually to an ever-deepening self-reflection in which we have tasted some of the delights of the pursuit of wisdom, about ourselves and about the world in which we find ourselves. He has awakened powers of mind and thought and introduced us to the joys of insight. The reason that a discussion of the philosophical life is deferred to the end of the *Ethics* is now clear, for to praise it at the beginning would strike us like an advertisement to eat in a restaurant

somewhere in Tashkent. By gradually giving us, through his book, our life to live over again in thought, by showing us both its ground and its perplexities and contradictions, and by inviting us to look yet more deeply into ourselves and our world, Aristotle provides us an appetizer from that wonderful restaurant in which everything thinkable is on the menu.

Most of us cannot devote our lives to philosophizing; but thanks to the blessings of freedom and the possibility of education that our wonderful country has provided us, all of us can exercise our intellect thoughtfully and in search of greater wisdom, and thus participate partially in that aspect of human flourishing which is philosophizing. A proper reading of Aristotle's *Ethics* proves also that happiness is an activity of thoughtful souls.

Greatness of Soul: The Peak of Moral Nobility

Despite this ringing endorsement of the excellent activity that is liberal education in pursuit of wisdom, I want to return to the virtues of character, the major preoccupation of the *Ethics*. As we are all citizens with an interest – or at least a stake – in politics and leadership, I would like to confront a democratic prejudice that keeps most modern readers from appreciating the peak of human excellence in the realm of action.

Among the ethical virtues discussed in the first five books of the *Ethics*, there are two pinnacles: greatness of soul (*megalopsychia*), also called "magnanimity" or "high-mindedness" (IV:3), and general or universal justice (V:1). What is true only of these two virtues is that each of them is said to include all the others. They differ in this way: greatness of soul is that aspect of complete ethical virtue seen as the perfection of the human being in himself, while justice is that aspect of complete ethical virtue seen as the perfection of the human being in his relation to others within the order of the political community. In greatness of soul, one is looking at the perfected soul of the agent; in justice, one is looking at the fittingness of his deeds to what the law, the city, and his fellow citizens require. Because the goodness of justice regarded as law-abidingness depends on the goodness of the city and its laws, only in the best city or polis will the great-souled man and the just man be one and the same.

Let us consider the great-souled man. In Aristotle's *Ethics*, greatness of soul is a singular virtue. It is the only virtue with "soul" in its name. Recalling the definition of happiness as "souling excellently," we see that if "great-souling" were all-complete excellent souling, then the activity of the great-souled man could be the most complete sort of human flourishing. Yet greatness of soul is the one virtue on Aristotle's list that none of us would have put on a list of our own. Indeed, most of my students find the great-souled man hard to take, obnoxious at best, or even vicious. They resent his disdain for lesser folk, they dislike his cool aloofness, and they proudly assert that they wouldn't want to have dinner with him – without considering that the feeling might, of course, be mutual. But the critique of greatness of soul has a venerable pedigree. It was almost certainly about greatness of soul, seen as noble pride, that St. Augustine said: "The virtues of the pagans are splendid vices." Can greatness of soul be a virtue? In what way is it good?

Let us look more closely at Aristotle's treatment. As in almost every discussion of a given matter, he starts from common opinion, only to refine that common opinion into the truer opinion toward which it points: "It is *believed* that great-souled is the one who deems himself worthy of great things and is worthy of them." The one who thinks he is worthy of much but in fact deserves little is vain and foolish; the one who thinks he is less worthy than he is in reality is small-souled. The virtue, even at first glance, seems to be related to ambition on a large canvas, but it also requires reflection that yields an accurate appraisal of self-worth.

The great thing that the great-souled man claims for himself is honor, said to be the greatest of the external political goods, "that which we assign to the gods, and which is most aimed at by those in high rank." Honor, *timê* in Greek, means not only recognition but also public office, just as our politicians still say when elected, "Thank you for the honor you have bestowed upon me." Moreover, because honor is the best thing a city can offer a human being, this virtue will show how the best of human beings stands with respect to his city.

Having begun with common opinion, Aristotle now starts to refine it. He moves from the vulgar emphasis on *claiming* honor and office, to his own preoccupation: being *deserving* of honor. There are three successive, rising formulations of Aristotle's emphasis on merit. First, "The great-souled man, if indeed he is to be worthy of the greatest things, must be the best man.... Therefore, it is necessary that one who is *truly* great-souled be good. And greatness in each of the virtues would seem to be characteristic of the great-souled man." Not only does he possess all the other moral virtues, but he possesses them in a superlative degree. For only on these grounds would he be deserving of the highest honor.

This leads to the second rise: "Greatness of soul, then, seems to be like a certain crowning ornament [a *kosmos*] of the virtues, for it makes them greater and does not come to be without them. Therefore it is hard to be truly great-souled; for it is not possible without perfect gentlemanship [*kalokagathia*, from *kalos*, noble, and *agathos*, good]."

What exactly is this crown or *kosmos* of the other virtues? It is a kind of noble pride, resting on a *proper awareness* of one's own true moral excellence, and manifesting itself in conduct that rests on the accuracy of this self-awareness. The great-souled man acts and holds himself in relation to knowing and esteeming his own capacity for great and excellent action. Knowing himself to be outstanding, he seeks to do the greatest deeds, commensurate with his own great excellence. And, as a result of this attitude, his other virtues are augmented by being mobilized into activity, as they are unified in him.

With this refinement of the popular notion of the virtue, Aristotle next looks at how the truly great-souled man stands with respect to honor. It turns out that the truly great-souled does not really care very much for honor, because (third rise) "there can be no honor worthy of all-complete (or all-perfect) virtue." Yes, he will accept honor, if it comes from a worthy source, partly to show that he does not care about it; for to reject honor, no less than to seek or claim it, is to give more honor to honor than it deserves. But in the end, honor, like all other external goods dependent on fortune, is to the truly great-souled man a petty thing. In fact, the virtue of greatness of soul finally consists in disdain for, or (better) indifference to, the external rewards of virtue (as well as the other vicissitudes of fortune). This highest temptation of the virtuous man is conquered in his peak and crowning virtue. External honor is unnecessary as proof of goodness for the man who is, and who knows that he is, truly good. Freed from enslavement to the love of honor and the opinion of his fellow citizens, the great-souled man accepts high office when it comes his way, in order to do great deeds as befits his perfect virtue and as conduces to his own flourishing. But you will not see him kissing babies or pandering to fashionable prejudice, as honor-loving and office-seeking democratic politicians do these days. Such vulgar practices are beneath his dignity. The great-souled man comes very close to being entirely self-sufficient.

What good, then, is greatness of soul? What good does it do its possessor, or the rest of us? One might think, quite rightly, of the great-souled man as one "born to command," as a Pericles or an Alcibiades, a Washington or a Lincoln. But Aristotle never directly mentions potential usefulness to the city, perhaps because his overarching concern here is personal rather than civic flourishing. Even more to be wondered at is the absence of any reference to the noble. Whereas the brave or the liberal or the magnificent man does what he does for the sake of the noble, nothing like this is said for the great-souled man. The reason seems to be this: The great-souled man does not act great-soulfully for the sake of the noble, because he himself *is* the noble. He is nobility and goodness incarnate (*kalokagathia*), the measure and standard for all human nobility. There is no external end of greatness of soul, any more than there is an external end of a *kosmos*; for greatness of soul, understood as crowning and ordering and making whole all-complete virtue, is *itself* an end. It is *the* pinnacle, or rather *a* pinnacle, of human being.

Consider some traits of the great-souled man. Everything he does, he does on a grand scale. There is nothing small or petty about him. He loves to benefit others, gives aid willingly, never asks for help. He is disdainful of the powerful, but he never lords it over the ordinary, being always courteous and measured in the presence of lesser people. He cares more for truth than opinion, refuses to flatter, and is open and frank. He bears no grudges, speaks and acts in the open, but is ironically self-deprecating when speaking to the many (think Abraham Lincoln, and the contrast with our present-day crowd-flatterers and braggarts). He engages in no small talk or gossip. He is a lover of beautiful things. Because nothing is great to him, he does not wonder or marvel. Except for this last matter – which suggests that his horizon is too limited – who can fault him? He has all-complete excellence. He is a unity, an ordered whole, a shining forth of beautiful human excellence of character. He goes, in a sense, in the place of a god, receiving from the community that which we usually reserve for the gods. At the very least, his existence – whether in concrete fact or only as an ideal type – inspires us by example, showing what human ethical perfection and the peak of human flourishing would look like. Is it merely our democratic intolerance of real superiority, grounded in an ideological disbelief in genuine inequality, and our envy in its presence that makes him obnoxious to our modern tastes? What is wrong with knowing how good you are, and acting accordingly, if you are truly excellent? Shouldn't we admire and look up to such people? Can we really do without such people?

Human Greatness and Modern Times

We liberal democrats, living in this great commercial republic and enjoying our freedom, peace, and prosperity, tend to take too much for granted. There come times of crisis – and who knows when the next one will arrive – in which the survival of the community devoted to comfort, health, and safety depends on the virtue of greater men who are devoted to something beyond comfort, health, and safety, men whose large ambition transcends mere popular acclaim. In times of greatest crisis, even egalitarians come to recognize the need for a great-souled man, a human being who really *is* superior and who will – confidently because deservingly – take the helm.

In my living memory, the liberal democracies of the world experienced precisely such a crisis, in the form of the threat of Nazi Germany. Hitler and his war machine were overrunning continental Europe, and the flame of human freedom and decency was in danger of being snuffed out. Fortunately – dare one say providentially? – a great-souled man was on hand to rally the still-free nations against the tyrant, also providing hope for the defeated that they would be rescued and that the flame of freedom would not be extinguished. As we face different but equally fanatical and increasingly threatening enemies, it is useful to be reminded of what genuine and confident human greatness looks like in times of crisis. Let us hear, from his *Memoirs of the Second World War*, Winston Churchill's own account of how, in the midst of the war, he acquired the highest office in the land, from which he carried the battle against Hitler and his barbarous tyranny to an improbably successful outcome.

May 10, 1940: Having been proved right in warning against Hitler's expansionist intentions, Churchill is back in the cabinet as First Lord of the Admiralty in the Tory government of Prime Minister Neville Chamberlain. He writes:

> The morning of the tenth of May dawned, and with it came tremendous news.... The Germans had struck their long-awaited blow. Holland and Belgium were both invaded.... The whole movement of the German Army upon the invasion of the Low Countries and of France had begun.
>
> At about ten o'clock, Sir Kingsley Wood [cabinet member and Chamberlain's trusted friend] came to see me, having just been with the Prime Minister. He told me that Mr. Chamberlain was inclined to feel that the great battle which had broken upon us made it necessary for him to remain at his post. Kingsley Wood had told him that, on the contrary, the new crisis made it all the more necessary to have a National Government, which alone could confront it, and he added that Mr. Chamberlain had accepted this view. At eleven o'clock, I was again summoned to Downing Street by the Prime Minister. There once more I found Lord Halifax. We took our seats at the table opposite Mr. Chamberlain. He told us that he was satisfied that it was beyond his power to form a National Government.... The question, therefore, was whom he should advise the King to send for after his own resignation had been accepted.... He looked at us both across the table.
>
> I have had many important interviews in my public life, and this was certainly the most important. Usually I talk a great deal, but on this occasion I was silent. Mr. Chamberlain evidently had in his mind the stormy scene in the House of Commons two nights before, when I seemed to be in such heated controversy with the Labour Party. Although this had been in his support and defence, he nevertheless felt that it might be an obstacle to my obtaining their adherence at this juncture.... His biographer, Mr. Feiling, states definitely that he preferred Lord Halifax. As I remained silent, a very long pause ensued. It certainly seemed longer than the two minutes which one observes in the commemorations of Armistice Day. Then at length Halifax spoke. He said that he felt that his position as a peer, out of the House of Commons, would

make it very difficult for him to discharge the duties of Prime Minister in a war like this. He would be held responsible for everything, but would not have the power to guide the assembly upon whose confidence the life of every Government depended. He spoke for some minutes in this sense, and by the time he had finished, it was clear that the duty would fall upon me – had in fact fallen upon me. Then, for the first time, I spoke. I said I would have no communication with either of the Opposition Parties until I had the King's commission to form a Government. On this the momentous conversation came to an end, and we reverted to our ordinary easy and familiar manners of men who had worked for years together and whose lives in and out of office had been spent in all the friendliness of British politics.

Later that day, at 6 p.m., Churchill was summoned to Buckingham Palace to meet with King George VI.

I was taken immediately to the King. His Majesty received me most graciously and bade me sit down. He looked at me searchingly and quizzically for some moments, and then said: "I suppose you don't know why I have sent for you?" Adopting his mood, I replied: "Sir, I simply couldn't imagine why." He laughed and said: "I want to ask you to form a Government." I said I would certainly do so.

The king had made no stipulation about the Government being national in character, and I felt that my commission was in no formal way dependent upon this point. But in view of what had happened, and the conditions which had led to Mr. Chamberlain's resignation, a Government of national character was obviously inherent in the situation.... I told the King that I would immediately send for the leaders of the Labour and Liberal Parties, that I proposed to form a War Cabinet of five or six Ministers, and that I hoped to let him have at least five names before midnight. On this I took my leave and returned to Admiralty.

In short order, the War Cabinet was successfully formed. Churchill tells us what it felt like to assume command.

Thus, then, on the night of the tenth of May, at the outset of this mighty battle, I acquired the chief power in the state, which henceforth I wielded in ever-growing measure for five years and three months of the war, at the end of which time, all our enemies having surrendered unconditionally or being about to do so, I was immediately dismissed by the British electorate from all further conduct of their affairs.

During these last crowded days of the political crisis, my pulse had not quickened at any moment. I took it all as it came. But I cannot conceal from the reader of this truthful account that as I went to bed at about 3 a.m., I was conscious of a profound sense of relief. At last I had the authority to give directions over the whole scene. I felt as if I were walking with Destiny, and that all my past life had been but a preparation for this hour and for this trial. Eleven years in the political wilderness had freed me from ordinary party antagonisms. My warnings over the last six years had been so numerous, so detailed, and were now so terribly vindicated, that no one could gainsay me. I could not be reproached either for making the war or with want of preparation for it. I thought I knew a good deal about it all, and I was sure I should not fail. Therefore, although impatient for the morning, I slept soundly and had no need for cheering dreams. Facts are better than dreams.

Winston Churchill died on Saturday, January 24, 1965. Britain and the world mourned. The next day, a great teacher of political science and a profound student of Aristotle's *Ethics*, Leo Strauss, began his class at the University of Chicago with the following impromptu remarks, with which I shall conclude:

> The death of Churchill is a healthy reminder to students of political science of their limitations, the limitations of their craft.
>
> The tyrant stood at the pinnacle of his power. The contrast between the indomitable and magnanimous [great-souled] statesman and the insane tyrant – this spectacle in its clear simplicity was one of the greatest lessons which men can learn, at any time.
>
> No less enlightening is the lesson conveyed by Churchill's fail-

ure, which is too great to be called tragedy. I mean the fact that Churchill's heroic action on behalf of human freedom against Hitler only contributed, through no fault of Churchill's, to increase the threat to freedom which is posed by Stalin or his successors. Churchill did the utmost that a man could do to counter that threat – publicly and most visibly in Greece and in Fulton, Missouri. Not a whit less important than his deeds and speeches are his writings, above all his *Marlborough* – the greatest historical work written in our century, an inexhaustible mine of political wisdom and understanding, which should be required reading for every student of political science.

The death of Churchill reminds us of the limitations of our craft, and therewith of our duty. We have no higher duty, and no more pressing duty, than to remind ourselves, and our students, of political greatness, human greatness, of the peaks of human excellence. For we are supposed to train ourselves and others in seeing things as they are, and this means above all in seeing their greatness and their misery, their excellence and their vileness, their nobility and their triumphs, and therefore never to mistake mediocrity, however brilliant, for true greatness.

CHAPTER FIFTEEN

The Ten Commandments

THE BIBLICAL BOOK of Genesis presents the story of how God's new way for humankind finds its first adherent in a single individual – Abraham, a man out of Mesopotamia – and how that way survives through three generations in the troubled households of Abraham, his son Isaac, and his grandson Jacob, who is renamed Israel. By the end of Genesis and the beginning of Exodus, the children of Israel are settled in Egypt, a land of good and plenty, where they are soon teeming and prospering – only, a brief time thereafter, to find themselves subjugated and enslaved. How this slavish multitude becomes transformed into a people, out of and against Egypt, is the subject of Exodus and the following books.

The central event in the national founding of the Israelite people is the giving of the Law at Mount Sinai. The Ten Commandments (Exodus 20:1–14), pronounced there by the Lord God to the assembled and recently liberated children of Israel, constitute the most famous teaching of the book of Exodus, perhaps of the entire Hebrew Bible. Prescribing proper conduct toward God and man, the Decalogue embodies the core principles of the Israelite way of life, and of what would later be known as the Judeo-Christian ethic. Even in our increasingly secular age, its influence on the prevailing morality of the West is enormous, albeit not always acknowledged or welcomed.

Yet despite its familiarity, the Decalogue is known only superficially, in part because its familiarity interferes with a deeper understanding of its teachings. This essay aims to develop such an understanding, and to build a case for the enduring moral and political significance of the Decalogue – a universal significance that goes far beyond its opposition to murder, adultery, and theft.

Structure and Context

We can begin by correcting some common misimpressions, starting with the name "Ten Commandments." Although most of the entries in the Decalogue appear to be in the imperative mode ("Thou shalt" or "Thou shalt not"), they are not called commandments (*mitzvot*) but rather statements or words: "And God spoke all these words (*devarim*)."[50] Later in the Bible we hear about the ten words – in the Greek translation, *deka logoi* or Decalogue – but whether the reference is to these same statements is far from obvious.

No help is provided by counting. Traditional exegetes derived as many as thirteen injunctions from God's speech in Exodus 20, and because internal divisions within particular statements are unclear, even those who agree on the number ten disagree on how to reckon them. Furthermore, no mention is made in Exodus 20 of the famous tablets of stone on which, in traditional imagery, we see the Decalogue inscribed, five statements on each. When such tablets are mentioned later on, we are not told what is written on them.

What then can we say about the structure of these pronouncements? First, they divide into two groups with distinctly different areas of concern. One group touches mainly on the relation between God and the individual Israelite: the first words spoken are "I *YHVH* (I the Lord) [am] thy God (*anochi YHVH elohekha*)," and within this group we hear the phrase "*YHVH* thy God" four more times. The second group (beginning with "Thou shalt not murder") touches primarily on conduct between and among human beings. In this section neither God (*elohim*) nor *YHVH* is mentioned, and the very last word of the Decalogue, "thy neighbor," marks a far distance from the opening "I *YHVH*."*

---

* We need to acknowledge the difficulty in translating the Tetragrammaton, the so-called "name" of the God of Israel. Most English translations will use "the Lord," and I will mostly (but not always) follow that less than satisfactory usage, even though it removes the sense in which the Tetragrammaton functions as a "personal name,"

Next, nearly all of the statements are formulated in the negative. The first few statements proscribe wrongful ways of relating to the divine: no other gods, no images, no vain use of the divine name. The last six begin with "not." Human beings, it seems, are more in need of restraint than of encouragement.

In this sea of prohibition, two positive exhortations stand out: the one about hallowing the Sabbath, and the one about honoring father and mother. Hallowing the Sabbath is also one of two injunctions that receive the longest exposition or explanation; the other one concerns images and likenesses. Clearly, these three – the positive commands and those with long expositions – deserve special attention.

Far more important than its structural features is the context into which the Decalogue fits. This is the new, people-forming covenant proposed by God through His prophet Moses to the children of Israel in the antecedent chapter of Exodus (19:5–6). The overall terms of that agreement are succinctly stated. If the children of Israel (1) "will hearken unto My voice" and (2) "keep My covenant," then, as a consequence, (a) "ye shall be Mine own treasure from among all peoples" and (b) "ye shall be unto Me a kingdom of priests and a holy nation." It is only here, with the offer of a divine covenant, that this motley multitude of ex-slaves learn for the first time that they can become a people, among the other peoples of the earth, and that they can become a special people, a treasure unto the Lord. Moreover, their special place is defined in more than political terms: they are invited to become a kingdom of priests and a holy nation (a subject to which we will return).

Yet the Decalogue is hardly the bulk of the Torah's people-forming legislation. All of the laws specifying proper conduct and ritual observance come later: first in the ordinances immediately following the giving of the Decalogue, then in the laws concerning the building of the tabernacle, and then, in the book of Leviticus, in the law governing sacrifices and the so-called Holiness Code. So the Decalogue functions rather as a prologue or preamble to the constituting law. Like the preamble to

---

and hence also the implication of singular and personal intimacy between the God of Israel and His people. I do so because, as I will suggest below, we should have scruples against trafficking in the so-called divine name, not least because, in the biblical account, the divine is ineffable and unfathomable, hence, beyond ordinary naming.

the Constitution of the United States, it enunciates the general principles on which the new covenant will be founded, principles that in this
case touch upon – and connect – the relation both between man and God
and between man and man. It is not so much a founding legal code as an
orienting aspirational guide for every Israelite, and perhaps for every
human heart and mind.

YHVH, Thy God

The Decalogue is introduced as follows: "And God spoke all these words,
saying" (Exodus 20:1). Unlike most biblical statements reporting a divine
act of speaking, this one does not identify the audience. But the omission
is fitting, for the speech appears to be addressed simultaneously to all the
assembled people and to each one individually: in fact, all of the injunctions are given in the second person singular. Moreover, although pronounced at a particular time and place, and uttered in the presence of a
particular group of people, the content of the speech is not parochial. It is,
rather, addressed to anyone and everyone who is open to hearing it –
including, of course, we who can read the text and ponder what it tells us.

If the identity of the audience is unspecified, that of the speaker is
plain: "I YHVH am thy God, who brought thee out of the land of Egypt,
out of the house of bondage" (Exodus 20:2). Later Jewish – but not Christian – tradition will treat this assertion as part of the first statement and
the basis of the first positive precept: to believe in the existence of the one
God, YHVH. But in context it functions more to announce the identity of
the speaker – who, as would have been customary in any such proposed
covenant between a suzerain and his vassals, declares the ruler-subject
relationship that governs everything that follows. In this understanding,
"I YHVH am thy God" emphasizes that the speaker is the individual hear-
er's personal deity: not just the god of this locale, capable of making the
mountain tremble, rumble, and smoke, but the very One who brought
you personally out of your servitude in Egypt.

Unlike God's self-identification to Moses at the burning bush (Exodus 3:6), there is no mention here of the patriarchs. The agreement
offered to the Israelites is a covenant not with the God of their long-dead
fathers but with the God of their own recent deliverance. The former cov-

enant was for fertility, multiplicity, and a promised land; the new one concerns peoplehood, self-rule, and the goals of righteousness and holiness. It rests on a new foundation, and it is made not with a select few but with the universal many.

Although the basis of the new relationship is historical, rooted in the Lord's deliverance of the Israelites from Egyptian bondage, the Lord's opening declaration also conveys a philosophical message. The Lord appears to be suggesting that for the children of Israel – if not also for other unnamed auditors – there are basically two great alternatives: either live freely in relation to the Lord, in Whose image humankind was created, or be a slave to Pharaoh, a human king who rules as if he were himself divine. Egypt, identified redundantly as "the house of bondage," is presented here not just as one alternative among many but as *the* alternative to living as men and women whose identity and whose freedom – from bondage not only to Pharaoh but to their own worst tendencies – seem to depend on embracing the covenant with the Lord.

How Not to Seek God

After the opening remark declaring God's relation to this people, the next statements concern how God wants them to conduct their side of the relationship. The instruction is entirely negative.

The first wrong way is this: "Thou shalt not have other [or strange, *aherim*] gods before Me" (Exodus 20:3). This is a declaration not of philosophical monotheism but of *cultural* monotheism. What is claimed precisely is an exclusive, intimate I-thou relationship like that of a marriage, requiring unqualified fidelity and brooking no other's coming between the two partners. One might phrase it this way: "*Thou* shalt look to no *stranger*-gods in My presence." This goes beyond turning an I-thou relationship into a "triangle." *Aherim*, the word translated "other" or "strange," suggests that any such putative deities would be alien not only to the relationship as such but specifically to its *human* partners. The only God fit for a relationship with beings made in God's image is the God whose being they resemble and whose likeness they embody. Only such a One would not be a "stranger."

Yes, powers regarded (not unreasonably) by other peoples as divine –
for example, the sun, the moon, the earth, the sea, the mountain, or the
river – may play a decisive role in determining the character and events of
human life. Yes, the powers that the Greek poets presented as anthropomorphic gods – Poseidon, earth-shaker; Venus, source of erotic love;
Demeter, source of crops; warlike Ares – must be universally acknowledged and respected for their place in human life. But one cannot truly
have a relationship with them, for they are strangers to all those who look
to them.* Only with YHVH is there the possibility of genuine kinship.

Having established the principle of exclusivity, God speaks next to
correct a second error, namely, the natural human inclination to represent the divine in artfully made visible images, and even to worship these
statues or likenesses:

> Thou shalt not make unto thee a graven [or sculptured] image,
> nor any likeness of any thing that is in the heavens above or that is
> in the earth below, or that is in the water under the earth; thou
> shalt not bow down unto them, nor serve them, for I *YHVH* your
> God am a jealous [or zealous] god, remembering [or visiting] the
> iniquity (*avon*) of the fathers upon the children unto the third or
> fourth generation of them that hate Me; and showing grace (*hesed*)
> unto the thousandth generation of them that love Me and keep
> My commandments. (Exodus 20:4–6)

Intended to proscribe the worship of idols, this injunction builds a
fence against such practices by forbidding even the making of sculpted
images or likenesses, especially of any natural being. It emphatically
opposes the practice, known to the ex-slaves from Egypt, of worshipping

---

* It is true that the Greek poets, by idealizing the human form in the ageless and
immortal gods, tried to bridge the gap between humankind and the indifferent eternal natural forces and heavenly bodies. It is also true that the anthropomorphic Greek
gods, according to Homer, had their favorites among the mortals. But these "relationships" were one-sided and based entirely on caprice and whim. By the very understanding of divinity, it was unthinkable that any eternal, beautiful, and self-sufficient
god would care a fig for us "creatures-of-a-day" – the weak, perishable, ugly, and
unlovable mortals they toyed with for sport.

natural beings – from dung beetles to the sun to the Pharaohs – and representing them in sculpted likenesses. But it also seems to preclude any attempt to represent God Himself in image or likeness. The overall message is clear: any being that can be represented in visible images is not a god. The unstated reason: God is incorporeal and transnatural.

What's wrong with worshipping visible images or the things they represent? Even if, as we have reason to believe, it rests on an error – mistaking a mere likeness for a true divinity – it seems harmless enough, at worst a superstitious waste of time. But the practice and the disposition behind it are hardly innocuous. To worship things unworthy of worship is in itself demeaning to the worshipper; it is to be oriented falsely in the world, taking one's bearings from merely natural phenomena that, although powerful, are not providential, intelligent, or beneficent. Moreover, paradoxically, such apparently humble submission masks a species of presumption. After all, human beings will have decided which heavenly bodies or which animals are worthy of being revered, and how these powers are to be appeased. In addition, the same human beings believe that they themselves, through artful representation, can fully capture these natural beings and powers, and then, through obeisance, manipulate them. Worse, with increased sophistication of the craftsmen comes the danger that people will come to revere not the entities idolized but the physical idols as well as the sculptors and painters who, in making them, willy-nilly elevate themselves.*

Perhaps the most important reason is that neither the worship of dumb nature nor the celebration of human artfulness addresses the twistedness and restlessness that lurk in the human heart and soul. To put it positively, neither nature nor artfulness teaches anything about righteousness, holiness, or basic human decency. Indeed, the worship of nature or of idols may contribute to the problem. Making the connection explicit, the Lord vows to visit the "iniquities" of the fathers on the sons, unto the third or fourth generation.

An iniquity (*avon*) in the Bible differs from a sin (*het*). To sin is to miss

---

* We now collect these statues in secular museums and admire their makers without a whiff of reverence for the divinity they allegedly represent. One suspects that when the ancient Athenians came to the Parthenon, temple of Athena on the Acropolis, what they most esteemed there was not the goddess but the sculptural genius of Phidias, who made her (and the political will of Pericles, who ordered the Parthenon built).

the mark, as an arrow misses the target. By contrast, to commit an iniquity is to do something twisted or crooked, to be perverse. Sin is not inherited, and only the sinner gets punished; iniquity, however, like "pollution," lasts and lasts, affecting those who come in its wake. It is not only that perverse fathers are likely to pervert their children; in addition, the children are inevitably stained by the father's iniquity.* How this comes about, the text leaves wonderfully ambiguous, thanks to the multiple meanings of the Hebrew verb *poqed*, which means both visiting and remembering; either the Lord promises to intervene directly, actively inflicting the father's twisted deeds on the sons, or He promises to allow those deeds to linger in the fabric of the world, contaminating the lives of the sons until repentance or cleansing is effected. Either way – and perhaps the two amount to the same thing – the perversity of the father's deeds will reverberate through the generations.[51]

The Israelites are not yet told what behavior they are to regard as iniquitous. Is it idolatry itself, or does idolatry lead to such twisted practices as incest, fratricide, bestiality, cannibalism, slavery? One way or the other, the fathers (and mothers) are put on notice: how they stand with respect to divinity will affect their children and their children's children. God and the world care about, retain, and perpetuate our iniquities.

But not indefinitely – only to the third or fourth generation, the limits of any father's clearly imaginable future. And overshadowing all is the promise of God's bountiful grace "to the thousandth generation of those who love Me and keep My commandments." Just as the sons of iniquitous fathers suffer through no direct fault of their own, so a thousand generations of descendants of a single God-loving and righteous ancestor enjoy unmerited grace. (By the way, it has been only two hundred generations since the time of Father Abraham, for whose merit the children of Abraham are still being blessed.)

From this little injunction on idol worship we learn that God and the

---

* The classic example is Oedipus, who unwittingly killed his father and married his mother. His deeds, committed in ignorance and violating no explicit law, nonetheless constituted a pollution that affected not only his children (who were also his half siblings) but also the entire land of Thebes, which suffered a plague on generation. We shall return to this primal iniquity when we examine the injunction to honor your father and mother.

world are not indifferent to the conduct of human beings; that our choice seems to be between living in relation to the Lord and worshipping or serving strange gods, between keeping His commandments and living iniquitously; that the choices we make will have consequences for those who come later; but that the blessings that follow from worthy and God-loving conduct are more far-reaching than are the miseries caused by iniquitous and God-spurning conduct. There will be perversity in every generation, but the world overflows with *hesed* or grace.

And this surprising turn in the comment on idolatry and iniquity highlights the decisive (and perhaps most important) difference between idols or strange(r) gods and "the Lord thy God": under the rule of no other deity could the world be seen to embody the kind of grace, kindness, and blessing here foretold. As earlier in the hope-filled rainbow sign after the flood (Genesis 9:1–17), the token of God's first covenant with humankind, here each and every Israelite learns that he will have reason to be grateful not only for his one-time recent deliverance from Egypt but also for the enduringly gracious (and not merely powerful or dreadful) character of the deity with whom he is covenanting.

The implications for how we are to live in the light of this teaching are clear. My children and my children's children are at risk from any iniquity I commit, but nearly endless generations will benefit from the good that I may do. An enormous responsibility, then; and yet we know also that we are not *solely* responsible for the world's fate, and that redemption is always possible. Even if we fail, there will still be *hesed*. To walk with hope in the light of *hesed* offers the best chance for a worthy life.

The final error to be corrected concerns the use of the divine name. For if visible beings are unworthy of worship, and if, conversely, "*YHVH* thy God" cannot be visibly imaged, all that remains to us of Him (when He is silent) is His name. Yet it is also not through His name that the Israelites are to enter into a proper relationship with the Lord:

> Thou shalt not take up (*nasa*) the name of the Lord thy God in vain, for the Lord will not hold guiltless the one who takes up His name in vain. (Exodus 20:7)

Without warning, and for no apparent reason, the Lord speaks now of Himself not in the first but in the distant third person. This personal dis-

tancing of divine speech echoes the growing distance in the several statements, from the opening "thy God," to "other/stranger gods before Me,"
to vain "images and idols" not to be made and worshipped, and now to
"the name of the Lord thy God" that is not to be taken in vain.

The prohibition itself, though seemingly straightforward, asks to be
unpacked. What, exactly, is being proscribed? What sort of use of God's
name is "in vain"? The concept embraces not only speaking falsely but
also speaking emptily, frivolously, insincerely. The most likely occasion
for such empty invocations of the divine name would be in swearing an
oath, calling on God to witness the truth of what one is about to say or
the pledge one is promising to fulfill. But the injunction seems to have a
larger intention, at the very least inviting us to ponder what would *not* be
a vain use of the Lord's name.

The real target of the injunction may be the attempt to live in the
world assuming that "God is on our side." That is, what is "vain" about
the forbidden speech may have more to do with an inward disposition of
the heart than with words overtly spoken. To speak the Lord's name,
unless instructed to do so, is to wrap yourself in the divine mantle, to
summon God in support of your own purposes. It is to treat God as if He
were sitting by the phone waiting to do your bidding. In the guise of
beseeching the Lord in His majesty and grace, you behave as if you were
His lord and master. You behave, in other words, like Pharaoh.*

There is a deeper issue, having to do less with misconduct and more
with the hazards of speech itself. Treating anyone's name as something

---

* This interpretation helps to make sense of the fact that the injunction is put not in
terms of "speaking" or "saying," but in terms of "carrying" or "bearing" or "lifting up"
the name of the Lord. This metaphor implies that the fault, deeper than the speech
itself, lies in the attempted appropriation of God's power and authority through the
name. It also makes sense of the second part of the verse, in which we are told the
consequence of disobedience: "The Lord will not acquit [cleanse, *naqah*] the one who
takes up His name in vain." The Lord will not claim or serve you just because you
claim the Lord or His assistance. And you will not be cleansed – not now, not ever –
from the stain of having done so. This injunction and its implications apply not only
to someone vainly swearing an oath, but also to anyone who might undertake to speak
in the name of God, including prophets and priests, who are susceptible to the occupational hazard of thinking that they speak for, or even in the place of, the divine. A
community whose members obey this injunction will be less likely to suffer the despotism of god-pretending pharaohs or the oppression of god-trafficking priests.

that one can "take up" or "lift" is to take him up, as if by his handle. Like making images of the divine, trafficking in the divine name evinces a presumption of familiarity and knowledge. To handle the name of the Lord risks treating Him as a finite thing known through and through. Even if uttered in innocence, the use of the Lord's name invites the all-too-human error that attends all acts of naming: the belief that one thereby grasps the essence.

Called by God from out of the burning bush, Moses, in the guise of asking what to respond when the Israelites inquire who sent him, seeks to know God's name. The profoundly mysterious nonanswer he receives – *ehyeh asher ehyeh*, "I will be what I will be," or "I am that I am" – is actually a rebuke: the Lord is not to be known or captured in any simple act of naming. The right relation to Him is not through naming or knowing His nature but through hearkening to His words. The right approach is not through philosophy or theology, not through speaking about God (*theo-logos*), but through heeding *His* speech.

This is not to say that the Decalogue proscribes all speaking about God. Later there will be instruction about times and circumstances in which the Israelites will be enjoined to call upon or to praise the Lord; and the mention of His name in regular rituals and prayers can hardly be taken as a violation of this injunction. At the same time, however, the proscription does serve to induce caution. By avoiding casual speech about the Lord, one leans especially against the cultivation of a childish view of the deity – a superpowerful fellow with a beard, accessible on demand, intelligible, familiar: a projection, in short, of our own needs and imaginings. And it makes clear that our relation to the divine is not to proceed by way of naming speech any more than by way of visible likeness.

Yet up to this point there has been no positive instruction regarding how one should relate to the divine. What does this God want of His people? The next utterance gives the answer.

The Sabbath Day

Of all the statements in the Decalogue, the one concerning the Sabbath is the most far-reaching and the most significant. It addresses the profound matters of time and its reckoning, work and rest, and man's relation to

God, the world, and his fellow men. Most important, this is the only injunction that speaks explicitly of *hallowing* and *holiness* – the special goal for Israel in the covenant being proposed. Here is the relevant text:

> Remember the Sabbath day, to keep it holy. Six days shalt thou labor and do all thy work. But the seventh day [is a] Sabbath to the Lord thy God.
>
> Thou shalt do no manner of work, thou, thy son and thy daughter, thy servant and thy maidservant, thy cattle and thy stranger that is within thy gates.
>
> For in six days made the Lord the heavens and the earth and the sea and all that is in them; but He rested on the seventh day; and therefore the Lord blessed the seventh day and He hallowed it. (Exodus 20:8–11)

The passage opens with a general statement specifying two obligations: to remember, in order to sanctify. Next comes an explication of the duty to make holy, comprising a teaching for the six days and a (contrasting) teaching for the seventh. At the end, we get the *reason* behind the injunction, a reference to the Lord's six-day creation of the world, His rest on the seventh day, and His consequent doings regarding that day.

Imagine ourselves "hearing" this simple injunction at Sinai. We might find every term puzzling: what is "the Sabbath day"? What does it mean to "remember" it? And what is entailed in the charge "to keep it holy" or "to sanctify it"? And yet the statement seems to imply that "the Sabbath day" is, or should be, already known to the Israelites. What might *they* have understood by it?

The word "sabbath" comes from a root meaning "to cease," "to desist from labor," and "to rest." Where, then, have the ex-slaves encountered a day of desisting? Only in their recent experience with manna.

After the Exodus from Egypt and their deliverance at the Sea of Reeds, the Israelites encounter shortages of water and food, and begin to murmur against Moses' leadership. Comparing unfavorably their food-deprived new freedom with their well-fed existence in bondage, they long for the fleshpots of Egypt and accuse Moses of bringing them into the wilderness to die of hunger. As if waiting for just such discontent, the Lord intervenes even without being asked. He causes manna to rain from heaven for the people to gather, "a day's portion every day," not only to tame their hunger but explicitly "that I may prove them, whether they will walk in My law or not" (Exodus 16:4). The restrictions placed on their gathering are threefold: each should gather only what he and his household need and can eat in a day; there is to be no overnight storage or waste; and there is to be no gathering on the seventh day, for which a double portion will be provided ahead of time on the sixth.

The provision of the manna, and the restrictions attached to its gathering and storage, teach several lessons: the condition of the world is not fundamentally one of scarcity but of plenty, sufficient to meet the needs of each and every human being; there is thus no need to hoard against the morrow or to toil endlessly, grabbing all you can; and there is no need to look upon your neighbor as your rival, who may keep you from a livelihood or whose need counts less than yours. Accordingly, one may – one should – regularly desist from acquiring and provisioning, in an expression of trust, appreciation, and gratitude for the world's bounty, which one also must neither covet beyond need nor allow to spoil. In all these respects, the provision of manna in the wilderness stands as a correction of fertile Egypt, where land ownership was centralized, acquisitiveness knew no respite, excesses were hoarded, the multitude sold themselves into slavery in exchange for grain, neighbor fought with neighbor, and one man ruled all as if he were a god.* Against the ex-slaves' despairing belief that food is preferable to freedom and that serving Pharaoh offered the surest guarantee of life, the children of Israel are taught that they live in a world that can provide for each and every person's needs, and also

---

* The provision of manna to sustain the children of Israel through their wilderness wanderings has political significance, in that economic matters are set aside so that moral and spiritual ones may be pushed to the fore. In keeping with its central mission to become a kingdom of priests and a holy nation, Israel will be the only people who become a people before inhabiting a land and before being required to provide for their common subsistence. (Whether the subordination of autochthony and political economy to morality and holiness has been politically good for the Jews is another question.) The provision of manna returns the Israelites to a gathering society, preagricultural, not unlike the Garden of Eden, before the division of labor and before the emergence of inequality that comes with landed property.

that the Lord helps those who will help themselves. They must work to gather, but what they gather is a gift. In a world beyond scarcity and grasping, the choice is not freedom versus food and drink, but grateful trust versus foolish pride or ignorant despair.

Aside from their experience of manna, the Israelites may have had another referent for a "Sabbath day." Before the coming of the Bible, many peoples in the ancient Near East already reckoned time in seven-day cycles connected with the phases of the moon. Among the Babylonians, these seventh days were fast days, days of ill luck, days on which one avoided pleasure and desisted from important projects out of dread of inhospitable natural powers. This was especially the case with their once-a-month Sabbath, *shabattu* or *shapattu*, the day of the full moon (that is, the fourteenth day from the new moon).

Against these naturalistic views, the Sabbath teaching in Exodus institutes a reckoning of time independent of the motion of the heavenly bodies, in which the day for desisting comes always in regular and repeatable cycles and is to be *celebrated* as a day of joy and benison. Readers of Genesis already know the basis of this way of reckoning time from the story of Creation, whose target was precisely those Mesopotamian teachings and the belief that the heavenly bodies are gods. But the children of Israel are only now learning that time in the world – and, hence, their life in the world – will be understood differently from the way nature-worshipping peoples understand it. The Sabbath day, blessed by the Lord, has existed from time immemorial, but the creation- and humanity-centered view of the world enters human existence only through the covenant being here enacted with the children of Israel.

The community can thus be founded not on organic economic growth, with households giving rise to villages and then cities (Aristotle); not on conquest or plunder by the strong or an act of patricide or fratricide (Machiavelli, the biblical example of Cain, the Roman example of Romulus); not on a social contract, entered into by fearful individuals aiming to escape the war of all against all (Hobbes), to protect private property (Locke), or to ratify a swindle pulled off by the rich against the poor (Rousseau); but on a covenant made by still-free and equal human beings with the Lord. The manna acknowledges the necessity of meeting necessity, but it does not put economics or the mastery of nature above the task of making men orderly and good. Getting the human beings out of slavery is easy compared with getting the inherent slavishness – and tyranny – out of the human beings.

What, then, is the duty to *remember* the Sabbath day? About some matters – such as their previous condition of servitude – the Israelites will be exhorted to keep in mind what they previously experienced. About the Sabbath day – whose original, of course, no human being could have experienced – the Israelites are told to keep present in their minds what the Lord is now telling them for the first time. Once they learn the reason for the injunction, the duty to remember will link their future mindfulness with their recall of the remotest past: the original creation of the world and the beginning, or prebeginning, of time. Each week, going forward, the children of Israel will be recalled to God's creation of the world and invited to relive it symbolically.

Much later, when Moses repeats the Decalogue in Deuteronomy, he will enjoin the Israelites to "guard" (or "keep" or "observe," *shamor*) the Sabbath day, to keep it holy, "as the Lord thy God commanded thee" (Deuteronomy 5:12). Guarding and keeping are duties for the Sabbath day itself, but remembering it can and should take place all week long, reconfiguring our perception of time and its meaning. Under this radically new understanding, the six days of work and labor *point toward* and are completed by the seventh day and its hallowing. Mindfulness of sanctified time makes an edifying difference to the manner and spirit in which one lives and works *all* the time; and the remembered change in the meaning of time transforms and elevates all of human existence. Work is for the sake of a livelihood, but a livelihood has a new meaning when staying alive is seen to have a purpose beyond itself.

The root meaning of *qadesh*, to make holy, is to set apart, to make separate. Other peoples have their own forms of separation or sanctity: sacred places, sacred rituals and practices, sacred persons or animals. But in Israel what is made holy is not a special object, place, or practice, but rather the time of your life.

How to make this time holy we learn in the sequel, but here the Israelite idea of holiness is connected to the distinction between work (or labor) and rest, as well as the distinction between the things that are yours and the things that "belong" to God. The six days of work appear to be for yourself and your own; by contrast, the seventh day is said to be a Sabbath unto the Lord thy God, when "labor" (*avodah*) for oneself is replaced by "service" (*avodah*) to the Lord.

Yet the form of devotion is odd. No rituals or sacrifices are specified;

on the contrary, what is required is an absence, a cessation, a desisting, and this obligation to desist falls on the entire household. From master to servant to beast and stranger, the worldly hierarchy is to be set aside; regardless of rank or station, all are equally invited to participate in the hallowing of the day. Nor do people need to travel or to sacrifice in order to encounter this sanctified time. Holiness has a central and ever-renewable place in their ordinary life at home, if they but keep it in mind.

And the key to the holiness that is the Sabbath's desisting from labor? It is nothing less than God's own doings in connection with Creation. Every week the children of Israel are, as it were, returned to the ultimate beginning and source of the world, summoned to remember and to commemorate its divine Creation and Creator.

This means, among other things, remembering that what we call "nature," once widely worshipped – heaven, earth, sea, and all they contain – is not itself divine but rather the aggregate of God's creations and creatures. At the same time, in remembering the majestic fact of creation and the world's plentitude and beauty, the Israelites are also taught not to disdain the world or regard it as hostile, malevolent, or inhospitable, but rather to see it as a generous gift for whose bounty and blessings all human beings can and should be grateful.

The Israelites are not only recalled to the Creation; their own weekly cycle of work and desisting is meant to reproduce it symbolically. Here is the most radical implication of the Sabbath teaching: the Israelites are, de facto, enjoined "to be like God" – both in their six days of work and especially on the day of desisting. Note well: their relationship to the Creator is no longer grounded solely in historical time and in their (parochial) deliverance from Egyptian bondage. It is also ontologically rooted in cosmic time and in the universal human capacity to celebrate the created order and its Creator, and in our special place as that order's godlike, God-imitating, and God-praising creatures.

It is, of course, peculiar to command us to rest as God rested, because it is peculiar to speak of God "resting." Nevertheless, we can conjecture something of what it might mean.

In the original account of Creation, at the end of the sixth day "God saw every thing that He had made and, behold, it was very good." But the true completion of Creation comes on the seventh day, only after the creative work has ceased:

> And the heaven and the earth were finished and all their host. And
> God finished on the seventh day His work which He had made and
> He desisted on the seventh day from all His work which He had
> made. And God blessed the seventh day and He hallowed it,
> because on it He desisted from all His work which God in creating
> had made. (Genesis 2:1–3)

Here there is no talk of resting but only of desisting, and in this way
blessing and hallowing (or setting apart) the seventh day. A complete
world of changeable beings has been brought into being by a divinity
Who then completes His creative makings by "standing down." In this
mysterious blessing and hallowing of time "beyond" the world of creative making, God, as it were, makes manifest in the rhythm of the world
itself that mysterious aspect of being that is beyond change.

Remarkably, this consecration of time – and this pointing to what is
"out of time" – is something we (and only we) humans can glimpse and
participate in. It is open to us if and when we set aside our comings and
goings, and turn our aspirations toward the realm beyond motion from
which motion derives. It is open to us when we are moved by wonder and
gratitude for the existence of something rather than nothing, for order
rather than chaos, and for our unmerited presence in the story.

It may seem similarly odd to suggest that human beings would be
imitating God by feeling gratitude: why, and for what, would God be
grateful? Yet gratitude for the created world is not itself part of the created world. It is literally a manifestation of grace, which stands us, however briefly, outside the world, beyond the flux of the world's ceaseless
motions and changes. Though ourselves beings of motion and change,
we alone, godlike among the creatures, are capable of standing outside
and contemplating the world, and of feeling gratitude for it and for our
place in it. In this respect, too, Sabbath remembrance and sanctification
permit us to be "like God."

The Sabbath rest thus offers a partial reprieve from the sentence of
unremitting toil and labor prophesied by the Lord at the end of the story
of the Garden of Eden – a "punishment" of the human attempt to become
like gods, knowing good and bad, undertaken in an act of disobedience.
According to that account, our prideful human penchant for indepen-

dence, self-sufficiency, and the rule of autonomous human reason led us into a life that, ironically, would turn out to be nasty, brutish, and short. This is still very much our lot. But here, with Sabbath desisting, we are not only permitted but obliged regularly to cease the life of toil, sorrow, and loss, and to accept instead the godlike possibility of quiet, rest, wholeness, and peace of mind.

And this rise to godlike peace, unlike the self-directed "fall" into the knowledge of good and bad, depends not on disobedience but on obedience: the only way a free and reckless creature like man can realize the more-than-creaturely possibility that was given to him at the Creation. It is not only or primarily in imitating God in our workaday labor, but mainly and especially in hearkening to a command to enter into sacred time, that we may realize our human yet godlike potential. Doing as I say, teaches the Lord, is the route to "doing as I did" (or "being as I am").

The Sabbath teaching has other profound implications for human life, especially for politics. Adherence to the Sabbath injunction turns out to be the foundation of human freedom, both political and moral. By inviting and requiring *all* members of the community to imitate the divine, it teaches the radical equality of human beings, each of whom may be understood to be equally God's creature and equally in His image, each of whom is entitled to leisure from toil and the freedom to exercise our peculiarly human capacities for appreciation and gratitude.

Sabbath observance thus embodies and fosters the principle of a truly humanistic politics. Although not incompatible with political hierarchy (including kingship), the idea behind the Sabbath renders illegitimate any regime that denies human dignity or that enables one man or some few men to rule despotically as if he or they were divine. And in reconfiguring time, elevating our gaze, and redirecting our aspirations, Sabbath remembrance promotes internal freedom as well, by moderating the passions that enslave us from within: fear and despair (owing to a belief in our lowliness), greed and niggardliness (owing to a belief in the world's inhospitality), and pride and hubris (owing to a belief in our superiority and self-sufficiency).

The deep connection between the Sabbath and political freedom is supported by the repetition of the Decalogue in Deuteronomy. There, the reason given for Sabbath observance rests not on God's creating the world but on the Exodus from Egypt:

> And thou shalt remember that thou wast a slave in the land of
> Egypt, and the Lord thy God brought thee out thence with a
> mighty hand and an outstretched arm; *therefore*, the Lord thy God
> commanded thee to keep the Sabbath day. (Deuteronomy 5:15;
> emphasis added.)

In place of the six days of God's creative work contrasted with the seventh day of divine rest and sanctification, the Deuteronomic version contrasts the Israelites' enforced labor in Egyptian servitude with the Lord's mighty deliverance. The substitution invites us to see the second justification for Sabbath observance as the logical analogue and consequence of the first. In a word, where men do not know or acknowledge the bountiful and blessed character of the given world, and the special relationship of all human beings to the source of that world, they will lapse into worship either of powerful but indifferent natural forces or of powerful and clever but amoral human masters and magicians.

These seemingly opposite orientations – the worship of brute nature and the veneration of clever and powerful men – amount finally to the same thing: both deny the special god-like standing and holy possibilities of every single human being, and of humanity as such. Called upon to remember what it was like to have lived where men knew not the Creator in whose image we humans are made, and called upon to remember the solicitude of the Creator for His suffering people, the Israelites will embrace the teaching about Sabbath observance, and their politics will be humanized and their lives elevated as a result.

Honoring Father and Mother

The Decalogue moves next to its only other positive injunction, which is also the first to prescribe duties toward human beings and the last to mention "the Lord thy God." Standing as a bridge between the two orders of duty – to God and to one's fellow men – it also invites us to consider what the one has to do with the other:

> Honor thy father and thy mother, so that thy days may be long
> upon the land which the Lord thy God giveth thee. (Exodus 20:12)

As children of the civilization informed by the Bible, we take for granted that the duty of honor is owed to both father and mother, and equally so. Yet this obligation is almost certainly an Israelite innovation. Against a cultural background giving pride of place to manly males and naming children only through their patronyms, the Decalogue trumpets a principle that gives equal regard to father and mother. Well before there is any explicit Israelite law concerning marriage, this singling out of one father and one mother heralds the coming Israelite devotion to monogamous union, with clear lines of ancestry and descent and an understanding of marriage as devoted to offspring and transmission. Moreover, the principle is stated unconditionally: God does not say, "Honor your father and mother if they are honorable." He says, "Honor them regardless." We will soon consider why.

As children of the civilization informed by the Bible, we probably also take for granted that our parents *should* be singled out for special recognition. But this is hardly the natural way of the world. The natural family is the nursery of rivalry and iniquity, even to the point of patricide and incest, and in most societies honor is usually reserved not for Mom and Dad but for people out of the ordinary, for heroes, rulers, and leaders who go, as it were, in the place of gods.

Calling for the honoring of father and mother is thus another radical innovation, a rebuke at once to the ways of other cultures, to the natural human (and especially male) tendency to elevate heroes and leaders, and to the correlative quest for honor and glory in defiance of human finitude. In place of honoring the high and mighty, the way of the Lord calls for each child's honoring his or her father and mother, in the service of elevating what they alone care for and do: the work of perpetuation. And by elevating equally the standing of both, each child also learns in advance to esteem his or her spouse, as well as their joint task as transmitters of life and a way of living in which perpetuation is itself most highly honored.

The Israelites will shortly be told more about what it means not to honor father or mother, and how seriously this failure is regarded. In the ordinances following the Decalogue, two of the four capital offenses (on a par with premeditated murder and kidnapping for slave trading) are striking one's father or mother and cursing one's father or mother. But exactly what it means positively to honor is unspecified, and perhaps for good reason. By not reducing that obligation to specific deeds or speeches, the injunction compels each son or daughter to be ever attentive to what honoring father and mother might require, here and now. What the Decalogue is teaching here is a settled attitude of mind and soul.

Consider two alternative terms that might have been used to describe what children owe their parents: love and/or obedience. One can love or admire without honoring, and, conversely, one can honor even without loving or admiring. Yet for the Israelite, the duty to honor parents persists even if love is absent. As for obedience, the duty to honor father and mother extends long beyond the time when we, their children, are under their authority. An adult child may disagree with his father and mother, and choose to act in ways they would not approve; yet even when he does so, his unexceptionable and enduring obligation to honor them is still intact and binding.*

Unlike the feeling of love, and unlike the wonder of admiration, both of which go with the grain, the felt need to honor (to give weight to; *kabed*) is not altogether congenial. For honor implies distance, inequality, looking up to another with deferential respect, reverence, and even something of fear. In this regard, honor is exactly like what is owed to a god, for it is rooted in the feeling of awe. Indeed, the link is later made explicit. When the Lord proclaims His central teaching about holiness, the injunction regarding the proper disposition toward father and mother is renewed, revised, and placed in remarkable company:

---

* The famous "love test" in *King Lear* (Act I, Scene I) illustrates an ethic of honoring parents, but with importance differences from the biblical one. Cordelia, Lear's youngest daughter, refuses to say how much she loves her father when he asks, but instead declares: "I love your majesty according to my bond, no more nor less." Prodded by her father to "mend your speech a little," she explains: "Good my lord, / You have begot me, bred me, loved me. I / return those duties as are right fit, / Obey you, love you, and most honour you." According to Cordelia, duty requires her to obey her father for begetting her, love him for "breeding" (that is, rearing) her, and honor him for loving her. Speaking in terms of her filial duties, Cordelia sees herself under obligation to her father, as the Decalogue teaches. But she has a non-Israelite understanding of the *ground* of the honor she owes, for she conceives it as repayment for love received. Moreover, her speech to her father "no more nor less" seems (to this reader) to fall far short of what honoring him requires.

ᴍ

Ye shall be holy; for I the Lord your God am holy. Ye shall fear [or revere] each man his mother and his father, and ye shall keep my Sabbaths. I [am] the Lord your God. (Leviticus 19:2–3)

Fear, reverence, and awe are, of course, precisely the disposition that is appropriate toward the Lord Himself: it was "fear/reverence of God" for which Abraham was tested and praised in the binding of Isaac on Mount Moriah (Genesis 22:12). Moreover, the command to fear/revere mother and father is now clearly coordinated with the command to observe God's Sabbath, making explicit the link between the two positive injunctions.

What, then, links the honoring of father and mother to keeping the Sabbath, and to "being holy"?

The teaching about "father and mother" comes right on the heels of the reason offered for sanctifying the Sabbath day: God's creation of the world and His subsequent setting apart and hallowing a time beyond work and motion. It thus extends our attention to origins and "creation," now in the form of human generating. God may have created the world, and the whole human race, but you owe your own existence to your parents, who are, to say the least, copartners – equally with each other, equally with God – in your coming to be. For this gift of life – and, one may pointedly add, for not aborting you or electing to contraceive the possibility of your existence – you are beholden to honor them, in gratitude.

Gratitude toward parents is owed not only for birth and existence, but also for nurture, for rearing, and especially for initiation into a way of life that is informed by the disposition to gratitude and reverence. The way of this "initiation" is itself a source of awe. For our parents not only teach us explicitly and directly regarding God, His covenant, and His commandments. They also, in their unmerited devotion to our being and well-being, serve as the embodiment of, and our first encounter with, the gracious beneficence of the world and of its bountiful Source.

Filial honor and respect are not only fitting and owed; they are also necessary to the parental work, whose success depends on authority and command. Exercising their benevolent power by invoking praise or blame, reward or punishment, in response to righteous or wayward conduct, yet forgiving error and fault and remaining faithful to their children, parents embody and model the awe-some, demanding, yet benevolent and gracious authority that characterizes the Lord God of Israel. In response, on the side of the child, filial piety expressed toward father and mother is the cradle of awe-fear-reverence (and, eventually, love) of the Lord. Even when we no longer need their guidance, we owe them the honor due their office.

So the injunction to honor father and mother is fitting and useful. But why has it such prominence in the Decalogue, and why, paired with the Sabbath, is it at the heart of God's new way and the summons to *holiness*? On the assumption that God reserves His most important teachings to address those aspects of human life most in need of correction, we need to remind ourselves of the problems this injunction is meant to address: the dark and tragic troubles that lurk within the human household and that, absent biblical instruction, imperil all decent ways of life. I refer to the iniquities of incest and patricide.

The Bible's first (and almost only previous) mention of "father and mother" is found in a comment inserted into the story of the Garden of Eden – after the man, seeing and desiring the newly created woman, expostulates, "This one at last is bone of my bone and flesh of my flesh," and then names her as if she were but a missing portion of himself: "She shall be called Woman (*ishah*) because from Man (*ish*) she was taken." At this point, interrupting the narrative, the text interjects:

> Therefore a man leaves his father and his mother and cleaves unto his woman, that they may become as one flesh. (Genesis 2:24)

Many commentators have seen here the ground of a biblical teaching about monogamous marriage. In my view, the context suggests something darker. The inserted exhortation comes right after a speech implying that love and desire – including especially (male) sexual desire – are primarily love and desire of one's own: "bone of *my* bone and flesh of *my* flesh." Leaving your father and mother in order to become "as one flesh" with an *outside* woman serves as a moral gloss not on monogamy but on the sexual love of your own flesh, which, strictly speaking, is the formula for incest.

The danger of incest, destroyer of the distance between parent and child, is tied to a second threat: resentment of and rebellion against paternal authority, up to and including murder. The Bible's first (and paradigmatic) story about the relation between father and sons, the story of Noah's drunkenness, is a tale involving at least metaphorical patricide. Told as the immediate sequel to the establishment of the Lord's first covenant with all humanity, the story serves as a crucial foil for the teaching about family life that God now, at Sinai, means to establish in the world.

Noah has just received the first new law, comprising the basis for civil society, away from the anarchic "state of nature" that was the antediluvian world. At its center is the permission to kill and eat animals but, in exchange, an obligation to avenge human bloodshed – an obligation that is said to turn on the fact that man alone among the animals is godlike:

> Whosoever sheds man's blood, by man shall his blood be shed; for in the image of God was man made. (Genesis 9:6)

And it concludes with the command to procreate and perpetuate the new world order:

> As for you, be fruitful and multiply, swarm through the earth, and hold sway over it. (Genesis 9:7)

We look to the sequel to see how well this creature, who now knows that he was made in the image of God, fares under the new covenant, and the result is not cheering. Noah plants a vineyard, gets blind drunk, and lies uncovered in his tent, stripped not only of his fatherly authority but even of his upright humanity. There he is seen in his shame by Ham, his hotheaded son, who goes outside and publicizes his discovery, celebrating his father's unfathering of himself, and without touching a hair on his head, commits metaphorical patricide. Ham's brothers, Shem and Japheth, enter the tent, walking backward, covering their father's nakedness without witnessing or participating in it. When Noah awakens, he curses Canaan son of Ham but calls forth a blessing on "the Lord, God of Shem," the son whose pious action restored him to his fatherly dignity and authority.

In explicating this story elsewhere (in *The Beginning of Wisdom: Reading Genesis*), I have suggested that it is intended to show how rebellion, incest, and patricidal impulses lurk in the bosom of the natural – that is, the uninstructed – human family. These dangers must be addressed if a way of life is to be successfully transmitted, especially a way of life founded on reverence for the Lord in whose image – as Noah and the human race have just discerned – we human beings are made.

The impulse to honor your father and mother does not come easily to every human heart. Indeed, twisted child-parent relations are the theme of other Genesis stories.* Yet some children appear to get it right, even without instruction. Shem, who restores his father's paternal standing, seems to have divined the need for awe and reverence for his father as a pathway to, and manifestation of, the holy. And Shem's merit, it turns out, is visited upon his descendants: he becomes the ancestor of Abraham, founder of God's new way. Ham, on the other hand, is the ancestor of the Canaanites and the Egyptians, whose abominable sexual practices will be the explicit target of the laws of sexual purity (in Leviticus 18) that are central to Israel's mission to become a holy nation. It is at the end of this list of forbidden deeds, each proscribed as an iniquitous "uncovering of nakedness," that the Lord pronounces the connectedness (mentioned earlier) of the call to holiness, awe and reverence for mother and father, and the observance of the Sabbath.

Summing up: The injunction to honor father and mother is not only a teaching about gratitude, creatureliness, and the importance of parental authority. It also insists on sacred distance, respect, and reverence, precisely to produce holiness, *qedushah*, in that all-too-intimate nest of humanity that often becomes instead a den of iniquity and a seedbed of tragedy. In Sabbath observance, a correction is offered against the (especially Egyptian) penchant for human mastery and pride that culminates in despotism and slavery. In honoring father and mother, a correction is offered against the (especially Canaanite) penchant for sexual unrestraint, including incest, that washes out all distinctions and lets loose a wildness incompatible with the created order and with living under the call to be a holy people. Adherence to these two teachings offers us the

---

* Among these are the incest practiced by Lot's (unnamed) daughters upon their father, whom they made drunk for the purpose; Jacob's deception of his father, Isaac, in stealing the blessing intended for Esau; Reuben's supplanting his father in an incestuous liaison with Jacob's concubine, Bilhah; and perhaps also Joseph's near-patricidal indifference to his aged father's heartache when he steals Benjamin away from Jacob for himself.

best chance for vindicating the high hopes the world carries for the creature who is blessed to bear the likeness of divinity.

Universal and Particular

The connections between the Decalogue's two positive injunctions, and
between both of them and the goal of holiness, shed light on the vexed
questions of the universality versus the particularity of God's teaching to
Israel and of Israel's special standing among the nations. Our interpretation implies that the call to holiness, although made only (or first) to the
people of Israel, seeks to produce on earth a perfection not just of one
people but of *human beings as such.* This is perhaps already implicit in the
Israelites' call to become a kingdom of priests, whether as example or as
minister to the other peoples of the world. The universality becomes
explicit with the reason for Sabbath remembrance and sanctification, as
the Israelites are summoned to adopt a godlike perspective on the nature
of time and the relation between motion and rest. All human beings can
appreciate and imitate the divine activities of creating and hallowing
because we are all equally related to the Lord whose divine image and
likeness each one of us bears.

Yet, paradoxically, we are immediately reminded that universality,
like holiness, requires remaining true to the necessary particularity of
our embodied existence. For what could be further from universality
than the utterly contingent and noninterchangeable relationship that
each person has to his singular father and mother? True, the parent-child
relationship bears certain deep similarities to the relationship between
the biblical God and any human being. But no one lives with the universal (or generic) Father and Mother, only with his own very particular
ones. A person shows reverence for fatherhood and motherhood as such
only by showing reverence for his own father and mother.

Beware the universalist who has contempt for the particulars; beware
the lover of all humanity, or of holiness, who does not honor his own
father and mother. For it turns out to be all but impossible to love your
neighbors as yourself if you treat lightly your most immediate "neighbors," those who are most emphatically your own and most able to guide
you to your full humanity. The case for a parochial community that bears

a universal way – hence the case for the distinctive nation of Israel – follows directly from these considerations.

From the Lord's (or the Decalogue's) perspective, indeed, the contingency and parochial character of our existence is not a misfortune or a defect. To the contrary, in the Torah it is an estimable blessing that we have bodies and live concrete and parochial lives, for it is only in and through our lived experiences, here and now, that we gain full access to what is universally true, good, and holy. Unlike a later scriptural teacher, the Lord of the Decalogue does not exhort you to leave your father and your mother, and follow him (Matthew 10:34–38; Luke 14:26). Instead, He celebrates the fact that grace comes locally and parochially, into the life each one of us was given to live as well as we can, embedded in the covenantal community into which we have been blessed to be born.

The "Second Table": Moral Principles for Neighbors

When we move to consider the statements of the so-called "second table" of the Decalogue, we find ourselves on more familiar legal and moral ground, which we can thus cover more expeditiously.

Murder, adultery, and theft are outlawed by virtually all civilized peoples. These legal prohibitions form the necessary condition of civil peace, erecting important boundaries between what is mine and what is thine: life, wife, property, and reputation. Because they stand to reason and because they were established already in the ancient Near East, they need no explanations, nor promises of punishment for violation or reward for compliance.

Yet the Decalogue is not a legal code, and it goes beyond existing law. These latter statements, in the lapidary two-word Hebrew style, are formulated as eternal and absolute *moral* principles. Being packaged within the God-spoken preamble to the specific covenant with Israel, moreover, the principles acquire elevated standing as sacred teaching, ordained by a divine lawgiver and resting on ontological ground firmer than mere human agreement or utilitarian calculation:

Thou shalt not murder.
Thou shalt not commit adultery.

Thou shalt not steal.
Thou shalt not bear false witness against thy neighbor.
Thou shalt not covet thy neighbor's house;
thou shalt not covet thy neighbor's wife, nor his [man-]servant
nor his maid-servant, nor his ox nor his ass, nor anything that is
thy neighbor's. (Exodus 20:13–14)

The first three absolutes defend the foundational – rather than the highest – human goods: life, without which nothing else is possible; marital fidelity and clarity about paternity, without which family stability and responsible parenthood are very difficult; and property, without which one's chance for living well – or even making a living – is severely compromised.* Further specification of these principles must and will be given later in Exodus when the ordinances of the covenant are pronounced.

The proscription of bearing false witness carries a moral message that goes beyond its clear importance in judicial matters. At stake are not only your neighbor's freedom, property, and reputation, but also the character of communal life and the proper uses of the godlike human powers of speech and reason. Echoing the earlier prohibition on taking the Lord's name in vain, this injunction takes aim at a deed of wrongful speech – speech that is, in fact, vain, light in weight and empty of truth. To speak falsely is to pervert the power of reasoned speech and to insult the divine original, Whose reasoned speech is the source of the created order and Who is Himself the model of which we are the image.

If most of the prohibitions in the second table are familiar, the Decalogue concludes in a surprising turn by focusing not on an overt action but on an internal condition of the heart or soul, a species of ardent desire or yearning. The uniqueness of this proscription of coveting is suggested both by its greater length and by the spelling out of the seven things belonging to your neighbor that you must not even long for.

---

* The triad of Life, Wife (or Marriage), and Property should be compared with the three foundational natural rights made famous by John Locke – Life, Liberty, and Property – which, suitably altered by Jefferson (Pursuit of Happiness instead of Property), became the bedrock of American political thought. What might it mean, in the long run, for a society to treat liberty rather than marriage as one of its inviolables?

What is this doing at the close of the Decalogue? As a practical matter, a prohibition against covetous thoughts and desires builds a fence against the other forbidden deeds, for if you do not covet the things that are your neighbor's, you will be less likely to steal, commit adultery, or murder; and you will be less tempted to make your neighbor suffer harm or loss by bearing false witness against him.

Beyond such practical considerations, the final injunction causes us to reflect on the meaning of possession and on the nature of desire and neighborhood. A man who covets what is his neighbor's suffers, whether he knows it or not, from multiple deformations of his own desire. Not content with his own portion of goodly things, he is incapable of seeing them in their true light: as means to – and participants in – a higher way of life.

Moreover, some of the same items occur on both the list of seven partakers in Sabbath rest and the list of seven "covetables," as if to indicate the mistaken direction of the coveter's desire. His heart is set on the possessions of another because he fails to realize that the things that matter most are not the unsharable things but rather the things we and our neighbors hold in common: knowledge of the Lord and what He requires of us, participation in His grace and the bounty of creation, and the opportunity to live a life of blessing and holiness, despite our frailty and our proclivity for error and iniquity.

Our neighbor's aspiration to, or possession of, these goods in no way interferes with our chances to attain them. On the contrary, to live among neighbors who yearn for the sharable goods is to live in a true community, in which each and all can be lifted up in the pursuit and practice of holiness. Such a polity, even if only an object of aspiration, is a veritable light unto the nations.

CHAPTER SIXTEEN

The Gettysburg Address

Abraham Lincoln's Refounding of the Nation

"IN THIS TEMPLE, as in the hearts of the people for whom he saved the Union, the memory of Abraham Lincoln is enshrined forever." This, I trust everyone knows, is the inscription on the back wall of the Lincoln Memorial, visible above the awe-inspiring statue of our greatest president, greeting us and inducing reverence as we enter what is, in my opinion, the finest public building anywhere. On the walls to the left and the right are carved in stone Lincoln's two greatest speeches, the Gettysburg Address and the Second Inaugural, Lincoln's personal contributions to his enduring memory. The world may little note nor long remember what exactly happened at Gettysburg, but it will never forget what Lincoln *said* there, or at his second appearance to take the oath of the presidential office.

The Gettysburg Address has been memorized, recited, and admired. (For those who do not yet know it by heart, the text is appended to this essay.) Countless scholars have discussed its rhetorical devices, literary merit, and political reception. But few have attended to the *thought* of Lincoln's speech and its deeper purposes – purposes that it continues to serve. Many people recognize that this funeral oration, honoring the Union dead in the battle that marked a turning point in the war against Southern rebellion, was clearly even more a war speech, a summons to the living to prosecute to victorious conclusion a war that, despite the victory at Gettysburg, was not going well enough. What Lincoln calls "the great task remaining before us" is, first and foremost, the winning of the war. But few people see that the speech offers Lincoln's reinterpretation of the American founding, his construal of the war as a *test* of that founding, and his own radical call for a second birth of our nation, a nation to be reborn through passing that bloody test. Central to Lincoln's declaration of America reborn is his revisionist reading of our original birth announcement, the Declaration of Independence, and with it his own baptismal teaching, as it were, on the relation between liberty and equality, crucial to our new birth of freedom.

The express rhetorical purpose of the speech is clearly evident on the surface. The occasion is the dedication of a Union cemetery at Gettysburg for the burial of the nearly 5,300 Union fallen (killed in three days; another 17,000 Union soldiers were wounded; 27,000 Confederate soldiers were killed or wounded). The main eulogy, two hours in length, had already been given by Edward Everett, a then famous, now forgotten Massachusetts orator. Lincoln, invited late to the event, was asked to offer a few ceremonial remarks, setting apart the burial ground as a sacred and hallowed place. Lincoln acknowledges that "it is altogether fitting and proper that we should do this." But as he himself immediately makes clear, he is much less interested in dedicating a patch of earth to honor the dead than he is in inspiring his listeners, "us the living," who are, in the face of dispiriting loss and grief, "to be dedicated here to the unfinished work which they who fought here have thus far so nobly advanced," dedicated to "the great task remaining before us," namely, victory in the war and the restoration of the Union, now on a more solid foundation.

It is the outer frame of the speech – especially its first and last sentences – that bespeaks Lincoln's larger purpose: to create for future generations an *interpretation* of the war, and especially the war's relation both to the once "*new* nation," brought forth by "our fathers" and "conceived in liberty," and to "*this* nation," which, through the sacrifice of war and our dedication and resolve, "shall have a new birth of freedom." Before turning to those passages at the beginning and the end, we need to see the relation of this speech to a concern that had preoccupied Lincoln for at least twenty-five years.

In January 1838, in a remarkable speech to the Young Men's Lyceum in Springfield, Illinois, Lincoln (age twenty-eight) worried about the perpetuation of our institutions, now that the founding generation had gone to rest and those who had known them were also dying out. It is an astonishing speech, informed by profound reflections on law and lawlessness, vaulting political ambition (including his own), and the vulnerability of free institutions in democratic times to both mob rule and tyranny. Here Lincoln asserts that perpetuating our political institutions requires the development of a "political religion," comprising reverence for the laws and, more generally, sober sentiments "hewn from the solid quarry of sober reason" – among them, the founding principles. As Lincoln put it,

> Passion has helped us; but can do so no more. It will in future be our enemy. Reason, cold, calculating, unimpassioned reason, must furnish all the materials for our future support and defense. – Let those materials be moulded into *general intelligence; sound morality;* and, in particular, *a reverence for the constitution and laws.*[Emphasis in original.]

Throughout his life, Lincoln remained obsessed with the problem of attaching his fellow citizens to the American republic. And one might well say that his speeches taken as a whole – unsurpassed in the annals of American political utterance – follow his advice in the Lyceum address: they articulate the clear rational principles of the American republic, they are molded into persuasive and sound moral arguments, and they are always in the service of enhancing reverence for the Constitution and its laws. But his *greatest* public utterances were prophetic speeches – speeches that soar and move the soul because they display powers higher than cold, calculating, unimpassioned reason. These supremely inspiring speeches, I submit, were crafted by Lincoln with a view to their becoming canonical texts of the much-needed political religion.

The Gettysburg Address is, in both form and substance, the perfect text for the "bible" of American political religion. It is short enough to be memorized: three paragraphs of progressively increasing length, ten sentences, 272 words (but 130 different words), three-quarters of which are monosyllables. The polysyllabic words stand out against the little words, and only a few pregnant longer words appear more than once. The disyllabic repeated words are *conceived, living, rather, people* (three times in the last clause), and especially *nation* (five times: "*new* nation" in paragraph 1; "that nation," "any nation," and "that nation" in paragraph 2; but "*this* nation" in the last sentence of paragraph 3, this nation that shall be reborn into freedom). Among the still-longer words, those that Lincoln uses more than once are *devotion* (twice), *consecrate* or *consecrated* (twice), and – the most important word in the speech – *dedicate* or *dedicated* (six times). Noteworthy also is the echoing of the word "here," used eight times – the importance of which will be clear by the end.

The three paragraphs of progressively increasing length refer to time periods and actors of progressively increasing rhetorical importance. First (30 words) is the *past*: "Four score and seven years ago"; "our fathers." Second (73 words) is the *immediate present*: "Now"; *we* who are engaged in a great civil war, but mainly a much smaller *we* who are, right *here* and right *now*, met on a great battlefield of that war, having come here, fittingly and properly, to dedicate a portion of that field. Third (169 words) is our *future* in relation to our present and our past: contrasting "the brave men" who fought and died, with "us the living"; and moving from (a) our inability through speech to dedicate ground better consecrated by the deeds of the brave men, to (b) "us the living" dedicating *ourselves* to the great task remaining before us, to (c) "*we* here highly *resolv[ing]*" to win the war, so that (d) certain great things will follow, both for this nation ("a new birth") and also for people everywhere and always. In this third paragraph, 82 of the 169 words constitute the last sentence, about our dedication. The speech, in its spatial references, has an hour-glass structure: it opens "on this continent," narrows at its center to "a great battle-field" and then down to "a portion of that field," but finishes by suggesting that our dedication "here" can ensure that popular government will never perish from the *whole earth*.

These are small formal details, important for the rhetorical effect but hardly enough to give the speech its canonical standing. That comes from both its content and its elevated tone and expression, and especially from its famous beginning and end. Let us examine them.

> Four score and seven years ago, our fathers brought forth on this continent a new nation, conceived in Liberty and dedicated to the proposition that all men are created equal.

Four score and seven years ago. Why does Lincoln begin with this expression? Scholars note that the language is biblical, and that it echoes the 90th Psalm:

The days of our years are three score and ten,
Or even by reason of strength four score years.

Few notice that Lincoln, with this pious biblical reference that summons listeners to reverence, is also making a crucial substantive point: the deed he is about to recount, he intimates, happened not in living memory, for none alive today (in 1863) had yet been born four score and seven years ago. Lincoln begins by reminding us of things we could not possibly remember, highlighting his longstanding concern about perpetuation in a fully postrevolutionary age.

The theme and imagery of the first paragraph, and indeed of the whole frame of the speech, is *birth*: the birth of the nation and, at the end, its *re*birth. Four score and seven (87) years identifies the birth year as 1776, the year of the Declaration of Independence, not 1775, the year of Lexington and Concord, and, more significantly, not 1787, the year of the Constitution. Lincoln gives no hint of the bloody war of American separation and secession that secured in deed the Declaration's verbal assertion of our independence from Great Britain. Instead, he gives us an image of quiet generative congress. According to Lincoln, *our fathers* brought forth or sired upon this continent (as mother) a new nation. After pointing out that we could not have known them, he brings us close to the founders in spirit by reverently calling them our *fathers* rather than our *grand*fathers or *fore*fathers, and invites pious gratitude for our patrimony. The nation they brought forth was new not only in historical fact, but also in principle. It was "conceived in Liberty, and dedicated to the proposition that all men are created equal." Several points deserve emphasis, especially when we compare Lincoln's description of the founding birth with the birth certificate language of the Declaration of Independence itself.

In the Declaration, the signers declare: "We *hold* these *truths* to be *self-evident*: that all men are created equal." In Lincoln's version, three important changes are made. First, Lincoln changes a "self-evident truth"

to a "proposition." Both notions come from geometry. (Lincoln had studied Euclid, mastering the first six books of the *Elements*.) A self-evident
truth is an *axiom*, which neither admits of proof nor requires proof, for it
contains its evidence in itself; for example, "The whole is greater than the
part," or "Things equal to the same thing are also equal to one another."
If you *understand* the statement, you are compelled also to affirm it as
true. According to the Declaration, human equality is held to be an axiom,
evident in itself: if one understands the meaning of "men," one must
immediately see that *all* men (both male and female;* white, black, and
red) are *equally human*; and, further, one must see that they *equally* possess, by virtue of their *equal* humanity, inalienable *rights*, among them
the right (that is, the rightful permission and claim) to defend their life
(when threatened), safeguard their liberty (against enslavement or despotism), and pursue their own happiness as they see fit. A proposition,
on the other hand, is like a geometric theorem. It is something now put
before us – a "pro-posit-ing" – whose truth must be proved; yet it may
turn out to be unprovable or even false. According to Lincoln, human
equality was not so much a self-evident *premise*† of the American founding as a proposition in need of future demonstration.

The significance of shifting "all men are created equal" from axiom to
proposition is revealed by Lincoln's second big change: according to Lincoln, "our fathers" treated "all men are created equal" not, as the Declaration states, as a *truth* that "we hold" (and that thus defines us as a distinct
people) but as a proposal to which they were *dedicated*. Lincoln shifts the

---

* The term "men" in the Declaration of Independence clearly means "human beings,"
and refers equally to male and female human beings. The same is true of both of the
putative sources for the Declaration's teaching of human equality: the natural rights
teaching of John Locke and the "created-in-the-image-of-God" teaching of the Bible
("God created man in his own image; male and female created He them").

† It is closely followed by assertions about (a) (equal) inalienable rights, (b) rights
secured by governments, justly instituted (only) by consent of the governed, and (in
the event that instituted governments become destructive of those ends) (c) the right
of revolution and of instituting a new government, according to principles and forms
deemed likely to effect the people's safety and happiness. In contrast to Lincoln's formulation in the Gettysburg Address, the Declaration's assertion of human equality
functions less as a national credo than as the beginning of a logical argument for legit-
imizing the American Revolution.

picture from theory to practice: the proposition is more than an intellectual matter that one holds as a belief and proves in speech; it is a practical and moral goal to which one must devote oneself in action. The effective truth of the proposition of human equality cannot be shown by Euclidean reasoning; it must be demonstrated through deed and devotion.

To avoid possible misunderstanding, we need to clarify what sort of human equality needs proof through deed and devotion. And, let me be clear, on this matter Lincoln and the Declaration of Independence are in full agreement. The propositional "created equal" clearly does not mean "created the same." Neither does it mean equal in every respect. We human beings naturally differ in body and mind, talents and character, desire and determination. Some of us are sturdy, swift, or striving; others are sickly, slow, or slothful. Some find success and happiness, others failure and misery. Some are rich, powerful, and in positions of authority; most people are not. But these natural, social, or economic inequalities in no way contradict the equal *humanity* of otherwise differing human beings. Neither do they refute the derivative – and politically relevant – idea of natural or God-given equal *rights*, including the rights of life, liberty, and the pursuit of happiness. It is the Declaration's (prepolitical) equality of intrinsic rights, not social or political equality, to which, according to Lincoln, our nation was dedicated and which, as a proposition, requires proof through deed and dedication.*

Third, and most subtly, Lincoln does not ask us to think of the proposition only as a universal truth that we too can try to prove in practice; he wraps that truth in the pious drapery of the dedication of *our fathers* – who, he subtly suggests by the use of biblical imagery, stand for us in the place of the patriarchs of Israel: Abraham, Isaac, and Jacob. We should take an interest in this proposition, he implies, not only because it might be true, but as a matter of honoring the memory of our remarkable fathers. In short, Lincoln has transformed a merely intellectual truth,

---

* It is commonly overlooked that, because of the great diversity of talents, ambitions, and efforts of human beings, securing these equal individual rights, especially the right to pursue happiness, virtually guarantees enormous inequalities of outcomes and achievements – economic, social, cultural, political. Neither Lincoln nor the signers of the Declaration of Independence were simple egalitarians. There is nothing un-American about *those* inequalities.

held as self-evident and accessible to universal human reason (the Declaration's formulation), into a truth requiring *practical* demonstration by *particular* people – our fathers – who dedicated themselves to doing so. In this way, Lincoln summons our ancestral and traditional piety and attaches it to the principles of an emerging political religion, whose creed he is here redefining. Yet ancestral piety alone cannot sustain us, as we shall see, and a new birth is necessary, in large part because our fathers did not get it exactly right, particularly in practice.

Why does Lincoln change the Declaration? In order to address and correct a deep difficulty regarding the relation between equality and liberty in our founding. A clue is provided in the other big idea in the first sentence, "conceived in liberty." We know the fathers, we know the mother continent, and we know the child nation and to what it is dedicated. But what is meant by "conceived *in* liberty," and how does this figure in Lincoln's revision of the story of America's birth?

Attending closely to the image of generation, we note that, because conception precedes birth, our fathers who brought forth the new nation, according to Lincoln, already enjoyed liberty when they conceived her. But the oddity of the "in" in the phrase "conceived in Liberty" has confused me for some time. One astute reader suggested that just as a natural child is "conceived in love," so the American national child was "conceived in love of Liberty." I myself have instead toyed with "conceived *freely*, conceived by *choice*," not by necessity or nature or in a fit of passion, or, alternatively, "conceived in an act of independence and liberation, from the rule of Britain." But an illuminating interpretation was given me by my friend Harvey Flaumenhaft of St. John's College, Annapolis. "In Liberty," he suggests, refers to the political matrix that characterizes both the before and the after of the "bringing forth" of the new nation, and that matrix is British liberty, the context also of the American colonies. Britain, like her colonies and the new republic, was a liberal polity, but British liberty was mixed with a hereditary principle – not only the monarchy, but especially a hereditary nobility of dukes and barons who lorded it over the commons. The true American innovation is the freely chosen replacement of the hereditary principle with the principle of equality and equal rights: governments, the founders declared, exist to secure the rights not only of the highborn of hereditary privilege but of *all* men, who are *equally* endowed with unalienable rights. Or, in Lincoln's formulation, our fathers exercised their liberty to dedicate a new nation to the principle of human equality, to secure the unalienable rights for *all* its people.

Today we take for granted the compatibility of political liberty and political equality. But this novel addition of the principle of equality to the principle of liberty was then an unprecedented experiment. Not unreasonably, it raised two big questions: Can a nation "so conceived and so dedicated long endure"? Can political equality be obtained without the *surrender* of liberty? Taking the second question first, Lincoln had been personally attacked as a tyrant who was destroying liberty in his pursuit of equality. "Maryland, My Maryland," the state song written in 1861, begins: "The despot's heel is on thy shore, Maryland! His torch is at thy temple door, Maryland!" And the alleged despot is none other than Lincoln! His later suspension of the writ of habeas corpus would eventually be ruled unconstitutional. Yet Lincoln teaches in this speech that commitment to the proposition of human equality is not only compatible with liberty, but is in fact freedom's only true foundation.

As to the first question, Lincoln says that the war is a test: a test of the durability of a nation committed to equality as well as to liberty.* And although he does not say so here, as he does in the Second Inaugural, the war is a test that is now upon the nation because of an offensive defect in the founding. The defect is not mentioned by name in the Gettysburg Address, but its name is slavery. (Lincoln, by the way, also does not mention either the North or the South – or the Union – nor does he here assign blame for the war; in the Second Inaugural he will explicitly suggest that the offense of slavery lies with the nation as a whole.)

The Declaration of Independence was a liberal document, not a republican (or democratic) one. It did not by itself specify any particular form of government: *any* government (including monarchy or aristoc-

---

* Lincoln insisted that the Civil War was a test also for durability of *any* nation so conceived and so dedicated. Why might our Civil War have such universal significance? In part, perhaps, because of the unprecedented character and great good fortune of America's founding: what other nation heretofore was founded in the name of certain abstract moral and political principles? But also, as we shall see, because the war was fought precisely to defend those principles against rebellious forces that denied them and sought to destroy the nation that rested on them. Victory against a rebellion based on denial of fundamental principles is surely evidence of durability.

racy) is legitimate so long as it secures the rights of all who live under its rule, and it rules by consent of the governed. Yet despite adding the egalitarian principle to the British liberal principle, and despite the fact that, in Lincoln's reformulation of the nation's birth, equality as the *goal* was to come out of liberty by way of dedication, the new nation was flawed and stained from the start by the institution of slavery.

Contrary to current opinion, many of the founders understood that America's practice fell short of its founding principles, and they devised instrumentalities that they hoped would place slavery in the course of its ultimate extinction. But by Lincoln's time the situation had deteriorated. Not only was the regime in contradiction with itself, falling short of its stated ideals; worse, the South in rebelling had given effect to the view that the principle of equality was not merely too lofty to realize but simply false as a proposition. Lincoln knew that this denial of human equality was the true cause of the war; and he understood that the bloody struggle over slavery was the true test of the nation. Now that the self-evident truth of equality had been turned into a proposition needing proof, and now that the rebels had repudiated the proposition and called it a self-evident lie, passing the test meant winning the war, in part because winning the war meant a repudiation of the repudiation, a vindication of the proposition of equality. And in practical terms, only through winning the war and restoring the Union could slavery be abolished and the equal humanity of all citizens be given enduring political legitimacy.*

This is made clear in the end of the speech, where Lincoln moves from honoring the deeds of the noble dead to summoning "us the living," and,

---

* This point is often poorly understood by Lincoln's critics, then and now. As in his own time, Lincoln is sometimes blamed for placing preservation of the Union ahead of ending slavery. But unlike many abolitionists, Lincoln understood that the moral goals could be accomplished only by an unconditional surrender of the rebels. Letting the South go would make everyone complicit in slavery's preservation and would accept the rejection of the idea that animated the founding of the United States. Even accepting the South's suit for peace, endorsed by many abolitionists in the face of the war's great carnage, would be to recognize the separate status and legitimacy of "the so-called Confederacy" and its explicit rejection of the idea of human equality and of self-government founded on that principle. As Lincoln rightly understood, that rejection could be repudiated only by a victory that restored the Union.

in consequence, from the religious language of dedication and devotion to the more political language of resolution.

> It is for us the living, rather, to be dedicated here to the unfinished work which they who fought here have thus far so nobly advanced. It is rather for us to be here dedicated to the great task remaining before us – that from these honored dead we take increased devotion to that cause for which they gave the last full measure of devotion – that we here highly resolve that these dead shall not have died in vain – that this nation, under God, shall have a new birth of freedom – and that government of the people, by the people, for the people, shall not perish from the earth.

The proper way to honor the sacrifice of the dead, Lincoln suggests, is not by speech, but by action: by *dedicating* ourselves to finishing their work and the great task of winning the war, by *devoting* ourselves to the *cause* for which they gave their lives, by our *resolving* that *we* will guarantee, by *our* deeds, that they will not have died in vain.

Why must "we *here* highly resolve that these dead shall not have died in vain," and what result of our resolution would so vindicate their sacrifice? The goal for which victory is indispensable, stated in Lincoln's conclusion, is twofold, both aspects transcending the mere restoration of the now dissolved Union: first, "that this nation, under God, shall have a new birth of freedom"; and second, "that government of the people, by the people, for the people shall not perish from the earth."

The new birth of freedom – for which Lincoln is here offering the baptismal blessing and explanation – is a birth made possible only through bloodshed, not through generative congress of ancestral patriarchs and mother continent, explained calmly on parchment in Philadelphia, 1776. More important, this new freedom will differ crucially from the British liberty in which the nation was first conceived. Here equality will not come out of liberty. Rather, if we adhere to our resolve, *freedom will be newly born out of equality*, because the inegalitarian principle and the practice of slavery will be repudiated and defeated as the necessary condition of rebirth. Everybody, masters as well as slaves, will share in this new birth of freedom, having shed the mutual degradation that enslavement brings to them both. Liberty has not been destroyed as the rebels claimed, says Lincoln, but rather it will be set for the first time on a truly secure foundation: the radical equality of all human beings, now thrice called "the people," who will govern and be governed for their own well-being – a result that can, fittingly, be achieved only by "us the living." We the people, we the living rededicating ourselves here on the graves of the fallen and resolving to act hereafter in service to the cause, become, under God, the nation's new patriarchs and founders.

But it is Lincoln's final words, those enunciating the second goal of the war, that show why the new birth of freedom goes beyond the mere abolition of slavery, and why the vindication of the principle of equality goes beyond securing the intrinsic human rights of the Declaration of Independence. "Government of the people, by the people, for the people" is Lincoln's final alteration and improvement of the Declaration, going beyond its neutrality on the form of government. To the Declaration's legitimating philosophical principle of consent of the governed, Lincoln adds the operative practical (and constitutional) principle of popular self-government. Not only are the people to be governed ("*of* the people"), but *they* are to do the governing ("*by* the people"). Also, the clear purpose of government is not the prosperity of the few, but the well-being of all ("*for* the people").* The new synthesis of freedom and equality, achieved by the popular and manly defense of the Constitution, takes the form of democratic self-rule – not just rule of the majority, but that special sort of democratic self-rule that is informed by the proposition of radical human equality and equal human rights.

The nation conceived in liberty got a new birth, a birth of freedom and popular self-government, thanks to the self-sacrificing deeds of "the brave men ... who struggled here" and thanks to the dedication of the

---

* I have here interpreted "government of the people" to mean "government *over* the people." But it could just as well, and perhaps better, mean "government *made* by the people," founded on their original choice and consent. In this section of the speech, with the Constitution very much on Lincoln's mind, the preamble's "We the People of the United States" who "ordain and establish this Constitution for the United States of America" could be Lincoln's reference for a government *of* popular *origin*. Be this as it may, the truly distinctive American feature of the triad is government *by* the people: their continuing *practice* of governing themselves, according to law and principle, and for the common good.

living, under Lincoln's leadership, to "the cause for which they gave their last full measure of devotion." But taking the long view, the nation became better able to attach the hearts and minds of its citizens thanks to the words fitly spoken at Gettysburg by Father Abraham, who presided over its refounding in speech no less than in deed, and whose words have inspired all who came afterward to dedicate themselves to preserve, protect, and perfect our political freedom and equality. Today and tomorrow, our attachment to the republic is greatly enhanced whenever we reanimate Lincoln's words and, under their still-living instruction, resolve to live up to his vision of our national purpose.

Appendix: The Gettysburg Address

Four score and seven years ago our fathers brought forth on this continent, a new nation, conceived in Liberty, and dedicated to the proposition that all men are created equal.

Now we are engaged in a great civil war, testing whether that nation, or any nation so conceived and so dedicated, can long endure. We are met on a great battle-field of that war. We have come to dedicate a portion of that field, as a final resting place for those who here gave their lives that that nation might live. It is altogether fitting and proper that we should do this.

But, in a larger sense, we can not dedicate – we can not consecrate – we can not hallow – this ground. The brave men, living and dead, who struggled here, have consecrated it, far above our poor power to add or detract. The world will little note, nor long remember what we say here, but it can never forget what they did here. It is for us the living, rather, to be dedicated here to the unfinished work which they who fought here have thus far so nobly advanced. It is rather for us to be here dedicated to the great task remaining before us – that from these honored dead we take increased devotion to that cause for which they gave the last full measure of devotion – that we here highly resolve that these dead shall not have died in vain – that this nation, under God, shall have a new birth of freedom – and that government of the people, by the people, for the people, shall not perish from the earth.

– *Abraham Lincoln*
NOVEMBER 19, 1863

ACKNOWLEDGMENTS

Thanks are owed to many people who helped me produce this book. Eric Cohen, Neal Kozodoy, Yuval Levin, Leon Wieseltier, Adam Wolfson, and the late Irving Kristol and Richard Neuhaus, friends and fine editors all, improved the original versions of these essays. My good friend Gertrude Himmelfarb urged me to collect some of my essays into a single volume. Eric Cohen read all those original essays and suggested a logical order that guided my rewriting; he also gave me permission to include the essay we wrote together, "For the Love of the Game." At Encounter Books, Roger Kimball, editor and publisher, graciously welcomed me again onto his list; Carol Staswick, my copy editor, read the manuscript several times, each time more carefully than its author, each time offering many fine suggestions for improvement; and Heather Ohle ably shepherded the volume through production. The United States Holocaust Memorial Museum kindly granted permission to use the two photographs that appear in Chapter Ten.

I am deeply grateful to Christopher DeMuth, Arthur Brooks, and Roger and Susan Hertog for providing me a most congenial home at the American Enterprise Institute, where this project was conceived and completed. I am indebted to my students and colleagues at the University of Chicago and to my colleagues at AEI and on the President's Council on Bioethics for their many contributions to my thinking.

I dedicate this volume to the memory of my best friend and wife of fifty-four years, Amy Apfel Kass (1940–2015), with whom I taught, wrote, raised a family, and savored what life has to offer—always Wing to Wing and Oar to Oar. The introduction to this volume is the first thing I have written in nearly fifty years that she did not read, discuss with me, and improve. A master teacher of great texts, from Homer and Sophocles to Shakespeare, George Eliot, and Melville, Amy opened the minds and nourished the souls of generations of students, inspiring and guiding their search for a life that makes sense. For all who knew her, she exemplified what it means to lead a worthy life.

May her memory be for a blessing, especially for our lovely grandchildren – Polly, Hannah, Naomi, and Abigail – to whom I also dedicate these reflections, in the hope that they too will find meaning in modern times.

–Leon R. Kass, *July 2017*

NOTES

CHAPTER 2 – THE END OF COURTSHIP

1   A fine history of these transformations has been written by Beth L. Bailey, *From Front Porch to Back Seat: Courtship in Twentieth-Century America* (Baltimore: Johns Hopkins University Press, 1988).

2   See my "Man and Woman: An Old Story," *First Things*, November, 1991. A revised version, "The Vexed Question of Man and Woman: The Story of the Garden of Eden II," is the third chapter of my book *The Beginning of Wisdom: Reading Genesis* (New York: The Free Press, 2003).

CHAPTER 3 – THE HIGHER SEX EDUCATION

3   The full text is available in Amy A. Kass and Leon R. Kass, eds., *Wing to Wing, Oar to Oar: Readings in Courting and Marrying* (South Bend, Ind.: University of Notre Dame Press, 2000), pp. 353–64.

4   Allan Bloom, *Love and Friendship* (New York: Simon & Schuster, 1993), p. 104.

CHAPTER 4 – VIRTUALLY INTIMATE

5   "Cybercheats Married – to Each Other," *Metro News*, September 17, 2007, http://metro.co.uk/2007/09/17/cyber-cheats-married-to-each-other-138650/. Thanks to Ed Whalen for introducing me to this story.

6   For a particularly comprehensive and lurid account, written with equal parts clinical detachment and voyeuristic enjoyment, and informed – in my opinion – by an appalling moral relativism, see Aaron Ben-Ze'ev, *Love Online: Emotions on the Internet* (Cambridge, UK: Cambridge University Press, 2004). Ben-Ze'ev is a professor of philosophy at the University of Haifa, specializing in human emotions. From 2004 to 2012 he was also the president of that university.

7   For a collection of timeless texts on these and related topics, see our *Wing to Wing, Oar to Oar: Readings in Courting and Marrying*.

8   Immanuel Kant, "Conjectural Beginnings of Human History," trans. Emil Fackenheim, in *Kant on History*, ed. Lewis White Beck (Indianapolis: Bobbs-Merrill, 1963), p. 57.

9   John T. Cacioppo et al., "Marital Satisfaction and Break-ups Differ across On-line and Off-line Meeting Venues," *PNAS* (National Academy of Sciences), vol. 110,

no. 25 (June 18, 2013), available here: http://www.pnas.org/content/110/25/10135.full.pdf. The study, which examined a nationally representative sample of 19,131 American respondents who married between 2005 and 2012, found that 35 percent met their spouse online. Among those, 45 percent met through an online dating service; among these, 25 percent met on eHarmony. Those eHarmony couples ranked first in marital satisfaction and were less likely to divorce or break up than couples who met on other online sites or through other methods. eHarmony's own press releases claim that 438 people marry every day in the United States as a result of being matched on eHarmony.

10   Erwin Straus, "Shame as an Historiological Problem," in *Phenomenological Psychology* (New York: Basic Books, 1966), pp. 217–24.

11   For a fuller examination of these matters, see Aristotle, *Nicomachean Ethics*, Book VIII, Chapters 1–6.

12   Straus, "Shame as an Historiological Problem," p. 219.

13   Ibid., pp. 220–21, emphasis added.

14   Kurt Riezler, "The Social Psychology of Shame," *American Journal of Sociology*, vol. 48, no. 4 (January 1943), p. 461. (This essay is anthologized in *Wing to Wing, Oar to Oar*, where the quoted passage appears on p. 183.)

15   Straus, "Shame as an Historiological Problem," pp. 222–23.

16   Roger Scruton, private communication to the author, responding to an earlier draft of this essay.

17   "The Master Speed," from *The Poetry of Robert Frost* (New York: Henry Holt & Co., 1969).

18   *Genesis Rabbah*, Chapter 68, section 4.

CHAPTER 6 – AGELESS BODIES, HAPPY SOULS

19   Michael J. Sandel, "What's Wrong with Enhancement," paper presented to the President's Council on Bioethics, December 2002, http://bioethics.georgetown.edu/pcbe/background/sandelpaper.html.

CHAPTER 7 – HUMAN DIGNITY

20   For a full text of the "First Arkansas Marching Song," by Captain Lindley Miller, see http://www.civilwarpoetry.org/union/songs/arkansas.html.

21   I have explored this subject at greater length elsewhere: See "Death with Dignity and the Sanctity of Life," Chapter 8 in *Life, Liberty, and the Defense of Dignity: The Challenge for Bioethics* (San Francisco: Encounter Books, 2002); and "Elementary Justice: Man, Animals, and the Coming of Law and Covenant," Chapter 6 in *The Beginning of Wisdom: Reading Genesis* (New York: The Free Press, 2003).

CHAPTER 9 – A DIGNIFIED DEATH AND ITS ENEMIES

22 Leon R. Kass, M.D., *Toward a More Natural Science: Biology and Human Affairs* (New York: The Free Press, 1985), particularly Chapters 6–9.

23 See my essay "Death with Dignity and the Sanctity of Life," *Commentary*, March 1990, pp. 33–43. Regarding the alleged "right to die," see my essay "Is There a Right to Die?" *Hastings Center Report*, vol. 23, no. 1 (January–February 1993), pp. 34–43. On the question of legalizing physician-assisted suicide and euthanasia, see also Leon R. Kass and Nelson Lund, "Courting Death: Assisted Suicide, Doctors, and the Law," *Commentary*, December 1996, pp. 17–29.

24 Yale Kamisar, "Some Non-Religious Views against Proposed 'Mercy-Killing' Legislation," *Minnesota Law Review*, vol. 42, no. 6 (May 1958), pp. 969–1042. Reprinted, with a new preface by Professor Kamisar, in *The Slide toward "Mercy Killing,"* Child and Family Reprint Booklet Series (Oak Park, Ill.: National Commission on Human Life, Reproduction and Rhythm, 1987).

25 Ibid., p. 990.

26 John Keown, "Some Reflections on Euthanasia in the Netherlands," in *Euthanasia, Clinical Practice, and the Law*, ed. Luke Gormally (London: Linacre Centre for Health Care Ethics, 1994), p. 209. Keown is citing F. C. B. van Wijmen, *Artsen en het Zelfgekozen Levenseinde* [Doctors and the Self-Chosen Termination of Life], (Maastricht: Vaakgroep Gezondheidrecht Rijksuniversiteit Limburg, 1989), p. 24, Table 18.

27 Data are from Paul J. van der Maas et al., *Euthanasia and Other Medical Decisions Concerning the End of Life* (New York: Elsevier Science Inc., 1992), as reported in John Keown, "Further Reflections on Euthanasia in the Netherlands in the Light of the Remmelink Report and the van der Maas Survey," in *Euthanasia, Clinical Practice, and the Law*, p. 224.

28 Gerrit van der Wal et al., "Evaluation of the Notification Procedure for Physician-Assisted Death in the Netherlands," *New England Journal of Medicine*, vol. 335, no. 22 (November 28, 1996), pp. 1706–11.

29 Herbert Hendin et al., "Physician-Assisted Suicide and Euthanasia in the Netherlands," *JAMA*, vol. 277 (1997), pp. 1720–22. For a fuller and chilling account of the Dutch practice, see Herbert Hendin, *Seduced by Death: Doctors, Patients, and the Dutch Cure* (New York: Norton, 1996).

30 Keown, "Further Reflections on Euthanasia in the Netherlands," p. 230.

31 See my essay on the Hippocratic Oath, Chapter 9 in *Toward a More Natural Science*, especially pp. 232–40. See also, in the same volume, Chapter 8, "Professing Medically: The Place of Ethics in Defining Medicine," especially pp. 217–23.

32 Franklin G. Miller and Howard Brody, "Professional Integrity and Physician-Assisted Death," *Hastings Center Report*, vol. 25, no. 3 (1995), p. 12; footnote quotation on p. 13.

33 Quoted in Alexander Morgan Capron, "Euthanasia in the Netherlands: American Observations," *Hastings Center Report*, vol. 22, no. 2 (1992), pp. 30–33.

34 See Robert J. Lifton, *The Nazi Doctors: Medical Killing and the Psychology of Genocide* (New York: Basic Books, 1986), pp. 32–48.

CHAPTER 10 – A MORE PERFECT HUMAN

35 René Descartes, *Discourse on the Method of Conducting One's Reason Well and Seeking Truth in the Sciences*, trans. Richard Kennington, ed. Pamela Kraus and Frank Hunt (Newbury Port, Mass.: Focus Philosophical Library, 2007), Part VI, paragraph 2.

36 Karl Binding and Albert Höche, "Permitting the Destruction of Unworthy Life: Its Extent and Form," trans. Walter E. Wright et al., *Issues in Law and Medicine*, vol. 8, no. 2 (1992), Essay One, p. 246.

37 Ibid., Essay Two, p. 265.

38 Robert L. Sinsheimer, "The Prospect of Designed Genetic Change," *Engineering and Science Magazine*, California Institute of Technology, April 1969. Dr. Sinsheimer subsequently had a change of heart and became one of the advocates for caution and sobriety.

39 Joshua Lederberg, "Unpredictable Variety Still Rules Human Reproduction," *Washington Post*, September 30, 1967.

40 Bentley Glass, "Science: Endless Horizons or Golden Age?" *Science*, vol. 171 (1971), p. 28.

41 Peter Singer, *Practical Ethics*, 2nd ed. (New York: Cambridge University Press, 1993), p. 186.

42 Marvin Olasky, "Blue-State Philosophy," *World Magazine*, November 27, 2004.

43 President's Council on Bioethics, *Beyond Therapy: Biotechnology and the Pursuit of Happiness*, October 2003, available in trade editions, edited by Leon Kass, published by Dana Press and by HarperCollins, or online at https://bioethicsarchive. georgetown.edu/pcbe/reports/beyondtherapy/index.html.

44 International Academy of Humanism, "Declaration in Defense of Cloning and the Integrity of Scientific Research," *Free Inquiry*, vol. 17, no. 3 (Summer 1997).

45 Steven Pinker, "A Matter of Soul," Correspondence, *Weekly Standard*, February 2, 1998, p. 6.

46 Prof. Pinker has responded to this critique (repeated in another essay of mine, "Science, Religion, and the Human Future," *Commentary*, April 2007) in the Letters section of *Commentary*, July–August 2007, which also contains, in response, my elaboration of this critique.

CHAPTER 11 – THE AIMS OF LIBERAL EDUCATION

47 Jean-Jacques Rousseau, "Discourse on the Origin and Foundations of Inequality Among Men," trans. Roger D. and Judith R. Masters, in *The First and Second Discourses*, ed. Roger D. Masters (New York: St. Martin's Press, 1964), p. 132.

48   Interested readers should see, among others, Hans Jonas, *The Phenomenon of Life: Toward a Philosophical Biology* (1966; University of Chicago Press, 1982); Adolf Portmann, *Animal Forms and Patterns* (1952; Schocken Books, 1967), and *Animals as Social Beings* (Viking Press, 1961); Erwin Straus, *Phenomenological Psychology* (Basic Books, 1966), and *The Primary World of Senses* (Free Press, 1963); Oliver Sacks, *Awakenings* (1973; Summit Books, 1987); E. S. Russell, *The Directiveness of Organic Activities* (Cambridge University Press, 1945); and Marjorie Grene, *Approaches to a Philosophical Biology* (Basic Books, 1968). For my own efforts, see *Toward a More Natural Science: Biology and Human Affairs* (Free Press, 1985, 1988), especially Chapters 10–13, and *The Hungry Soul: Eating and the Perfecting of Our Nature* (Free Press, 1994, 1999).

49   See "Awesome Beginnings," Chapter 1 of my *The Beginning of Wisdom: Reading Genesis* (New York: Free Press, 2003, 2006); and my "Evolution and the Bible: Genesis 1 Revisited," *Commentary*, November 1988.

50   Those "Thou shalt" and "Thou shalt not" formulations are not expressed with the imperative particle *'al*, "don't do X," but with the particle *lo*, which negates a future tense, "you shall not do X." Rémi Brague suggests: "Perhaps we should somehow take grammar more seriously than it deserves and understand the commandments as real future forms. They are the logical consequences of the liberation wrought by God. In this way, they can be understood as follows: Since you are now free people, you will not have to do anymore what slaves do; that is, you will not kill, you will not steal, and so forth. The word 'commandment' has the ring of submission. But the Decalogue is not about submission at all. What we call the laws are the codification of liberty. They do not limit freedom by setting rules that we are not allowed to trespass. Abiding by the law is nothing more than remaining faithful to the logic of liberation, taking one's freedom seriously and drawing whatever consequence it can have. In fact, the 'commandments' are something like the code of free people, of gentlemen who are aware of 'what is not done.'" Rémi Brague, "God and Freedom: Biblical Roots of the Western Idea of Liberty," in *Christianity and Freedom*, vol. 1, *Historical Perspectives*, ed. Timothy Samuel Shah and Allen D. Hertzke (New York: Cambridge University Press, 2016), p. 395.

51   My friend and former colleague Michael Fishbane, as part of an overall critique of my humanistic reading of the text, has rightly pointed out that my interpretation of these passages underemphasizes the stark and painful fact that innocent children will have the iniquities of their fathers and grandfathers visited upon them. His comments can be found here: "What Does the God of Israel Demand?" *Mosaic*, June 5, 2013; and my response here: "A Reply to My Respondents, and My Friends," *Mosaic*, June 26, 2013.

INDEX

First American edition published in 2017 by Encounter Books, an activity of Encounter for Culture and Education, Inc., a nonprofit, tax exempt corporation.
Encounter Books website address: www.encounterbooks.com

Portions of this book have appeared in *Commentary*, *First Things*, *Mosaic Magazine*, *National Affairs*, *The New Atlantis*, *The New Republic*, and *The Public Interest*.

Photo Credits—*Glass Man* (p. 231): United States Holocaust Memorial Museum, courtesy of National Archives and Records Administration, College Park. *Maimed soldiers* (p. 233): United States Holocaust Memorial Museum, courtesy of Library of Congress.

Manufactured in the United States and printed on acid-free paper.
The paper used in this publication meets the minimum requirements of ANSI/NISO Z39.48–1992 (R 1997) (*Permanence of Paper*).

FIRST AMERICAN EDITION

LIBRARY OF CONGRESS CATALOGING-IN-PUBLICATION DATA

Names: Kass, Leon, author.
Title: Leading a worthy life : finding meaning in modern times / Leon R. Kass.
Description: New York : Encounter Books, [2017] | Includes bibliographical references and index.
Identifiers: LCCN 2017031502 (print) | LCCN 2017043096 (ebook) | ISBN 9781594039423 (Ebook) | ISBN 9781594039416 (hardback : alk. paper)
Subjects: LCSH: Meaning (Philosophy) | Life.
Classification: LCC B105.M4 (ebook) | LCC B105.M4 K37 2017 (print) | DDC 170/.44–dc23
LC record available at https://lccn.loc.gov/2017031502

A NOTE ON THE TYPE

Leading a Worthy Life has been set in Kingfisher, *a family of types designed by Jeremy Tankard. Frustrated by the paucity of truly well-drawn fonts for book work, Tankard set out to create a series of types that would be suitable for a wide range of text settings. Informed by a number of elegant historical precedents – the highly regarded Doves type, Monotype Barbou, and Ehrhardt among them – yet beholden to no one type in particular, Kingfisher attains a balance of formality, detail, and color that is sometimes lacking in types derived or hybridized from historical forms. The italic, designed intentionally as a complement to the roman, has much in common with earlier explorations in sloped romans like the Perpetua and Joanna italics, yet moderates the awkward elements that mar types like Van Krimpen's Romulus italic. The resulting types, modern, crisp, and handsome, are ideal for the composition of text matter at a variety of sizes, and comfortable for extended reading.*

DESIGN & COMPOSITION BY CARL W. SCARBROUGH